THE PATH

One Man's Quest on the Only Path There Is

J. Donald Walters
(swami Kriyananda)

Second Edition, 1996

THE PATH

One Man's Quest on the Only Path There Is

by J. Donald Walters

(Swami Kriyananda)

With a Preface by
John W. White

CRYSTAL CLARITY
PUBLISHERS

14618 Tyler-Foote Road, Nevada City, CA 95959
1-800-424-1055

About the cover:

This is a watercolor I did in December 1953, of a devotee aspiring to merge into the spiritual eye. Paramhansa Yogananda explained that the golden outer ring of the spiritual eye vibrates with the astral universe; the blue field within the ring, with the causal universe and the Christ Consciousness; and the five-pointed star, with cosmic consciousness, or God the Father beyond all vibratory creation.

First Printing 1977
Revised Edition 1996

© Copyright 1996
J. Donald Walters (Swami Kriyananda)

ISBN 1-565-89-733-1

Printed in Canada

Cover painting by J. Donald Walters
Cover design by Christine Starner Schuppe
Back cover photo by Norman Seeff
Frontispiece photo by Mel Bly

Special thanks to Jeffrey Philpott, Mel Bly, and John Novak for their photographs in the Ananda chapter.

To the sincere seeker,
whatever his chosen path.

A group of Paramhansa Yogananda's disciples had gone with him to see a movie about the life of Gyandev, a great saint of medieval India. Afterwards they gathered and listened to the Master explain certain, subtler, aspects of that inspiring story. A young man in the group mentioned another film he had seen years earlier, in India, about the life of Mirabai, a famous woman saint.

"If you'd seen *that* movie," he exclaimed, "you wouldn't have even *liked* this one!"

The Guru rebuked him. "Why make such comparisons? The lives of great saints manifest in various ways the same, one God."

OTHER WORKS BY SWAMI KRIYANANDA

MEDITATION FOR STARTERS

SUPERCONSCIOUSNESS
A Guide to Meditation

THE ESSENCE OF SELF-REALIZATION
The Wisdom of Paramhansa Yogananda
Edited by Kriyananda

ANANDA YOGA FOR HIGHER AWARENESS

ANANDA COURSE IN SELF-REALIZATION

INTENTIONAL COMMUNITIES
How to Start Them, and Why

Do It NOW!
A Perennial Calendar and Guide to Better Living

AFFIRMATIONS FOR SELF-HEALING

Descriptions of these and
other books and music can be found in
the resources section at the end of this book.

PREFACE

by John W. White, M.A.T., Yale University

author, *Everything You Want to Know about TM;*
editor, *The Highest State of Consciousness,*
Frontiers of Consciousness, What Is Meditation;
associate editor, *New Realities Magazine*

When one has been moved to laughter and tears, deep contemplation and joyful insight, as I have been while immersed in *The Path*, it is hardly possible to find a word or a phrase sufficient to encompass the enriching experience. "Deeply inspiring"—though hardly adequate—is the best way I can find to describe it.

Briefly, *The Path* is a story of one man's search for God through the path of yoga. It tells how American-born Donald Walters became universally-born Swami Kriyananda. At the same time, it serves as a practical manual of instruction for others in search of God-realization, no matter what tradition or path they follow. As an exceptionally lucid explanation of yogic philosophy, *The Path* will also be a valuable resource for those intellectually curious, but not consciously committed to spiritual growth.

The catalyst in Kriyananda's transformation was his guru, the well-known yogi, Paramhansa Yogananda, author of *Autobiography of a Yogi*. In fact, it is accurate to say that *The Path*, subtitled *"Autobiography of a Western Yogi,"* is as much about Yogananda as about Kriyananda. For, in truth, the two are one. That is part of the inspirational quality of *The Path*—the selfless devotion to guru which Kriyananda displays throughout the book. At the same time, he makes clear that Yogananda did not want devotion for himself. Rather, he would lovingly redirect his disciples' devotion to God.

This brings me to another element of the book which helped produce my feeling of inspiration—its abundant wisdom. Kriyananda's commentaries on spiritual unfoldment and his lucid explanations of yogic concepts are profoundly instructional. Moreover, like a true teacher he blends theoretical presentations and practical advice with personal anecdotes and illustrative stories in a way that is altogether engaging. Last of all, he presents us with much previously unpublished conversation from Yogananda, whose words are always enlightening.

Kriyananda's freedom from sentimentality is still another appealing aspect of his account. In creating this self-portrait, he speaks frankly about his failings, his ignorant shortcomings, his periods of doubt and depression, his moments of thralldom to spiritual pride. He doesn't attempt to romanticize the path he followed nor gloss over the difficulties he encountered within himself and in relation to others.

I have mentioned devotion, honesty, and wisdom as three characteristics of *The Path,* that give it an uplifting quality. There are others just as important—transpersonal love, for example, and the constant emphasis on attunement to God as the solution to all our problems. However, it also important to note that *The Path* is not only spiritual—it is spiritual *literature.* The literary style with which Kriyananda reveals himself is worthy of study by authors as well as spiritual seekers. It is by turns elegant, graceful, supple, delicate and always clear—a verbal elixir that would work powerfully on the consciousness of readers even if the theme were profane instead of divine.

The final quality of *The Path* which I want to note is its planetary vision of society. Yogananda encouraged his followers—and I quote him here—"to spread a spirit of brotherhood among all peoples and to aid in establishing, in many countries, self-sustaining world-brotherhood colonies for plain living and high thinking."

Today, Ananda World Brotherhood Village, established by Kriyananda and dedicated to human upliftment in accordance with Yogananda's teachings, is part of a growing global network of spiritual communities from many traditions and teachings which are linking together ever more intensively to become the seedbed for a new world—rooted in a vision of humanity's oneness rather than in the warfare and competition that has characterized this century heretofore.

The Path chronicles the establishment of Ananda. In so doing, it provides useful instruction in still another dimension that the dedicated spiritual seeker must come to face—his or her relation to society in general. The solution proposed in the life and teaching of Paramhansa Yogananda, as carried forward by Swami Kriyananda, is still another reason why *The Path* is so worth reading. The integral relation between spiritual practice and worldly affairs becomes abundantly clear through Kriyananda's words and deeds.

'Not only is *The Path* inspirational—urging you to "go and do thou likewise"—it also gives the pragmatic technical instruction needed to put principle into action. Moreover, it does so with a beauty and simplicity that is the verbal embodiment of the yogic approach to God-realization. I trust that you will find *The Path* to be a major resource in your life and that you will, in accord with yogic tradition, lovingly share it with others as part of your service to the world. For an inspired work such as this, that is the only proper response.

Cheshire, Connecticut
June 1, 1977

ACKNOWLEDGMENTS

Many people, by their suggestions, encouragement, and support, have helped bring this book to completion. To thank most of them is possible only in silence. I would particularly like, however, to express my thanks to Marsha Todd, Asha Savage, Fern Lucki, and Kathleen Stark for their helpful editorial suggestions; to Asha also for endlessly typing and retyping the manuscript; to Margie Stern for her long labors in preparing the index; to Robert Fite and Ben Davis for suggesting the title; to Bob and June Moody for placing their apartment on Hawaii's beautiful Kona Coast at my disposal for the editing of Part One of the book, and to Paul and Jan Weber and Charlotte Weber, too, for helping to make my stay there possible.

I would like also to express my deep appreciation to those in Ananda Publications who worked long and patiently on the production of the book: George Beinhorn, photography; Alan Gosink, camera work; Janice Hart and Nancy Raynes, design and layout; Kathy Mohr, typesetting. For their innumerable proofreadings of the manuscript during its various phases of development, I would also like to thank Peter Altman, Cynthia Brooks, Carolyn Escobar, Nancy Estep, Anita Miller, Julia Beakley, Pamela Pardridge, Patricia Ryan, Suzanne Simpson, Sally Smallen, Jim Van Cleave, and Sonia Wiberg.

Without the help of these many friends the book would have taken years longer to complete.

Swami Kriyananda

Ananda World Brotherhood Village
April 3, 1977

Contents

PART III

Illustrations

PART I

CHAPTER 1

The Pilgrim Whittles His Staff

THERE ARE TIMES when a human being, though perhaps not remarkable in himself, encounters some extraordinary person or event that infuses his life with great meaning. My own life was blessed with such an encounter nearly thirty years ago, in 1948. Right here in America, of all lands the epitome of bustling efficiency, material progressiveness, and pragmatic "know-how," I met a great, God-known master whose constant vision was of eternity. His name was Paramhansa Yogananda. He was from India, though it would be truer to say that his home was the whole world.

Had anyone suggested to me prior to that meeting that so much radiance, dynamic joy, unaffected humility, and love might be found in a single human being, I would have replied—though perhaps with a sigh of regret—that such perfection is not possible for man. And had anyone suggested to me, further, that divine miracles have occurred in this scientific age, I would have laughed outright. For in those days, proud as I was in my intellectual, Twentieth-Century "wisdom," I mocked even the miracles of the Bible.

No longer. I have seen things that made a mockery of mockery itself. I know now from personal experience that divine wonders do occur on earth. And I believe that the time is approaching when countless men and women will no more think of doubting God than they doubt the air they breathe. For God is not dead. It is man only who dies to all that is wonderful in life when he limits himself to worldly acquisitions and to advancing himself in worldly eyes, but overlooks those spiritual realities which are the foundation of all that he truly *is*.

Paramhansa Yogananda often spoke of America's high spiritual destiny. When first I heard him do so, I marveled. *America?* All that I knew of this country was its materialism, its competitive drive, its smug, "no-nonsense" attitude toward anything too subtle to be measured with scientific instruments. But in time that great teacher made me aware of another aspect, an undercurrent of divine yearning—not in our intellectuals, perhaps, our so-called cultural "leaders," but in the hearts of the common people. Americans' love of freedom, after all, began in the quest, centuries ago, for *religious* freedom. Their historic emphasis on equality and on voluntary, friendly cooperation with one another reflects principles that are taught in the Bible. Americans' pioneering spirit is rooted in these principles. And when no frontiers remained to our people on the North American continent and they began exporting their pioneering energies abroad, again it was the spirit of freedom and of willing cooperation that they carried with them, setting a new example for mankind everywhere. In these twin principles Paramhansa Yogananda saw the key to mankind's next upward step in its evolution.

The vision of the future that he presented to us was of a state of world brotherhood in which all men would live together in harmony and freedom. As a step toward this universal fulfillment he urged those people who were free to do so to band together into what he called "world brotherhood colonies": spiritual communities where people, living and working together with others of like mind, would develop an awareness of the true kinship of all men as sons and daughters of the same, one God.

It has been my own lot to found such a "world brotherhood colony," the first of what Yogananda predicted would someday be thousands of such communities the world over.

Because the pioneering spirit is rooted in principles that are essentially spiritual, it has not only expanded men's frontiers outwardly; in recent decades especially, it has begun to *interiorize* them, to expand the inward boundaries of human consciousness, and to awaken in people the desire to harmonize their lives with truth, and with God.

It was to the divine aspirations of these pioneers of the spirit that Paramhansa Yogananda was responding in coming to America. Americans, he said, were ready to learn meditation and God-communion, through the practice of the ancient science of yoga.* It was in the capacity of one of modern India's greatest exponents of yoga that he was sent by his great teachers to the West.

In my own life and heritage, the pioneering spirit in all its stages

---

* Yoga: a Sanskrit word meaning "union." Yoga is also a system of psycho-physical techniques for helping man to achieve conscious union with the Infinite Spirit, God. The yogi, a practitioner of the yoga science, acquires outwardly also a vision of the underlying unity of all life.

of manifestation has played an important role. Numerous ancestors on both sides of my family were pioneers of the traditional sort, many of them ministers of the Gospel, and frontier doctors. My paternal grandparents joined the great land rush that opened up the Oklahoma Territory in 1889. Other ancestors played less exploratory, but nonetheless active, roles in the great adventure of America's development. Mary Todd, the wife of Abraham Lincoln, was a relative of mine. So also was Robert E. Lee, Lincoln's adversary in the Civil War. It pleases me thus to be linked with both sides of that divisive conflict, for my own lifelong tendency has been to reconcile contradictions—to seek, as India's philosophy puts it, "unity in diversity."

My father, Ray P. Walters, was born too late to be a pioneer in the earlier sense. A pioneer nevertheless at heart, he joined the new wave of international expansion and cooperation, working for Esso as an oil geologist in foreign lands. Mother, Gertrude G. Walters, was a part of this new wave also: After graduating from college she went to study the violin in Paris. Both my parents were born in Oklahoma; it was in Paris, however, that they met. After their wedding, Dad was assigned to the oil fields of Rumania; there they settled in Teleajen, a small Anglo-American colony about three kilometers east of the city of Ploeşti. Teleajen was the scene of my own squalling entrance onto the stage of life.

My body, typically of the American "melting pot," is the product of a blend of several countries: England, Wales, Scotland, Ireland, Holland, France, and Germany. It was little Wales, the smallest of these seven, that gave me my surname, Walters. For Kriyananda is a monastic appellation that I acquired only in 1955, when I was initiated into the ancient Swami order of India.

The human body, through the process of birth, is a new creation. Not so the soul. I came into this world, I believe, already fully myself. I chose this particular family because I found it harmonious to my own nature, and felt that these were the parents who would best afford me the opportunities I needed for my own spiritual development. Grateful as I am to my parents for taking me in, a stranger, I feel less indebted to them for making me what I am. I have described them, their forebears, and the country from which they came to show the trends with which I chose to affiliate, for whatever good I might be able to accomplish for myself, and perhaps, also, for others.

For everyone in this world is a pilgrim. He comes alone, treads his chosen path for a time, then leaves once more solitarily. His is a sacred destination, always dimly suspected, though usually not consciously known. Whether deliberately or by blind instinct, directly or indirectly, what all men are truly seeking is Joy—Joy infinite, Joy eternal, Joy divine.

Most of us, alas, wander about in this world like pilgrims without a map. We imagine Joy's shrine to be wherever money is worshiped, or power, or fame, or good times. It is only after ceaseless roaming that, disappointed at last, we pause in silent self-appraisal. And then it is we discover, perhaps with a shock, that our goal was never distant from us at all—indeed, *never any farther away than our own selves!*

This path we walk has no fixed dimensions. It is either long or short, depending only on the purity of our intentions. It is the path Jesus described when he said, "The kingdom of God cometh not with observation: Neither shall they say, Lo here! or, lo there! for, behold, the kingdom of God is within you."* Walking this path, we yet walk it not, for the goal, being inward, is ours already. We have only to claim it as our own.

The principal purpose of this book is to help you, the reader, to make good that claim. I hope in these pages, among other things, to help you avoid a few of the mistakes I myself have made in the search. For a person's failures may sometimes be as instructive as his successes.

I was born in Teleajen on May 19, 1926, at approximately seven in the morning. James Donald Walters is the full name I received at christening in the little Anglican church in Ploeşti. Owing to a plethora of Jameses in the community, I was always known by my second name, Donald, in which I was the namesake of a stepuncle, Donald Quarles, who later served as Secretary of the Air Force under President Eisenhower. James, too, was a family name, being the name of my maternal grandfather. It was my ultimate destiny, however, to renounce such family identities altogether in favor of a higher, spiritual one.

Mother has told me that throughout her pregnancy she was filled with an inward joy. "Lord," she prayed repeatedly, "this first child I give to Thee."

Her blessing may not have borne fruit as early as she had hoped. But bear fruit it did, gradually—one might almost say, relentlessly—over the years.

For mine is the story of one who did his best to live without God, but who—thank God—failed in the attempt.

* Luke 17:20,21.

CHAPTER 2

He Sets Out from Home

J OY HAS ALWAYS been my first love. I have longed to share it with others.

My clearest early memories all relate to a special kind of happiness, one that seemed to have little to do with the things around me, that at best only reflected them. A lingering impression is one of wonder to be in this world at all. What was I doing here? Intuitively I felt that there must be some higher reality—another world, perhaps, radiant, beautiful, and harmonious, in relation to which this one represented mere exile. Beautiful sounds and colors thrilled me almost to ecstasy. Sometimes I would cover a table down to the floor with a colorful American Indian blanket, then crawl inside and fairly drink in the luminous colors. At other times, gazing into the prism formed by the broad edge of a mirror on my mother's dressing table, I would imagine myself living in a world of rainbow-colored lights. Often also, at night, I would see myself absorbed in a radiant inner light, and my consciousness would seem to expand beyond the limits of my body.

"You were eager for knowledge," Mother tells me, "not a little willful, but keenly sympathetic to the misfortunes of others." Smiling playfully, she adds, "I used to read children's books to you. If the hero was in trouble, I would point pityingly to his picture. As I did so, your lips quivered. 'Poor *this!*' you exclaimed." Mother (naughty *this!*) found my response so amusing that she sometimes played on it by pointing tragically to the cheerful pictures as well—a miserable ploy which, she informs me, invariably succeeded.

As I grew older, my inner joy spilled over into an intense enthusiasm for life. Teleajen gave us many opportunities to be creative in our play. We were far removed from the modern world of frequent movies, circuses, and other contrived amusements. Television was, of course, unknown at that time even in America. As a community composed mostly of English and American families, we were remote even from the mainstream of Rumanian culture. Our parents taught us a few standard Anglo-American games, but for the most part we invented our own. Our backyards became transformed into adventure lands. A long stepladder laid sideways on the snow became an airplane soaring us to warmer climes. A large apple tree with hanging branches served a variety of useful functions: a schoolhouse, a sea-going schooner, a castle. Furniture piled high in various ways in the nursery would become a Spanish galleon, or a mountain fortress. We blazed secret trails through a nearby cornfield to a cache of buried treasure, or to a point of safety from the pursuing officers of some unspeakably wicked tyrant. In winter, skating on a tennis court that had been flooded to make an ice rink, we gazed below us into the frozen depths and imagined ourselves moving freely in another dimension of wonderful shapes and colors.

I remember a ship, too, that I set out to build, fully intending to sail it on Lake Snagov. I got as far as nailing a few old boards together in nondescript imitation of a deck. In imagination, however, as I lay in bed at night and contemplated the job, I was already sailing my schooner on the high seas.

Leadership came naturally to me, though I was unwilling to exert it if others didn't share my interests spontaneously. The children in Teleajen did share them, and accepted my leadership. More and more, however, as I grew older, I discovered that people often considered my vision of things somewhat peculiar. I noticed it first in some of the newly arrived children in Teleajen. Accustomed to the standard childhood games of England and America, they would look puzzled at my proposals for more imaginative entertainment—like the time we gazed into unfamiliar dimensions in the ice while skating over it. Unwilling to impose my interests on others, I was equally unwilling to accept their imposition in return. I was, I suppose, a nonconformist, not from conscious desire or intent, but from a certain inability to attune myself to others' norms. What was important to me seemed to them unimportant, whereas, frequently, what they considered important seemed to me incomprehensible.

Miss Barbara Henson (now Mrs. Elsdale), our governess for a time, described me in a recent letter the way she remembers me as a child of seven: "You were certainly 'different,' Don—'in the family but not of it.' I was always conscious that you had a mystic quality which set you apart, and others were aware of it, too. You were always the observer, with an extraordinarily straight look in those blue-grey eyes which made you, in a sense, ageless. And in a quiet, disconcerting way, you made funny little experiments on other people as if to satisfy your suspicions about something concerning them. Never to be put off by prevarication or half-truths, you were, one felt, seeking the truth behind everything."

Cora Brazier, our next-door neighbor, a kind, sympathetic lady, once remarked to Miss Henson, "I always try to be especially nice to Don, because he's not like the others. I believe he knows this, and is lonely."

Although this knowledge was not to dawn on me fully until after I left Teleajen, there was even there a certain sense of being alone. It was held in abeyance, however, by the presence of good friends, and by a harmonious home life.

My parents loved us children deeply. Their love for each other, too, was exemplary, and a strong source of emotional security for us. Never in my life have I known them to quarrel, or to have even the slightest falling out.

My father was especially wonderful with children. Rather reserved by nature, he yet possessed, and possesses to this day, a simple kindness and a sense of humor that enabled him to appreciate young minds. At bedtime he would invent hilarious stories for us that were continued night after night, frequently with additions from his enthusiastic listeners. Then, as my brothers and I were ready to fall asleep, he would arrange us at one end of the bed or the other depending on whether we said we wanted to travel in sleep to Australia, America, or to some other distant land.

He taught us much, by example as well as words. Above all what we learned from him came from observing in him a nature always humble, honest, truthful, honorable, kind, and scrupulously fair. I would go so far as to call him, in his quiet, rather shy way, a great man.

But in my own relationship with him there was always a certain sadness. I could not be to him the kind of mirror a man naturally hopes for in his sons, especially in his first-born. I tried earnestly to share his interests, but where he was attracted to the "hows" of things, I was attracted to the "whys." He was a scientist, and I, instinctively, a philosopher. He tried to interest me in the way things worked. (I still remember a dusty expedition under the house, where he showed us boys what made the front doorbell ring. I at least *tried* to feel grateful!) But I was only interested in what things meant. My inability to communicate with him on those subjects which interested each of us most deeply was the first indication I had that his world—which I considered, by extension, the normal world—could never truly be mine.

Mother and I understood one another intuitively; ours was a communication of souls, less so of speech. Though she never spoke of praying for us children, I know that her prayers and love for me were my greatest blessing during the formative years of my life.

Rumania was still a feudal land. Its people, gifted artistically, tended otherwise to be somewhat inefficient and unhurried. The country was an anachronism in this busy Twentieth Century. Its workmen could spend fifteen years with picks and shovels digging a tunnel under the railway tracks at the main station in the capital. One summer, eager to follow the example of the rest of the modern world, the whole nation went on Daylight *Losing* Time, by official mistake! Drivers' tests included such penetrating questions as "What goes on the front of a car?" (Headlights, naturally.) Years later, Indra Devi, the well-known yoga teacher,* told me that while traveling by train through Rumania she had once been asked by the conductor what she was doing in a second-class compartment.

"Why, can't you see? I have a second-class ticket!"

"Oh, that doesn't matter in *Rumania!* Please, just go sit in first class where everyone else is."

Inattention, however, to the petty details of modern commerce and efficiency seemed somehow appropriate in a land that inspired thoughts of music and poetry. Rumania was one of the most fascinatingly beautiful countries I have ever seen: a land of fertile plains and soaring mountains, of colorfully clad peasants and musically gifted gypsies, of hay carts on the highways vying with automobiles for the right of way, of giggling, naked children, of gay songs and laughter. Frequently, outside our colony in the evenings, we would hear bands of gypsies conversing, singing, or playing the violin: the sad, haunting melodies of a people forever outcast from their true home, in India. These gypsies were my first contact with the subtly subjective moods of the Orient—moods that, I was to learn, are reflected in many aspects of life in Rumania. For centuries Rumania had been under Turkish rule. Now a proud and upcoming Western nation, there still clung to her something of the aura of the mystical East.

Rumania was a kingdom. King Carol II had his summer home about sixty kilometers (forty miles) northwest of us, in Sinaia, a lovely hill station in the Transylvanian Alps. Though I never saw him there, we, too, spent many vacations in Sinaia, and in other quaint towns and villages nearby: Buşteni, Predeal, Timiş, Braşov. In winter we often skied; in summer we hiked, or waded and

---

* Author of *Forever Young, Forever Healthy,* and other books.

swam in friendly, chuckling brooks, or played in fragrant meadows. Many times these mountain trips were taken because of my health, which was precarious. I was skinny as a pencil, and forever coming down with a variety of obscure ailments. Timiş was my favorite spot. There we always stayed at a guest lodge run by a German lady, Frau Weidi, whose husband kept bees that produced the best honey I have ever eaten.

Sixty kilometers to the south of Teleajen was Bucharest, Rumania's capital: a clean, modern city that rose like a prophetic dream in the mind of a nation still asleep in the Middle Ages. Ploeşti remained for me, however, the Big City for the first nine years of my life: a not-very-attractive jumble of dirty streets and uninteresting houses. My recollections of it are few: visits to Ghiculescu, the grocer; Sunday services at the Anglican church; and very occasional outings to the movies—Walt Disney cartoons, mostly, and comedies featuring Laurel and Hardy, whom the Rumanians had renamed fondly, Stan and Bran.

The church served as a focus for Mother's piety. In this area of her life Dad played the role of disinterested spectator. Though he respected Mother's religious inclinations, and went with her to church more or less regularly, I never observed that liturgy held any attraction for him. His own natural concept of reality was more abstract. Nothing, I think, so inspired him as the contemplation of vast eons of geologic time. The thought of a God sitting somewhere on a heavenly throne, bestowing favors on special groups of worshipers, struck him, I suspect, as faintly barbaric.

My own natural bent lay somewhere between these two, the pious and the abstract. Like Dad, I was not greatly attracted to the church worship services. The hymns seemed to me rather dull and sad. The minister I considered a good man, but certainly not an inspired one. I suppose I accepted the rituals as good things to do; beyond this pale recognition, however, they held little meaning for me. I wish I could report that the life of Jesus at least made a strong impression on me. I am moved by it now. But then it reached me through a filter of wooden traditionalism, robbed of immediacy. I'm sure I couldn't have defined my feelings at the time, but I think what I missed most of all in our church services were love and joy. Mother had these qualities. What impressed and touched me about her was not religion as she defined it, but as she lived it.

Like Dad, I found it difficult to believe in a God who loved each human being personally. That God was impersonal seemed to me self-evident, when I considered the vastness of the universe.

How then, I thought, could He be interested enough to listen to us mortals when we prayed? It was only many years later, in the teachings of India, that I found reconciliation for these seemingly incompatible concepts of a God both personal and impersonal. For the Infinite Spirit, as my guru was to explain with perfect simplicity, though impersonal in its vastness, has become personal also, in creating individual beings. Infinity, in other words, implies infinitesimal littleness as well as infinite immensity.

Though I found it difficult to address God personally, I always felt that reality must be *spiritual,* that it must have some high meaning and purpose. I remember a discussion I had once with Dad. I was about six years old at the time; we were standing on the terrace of our Teleajen home, watching the birds at play in the large apple tree.

"In the hundreds of millions of years," Dad said, "since the world was created, every species has had its turn at being the master of this planet, except the birds. First there were the fishes, then the insects, then reptiles, and now man, who represents the mammals. Perhaps, millions of years from now, man, too, will be pushed aside, and the birds will get their turn at being the earth's masters."

How appealing I found this picture of the vast reaches of time! But then a doubt occurred to me: Is there no *meaning* to it all? Is life nothing but a process of endless change, with different species ruling for no better reason than that their turn has come? Surely there must be some higher purpose—hidden, perhaps, but divine.

My questioning mind must have made me something of a trial to my parents. Mother, on a visit to Italy in 1933, wrote to Miss Henson: "Please tell the boys that I want them to try to be very good and that will help both them and me to have a good time. (Donald is sure to find a flaw in that argument, but you might try it!)"

Fortunately for me, Mother and Dad never discouraged my questioning. I remember one day, at the age of five, standing in the bathroom, watching Dad shave. I was pondering one of the profound mysteries of childhood: How can Santa Claus reach every home in the world in a single night? Suddenly the answer dawned on me.

"Daddy, there isn't really a Santa Claus, is there?"

Dad, too honest to insist there is, but too considerate of the sweet myths of childhood to admit that there isn't, hedged his reply. I understood him perfectly. Then and there I decided that it really would be much nicer to go on believing in Santa Claus anyway. In that spirit I believe in him still.

Myths are an important part of life. Paradoxical as it seems, they are important to man's search for reality as well, for they help to give his mind the elasticity it needs to imagine new solutions to old problems.

Myths (in fact!) formed a large part of my education. I loved Greek mythology, the adventures of King Arthur and his knights of the Round Table, the legends of Robin Hood and Peter Pan, Grimm's fairy tales, stories from the Old Testament—myths, all, in which goodness, courage, and honor win in the end. One's life experiences may not always endorse such moral preachments, but wise men and women have ever insisted that justice does prevail, eventually, even if the time of reckoning stretches far beyond man's present horizons. *"Yato dharma, tato jaya,"* say the Indian Scriptures: "Where there is righteousness, there is victory." Fact may well, as people claim, be stranger than fiction, but fiction very often is, in a deeper sense, truer than fact. I think it a pity that the ancient myths are not given more emphasis in modern education. Certainly they enriched my own upbringing.

But then, the culture of Rumania was more conducive than pragmatic America's to the art of legend-telling. As children, my brothers and I got periodic opportunities to compare these two countries. Every three or four years Dad received a three-months' vacation, all expenses paid, in America. My first journey here was when I was six months old, then three years, seven, ten, and thirteen. It was after I turned thirteen that we settled here.

I still recall my amazement, at the age of three, on reaching London and finding waiters, taxi drivers, the man in the street—all speaking English! I'd supposed English was spoken only by parents and their friends. Nurses, of course, spoke German, but wasn't it a law of life that practically everyone else spoke Rumanian? I suppose by so compartmentalizing these languages I managed to keep from confusing them—a further example, perhaps, of the value of the myth-making process. Once Mother addressed me in Rumanian, and I replied in shocked tones, "Mother, don't talk to me like that!"

Looking at America with eyes that were partly Rumanian, I gained insights that sometimes conflicted with my pride in being an American. I deeply loved America. I admired its dynamic energy, and stood almost in awe of its constant emphasis on common sense: The Americans I met seemed to know exactly what to do in every situation. I loved them, too, for their kindness—whenever they took the time from constant, driving activity to be kind. But on the other hand, I found myself puzzled by what often struck me in their conversation as "big talk." I'd noticed it in a few of the Americans in Teleajen, especially in the newcomers. In America even the children, it seemed, were always trying to demonstrate how grown-up they were, how sophisticated, how important. It was as though they had no patience with childhood. What, I wondered, was all that *important* about being important?

Compared to America, Rumania is a little country. Though independent in spirit, its people have a less exalted image of themselves. Americans, with their four million territorial square miles, fall more easily a prey to the thought of self-importance, a temptation which seems to accompany bigness whether in nations, institutions, or individuals.

Vacations in America entailed visits to our various relatives. My earliest memories include Mother Ella, my maternal grandmother, who died while I was still young. I remember best her sweet smile, so loving it seemed almost saintly. My paternal grandparents, who lived longer, were simple, good people too. It was in these relatives, and in many other people like them, that I caught my first glimpse of the particular spiritual genius of America: childlike innocence and simplicity, a predisposition to see goodness in others, a love of freedom tempered by a desire to live in harmony with man and God.

Granddad introduced me also to another American trait: the tendency to dignify inconsequential matters, humorously, by pretending that more serious issues are at stake. It is a trait that can, and sometimes does, lead to misunderstandings.

Once in Tulsa Dad paid a minor traffic fine. Granddad remarked to me afterwards, straight-facedly, "Well, I guess your Dad escaped prison this time." I took him literally. Several days later we were eating in a crowded restaurant. As sometimes happens in a crowd, there occurred a brief interlude when, for no apparent reason, everyone in the room stopped talking—everyone, that is, but young Donald.

"Daddy!" I cried, "tell us about the time you escaped from prison!"

Momentarily the room was in shock. Then suddenly everyone was laughing. (Why, I wondered, was Dad blushing so furiously?)

Trips to and from America must have been something of an ordeal for our poor parents. We were three brothers. Dick, the youngest, wasn't old enough to engage in much fraternal rivalry, but Bob and I were close to the same age, and when we weren't cooperating in some misadventure (like the time we upset a traveling prince and his retinue by scrambling their shoes, left overnight in the corridor to be shined), we often wrestled each other to work off excess energy.

Bob was born a year and a half after me, but soon grew to my height, and occasionally surpassed it. He felt little hesitancy in challenging a seniority which I had no intention of relinquishing. Temperamental differences existed between us, too. Bob was impulsive, outgoing, fond of popularity, demonstrative of his feelings. I was in many ways quite the opposite: reserved, rather shy, pensive, forever questioning. Bob once picked up a caterpillar from a path with the loving cry, "There, there, you poor little worm! I'll put you over here so no one can step on you." He then ran off gaily, quite forgetting the incident. Had I helped the same caterpillar, I would have pondered the incident for days, wondering what it was that made certain creatures defenseless, and why this particular insect, out of millions, should have received help. Beside Bob I'm afraid I sometimes felt myself rather a lump. As a matter of fact that thought seemed sometimes to bother him, too. His spirit of rivalry was, I think, rooted partly in unconscious disapproval of me for not being more like others. But for all that we managed to be good friends. And always, where the rest of the world was concerned, we stood together in brotherly solidarity, never more so than when either of us was being threatened.

Fighting is, I suppose, an inextricable part of the process of growing up, particularly so for boys. I recall what might be considered my fair share of boyhood scraps, though I don't remember ever instigating one. (In this respect I was unlike my cousin Ed, who made full, aggressive use of nature's gift to him of a strong body. "Eddy," his mother once admonished him, "don't you know that when another boy hits you, you shouldn't hit back?" "Oh, but Mother," Ed remonstrated self-righteously, "I *never* hit back. I always hit first!")

Though I myself never "hit first," if ever it seemed important to me to demonstrate to others, or to myself, that I was no coward I was not one to turn the other cheek. Several fights, in fact, far from stirring me now to repentance, stand out in my memory as having helped me to learn worthwhile lessons.

It was because of a fight that I first learned something of the fickleness of human loyalties. I was seven or eight at the time. Alvin, a big boy who was visiting Teleajen with his parents, determined to impose his command on our group. Brawn, fortunately, was not important to our "group dynamics." I knew that the support I had from my friends was born of mutual affection, not of fear. But when Alvin challenged me, his victory seemed so much a foregone conclusion that most of the children, fearing later retribution, sided with him. Bob was the sole exception. I, furious with the rest of them for their fickleness, determined to teach them a good lesson by beating Alvin.

It was a long, somewhat bloody battle. Every shout for Alvin only goaded me to renewed efforts. Gradually his strength flagged. As it began to look as if I might win after all, first one of the children, then another, joined Bob in rooting for me. At last Alvin's courage crumbled altogether. By this time everyone was enthusiastically on my side.

Victory was bitter-sweet for me that day, however. I knew my friends had really wanted me to win all along. But I also understood a little bit what an unreliable thing is the support of one's fellow creatures.

Wise indeed is he who discovers that God's friendship *alone* can never fail him.

But disappointment is a good teacher; it helps us to take our first, faltering steps out of childhood toward maturity. For the world is frequently at odds with our desires. The sign of maturity is a willingness to adjust to realities broader than one's own. It is how we react to disappointment that determines whether our development will be a shrinking towards bitterness and cynicism, or an expansion towards acceptance and wisdom.

CHAPTER 3

Storm Clouds

I T WAS SUMMER, 1935. I was nine years old. Vacationing in the quaint mountain village of Buşteni, I was enjoying a happy season of games, picnics on grassy meadows, and carefree laughter.

One afternoon I went to my room to read a book. Sitting in a chair, I suddenly felt dizzy. I lay down on the bed, but even from this position the room seemed to be spinning. I cried weakly for help, but no one came. At last, summoning all my strength, I struggled to the door, leaning against the wall for support, and called again. This time I was heard.

A doctor was hastily summoned. A large, loud-voiced, over-confident lady, she was evidently determined to prove that I had appendicitis. (*Prod.* "Does it hurt here?" *Prod again.* "How about here?") Minutes of this diagnostic predetermination made me hurt all over. Finally, deciding, perhaps, that it would be no use operating on my entire abdomen, she gave up.

I came near dying in that little village. As it was, though I survived, the happy world I had known for the first nine years of my life died for me with this illness. Back home in Teleajen, all I remember "clearly" are long stretches of delirium: Dad reading to me from Mark Twain's *Huckleberry Finn,* and the drunken fits of Huck's father returning to me at night in a terrifying garb.

"I don't *want* to be a drunkard!" I cried, wrestling with my own delirium. "I don't *want* to be a drunkard!"

At last I came to associate *any* unusual mental state with delirium. The very soul-expansion which, until this time, had visited me so often at night, now filled me with a nameless dread.

Because of this fear, I now began making a conscious effort to adjust to the norms of others. For the better part of a decade, insecurity and self-doubt left me anxious to prove to myself that I was not in some indefinable way abnormal.

Dr. Stroyei, a pediatrician in Bucharest, finally diagnosed my illness as colitis. He forbade me all dairy products, and put me on a bland diet of soft-cooked foods that almost robbed me of all interest in eating. When I'd recovered sufficiently, my parents decided to send me to the salubrious climate of Switzerland. Dr. Winthrop Haynes, my godfather, recommended a small Swiss-English boarding school where his own sons had studied for a time, in Chesières, a mountain village in French Switzerland. The school was named, perhaps a trifle pretentiously, *L'Avenir* ("The Future").

My own future here, eighteen long months of it, was somewhat bleak. Only nine years old when I arrived, never before away from my family, and unfamiliar with French (the language commonly spoken at L'Avenir), I was homesick much of the time. Throughout my stay, moreover, I was afflicted with a series of fairly serious illnesses, stemming from the colitis.

L'Avenir was owned and run by a kindly couple, Mr. and Mrs. John Hampshire. Mr. Hampshire was English; his wife, whom we children knew affectionately as Tante Béa (Aunt Beatrice), was French-Swiss. The students themselves were a mixed bag of Swiss, English, American (me), Italian, and French.

Unhappy though I was, my stay there did have its compensations. The scenery, for one thing, was stunningly beautiful. Across the valley from us loomed the famous Alp, Les Dents du Midi. In winter we skied daily. In warmer weather, frequent walks led us through flowered pastures and quiet, discreet woods—all very properly Swiss. I still recall the herds of cows passing our chalet school in the early mornings, their bells ringing melodiously.

Gradually, too, as I learned to speak French, adjustment became easier for me. The teachers, able to communicate with me now, grew quite fond of me. (Grownups were touched, generally, because I treated them like *people*.) Even our frosty German teacher, to whom I'd seemed merely stupid as long as I couldn't speak French, eventually thawed.

My long illness coincided with the growing political malady of Europe. In Vienna, where Mother and I stopped on our way to Switzerland, we were warned by friends not to criticize Nazi Germany except in safe places, and then only in whispers. Austria had not yet been annexed, but one saw Nazi officers everywhere, marching about, challenging people with the Nazi salute, sternly shouting, *"Heil Hitler!"* ("Hi," I would reply, waving a hand nonchalantly.) Storm clouds were gathering. In the bluster of bullies everywhere one saw the arrogance of men newly justified in their own eyes. And, growing in the hearts of peace-loving people everywhere, there was fear.

One of the students at L'Avenir was an Italian boy, larger by a head than most of us, and a braggart. Guido tried to ingratiate himself with us by laughing loudly at everything, and at nothing. But he was a bully, and nobody liked him. He was also—naturally enough, considering his own insensitivity—an ardent supporter of Italy's dictator, Mussolini. We were never allowed to forget his country's "glorious" conquest of poor, backward Abyssinia.

Little cogs in a big wheel! But it took those little cogs to make the wheel turn. Individual bullies, each insignificant in himself, were banding together on the stage of history, and imagined in their swelling ranks that fate had given them the power to change the world. For them it was a heady hour. Such, indeed, is the power of mass hysteria that ere long many others, too, peace-loving formerly, were striding about behaving like petty dictators.

An Austrian friend of ours in Teleajen, pleasant enough when he first came there, caught the bully fever. From then on, normal conversation with him was impossible; all he ever spouted was a succession of grim boasts. "We Germans," it seemed, would soon be marching in to subjugate everyone and his dog.

This man's chief weakness was simply, I think, that he lacked a sense of humor. I've never known a bully to possess one. I don't mean they can't laugh *at* people; that they do readily enough. It's that they can't laugh *with* others. Humor certainly was conspicuous by its absence among those who succumbed to the disease of Naziism.

I even wonder whether the evolution of tyranny isn't reducible to some kind of law, in which humorlessness plays an essential role. First, it seems, in the line of converts to tyranny come the true bullies—the sadists, the mentally crippled and vengeful, the criminal. Then, as the spirit of arrogance spreads, well-meaning but essentially humorless people enter to swell the tide. Finally come the well-meaning, but stupid. At this point, anyone with any true values has little choice but to flee, to go underground, or to maintain a resolute silence in the face of general insanity. Or—he can laugh.

One evening in Germany a famous comedian appeared on stage before a large audience. Clicking his heels together, he raised his right arm high above his head. Several people in the audience leapt to their feet and returned the Nazi salute.

"That," said the comedian, "is how high my dog jumped yesterday."

This man knew the probable consequences of his brave gesture, but his sense of humor in the face of those probabilities revealed that indomitable spirit in human nature before which tyranny must ever succumb in the end.

In the summer of 1936 we traveled through Germany on our way to America. A stranger sharing Bob's train compartment was arrested at the German border by the Gestapo. Perhaps he was Jewish. Or perhaps, like thousands of others, he was merely trying to flee despotism. But, young as we were at the time, we knew the likely outcome of his arrest: imprisonment, and then death.

In Rumania I had a governess for a time who, like our friend in Teleajen, was an Austrian Nazi. Also like him, she was quite devoid of any sense of humor. Miss Annie assured us constantly, whenever our parents weren't there to hear her, that Japan would never lose in any war against America, having never lost one in its long history. The German people, moreover, in league with the Japanese and the Italians, were destined to rule the whole world. It seemed peculiarly fitting to us when Miss Annie was found to be a kleptomaniac.

Whenever we traveled through Germany, however, all the people we met proved exceedingly kind and hospitable, eager to help us in every way they could. Were *these* people Nazis? Some, I suppose, were; the worst bully, after all, is still a child of God, and cannot but reflect something of the Divine Goodness. But I think most of them were simply normal, good people caught up in the flood of a national tragedy. We loved them almost more, I think, for the sadness of their plight. What country, after all, is in a position to be able to say honestly, "*Our* people would never sink so low"?

The plight of Europe affected me deeply. Why, I wondered, can't people learn to live together in harmony? What is it in human nature that courts, that seems almost to *demand,* tragedy?

Perhaps my gloomy reflections were aggravated by my own unhappiness. One day I was standing alone on the balcony of our chalet school. Mr. Hampshire came out to find me weeping silently.

"What's the matter?" he inquired gently.

"I'm homesick!" I sobbed.

Kindly, he wrote that day to my parents. Soon it was decided that I should return home.

During my stay in Switzerland Dad had been transferred to Bucharest. Our new residence was on the outskirts of the city, at Strada Capitan Dimitriade N⁰ 10. Here I got six months' respite before resuming my formal education. It was during this period that Miss Annie tutored me.

My health through this winter of 1936–37 was still precarious. Occasionally the pain was intense, though I remember now, more clearly than the pain, the tears in Mother's eyes as she suffered with me in her love.

Sometimes, when I was well enough, I played football on an empty lot with the neighborhood children. One of these was a boy from a slum area across Boulevard Bușteni. His family were so poor they couldn't even afford window panes, but covered up the window openings in winter with newspapers. I took intense pity on him, invited him frequently to my home, and gave him freely of my toys. I was his friend. He, I assumed, was my friend.

One day he and a few of the boys in our own neighborhood taught me a hard lesson. Dissembling camaraderie, they invited me to join them in the courtyard of a nearby home. The gate closed quietly behind me; someone locked it. Then, to my surprise, they backed me against a fence and began kicking a football at me, trying to hit me with it. Obviously, they were working up the courage for an attack.

I stood my ground and waited quietly, struck the football aside whenever it came too near, and affected an attitude of indifference. Minutes passed. At last the boys changed their minds about the merits of this afternoon's entertainment. The gate was opened, and I was allowed to walk out unscathed.

Though physically unhurt, I thought my heart would break. Back home, I wept inconsolably. Why, I asked Mother through tears, had my "dearest" friend, and my other good companions, so betrayed my love for them? It was small comfort to reflect that war hysteria had by now made Rumanians suspicious of *all* foreigners.

Painful though this experience was, it proved an excellent lesson. From it I learned that it isn't enough to give to others, even with love. If one would not beggar them in their own eyes, one must make it in some way possible for them also to reciprocate.

My absence in Switzerland, which had relieved Bob of the restraining presence of an older brother, had left him by no means languishing in his new freedom. Gleefully in fact, from then on, he insisted that every important event in our family must have occurred "while you were in Switzerland."

My absence from home had had its effect on me, too. Whether I liked it or not, I now was a little less dependent on the home for which I had so recently been feeling homesick. God was weaning me from dependence on earthly security. My illness; my consequent absence, in that condition, in a far land; my growing sense of aloneness: These were, I think, meant only to help me realize that my true home is not here, on earth, but in Him.

Indeed, this is for all men an eternal truth: God is our reality. Ineluctably we are led, quickly or slowly, by one path or another, towards this divine understanding.

In this thought I am reminded of a brother disciple who once asked our guru, "Will I ever leave the spiritual path?"

"How could you?" the Master answered. "Everyone in the world is on the spiritual path."

My parents, Ray and Gertrude Walters, in Teleajen, Rumania, a few days after my appearance on the scene, May 1926.

My mother, my brothers Dick and Bob, and I (*right*). If Dick was one year old at the time, I was five.

Chesière, Switzerland, where I went to school in 1935 and 1936.

With schoolmates at L'Avenir, my school in Switzerland. Skiing was our favorite winter pastime. I am standing third from the right.

Me, at four years old . . .

. . . at ten in Bucharest,

. . . at fifteen,

and at nineteen.

26

The Downs School, Colwall, England, where I studied from 1937 to 1939. The school still looks the same today, forty years later. *(insert)* I, during my days at The Downs.

A photograph of my parents in 1976, taken outside their home in Atherton, California.

A typical scene of rural Rumania as it was when I lived there.

CHAPTER 4

A Temporary Haven

PERHAPS THE DIVINE FISHERMAN was thinking this poor fish had better not be pulled in too forcibly, lest he break the line. At any rate, the process of dragging me out of my little pond of earthly security became, for a time, relatively pleasant for me. After six months in Bucharest my health was greatly improved. I was eleven years old now, and my parents were anxious to see me resume my formal education.

A Quaker boys' school in England had been highly recommended to us. Nestling snugly in the heart of the Malvern Hills near the village of Colwall, The Downs School was surrounded by verdant, rolling fields, and by narrow country roads that wound their way carefully between clipped, very *English* hedges. The buildings were attractive, and the grounds spacious. I was steeled to the idea, which months earlier had been so painful to me, of living away from home. The Downs seemed a better place than most in which to spend my exile.

The English have many wonderful traits: honor, loyalty, a sense of duty and fair play. Since, however, this is a chronicle of my spiritual search, I cannot in good conscience ignore what comes across to me as a certain blind spot in their national temperament: a reliance so complete on the ordinary that it gives almost no credence to the extraordinary. Something there is about the religious spirit of England that tries to mold Jesus Christ himself into the very proper image of an English gentleman, and casts the Old Testament prophets as fellow club members with him, perhaps writing occasional letters to the *Times* in protest against the lamentable want of good form in a few of their countrymen. Whether members of the Church of England or of any other sect, the English give one the impression of having neatly clipped and trimmed their religion, like a hedge, to protect values that are primarily social. I refer not to the courageous, free-thinking few, but to the

28

many whose worship seems to close, rather than open, windows onto infinity.

I hope I am wrong. At any rate, the only memorable religious event for me during my two years at The Downs occurred one Sunday evening when the father of one of our students, an Anglican minister, delivered a sermon. This man's body, almost perfectly round, was surmounted by a face that was dangerously suggestive of a pig's—dangerously, I say, because his porcine appearance, combined with a spirit of immense dignity, reduced me and a friend beside me to helpless fits of merriment. All I remember clearly now is looking up at one point, through tears, to see "the pig" describing a wide circle with his arms. "And the whole world . . ." he cried feelingly. His gesture so perfectly outlined his own global figure that fresh paroxysms of mirth overwhelmed us. The row directly behind ours was filled with faculty members, but to my surprise none of them endeavored to discipline us. Perhaps they, too, were finding self-control difficult!

The Downs was easily the best school I ever attended. Religious teaching there may not have been exactly ponderous, but in other respects the teachers knew how to draw the best out of their students. Character building is more basic to the English educational system than to the American. At The Downs, honor, fair play, truthfulness, and a sense of responsibility were given strong emphasis. To tell a lie was considered almost beneath contempt. A boy was once caught stealing sixpence and a little candy from another boy's locker, and so shocked everyone that he was expelled from the school.

In sports, too, though we did our best to win, we were taught that the game itself, not its outcome, was what really mattered. After rugby matches with other schools the members of both teams dined together, rivalry forgotten, new friendships affirmed. I have sometimes wondered what would happen if opposing teams in America were to dine together following a game. Given our national emphasis on winning, I suspect there might be a free-for-all.

Once, in punishment for some peccadillo, a group of us were told to run several miles around a course of country roads. No one checked up on us to make sure we didn't spend that time lying under some tree instead. Mr. Hoyland, the headmaster, knew it wouldn't occur to us to break our word to him.

Another time, as punishment for some infraction, I was told not to go swimming on three occasions when I really wanted to. The trust implied in this condition helped me to live up to it, though I must admit that on one of those occasions it was raining, so I wouldn't have been able to go anyway.

Needless to say, idealism didn't always win out over basic human weaknesses, nor propriety over boyhood's natural exuberance. But on the whole I am impressed with what the English school system was able to accomplish.

The Downs School had a number of innovative features of its own: two kinds of marks, for example, one of them in Greek letters, to show how well we'd done in the subjects themselves; and the other in colors, to show how earnestly we'd applied ourselves to those subjects. Those bright colors seemed somehow even more worth striving for than the letter grades.

Wednesday afternoons were our hobby time. We were allowed to select our own hobbies, on approval, and were given qualified instructors for them. My first year there I studied sculpture; my second, painting. For what would have been my third year, a group of us generated enough interest to get astronomy approved. But for me, as will become clear later on, that year was not destined to be.

In addition to sculpture and painting I studied piano, and also sang in the choir. Our choir instructor, a puffy-cheeked, solemn, but good-natured lady, would peer at us myopically as she waved her baton. With great earnestness she taught us to sing:

> Bach and Handel, as you know
> Died and were buried long ago.
> Born in the year one-six-eight-five,
> Still they're very much alive.

If this ditty fell short of the musical standards it celebrated, we had no quarrel with the sentiment it expressed. For we loved classical music. Actually I seldom heard popular music until we moved to America. My parents and their friends occasionally threw parties and danced to records, but to us boys this was just "grown-up nonsense." I remember how we shook with merriment the time I imitated for my brothers a recording I'd heard in England of "My Dear Mister Shane," sung in extravagantly nasal accents by the Andrews Sisters. At The Downs, too, tastes ran generally to classical music, except perhaps among the older boys. It was quite unselfconscious on our part; we simply liked it.

Too many people treat the classics as though they were something to be bolted down with water and a wry face. But if children's tastes weren't conditioned otherwise by their sexually awakened elders, I think most of them might grow up loving great music.

Life in England exposed me also to another kind of sound: the British accent. Not that I was unfamiliar with it; many of our friends in Rumania were English. But there at least we mixed with them on neutral ground. Here only I was a foreigner. Placed at such a disadvantage, I worked hard to overcome it. By the time I returned home for my first vacation I was already saying "ne-oh," and "shahn't" with the best of 'em—much to the dismay of my parents.

At first I tried awkwardly to cloak my shyness under a somewhat ill-fitting mantle of jocularity. A boy named Randall decided my behavior lacked proper dignity for a Downs boy. When I passed off his scolding with another joke, he became so irritated that he challenged me to a fight. Randall was the accepted leader of our form,° and was accustomed to being obeyed.

Grudges at The Downs weren't supposed to be settled on the spot. To win time for a possible reconciliation, the rule was to submit a formal challenge, after which a boxing match was arranged in the gym, complete with seconds and a referee.

I accepted Randall's challenge. The date for the match was set. As the days passed, and Randall observed in me no sign of fear, his attitude toward me gradually changed.

"Let's be friends," he suggested one day. I assured him I'd never felt we were enemies. In time our friendship developed into one of the happiest I have ever known.

Randall was good-natured, highly intelligent, sensitive yet practical, and intensely earnest in everything he did. His friendship opened for me the door to acceptance by the other boys. Once accepted, I brought to them a lighter spirit—the ability, for example, to laugh at oneself. Our Latin teacher, Mr. Days, a formidable man whose bluff I somehow managed to penetrate, wrote to me years later, "Yours wasn't, perhaps, the brightest class I ever had, but it was certainly the happiest."

Days passed in study, good fellowship, and sports. A fast runner, I managed to play wing three-quarter (the principal running position) in several of the rugby games with other schools. Cricket, however, I considered an utter waste of a sunny afternoon. In practice sessions, which were obligatory, I would lie down in the outfield and wait comfortably for someone to shout, "Walters, get up! The ball's coming your way!"

Sometimes there were inter-form "wars"—in fun, not in anger. One form would "board" the other, perhaps through windows that hadn't been secured quickly enough. Fights at The Downs, even those initiated in anger, commonly strengthened the spirit of friendship.

° The English equivalent of *grade.*

This was an outcome that, to my surprise, I never encountered in the schools I attended later in America.

But while we scrapped and competed merrily in classrooms and on the playing fields, another more serious conflict was developing in Europe. The relentless approach of World War II made a somber backdrop to our school days, one that was never very far from our thoughts. Many of us, we realized, might have to fight in the next war. Many of us would probably be killed.

The pride of the English is intense. One boy, dignifying with the label of patriotism what was really only a mean nature, once called me a "dirty foreigner." I was inured to the second half of this role, so didn't feel greatly offended. "If I'm a dirty foreigner," I replied, smiling, "perhaps you're a dirty Englishman." Outraged, the boy leapt at me. I proved stronger than he, and had no difficulty in holding him down till he tired of hurling imprecations and cooled off. Later I related the incident to Randall and one or two other friends, and was impressed at the depth of their patriotic feeling. Their laughter at the outset was generous; none of them liked the boy, and all of them liked me. But it subsided when I reached the point where I'd said, "Perhaps you're a dirty Englishman." Their sympathy returned only when I explained that it was purely a question of whether or not the other boy had recently bathed.

England's Prime Minister, Sir Neville Chamberlain, went to Germany in 1938, and returned with the welcome proclamation "Peace in our time." Much was made in the press of his glad tidings, though I don't think people put much faith in them. At any rate, gas masks were soon passed out to each of us at school. On a trip to Rumania with Roy Redgrave, the son of family friends of ours there, we sang the English national anthem loudly in the streets of Nuremberg, feeling very brave, though I don't suppose the Gestapo felt particularly threatened by a couple of skinny English schoolboys. What children do, however, reflects the spirit of their elders. Throughout Europe, defiance was now in the air. It could only be a matter of time before open conflict broke out.

My two years in England gave me much to be grateful for. The friendships I formed there, and the good times we had, left me with many happy memories. Though circumstances prevented me from returning for my third and final year, Mr. Hoyland had selected me for the second half of that year to be the head boy. But my gain was not only in the form of memories. I also learned many worthwhile lessons, particularly on the correctness or incorrectness of different patterns of behavior. Such teaching borders on an important spiritual principle. For as my guru was to emphasize later, it is not enough to be guided by high ideals: One must also "learn to behave." That is to say, one must know how to relate properly to every reality on its own level.

This balance of the inner and outer aspects of one's life is not easy to achieve. My two years in England helped me toward this fulfillment. Partly for this reason, England has always held a warm place in my heart. So great is my regard for the fine characteristics of her people, and so loving were the friendships I formed there, that I think I shall always remain, in part, an Englishman.

CHAPTER 5

The Storm Breaks

IT WAS SPRING, 1939. Dad, after fifteen years in Rumania, had risen to become head geologist for Esso in Europe. Now he was being transferred to Zagreb, Yugoslavia, there to be Esso's exploration manager. All our belongings were packed and stored in Bucharest, ready for shipment. In March Dad rented an apartment in The Hague, Holland, on Koninginnegracht. We spent our Easter vacation there. (Fond memories of picturesque streets, acres of tulips, and smiling, friendly people!)

Summer came, and with it another visit to America. The weeks passed quietly for us among relatives in Ohio and Oklahoma. August was about to close its ledger; it was time for us to return to Europe. We entrained at Tulsa for New York.

As we stepped out onto the station platform in Chicago, the headline struck us with all the force of an ocean wave: *WAR!* Hitler had invaded Poland. Hopes for peace had been smashed on rocks of hatred and nationalistic greed. To return now to a war-torn continent would be foolish. Dad was transferred to the head offices of Esso at Rockefeller Center, in New York City. Our belongings, packed and ready for shipment to Zagreb, had only to be rerouted to America.

We settled eventually in the New York suburb of Scarsdale, at 90 Brite Avenue, in the Foxmeadow section. For the next nine years this was to be my home, or rather my point of perennial departure.

While I was still a small child my parents had enrolled me at Kent School, in Kent, Connecticut. This was a church school for boys, run by Episcopalian monks. I was not scheduled to enter Kent for another year, however, and was placed meanwhile at Hackley, a boys' school near Tarrytown, New York.

And now the Divine Fisherman began once again to reel in His line determinedly. Looking back after all these years, it is easier for me to summon up a certain proper sense of gratitude to God for holding me so closely in check. At that time, however, I'm afraid gratitude was not my uppermost sentiment. A month earlier my expectations had been glowing. I was returning to The Downs for a happy final year there, surrounded by good friends. Now suddenly I found myself, at thirteen, the youngest boy in the lowest grade of a high school where the only familiar feature was my own perennial status as a "foreigner," a status which, as a born American returning to his own country to live, I found particularly distasteful.

Even my accent, now English, set me apart. But whereas formerly, in England, my American accent had occasioned little more than good-natured amusement, here my English accent marked me for derision. It took me at least a year to learn to "talk American" once again.

Heretofore in my life I had never heard a dirty word. At Hackley it seemed, once I'd been initiated into the new vocabulary, that I heard little else. In the past, swing music had been only an amusing game. Here, it was practically a religion. Sex had never before figured in our conversations. Here, it was virtually an obsession. Aggressive behavior, rudeness, insensitivity to others as an affirmation of one's own independence—these, it seemed, were the norms. School "wisdom" included such precious advice as "Silence is golden—and also healthy."

The fact that I was just entering puberty made the problem of adjustment all the more difficult. In truth, I could see no good reason to adjust. Rather, I tended to enclose myself defensively within psychic walls, like a medieval town under attack. One or two of the boys were friendly to me, but to the others I seemed merely an import, dumped on American soil quite unnecessarily, and, considering the solid worth of the domestic article, even presumptuously.

In the room next to mine there was a boy of fifteen, named Tommy, who weighed two hundred and twenty pounds to my one hundred and seven. Tommy was a bully. My "English ways" were, to him, an insult to the glory of America. It wasn't long before, dissatisfied with merely voicing his disapproval, he advanced to open threats.

I'm not sure he was quite sane. One morning I awoke to see him peering in my window, an air pistol in his hand. As I leapt to safety behind my desk, a bullet struck the other side of it with a thud.

What bothered Tommy about me, I think, was not only the implied insult of my un-American ways, but the fact that I wouldn't acknowledge my self-evident inferiority by cringing before him. Later that day he made it a point to sit next to me at lunch, the better to express his opinions. Throughout the meal he criticized my appearance, my vocabulary, my table manners. ("Don't you know you should spoon your soup toward the *far* side of the bowl—peasant?") I paid no attention to him. Finally he muttered, "Boy, am I going to get you!"

I knew he meant it. Back in my room after lunch I pushed the dresser up against the door, which was without a lock. Tommy arrived shortly afterward, breathing threats. He rattled the doorknob, then leaned heavily against the door, puffing dire predictions with mounting fury. At last, succeeding in shoving the door open, he rushed into the room like an enraged bull and proceeded to beat me with such uncontrolled rage that it really seemed as if he wanted to kill me.

"I'm going to throw you out that window!" he panted again and again. (We were three storeys above the ground.) Throughout the beating he kept his voice low for fear of attracting the attention of others on our floor. Somehow the ferocity of his whisper sounded more invidious than an angry shout.

What could I do, small as I was? I lay motionless on the bed, face down, waiting for him to exhaust himself.

"Why didn't you cry for help?" a friend asked me the next day.

"Because I wasn't afraid."

Interestingly, the fact that I took Tommy's beating calmly, and never thereafter altered my attitude toward him, left him without another weapon to use against me.

People commonly see physical victory as conclusive. But true victory is always mental. One's conqueror may feel conquered in turn by a spirit that he finds he cannot reach with physical weapons.

Tommy, from this time on, gave me a wide berth.

Though I was released now from his bullying, in other respects my life at Hackley grew no happier. I sought escape in the music room, where for hours at a time I practiced the piano. My unhappiness stirred me also for the first time to a longing for the religious life. Perhaps, I thought, I would become a missionary. I expressed these aspirations, somewhat hesitantly, to my cousin Betty, when both of us were at my parents' home in Scarsdale. She was horrified.

"Not a missionary, Don! There's too much to *do* in this world. You wouldn't want to bury yourself on some primitive island!"

The vigor of her reaction shook me in my still-frail resolution.

What, after all, did I really know about the missionary calling? Self-doubt was in any case becoming my own private hell.

After a year at Hackley School, the time came for me to enter Kent.

Kent is an Ivy League prep school that ranks high, scholastically and socially. I entered it with high hopes. But I soon found that the general interests of the boys here were essentially what they had been at Hackley, with the addition of a sort of "All for God, Country, and Our School Team" spirit in which arrogance played the leading part. The Kent student was expected by his peers to embrace every social norm, to like or dislike all the "right" people, and to boast of his proficiency in all the "right" activities, particularly those related to sex and drinking. Woe betide that hapless youth who danced to a different piper. To laugh with the loudest, to tell the dirtiest jokes, to shout boisterously when merely passing the time of day, to smile expansively at everyone ("Oh, *hi*, Don!") in a bid to get *others* to like *you:* These were the banners of success. Conformity made one eligible for that supreme reward: popularity. Nonconformity exiled one to a limbo of disapproval and contempt.

Experience had shown me that I had the ability to make friends. But what was I to do when, try as I might, I simply couldn't share the enthusiasms of my fellow students? It was not a question, as it had been in England, of relating to new realities on their own level. In England, principles at least had been concerned. Here I could find none—only egotism, selfishness, and self-interest. I might have been able to stand my ground firmly had I been able to out-shout, out-boast, and out-laugh others. As it was, being naturally somewhat shy, I was unwilling to offer my ideas where I felt they were unwelcome.

Instead I became intensely introverted, miserable with myself, certain that my life was already, at its outset, a failure. In an environment that demanded absolute conformity, an inability to conform seemed like failure indeed. Gradually it became as evident to others as it already was to me that I was simply one of that unfortunate breed, of which the human race will ever produce its allotted few: a misfit, a general embarrassment, a creature of subnormal ability.

Yet in my heart I knew this judgment to be false.

I tried my best to enter into the life of the school. I joined the school paper, reporting sports events with a hopeful heart. But my first two articles spelled my undoing; my humorous touch on so sacred a subject as *sports* was considered tantamount to blasphemy. The editor smiled with amusement, then appeased his conscience by withholding further assignments from me. I joined the debating society, but found I couldn't speak in defense of issues to which I wasn't sincerely committed. I became a member of the French club, but my fellow members were for the most part lonely outcasts like me. I played football. I rowed. I sang in the glee club.

Nothing worked. There was almost a kind of shame in the few friendships I did form, a tacit understanding that ours was a companionship in failure.

At times I was actually afraid to leave a roomful of boys, lest my departure give them the opportunity to talk against me. Nor were my fears groundless: I knew, from the times when I stayed, what uncomplimentary things they could say about those less popular boys who happened to be absent. One day, after passing a couple of classmates on the stairway in our dormitory, I overheard one of them, obviously not caring whether I heard him or not, laugh derisively, "What a sad case!"

The worst of it was, I had no clear grounds on which to refute him.

During this gloomy period, religion might have been the comfort for me that it had been at Hackley. Kent was, after all, a church school, and most of the boys there were moderately religious; at least, I recall none of them grumbling over the required attendance at worship services. But religion at Kent seemed as though it were being kept preserved in formaldehyde. With the exception of one jolly, elderly brother who taught no classes, and who was, I'm afraid, a little foolish, the monks seemed a joyless lot, uninspired and uninspiring in their calling. The church services were heavy with the consciousness that one went through all this merely because it was *done*. Religion at Kent inspired me to look almost anywhere but to God for solace and enlightenment.

Soon I was seeking both of these fulfillments in the realm of ideas. Always a bookworm, I began diving into the worlds of James Fenimore Cooper, Sir Walter Scott, Keats, Shelley, Shaw, and other great writers.

At fourteen I began writing a novel of my own. The influence of Cooper was evident in my setting: A pioneer family, living on an isolated farm in Oklahoma, was attacked by red Indians. Only two boys escaped massacre, by fleeing during the confusion. Earnestly, at this point, I counseled the reader not to think harshly of the Indians, "for they had been oppressed by the white man ever since he came to this continent, and had had their hunting grounds taken away and changed into towns and places of civilization. . . . Nor must you think ill of their scalping methods, for that was just the coustom [*sic*] among the indians, and though we may think it cruel or repulsive, surely some of the things we do are just as bad, if not more so."

The two boys escaped into a nearby forest, pursued by Indians. Deep in the forest they discovered a cliff, scaled it to a high ledge, and there rested, thinking they'd arrived unobserved. Minutes later, one of them happened to look down from their ledge, "and drew back in astonishment, for there, not five feet below him, was an Indian, and following him came three more, the last two carrying guns, but the others without them for greater agility. Just then the foremost one heard him and uttered a word that would correspond to our word 'Shucks!' For they had planned on a surprise." (How I've laughed over that Indian's disappointed exclamation!)

The boys, having nowhere else to go, fled into a nearby cave. Down and down it led them, deep under the surface of the earth. At last, to their amazement, they emerged into another world, inexplicably sunlit and beautiful. Here Indians and white men lived happily together in perfect brotherhood: hence the title of the novel, *The Happy Hunting Grounds.*

This was all, of course, pure escapism. Yet it also reflected a feeling which I think comes to many people from time to time in their lives: the deep, inner certainty that their true home *is* elsewhere, that they belong in heaven, and that the present world is only a proving ground for the soul. As Jesus said, "No man hath ascended up to heaven, but he that came down from heaven."* This certainty is born not of speculation, but of deep astral memories that have been dimmed by more recent, earthly experiences.

Unhappiness and suffering are necessary for the soul's unfoldment. Without them we might remain satisfied with petty fulfillments. Worse still, we might remain satisfied with *ourselves.*† My personal unhappiness at Kent School inspired me to meditate on the sufferings of mankind everywhere. Could anything, I wondered, be done to improve the human lot?

Surely, if all men would truly accept one another as equals they would be much happier. I laboriously worked out a system of government in which no man possessed any personal property, all things being owned in common. Though I don't think I realized it at the time, my ideas were similar in several respects to those preached, though hardly practiced, under modern communism. But

---

* John 3:13.
† "Because thou sayest, I am rich, and increased with goods, and have need of nothing; and knowest not that thou art wretched, and miserable, and poor, and blind, and naked: I counsel thee to buy of me gold tried in the fire . . . and anoint thine eyes with eyesalve, that thou mayest see" (Revelation 3:17,18).

as I pondered the matter more deeply, I came to realize that most men are not capable of living in a voluntary state of nonpossession. A few people—monks, for instance—might be non-attached enough to consider nothing their own, but to *force* nonpossession on humanity at large would be tyranny. Dictatorship, even in the name of the common weal, would inflict more abuses than it could alleviate.

At this time also I wrote a one-act play, titled *The Peace Treaty*. Its subtitle was "Every Man for Himself." It was about a group of cave men, tribal chieftains, who got together after a war to determine the conditions for peace. One of them, like all visionaries ahead of his times, proposed an idea that he claimed would banish war forevermore. His plan demanded a generous spirit of international cooperation among the different tribes to replace the inter-tribal rivalries and selfishness that had prevailed hitherto. The other chieftains professed great admiration for his ideas. But it soon became clear that they understood him not at all, for when it came to the question of what sacrifices each would have to make to ensure peace, each suggested a few "minimal" improvements in the original plan, with a view to getting as many concessions as possible for himself. The peace treaty was finally thrown out as chieftains scrambled for whatever booty each could grab for himself.

At the close of the play the hero soliloquized: "If God existed, would He allow all this? . . . But—of course He exists! How could life have come to this earth without Him? Ah! I see it all now. Yes, God exists, but He wishes mankind to live under hard conditions, for it is only under such that Man can prove himself worthy of the Kingdom of Heaven." God cares, I concluded, but wants man to *earn* His blessings, for without victory over greed, paradise itself would become but another battleground. Man, I was saying, is not perfectible through outward systems, but only in himself. The play ended with blows and shouts offstage, followed by gunshots, then cannonades, then bombs, and finally one bomb, mightier than all the rest. And after that: *silence*.

The hard reality of human greed was the stumbling block on which my dreams of political salvation became shattered. At fifteen I began writing another novel, about a man who foresaw the destruction of modern civilization, and decided to do what he could to preserve its most constructive elements. Far out into the wilderness he went, and there built a utopian community. Aiding him were experts in various fields, men and women who understood that expertise must be rooted in wisdom and love, not merely in knowledge. This little community kept the lamp of civilization burning while the rest of humanity bombed itself back to the caves. The group then returned to their fellow men to teach them a better, more constructive way of life.

The more I thought about my visionary community, the more compellingly it attracted me. From an escapist dream my concept evolved gradually to a spreading network of intentional villages *within* the framework of present-day civilization. Someday, I resolved, I would start such a community myself.

It isn't often that one's boyhood dreams are later fulfilled. With God's grace, this one has been. That tale, however, must await its telling until a later chapter.

I gave much thought also at Kent to the possibility of paranormal phenomena—prophecy, telepathy, and the mental control of objective events—and to the question of what life is like after death. I wondered whether I might serve my fellow man better if I tried to develop extra-sensory powers myself. But no, I decided, this whole subject was too remote from common experience to be meaningful to most people. Instead I would become a writer; through words perhaps I would be able to inspire others to a loftier vision.

While I was mentally improving the world, however, my own little world was deteriorating rapidly. A few of the older boys conceived what must have been almost a hatred of me. Ineptness I suppose they might have excused; not everyone, after all, could hope to match them in their excellence. But while self-admittedly inept in their ways, I had gone on from this recognition of failure to develop other—to them, inadmissible—interests. Was not this implied rejection of their standards unthinkably presumptuous? They began openly threatening to make my life "really miserable" next year, when a few of them would be returning to Kent as student body leaders.

I felt I could take no more. In tears that summer I pleaded with Mother to take me home.

Stroking my head tenderly, she said, "I know, dear. I know. You're like your Dad. He's always been shy when people didn't want what he had to give them. Yet he has so much to offer. And so do you. People haven't understood it, but never mind. Stay home now, and live with us who love you. Here you'll be happy."

What relief flooded my heart! I never saw Kent again. Who can say whether I might yet have coaxed a few useful lessons from its dreary walls? But I felt I had taken from them every blessing that I possibly could. I was ready now, inwardly as well as outwardly, for a different kind of schooling.

At age fourteen, when I was attending Kent School.

Our home at 90 Brite Avenue, Scarsdale, New York.

CHAPTER **6**

A Paper Rest House:
the "Popularity Game"

MOST OF THE YOUNG PEOPLE I met during my adolescence seemed secure in their values. The 1940s were unlike today, when it is common for young people to question society's values, to seek Meaning, to ponder their relationship to the universe and to God. When I was in high school, as nearly as I could tell I walked alone in such questing. I knew no guidelines to follow. I wasn't even sure what it was I was seeking. All I knew definitely was that I wanted *something,* and that that something didn't seem to be what anyone else wanted.

Others had already planned their lives more or less confidently. They would get good jobs, make money, get ahead in the world, marry, settle down in Scarsdale or in some other wealthy community, raise children, throw cocktail parties, and enjoy the fruits of a normal, worldly life. But I already knew I didn't want money. I didn't want to "get ahead" materially. I wasn't interested in marrying and raising a family. I knew well enough a few of the things I *didn't* want, but had no distinct notion of what it was I *did* want. And in this uncertainty I sometimes doubted whether my disinclination for the things others prized wasn't proof of some inadequacy in myself.

Had others, I wondered, secure as they evidently were in their norms, achieved some insight to which I was blind? Certainly my lifelong inability to adopt a conventional outlook had for years been a source of intense unhappiness to me.

Now that I had left Kent, and was enrolled as a senior in Scarsdale High School, I determined to overcome what was surely a defect in my character. This new school year, I decided, I would try a great experiment. I would pretend to myself that I *liked* what everyone else liked, that their values were my values, their norms mine. I would see whether, by deliberately adopting their outlook, I could not begin at last to feel at home with it. If I succeeded, how easy my life would become! Resolutely I set my sights. This last year of high school would mark my giant step forward into normality.

As a first step toward "swinging with the crowd," I seized energetically on swing music. Every week I listened eagerly to the radio with my brothers to learn which popular songs had made it onto the Hit Parade. I put on crowd-consciousness like a suit, and soon found that it fit snugly enough. In shouting competitions I pitched in and shouted. In laughing I bubbled with the best. I dated. I danced. I became the vocalist for a local dance band. And as I made a great noise I found, incredibly, that I both liked it and was liked for it.

I began the school year with a major advantage: Both of my brothers were popular. Bob, who was in the tenth grade, was loved by everyone, including upperclassmen. His was not the typical attitude of the Big Man on Campus—more interested, that is to say, in being loved than in loving, and ever careful to associate with only the "right" people. Bob genuinely liked *everyone*. It made no difference to him whether they were looked up to or down on by others. He was their friend, and they knew it. Unable to tone his voice lower than a gentle boom, he dominated every gathering, but no one seemed to mind. Somehow in his company they felt more generous, more sure of their own goodness.

His enthusiasm for life was boundless. One day, coming home from playing in a football game, he was found to have a fever of 105°. Ill as he was, he had insisted on finishing the game.

They called him "Bucky," after Bucky Walters, the famous baseball player. Though the nickname has remained with him, I myself have never used it, for I know that he has also a deeper side, one that he doesn't often reveal to others—a refined sensitivity to music, a deep gentleness, a certain nobility of character, all of which seem to me rather betrayed by the hail-fellow-well-met implications in that nickname.

From the start it was obvious to everyone that Bob and I were very different specimens. A few of my classmates, besides, had heard from Phil Boote, my ex-roommate at Kent. Phil also lived in Scarsdale, and had shown enough sense of community responsibility to warn them what a social disaster I was. For Bob's sake, however, and because I was so obviously determined to mend my unconventional ways, they gave me the benefit of the doubt, and accepted me kindly enough into their midst.

Scarsdale High was much larger than Kent, a fact which permitted many different types there to mix happily without the same pressure being placed on them to conform as there had been at Kent. Being Bob's brother automatically threw me into the "in" group, a position I boldly accepted as the kind of challenge I needed to bring off my "great experiment" with a maximum of success.

I tried out for the football team. At 136 pounds, I was hardly first-string material. Still, I played hard during practice sessions, and at the games ardently supported our team from the bench. Unfortunately for my dreams of glory, I was a halfback, and so also was Charlie Rensenhouse, the team captain. Openings in that position were rare. The only time I actually made it onto the playing field during a game was once when Rensenhouse got hurt.

"Walters!" Coach Buchanan shouted.

My big opportunity? "Yes, Sir!" I cried, leaping eagerly to my feet.

"Walters, get out there and help Rensenhouse off the field."

In track I did better. We hadn't had a track team at Kent, so I was unfamiliar with the proper starting techniques, but I was a fast runner, and managed to acquit myself creditably. I actually ran the 100-yard dash in only 10.2 seconds at my first meet. Unfortunately, I pulled a ligament early in the season and was out of the running for the rest of the school year.

Of my classes, my favorite was English. Lucyle Hook, our English teacher, took a keen interest in her subject, loved her students, and obviously wanted with all her heart to share her knowledge with us. She was as much our friend as our teacher. With her encouragement I wrote short stories and poems. While none of them was particularly consequential, they were good enough at least to gain me a reputation as a budding talent, and fanned my determination to become a writer.

One of the students in my French class was a girl named Ruth, later voted the most beautiful girl in our senior class. I dated her frequently, and became as infatuated with her as any boy is likely to be with his first girlfriend. But there were potholes on the highway of our romance.

Dad, for fear of spoiling us boys, gave us a weekly allowance of only fifty cents. I had to save for two weeks merely to take Ruth out to the movies. Even then, we usually had to walk the several miles to White Plains and back. It wasn't the best possible setup for making a good impression on a girl.

Worse still, when it came to something so deeply personal as

romance I couldn't put on my extroverted bluff, which was carrying me along successfully enough in other departments of my life.
Somehow I'd conceived the notion that I was physically unattractive,
and that I had nothing worthwhile really to offer anyone. Because
I doubted my own worth, moreover, I was afraid to trust myself to
another person's feelings about me. When another boy, a large,
perennially joking, popular football star, began dating Ruth, I
hadn't the self-confidence to compete with him. For that matter, I
wouldn't have competed with him even if I'd been bursting with
confidence, for I could never see love in the light of self-imposition
and conquest.

Singing I found a joy. Mr. Hubbard, our chorus director, tried
to persuade me to take it up as a career. "There's money in your
voice," he would insist, not realizing that money was probably the
poorest lure he could have dangled before me. That year I sang in
Handel's *Messiah,* and in Gilbert and Sullivan's *Yeomen of the Guard.*
At our Church of St. James the Less, my brothers and I also sang
the roles of the three wise men in the Christmas pageant, an event
which, I was surprised to learn recently, is still remembered by
some old-timers in Scarsdale.

Other activities at the church, I must admit, held less appeal for
me. Our minister, Father Price, kept threatening us in his sermons
that if we didn't toe the straight and narrow we'd soon end up
"right in the lap of the Nazis."

Instead, I began bending rather too far in another direction.
Doug Burch, a friend of Bob's and mine, introduced me to Nick's,
a night club in Greenwich Village, famous as a hangout for
Dixieland jazz enthusiasts. Eddie Condon, Peewee Russell, and
other jazz "greats" played here with such consummate skill that I
actually found myself growing to like jazz. Fascinated with this new
"scene," I absorbed all its trivia: how the wife of one of the taller
players used to beat him up; how the band ate in a night club
across the street because Nick wouldn't feed them properly; how a
little old lady showed up on Saturday nights, took a front table,
and clapped her hands enthusiastically to the music, shouting,
"Yeah! Yeah!" like any teenager. It is amazing that people can
make as much as they do out of this kind of "news," merely because celebrities are involved. But they do. And we did.

It was at Nick's that I took my first alcoholic drink. Of all the
foolish pastimes to which mankind is given, drinking must surely
rank near the top of the list. Few people, I imagine, take up either
drinking or smoking for pleasure alone. It seems more a question
of not wanting to appear gauche. At any rate, those were my

motives. Alcohol I found at least not positively sickening, but smoking was like learning to enjoy rotten food.

I remember clearly the first time I learned to inhale. A girl at a party in Scarsdale showed me the knack. One drag made me so dizzy I almost slipped to the floor. Then, with the kind of inverted idealism that marked most of that year for me, I told myself sternly, "I'm going to *master* this thing if it kills me!" Little did I realize that *true* mastery would have meant not succumbing to such silliness in the first place. That evening I succeeded in "mastering" smoking, but I'm afraid it wasn't long before smoking mastered me.

The worst of drinking, from a spiritual standpoint, is not the temporary stupor it may induce, nor the hangover that sometimes follows an indiscreet "night on the town," but the long-range effect that alcohol exerts on the personality. In some subtle way it seems to make one more worldly; one's perceptions become less refined; one inclines, if ever so slightly, to scoff at things that he formerly considered sacred. The ego, in becoming less sensitively responsive to its environment, becomes more self-assertive and aggressive. It is as if it were gripping harder in an effort to compensate for the diminution of its natural powers. These effects, as I say, may be observed not only during hours of inebriation, but as actual, long-term personality changes.

The explanation may be that things, inert though they seem, actually serve as media for various states of consciousness. We may scoff, as I used to do, at "holy Joes" in church who denounce "likker" as a tool of Satan, but many a truth has been hooted down with laughter. The very inclination, so common in societies where drinking is popular, to tell jokes about drunkenness suggests a subconscious desire to silence the whisper of conscience. For every man must know deep inside him that drunkenness is an insult to his true divine nature.

Another "thing" through which consciousness often gets changed is music. Looking back, I am astonished to see how quickly, by my constant, *willing* exposure to swing music, I came to assume attitudes that I had thought formerly quite foreign to me. As months passed it became more and more my second nature to see life in terms of sports, romance, and good times, to laugh with the loudest, roam hither and yon with the most restless, and give and take in the youthful exuberance of an ego competing more or less insensitively with other egos.

Yet somewhere, deep inside me, there was a watchful friend who remained unimpressed, who questioned my motives, observed my follies with detachment, and demanded of me with a sad smile of reproach, "Is this what you *really* want?" I was frank enough with myself to admit that it wasn't.

Gradually the longing grew within me to stop wasting time. I could see that there was too much in life to learn, too much towards which to grow. For my English source theme at the end of the school year I elected to write on the subject *The Different Concepts of the Universe that Were Held by Ancient Civilizations, and the Quality in Each Civilization that Influenced the Development of Its Particular Concept.* Questions that had no part in my Great Experiment returned insistently to my mind: What is life? What is the universe? What is the purpose of life on earth? Such issues could not be laughed away with another night at Nick's.

One evening a classmate and I visited a local diner, an "in" place with the high school crowd. While we were waiting for seats, my friend began making impromptu additions to the music that was playing on the juke box. Laughingly I encouraged him. All the while, however, my silent inner "friend" demanded of me indignantly, "What is all this jerking about, this nodding of the head up and down like an animated puppet, this contortion of the facial muscles? Is not this, too, a kind of drunkenness?"

My outer friend wrote afterwards in my year book how much he had enjoyed our little "jam session" together. But I felt merely embarrassed by it, as though I had been the plaything of a rhythm-induced hysteria.

At Scarsdale High I learned that I could, if I wanted to, play the Great American Popularity Game and come out, in a sense, a winner. But my success had not made me any happier. If I felt that I now understood something of what other young people wanted from life, I couldn't say that I was any more attracted to their vision.

I was back almost at the beginning. The one thing I had learned this year was how to wrap a veil around myself and hide my true feelings. Well, perhaps after all this was a useful lesson. There can be little merit in exposing one's highest aspirations to people who don't appreciate them. But it wasn't much of a step towards *fulfilling* my aspirations. My next step, I realized, must be more deliberately in the direction of that fulfillment.

CHAPTER 7

To Thine Own Search Be True

I GRADUATED FROM Scarsdale High School in June 1943, shortly after turning seventeen. Bob and I were invited by George Calvert, a school friend of ours, to work with him on his father's farm in upstate New York. That summer we picked strawberries and pitched hay. The work was vigorous, healthful, and good fun. After six or seven weeks as a farm hand, I decided to take advantage of my vacation to broaden my experience of the world. The change I hit upon was radical: from bucolic pastures to grey skyscrapers and acres of sterile concrete.

New York! I worked there as a messenger boy for the *Herald Tribune*. Every day, dodging determined cars, trucks, and buses, and weaving through impatient hordes of shoppers, my fellow messenger boys and I visited the inner sanctums of well-known department stores, delivered advertising copy to and from countless corporations, and swept pellmell through the rushing bloodstream of big-city life. The myriad sense impressions were stimulating, almost overwhelming. In madly bobbing faces on crowded sidewalks, in pleading glances from behind drugstore counters, in fleeting smiles, frosty stares, angry gestures, twitching lips, and self-preoccupied frowns, I saw mankind in virtual caricature, exaggerated out of all credible proportion by the sheer enormity of numbers. Here were tumbling waves of humanity: the youthfully exuberant, the sad and lonely, the stage-struck, the grimly success-oriented, the hard and cynical, the fragile, the lost. All looked hurried and nervous. All seemed harassed by desire.

New York! Its heaving sea of humanity charms and repels in the same instant. It encourages a sense of exaggerated self-importance in those who pride themselves on living in one of the largest, most vital cities in the world. But, in the anonymity it imposes on its faceless millions, it also mocks at self-importance. New Yorkers face a perennial conflict between these opposing challenges to their egos, a conflict that is resolved only by those who seek a broader, spiritual identity. For in the frenzied pace of big-city life it is as if God were whispering to the soul: "Dance with bubbles if you like, but when you tire of dancing, and your bubbles begin bursting one by one, look about you at all these other faces. They are your spiritual brothers and sisters, mirrors to your own self! They *are* you. O little wave, transcend your littleness. Be one with all of them. Be one with life!"

When autumn came I began my higher education at Haverford College, a small men's college on the Main Line to Paoli from Philadelphia. At that time, owing to the war, it was smaller than ever.

The students were bright-eyed, enthusiastic, and intelligent; the professors, quiet, sedate, seriously concerned for their students' welfare. Haverford, a Quaker college, conveys the simple, serene dignity that is to be expected of institutions run by that pacific sect. I don't mean we students didn't have our normal boys' share of high times, but these were always inflicted on a background of gentle disapproval from the discreet greystone-and-ivy buildings, and of restrained dismay from our ever-concerned faculty.

The diminished student body was composed mostly of freshmen, a fact which didn't conduce greatly to the maintenance of certain hallowed college traditions, such as freshmen hazing. When a handful of upperclassmen appeared one day in our dormitory to subject us to that ancient rite, we met them with another venerable American institution: the bum's rush. With whoops of joy, flying pillows, energetic shoves, and a solid phalanx of inverted chairs, we drove them down the stairs and out of the building. Thereafter they left us strictly alone, concluding, no doubt, that in wartime there are certain sacrifices which older and wiser heads must make in the name of peace.

We freshman were so dominant numerically that I actually made the football team. One of my problems at Scarsdale High, apart from my light weight, had been that I could never throw the ball properly; my hands were simply too small to get a grip on it. At Haverford our coach, "Pop" Haddleton, solved this problem by making me a running guard. Counting on speed rather than weight, I found I could pull larger opponents off balance while they were still shifting their bodies into position to block me. I would then dash through the line and catch many a runner before he'd got off to a good start with the ball. The left guard, a boy named Mason, was as lightweight as I. Our college newspaper was soon dubbing us "the watch charm guards."

My big play of the season came near the end of a game. Up to that point neither team had scored. In a last, desperate maneuver we were going to try an end run down half the length of the field. I was to run interference. We cleared the end safely, and were well on our way into "enemy territory," when two men rushed to intercept us. I prepared to block the first of them, hoping our runner would be able to dodge the second. Just then I tripped on a dangling shoelace! Sprawling full length onto the ground, I made a perfect, though involuntary, double block. Our man went on to make the touchdown. And I was the hero of the hour. I tried to explain what had really happened, but no one wanted to believe me.

We won every game that season. And so it was that my school athletic career reached a happy climax—before petering out altogether.

For not long after this, college sports and I came to a rather cool parting of the ways. Our separation was due partly to my increasing preoccupation with the search for meaning, and partly, I'm afraid, to the fact that I was attaching "meaning" to a few of the wrong things—like sitting in local bars with friends, nursing a variety of poisonous decoctions, and talking philosophy into the wee hours.

I began devoting much of my free time also to writing poetry, the themes of which related to questions that had long been bothering me: Why suffering? Why warfare and destruction? How is it that God countenances hatred and other forms of human madness? Surely, I thought, suffering can't be His *will* for us? Must it not be a sign, rather, that man is *out of harmony* with God's will?

And what of eternal life? Not even matter or energy can be destroyed. Was it not reasonable, then, to suppose that life, too, is eternal? And if eternal, what about heaven and hell? I wrote a poem at this time in which I postulated a world after death that is perceived differently by each individual, seeming to be either beautiful or ugly, happy or sad, according to the state of consciousness he brings with him from this world.

At this point in my life I might easily have embraced a religious calling. But I knew too little about it, and found no guidance from others in directions that were meaningful to me. Haverford College is a prominent center of Quakerism. In my time there, leading members of this society were on the faculty: Douglas Steere, Rufus Jones, Howard Comfort. I was impressed by their transparent earnestness and goodness. I also liked the Quaker practice of sitting quietly in meditation at the Sunday services—"meetings," as they were called. Above all, I liked the Quakers for their simplicity. All that they did seemed admirable to me. But somehow I could find no challenge in it. I was seeking a path that would engross me utterly, not one that I could contemplate benignly while puffing on a pipe.

Sunday meetings became all too frequently the scene of genteel competition. The Quakers have no ordained ministers; their members sit in silence on Sunday mornings until one of them feels moved "of the Spirit" to rise and share some inspiration with others. Haverford being an intellectual community, our Sunday meetings were more than usually taken up with this kind of "moving." Hardly a minute passed in silence before someone else was on his feet, sharing with everyone else. Sometimes two or more were moved simultaneously—though, in such cases, courtesy always prevailed.

I'll never forget Douglas Steere rising one day to inquire brightly, "Is there a little bird in your bosom?" Involuntarily my hand went to my chest. The solemnity of the occasion, and my own respect for him, prevented me from succumbing to hilarity on the spot, but afterward my friends and I made up delightedly for our heroic repression.

Doubtless I had much to learn, not the least being reverence and humility. It may be that those religious leaders had more to teach me than I knew. But since I didn't know it, I had no choice but to follow my own star.

Early during my first semester at Haverford I made friends with Julius Katchen, who later acquired fame as a concert pianist in Europe. I loved his intensity and enthusiasm. And though I was less agreeably impressed by his egotism, I found compensation for it in his romantic devotion to every form of art, music, and poetry. Our friendship flourished in the soil of kindred artistic interests. In this relationship, Julius was the musician, and I, the poet. Through our association my feelings for poetry became more musical, artistically more romantic. Julius's mother, too, had been a concert pianist. When I visited the Katchen home in Long Branch, New Jersey, I was caught up in his entire family's devotion to the arts.

At this time, also, I took a course in poetry composition at nearby Bryn Mawr College under the famous poet, W. H. Auden. Auden encouraged me in my poetic efforts. For some time thereafter, poetry became my god.

Yet there was another side of me that could not remain satisfied for long with Keats's romantic fiction, "Truth is beauty, beauty, truth." In every question, what mattered most to me was not whether an idea was beautiful, but whether in some much deeper sense it was *true*. In this concern I found myself increasingly out of tune with the approach our professors took, which was to view all intellectual commitment with suspicion. Scholarly detachment, not commitment, was their guiding principle.

"That's all very well," I would think. "I want to be objective, too. But I don't want to spend my life sitting on a fence. Even objectivity ought to lead one to conclusions of *some* kind." To my professors, scholarly detachment meant holding a perennial question mark up to life. It meant supporting, "for the sake of discussion," positions to which they didn't really subscribe. It meant showing equal interest in every argument, without endorsing any. I was impatient with their indecisiveness.

My need for truths to which I could commit myself had posed a problem for me in our debating society at Kent School. It made me a failure in public speaking classes during my freshman year at Haverford, and a bad actor in the plays in which I occasionally took part, during college and afterward. It ruined my chances, years later, as a radio announcer. More and more it was to give me difficulties as a student as well, particularly in such subjects as English literature and philosophy. I *had* to know whether what we were considering was true. In reaction against my professors and their insistence on a spirit of polite scholarly inquiry, I gradually developed a rebellious attitude toward college in general.

It was at about this time that I met a student at Haverford whose search for truth coincided more nearly with my own. Rod Brown was two years older than I, exceedingly intelligent, and a gifted poet. At first our relationship was one of learned sage and unlettered bumpkin of a disciple. Rod treated me with a certain amused condescension, as the ingenuous youngster that I was. My poems he read tolerantly, never lavishing higher praise on them than to call them "nice." *His* poems I couldn't even understand. He would quote at length from countless books I'd never heard of, and could make each quotation sound so important that one got the impression that only a confirmed ignoramus would dare to face life without at least the ability to paraphrase that passage.

Rod was a sensitive young man who had learned early in life to fend off others' rejection of him by treating them with disdain. It was purely a defense mechanism, but he carried it off well. I was as intrigued by his superior attitude towards me for my ignorance as I was captivated by his single-minded devotion to philosophical realities. Surely, I thought, if he knew enough to look down on me, it behooved me to learn what the view was from his altitude.

In time we became fast friends. I discovered that, besides his
enthusiasm for truth, he had a delightful sense of humor, and was
eager to share his ideas and opinions, always fresh and interesting,
with others. Rod only raised a supercilious eyebrow at my theories
about God, suffering, and eternal life. Rhetorically he would ask,
"How can anyone ever know the answers to such questions?" But
he directed my thinking constructively into more immediate channels. For the time being the quest for religious truths dropped out
of my life. But where the search concerns truth, can *true* religion be
very far away?

Indeed, Rod's thinking and mine verged constantly on the spiritual. He introduced me to Emerson and Thoreau. I drank eagerly
at the fountain of wisdom in "The Over-Soul," in "Self-Reliance,"
and in *Walden*. These writings were the closest I had come so far
to the expansive vistas of Indian thought,° for though I didn't realize it at the time, Emerson and Thoreau were both admirers of
India's Scriptures, and echoed in their own writings the lofty teachings of the *Upanishads* and the *Bhagavad Gita*.

Rod prompted me to stop concerning myself with life's meaning
as an abstraction, and to face the more concrete problem of how to
live wisely among men. One of the principles we discussed night
after night was non-attachment. Another was the courage to reject
values that we considered false, even if all other men believed in
them. Amusing as it seems now, we spent hours discussing intellectually the uselessness of intellectualism. And, deciding that the un-
educated masses were surely more genuine than we in their simple,
earthy attitudes, we set out with pioneering zeal to frequent the
haunts of truck drivers and manual laborers. No deep wisdom was
ever born of these outings, but then, people who hold cherished
theories rarely feel a need to sustain them on the coarse fare of
facts!

Not everything Rod said or did won my support. He told me
approvingly, for instance, of an older friend of his who had an
unnaturally small heart. To Rod and his friend this fact suggested
a lack of emotional capacity, and, therefore, a nature truly non-attached. But I disagreed with their equation, for I considered non-
attachment and feeling not at all incompatible with one another. The
important point, rather, I felt, was that one's feelings be *impersonal*.

° In those days, courses in Indian studies were comparatively rare. The only actual exposure I ever got to them was from Douglas Steere, in his freshman
course on the history of philosophy. For the first twenty minutes of his first class
Dr. Steere touched lightly on the *Veda*s, giving us the impression, merely, that
there *was* such a thing as Indian philosophy.

Non-attachment releases one from identity with a mere handful of things, and should therefore permit an *expansion,* an *increase,* of feeling.

Rod also believed that, armed with a genuine spirit of non-attachment, one could behave in as worldly a manner as one pleased. But this argument struck me as too convenient a rationalization for his own worldliness. For Rod, despite his disdain for middle-class values and his praise of lower-class simplicity, betrayed a marked fondness for upper-class luxuries. Though he often mocked me for my innocence, I myself looked upon innocence as a truer safeguard of non-attachment.

Rod, like all men, had his shortcomings. He was, among other things, somewhat intolerant of disagreement, proud of his own brilliance, and unabashedly lazy. But for all that he was at heart a loving and true friend, deeply concerned about countless others despite his vaunted indifference, more hurt by people's rejection of him than honestly disdainful of them in return, and a great deal more conservative in his values than he would ever have admitted. While others clucked disapprovingly at him, I saw him as one person who could really help me to think boldly for myself. For this reason above all, I was grateful for his friendship.

Yet in my association with him I also acquired some of the very traits I disapproved of in him. Such, indeed, is the power of all human association. Like Rod, I developed intellectual pride as a defense against rejection and misunderstanding. Perhaps worst of all, I acquired some of his worldliness, though never so much so that Rod ceased to twit me for what he called my naiveté.

In those days it was Rod who gave me my real education. My classes formed a mere backdrop; they taught me facts, but in discussions with him I learned what I would do with facts. Night after night we sat discussing life over pots of coffee in our rooms, or in bars, or in an off-campus restaurant with the engaging name "The Last Straw." We had few friends, but that no longer really mattered to me. I was seeking truth now, not the mere opinions of men.

The pond and some of the buildings at Haverford College, Pennsylvania, where I spent two years.

My college friend, Rod Brown, and I in Wellesley, Massachusetts.

My cousin Bet, at Wellesley College,
Massachusetts.

Our Haverford football team. I am in the front row, third from left.

CHAPTER 8

Joy Is the Goal

M Y FIRST YEAR AT Haverford was one of joyous sifting of new ideas. During my second year there, I tried to digest those ideas and make them my own. The digestive process took place on two levels, the one abstract, and the other deeply personal.

On the abstract level, association with Rod had coaxed me out of my former preoccupation with suffering, and with the essential unreality of this world. I was beginning to see the world more affirmatively. Even suffering seemed to me conquerable now, by the simple—and perhaps simplistic—expedient of strong, positive affirmation.

On the personal level, I was learning to affirm my own worth, a worth I had doubted during my years at Hackley and Kent, then affirmed artificially at Scarsdale High. Now, at Haverford, in the company of friends who shared many of my ideals, I was discovering in myself a basis for genuine self-acceptance.

Once I had somewhat digested my new attitudes, my two-fronts advance converged on a single point. For both abstract and personal reasons, I began to find myself able to express once again that most battered of virtues: trust. In the words of Emerson, I was beginning to feel that the world was my "oyster," that life was basically sunny, right, and beautiful. Even the disapproval of worldly people could no longer dampen my expanding trust in life, and, on a certain level, in them. For I felt they merely lacked the courage to live up to a truth which, deep in their hearts, they believed in. I longed for the power to bring them joy.

Trust! This joyful offering I now made to life was selfless and pure. Yet the wise have ever said that one should trust fully only in God, that to place faith in earthly accomplishments is like expecting perpetual stability of a ship at sea. Alas, I hadn't their wisdom to guide me. All my faith now I flung with ardent enthusiasm into the fragile basket of this world.

For my sophomore year I was assigned to a suite in Lloyd Hall, which in normal times was reserved for upperclassmen. My roommate was from Argentina. Roberto Pablo Payro was his name; I understand he has since become a successful novelist in his country. Roberto was quiet, dignified, and ever courteous: ideal qualities in a roommate. We got along well together, though the goals we pursued were different. Roberto's social life was as quiet as he was. He liked sophisticated, serious discussions, mostly on such down-to-earth subjects as politics and sociology, and rather marveled that such abstractions as "life" and "truth" could command from me the intense enthusiasm that they did. My tendency was to seize a thought firmly, wrestle with it for days until I felt I'd mastered it, and then to dash out, laughing, in search of friends with whom I could celebrate my victory. To Roberto I must have seemed alternately far too intense, and inconsistently frivolous.

But thought itself was, for me, a joyous adventure. It was only years later, after I met my guru, that I learned that thinking is but a by-path to truth, and that the highest perceptions are possible only when the fluctuations of the mind have been stilled.

Rod was the best friend I had found so far in this country. We spent much time together, continuing our nocturnal rounds of coffee, drinks, and wee-hour philosophizing. But I was beginning also to spend more time now seeking truth on my own.

For my college major I selected English literature. I loved reading the great works that comprise our true heritage—a heritage of insights and inspiration, not of mere worldly accomplishments. Reading Shakespeare, Donne, and numerous others, I pondered a new question: In what ways has great literature served the cause of truth? As an aspiring writer myself, I hoped to make whatever I wrote serve as an instrument of the highest vision.

But there was buoyant good humor, too, in our seeking. Rod and I could laugh merrily over the gravest of issues. A few somber souls there were who viewed our unconventional levity with dismay. I think they considered it a proof that we were dissolute, misspending our youth in drunkenness and debauchery. But we had little patience with people who equated seriousness with joylessness. Taking my cue from Rod, I would sometimes delight in pretending we were in league with forces unspeakably dark. (The effort to imagine such forces I left entirely to our critics!)

One of our fellow students, with the appropriate last name of Coffin, used to carry a Bible around with him wherever he went, the more sadly to reproach anyone who showed a disposition occasionally to kick up his heels. "The wages of sin," Coffin would remind us sinners gravely, citing chapter and verse, "is death." As my own reputation for cheerful irreverence spread, he took to bringing me, particularly, the Good News. Entering my room one morning before I'd fairly tested the world to make sure it was still there, he sat on the edge of my bed, the Bible open in his hands, looked at me dolefully, and—sighed.

If only religion weren't made so lugubrious, I think many people might be inspired to seek God who presently confuse ministers with undertakers. It was years before I myself learned that religious worship needn't verge on the funereal—that it can be, as Paramhansa Yogananda put it, the joyous funeral of all sorrows. As it was, I satisfied a natural craving for religious inspiration by laughing at the lack of it in religion as I found it practiced. Had I known better, I might have sincerely worshiped.

During our second year at Haverford someone gave Rod a few guppies in a glass bowl. *Guppy,* we decided, was far too undignified a name even for so nondescript a creature. We renamed his new pets, accordingly, "The Sacred White Fish." Soon, enlarging on this grand concept, we created an entire religion, complete with ceremonies, dogmas, and ritual responses. I even found a partially completed, abandoned chapel for our rites. Needless to say, our comedy never advanced beyond the playful planning stage, but we had great fun with it.

One day Rod was summoned into the dean's office. "What's this I hear, Mr. Brown," began Mr. Gibb cautiously, "about . . . . ah . . . how shall I put it? . . . a new religion? Something about the . . . ah . . . sacred . . . ah . . . white . . . ah . . . *fish?* Have I heard this incredible tale correctly?" We never learned whom it was we'd shocked into reporting us to the dean, but even this anonymous outrage added fresh zest to our game.

Yet I also felt, inexplicably, a deep, almost wistful thrill at the thought of helping to found a new religion. Perhaps it was because the fun we were having with those guppies underscored for me the joy that I missed in the churches. But to me it was more than fun. My search for truth, and for joy as the very essence of truth, held an almost life-or-death earnestness.

On another matter I felt less keenly the need to cloak my interest under a guise of playfulness. A continuous aspiration of mine since the age of fifteen had been the founding of a "utopian" community. Utopia literally means "not a place"; the word is generally used to describe any impractical communitarian dream. But I was convinced that an intentional community founded on high ideals could be made viable, with sufficient realism and foresight.

During this period at Haverford, and for years thereafter, I devoted considerable time to studying and thinking about the problems connected with such a project. On some deep level I believed it was my duty someday to found such a community.

Among my friends, however, I encountered little sympathy for the idea. When I spoke of it to a few of them, they expressed mild interest, only to lose it altogether when they realized I was completely in earnest. After that, they left me to do my dreaming alone.

Undaunted by their lack of interest, I simply broadened my horizons to include the rest of the human race! The more I thought about intentional communities, the more clearly I saw them not as a step backward into primitive simplicity, but as a step *forward* in social evolution, a natural progression from machine technology and the self-defeating complexity of modern life to a new kind of *enlightened* simplicity, one in which technology served human, not merely mechanical or economic ends.

Decentralization seemed to me a growing need, too, in this age. The essentially sterile demands for efficiency that are served by centralizing power in big industry and big government would, I believed, be balanced by the human and idealistic values that would be emphasized in small, spiritually integral communities.

With my growing enthusiasm for life I also took increasing pleasure in singing. At last I resolved to take singing lessons. Dr. Frederick Schlieder, the noted pianist and organist, recommended to Mother that I study under Marie Zimmerman, a singing teacher in Philadelphia. "She is a real musician," he assured Mother. "Your son is fortunate to be in college so nearby."

One day I took a train into Philadelphia and visited Mrs. Zimmerman in her studio. Seventy-five years old she must have been at that time. A concert singer in her younger days, her voice, now no longer beautiful, was still perfectly placed.

"The voice," she explained to me, "is an instrument that can't be seen. I can't *show* you how to use it, as I could how to play the piano. You'll have to listen sensitively as I sing a note, then try to imitate the sound that I make. The more perceptively you listen, the more quickly you'll learn."

Next she placed my right hand over her stomach. "I'm going to show you how to breathe properly," she explained. As she inhaled, her diaphragm moved downward, pushing the stomach out. I prepared to listen to a full, operative tone.

"Mooooooooooo!" came the feeble croak, its sound hardly powerful enough to fill a pantry, let alone a concert hall. I fought to suppress my mirth.

But her voice *was* well placed. Recalling Dr. Schlieder's high recommendations, I decided to study with her.

"You will pay me five dollars a lesson," she announced firmly. "It isn't that I need the money. I don't. But *you* need to pay it. It will help you to take your lessons seriously."

I didn't want to bother Dad for the weekly fees, so I took a job waiting on tables one night a week at The Last Straw. From those earnings I paid for my lessons.

Marie Zimmerman proved an excellent teacher. Unlike most voice teachers, she wouldn't let me sing on my own for the first weeks. Gradually only, as my placement improved, she allowed me to practice a little at home, then a little bit more. The farther I progressed, the more I grew to enjoy these lessons, until at last they became the high point of my week.

Marie Zimmerman was not only an excellent teacher and a fine musician; she was also a remarkable woman. Deeply, calmly religious, she was content with only the highest and noblest in everything. She was, in fact, an impressive example of a truth that was becoming increasingly clear to me, that the chief masterpiece of an aspiring artist must be *himself.*

One day at about this time I had what was, to me, a revelation. Sudden, vivid, and intense, it gave me in the space of a few minutes insights into the nature of art, and of art's relationship to truth, that have guided my thinking ever since.

The word *art,* as Rod and I used it, encompassed *all* the creative arts including music and literature. We had pondered authorities whose claim was that art should be for art's sake alone; or that it must capture reality as a camera does, literally; or that it ought to reflect a sense of social responsibility; or be a purely personal catharsis; or express the spirit of the times in which the artist lives.

Suddenly I felt certain of a truth deeper than all of these. Most artistic theories, I realized, emphasize primarily the *forms* of art. But art is essentially a human, not an abstract phenomenon. A man's intrinsic worth is determined not by his physical appearance, but by his spirit, his essential attitudes, his courage or cowardice, his wisdom or ignorance. With art, similarly, it is the artist's vision of life, not his medium of expression, that determines the validity of his work. Inspiration, or sterility: Either can be expressed as well through realism as through impressionism. The essential question is: *How great does the artist's work reveal HIM to be, as a man?* Only if *he* is great will his work stand a chance of being truly great also. Otherwise it may reveal superlative craftsmanship, but lest plumbers, too, deserve acceptance as artists, mere skill cannot serve to define art.°

My first task as a writer, I decided, was no different from my first task as a human being. It was to determine what constitute ideal human qualities, and then to try to develop *myself* accordingly.

At about this time we were given the assignment in English class of writing an essay on our personal criteria of greatness in literature. Not feeling competent as yet to explain some of the subtler nuances of my revelation, I confined myself to one aspect of it— one perhaps subtler than all the rest! I wrote that, after reading Homer's *Iliad,* I had sensed a blazing white light emanating from it. Later, as I contemplated other great works, I had sensed again in each case a bright light, though in no case so intense as Homer's. Chaucer's light seemed of a duller hue than Milton's, Dante's or Shakespeare's. From still lesser works I sensed no light at all; it was as though they were spiritually dead. I admitted that I saw no objective reason for giving Homer the highest marks; his epic seemed to me, on the surface, only a good, rousing war story. But I knew from its light that it must be a work of superlative greatness. †

My poor professor! Shaking his head in bewilderment, he gave me a flunking grade. Yet even today I consider the criterion of greatness that I described in that paper to have been just and valid.

Rod and I continued our discussions on philosophical matters: intellectual integrity, for example, and living in the *now,* and the importance of non-attachment. Non-attachment, I was coming to realize, is crucial to human happiness. No one can truly enjoy what he fears to lose.

One evening my non-attachment was put to an unusual test. I was sitting in my bedroom, studying for a philosophy exam. The textbook was exceptionally dull. Midway through my study, as I was reflecting glumly that this author valued pedantry over clarity, I heard footsteps approaching stealthily over the dry leaves on the ground outside my window. I glanced at my watch. Nine-thirty: the hour the library closed. One of my friends must be planning to play a joke on me on his way back from there. Smiling, I stepped over to the window to show him I'd caught him at his little game.

At once the footsteps fled into the night. Whoever it was would, I assumed with a smile, come around through the front door and

---

° I discuss this subject in a book of mine, *The Artist as a Channel* (Crystal Clarity, Publishers, 1988).

† Homer was customarily referred to by ancient Greeks as *"divine* Homer."

we'd enjoy a friendly chuckle before he returned to his own room.

To my surprise, no one came.

Smiling at the improbable fancy, I thought, "Maybe someone wanted to shoot me!"

Twenty minutes passed. Again the footsteps came, this time even more softly over the dead leaves.

Who could it be? My friends weren't this persistent at *anything!* Perhaps it really *was* someone wanting to shoot me. Silently I stepped to the window. Once again the steps faded hastily into the darkness.

By this time my curiosity was thoroughly aroused. How would I ever know who this mysterious intruder was, or what he wanted, if I persisted in frightening him off? If he returned a third time, I decided, I would pretend I hadn't heard him.

Another twenty minutes passed. Finally once again: footsteps, this time more stealthy than ever. Moments later, a shoe scraped lightly on the ledge below my window. A hand grasped the metal grating over the window.

Suppressing a smile, I kept my eyes glued on the page before me.

Suddenly: an ear-splitting shot! For several seconds I heard nothing but the ringing in my ears; then, gradually, the ticking clock on my dresser; a car in the nearest parking lot revved its motor and roared off the campus at high speed.

Amazed, I leaned back in my chair and—laughed delightedly! It seemed incredible that such a thing could have actually happened. I checked my body: No holes anywhere. No blood. No pain. What? *Nothing* to show for this absurd adventure? I stepped over to examine the window. The screen was intact. What did it all mean?

Days later I learned that that evening had been Halloween! Evidently some village boy had decided, as a Halloween prank, to put the fear of God into a college student. He'd fired a blank cartridge!

I knew one ought to show a greater sense of responsibility toward one's body than I had. But I was happy at least to have had this experience as evidence of some definite measure of my non-attachment.

Soon, however, I received another test of my non-attachment, and this one I didn't pass so easily. It was a test of my developing ability to offer trust unreservedly.

Haverford boys usually dated Bryn Mawr girls. I did too, whenever I had the inclination for it—and the money, which was seldom. I finally met a girl at Bryn Mawr named Sue, who came to epitomize for me everything that was good, kind, and holy in life. Her tastes were simple. Her smile expressed so much sweetness that, whether blindly or with actual insight, I could not imagine her holding a mean thought. Our joy in each other's company was such that we never felt the need to go anywhere in particular. A quiet walk through green fields, a friendly chat, a communion of hearts in precious silence: These were the essence of a relationship more beautiful than any I had ever before known.

I had no thought of marriage, of long years spent together, or of anything, really, beyond the present. Sue was for me not so much a girlfriend as a symbol of my new gift for trust, for giving myself to life joyously, without the slightest thought of return. How she felt toward me seemed almost irrelevant. It was enough, I felt, that my own love for her was true.

Yet there were times, in the happiness of moments together, when she would gaze at me sadly. She wouldn't say why. "Never mind," I would think, "I will only give her the more love, until all her sadness is washed away."

For Christmas vacation I went home. Shortly after the New Year I received a letter from Sue. Eagerly I tore it open.

"Dear Don," it began, "there is something I've been needing to tell you. I realize I should have done so early in our friendship, but I enjoyed your company and didn't want to lose it." She went on to say how deeply she had come to feel about me, and how sad also, that the realities of her life were such that she could never see me again. She was married, she explained, and was even then carrying her husband's baby. Her husband was stationed overseas in the Navy. She had realized she would not be allowed to return to college once it became known she was pregnant; hence her resolution of silence. But she had been feeling increasingly unhappy about this resolution insofar as I was concerned. She realized she should have had the courage to tell me sooner. Now she would not be returning to Bryn Mawr to finish the school year. She hoped I would understand the loneliness that had motivated her to go out with me. She had never wanted to hurt me, and was unhappy in the knowledge that such a hurt now was inevitable.

The effect of her letter was devastating. I didn't blame Sue, but rather sympathized with the predicament she'd been in. I reminded myself that I had never asked her to return my love, that in fact I'd never contemplated marriage to anyone. But, oh, the pain! And had I, I asked myself, been wrong to trust so completely?

Put differently, was the whole structure of my inner development, in which trust played so vital a role, made of sand?

Much time was to pass before I understood that life, without God, is *never* trustworthy. It is not earthly fulfillment that deserves our faith, but God alone; not outer circumstances, but His inner blessings in the soul. These alone can never fail, can never disappoint. For God is our only true love. Until we learn to place ourselves unreservedly in His hands, our trust, wherever else we give it, will—*must,* indeed—be betrayed again and again.

Can a boat ride calmly in a storm? How can a world in constant flux offer more than delusive security?

For months to come my problem was not disillusionment, for I determined with all my heart to trust life in spite of anything else that might come to hurt me. My problem, rather, was how to find a firm base on which to repose my trust.

I blessed Sue when I received her letter. I bless her even more now. For through our friendship, and even more through our parting, I was brought closer to God.

CHAPTER 9

He Gathers Strength for the Climb

AT ABOUT THIS TIME in my life I had an interesting dream. I was living with many other people in a torture chamber. For generations our families had lived here, knowing no world but this one; the possibility of any other world simply never occurred to us. One awoke, one was tortured, and at night one found brief respite in sleep. What else could there be to life? We didn't particularly mind our lot. Rather, we imagined ourselves reasonably well-off. Oh, there were bad days to be sure, but then there were also good ones—days together, sometimes, when we were less tortured than usual.

The time came, however, when a handful of us began thinking the unthinkable. Might there, we asked ourselves, just possibly be *another,* a better way of life? Moments snatched when our torturers were out of earshot served to kindle our speculations. At last we determined to rebel.

We laid our plans carefully. One day, rising in unison from our tasks, we slew the torturers and escaped. Slipping out of the great room cautiously, lest armies of torturers be waiting for us outside, we encountered no one. The torture chamber itself, it turned out, occupied only the top floor of a large, otherwise empty building. We walked unchallenged down flights of stairs, emerging from the ground floor onto a vast, empty plain. Confined as we'd been all our lives in the torture chamber, the horizon seemed incredibly distant. Joyfully we inhaled the fresh air. Gazing about us, we all but shouted the new word: Freedom!

Before departing the building forever, we glanced upward to the top floor, scene of the only life we'd ever known. There, to our astonishment, were the very torturers we thought we'd slain, going about their business as though nothing had happened! Amazed, we looked to one another for an explanation.

And then the solution dawned on me. "Don't you see?" I cried.

"It's ourselves we've conquered, not the torturers!"

With that realization I awoke.

I felt that this dream held an important meaning for me. The prison, located as it had been on the top floor of the building, symbolized for me the human mind. The torturers represented our mental shortcomings. The emptiness of the rest of the building meant to me that once one overcomes his mental torturers, he finds no more enemies left to conquer. All human suffering, in other words, originates in the mind.

My dream, I felt, held a divine message for me. Its implication was that the time had come for me to seek a higher life. But *how* was I to seek it? I knew nothing of great saints who had communed with God. To me this very word, saint, connoted only a person of frail goodness, not one filled with divine love, and certainly not with ecstasy. All I knew of religion were the stylized church services I had attended, the uninspired ministers I had listened to—insecure men who sought support for their faith in the approval of others, not in the unbribable voice of their own conscience.

Though I didn't realize it at the time, my ignorance concerning the spiritual path was my own chief "torturer"; it hindered me from seeking the good for which my soul longed. Subordinate to ignorance there were other, more evident, failings—doubt, for example. Had I approached truth by love I might have gone straight to the mark. But I was trying to *think* my way to wisdom. God I looked upon as Something to be thought about, not Someone with whom one could commune. I wanted desperately to trust, even to love, but had no idea what, specifically, to trust or to love. I had reached a point where I thought about God almost constantly; but He remained silent, for I never called to Him.

Another of my mental torturers was fear. Certainly I had never considered myself a fearful person, but that was because in most matters I was non-attached. In one test of my non-attachment, however, I had shown myself exceedingly vulnerable: I feared disappointment from others.

Peace in this world depends on cheerfully relinquishing attachment to all things, even to ego. As long as I strove to protect my sense of personal worth, I would suffer again and again, ever in essentially the same ways.

I was not yet wise enough to see clearly, but at least my vision was improving. My dream about the torture chamber, conveying as it did a sense of divine guidance, had made me more aware of realities beyond those known through the senses. This awareness, coupled with the trust and affirmation that I had worked on developing earlier, led me now to an interesting discovery.

I hit upon what was, as far as I knew then, a novel theory: To be lucky, *expect* luck; don't wait passively for it to come to you, but go out and meet it halfway. With strong, positive expectation, combined with equally positive action, success will be assured. With this simple formula I was to achieve some remarkable results.

Not long after the New Year our first semester ended. At that time Rod, and one or two other friends, flunked out of college. It was hardly surprising, considering the disdain all of us felt for "the system." Their departure put me on my own now in my efforts to understand life more deeply. My independence proved a wholesome opportunity.

I visited Sue's dormitory occasionally, hoping in chats with a few of her friends to relive a little of the happiness I had known with her. But the pain of not finding her there was too keen.

Marie Zimmerman, noticing my low spirits, inquired about them one day. I told her of my little tragedy.

"Ah!" she exclaimed impatiently. "Puppy love! I lived with my husband nearly fifty years. In all that time our friendship kept growing deeper. Since his death we are closer than ever. *That* is love!"

Offended, I told myself she simply didn't understand. But her words remained with me, gently reminding me in my deeper self that I probably had much in life yet to learn.

My college classes had lost all appeal for me. I seldom mixed with the other students. To protect my unhappiness over Sue, I put on an over-intellectual front, did frequent battle with words, and assumed an air of self-assurance in which there was considerably more affirmation than self-recognition. My heart was vulnerable, but not my reason or my will.

Mainly, however, I spent my days thinking, thinking, thinking, as if to wrest from life insights into its farthest secrets. Why was the promise of joy so often a will-o'-the-wisp? And was it not essential to a well-ordered universe that love given be in some way returned? Again, where lay the pathway to true happiness?

"Relax!" cried Roberto one day, seeing me staring sightlessly out the window. "Can't you ever relax!"

So the semester passed. In recollection it all seems a grey fog.

My draft board called me for an examination, which I failed because of poor eyesight, thereby resolving the dilemma of whether or not to register as a conscientious objector. I had doubted whether I could register thus in completely good conscience, since it wasn't a matter of my religious convictions; I simply knew with perfect certainty that, even if my own life depended on it, I could never take the life of another human being.

In April, Dad was sent to Rumania as petroleum attaché to the U.S. diplomatic mission in Bucharest.

My job at The Last Straw convinced me, and everyone else (especially my employer!), that whatever my mission in life was, it was not to be a waiter. I kept absent-mindedly sitting down with customers, quite forgetting that there were other tables to be served; then forgetting to change the bill when customers increased their orders. I'm afraid I was almost The Last Straw's last straw!

My singing lessons were the only really bright spot in my life. Marie Zimmerman was a demanding teacher. After six months of weekly lessons she stopped me one day in the midst of a song.

"There!" she cried triumphantly. "*That note.* That's how all of them should sound!"

There were other compensations besides the sheer joy of learning to sing from her. Once she said to me, "If any singing teacher worthy of the name—I mean a real *musician*—were to hear you now, he would be impressed."

And toward the end of the college year, she told me softly, "I am living for only one thing now: to see you become a *great* singer! It isn't only your voice; others have good voices, too. But you have a mind; you *understand*."

Dear Marie! (May I call you that, now that you've left this world? To call you Mrs. Zimmerman seems too formal when addressing your soul.) How sad I have been that I had to disappoint you. That was our last class together. I *couldn't* go back to you. I knew that to be a singer, even a world-renowned one, was not at all my calling. But maybe you are pleased with the fact that I *have* touched people with my gift—not for money, but for love. And maybe someday, too, if we meet in heaven, or in some other life on earth, I can sing for you again. One of my deepest prayers on the spiritual path has been that all whom I have ever loved be blessed with divine peace and joy. May you be so blessed also.

As the college year began drawing to a close, my prolonged inattention to the daily class routine brought me to a rather awkward predicament. Most of my courses I was at least confident of passing, though barely. Greek, however, was a downright embarrassment. It became a standard joke in class to see whether I would recognize one, or two, Greek words in a paragraph when called upon to translate. The entire semester I did hardly three assignments. As we prepared for the final exam, Dr. Post, our professor, remarked more than once, "Not everyone in this room need trouble himself to appear for that event." Whenever he said this, the other students glanced at me and laughed.

But I determined to show up for the exam, and to pass it. It might take a bit of luck not to flunk, but then, I reminded myself, I also had my new theory on how to attract luck: *Expect* to be lucky, then meet luck halfway with a vigorous, positive attitude.

Unfortunately, I felt anything but vigorous and positive towards the one activity that really mattered: study. A week before the test I finally picked up the textbook and glanced half-heartedly at the first page. It was no use. Giving up, I flung the book aside. "To-morrow," I consoled myself, "I'll study *twice* as long as I was going to today." But the next day my good intentions were again routed ignominiously. For the rest of the week I showed persistence only in my continued willingness to procrastinate.

Almost before I knew it, the last evening was upon me. And I hadn't studied at all! Even now I fully intended to pass, but I can't imagine anyone in his right mind endorsing these roseate expectations.

Necessity, it is said, is the mother of invention. Fortunately for me, my present extremity displayed the right, maternal instinct. Out of the blue an inspiration appeared.

"You are a Greek," I told myself with all the concentration I could muster, adjusting myself resolutely to this new identity. The results were astonishing.

As an American, I had found the study of Greek difficult. But now as a Greek "my own" language came surprisingly easily. Through some subtle channel in the network of consciousness that binds all men together, I felt myself suddenly in tune with Greek ways of thinking and speaking. Approaching this new language as an old friend, moreover, I no longer faced the age-old problem of the student who, while attracting knowledge with one half of his mind, pushes it away with the other half by his unwillingness to learn. My entire mental flow was in one direction. For two hours I absorbed Greek grammar and vocabulary like a dry sponge in water, until I could hold no more.

The following morning, "Mother Necessity" gave birth to an-other inspiration. Our class had been studying the New Testament in the original Greek. Dr. Post had told us that we'd be asked to translate a portion of it into English. This morning, then, mindful of my theory on attracting luck, it occurred to me to turn to the King James translation of the Bible. Only enough time remained for me to read one chapter, but if my luck held, this would be the chapter from which the passage would be selected.

It was! The exam that year as it turned out was exceptionally difficult: Only two students passed it. But my theory on luck was vindicated: I was one of them.

From this experience I learned several useful lessons: for one, the mind's power for positive accomplishment, once it learns to resist its own "no"-saying tendency. Much, indeed, of what people do amounts to pushing simultaneously on opposite sides of a door. Working themselves to exhaustion, they yet accomplish little, or nothing. If they would only learn to say "Yes!" to life with all the conviction of their being, their capacity for success might be expanded almost to infinity.

This discovery of the latent power within me, and within every man, was important for me, but even so its interest was secondary to another problem that eluded me still: the secret of happiness.

Is not joy, I asked myself, what all men are really seeking, in their heart of hearts? Why, then, do so few experience it? And why is it so common for people to suffer in the very pursuit of happiness? Toward the end of the semester it occurred to me that perhaps the fault lay with our life-style in America. How, I asked myself, could anyone find true happiness while satiating himself on physical comforts? Thoreau's statement in *Walden* impressed me: "Of a life of luxury the fruit is luxury." For the materialist, the heights of inspiration are unimaginable. The worst disease of modern life, I concluded, is complacency. True joy is ever creative; it demands fresh, vital, *intense* awareness. How, I thought impatiently, will happiness worthy of the name ever be felt by people who are too complacent to hold an unconventional thought? Materialism cannot buy happiness.

It is not unusual for this kind of judgment to be met with indulgent smiles, as though the sheer frequency with which it is made, by young people especially, rendered it invalid. But considering the fact that it is arrived at more or less independently by so many seekers after honest values, I think it might be wise to ponder whether it contains an element of truth.

At any rate, my own solution that year to the shortcomings I identified with life in America was to travel abroad. I imagined people in less industrialized countries turning to their daily tasks with a song on their lips, and inspiration in their hearts. Mexico was such a country. I would spend my summer vacation there among simple, happy, spontaneous, *genuine* human beings.

Getting there was my first problem. If I took a job to earn the money for the journey, my vacation might end before I'd saved enough. How, then—short of robbing a bank—could I "get rich quick"? What was called for, obviously, was another application of my theory on luck.

Affirming a bright, positive attitude, I cast about hopefully for a solution. Our college yearbook, I remembered, offered cash prizes for a variety of literary contributions. If only I could win a large enough prize, my problem would be solved! I leafed through the book. Most of the prizes listed were small: ten, fifteen, twenty-five dollars. But then a more promising figure caught my eye: one hundred dollars! This amount would take me far, indeed. Eagerly I checked to see what I must do to win it. Then my heart sank. The requirement was for an essay on the subject "The Basic Principles Underlying the Government of the United States." Some law professor, probably, dreamed up this legal gem! Why, I thought with a sigh, must educators continually place the highest price on the driest matter? Who would ever write on such a ponderous subject?

I was about to pass on to other prospects when the answering thought came: "That's right: Who *would?*" Examining the information more closely, I found no one listed as having won this prize the previous year. I checked several earlier yearbooks: None of them showed a winner. Perhaps after all there *was* hope! Ignorant though I was of the fine legal or historical points implied in the topic, if mine was the sole entry. . . .

Anyway, I reflected, I wasn't *completely* ignorant. At least I knew America's basic principles as they are popularly defined: *Life, liberty, and the pursuit of happiness.* That brief phrase might not make much of an essay, but what if I took a fresh approach to it? Would the judges decide I'd skirted the issue if, for example, I examined our present-day society in the light of how truly it was living up to those principles? Here at least I'd be walking familiar ground.

Dividing my essay into three chapters—"Life," "Liberty," and, "The Pursuit of Property"—I sought to demonstrate how, by our relentless acquisitiveness, we were depriving ourselves of all three of our basic rights: life and liberty, as well as happiness.

My paper was the sole entry. It won the prize.

Another prize offered in the yearbook was of fifteen dollars for the best poem submitted. Though this was hardly "big money," it seemed worth a light stab; I already had a few poems written that I could submit. In this effort, I knew, I faced competition. The campus poetry club had been debating which of its members would walk away with the prize; they'd already made clear their view that I, who wasn't a member, didn't stand a chance. In the past we'd crossed swords on the subject of solitary, versus group, creativity. To me a poetry *club* seemed a contradiction in terms. I saw it as a victory for my own point of view when this prize came to me.

Thus, with $115 in my pocket before the vacation had even started, I decided I had enough money for the journey. If I found later that I needed more, Lady Luck would no doubt provide it. Barely nineteen years old, never before on my own, and with my parents far away in Rumania: I considered myself an adventurer indeed!

Before leaving for Mexico, I took a short trip north to Massachusetts to visit Rod. Soon thereafter my great odyssey began. Heading south, I made use of a return-trip train ticket that I was holding from New York to Philadelphia. From Philadelphia I planned to hitchhike, armed with my so-far-successful formula for attracting luck, and burdened with nothing but a knapsack.

A young couple seated behind me in the train noticed the knapsack, and engaged me in conversation. Was I a hiker? They themselves were enthusiastic youth hostelers. We chatted pleasantly; soon we were singing folk songs. By the time we reached Philadelphia we felt like old friends. They invited me to spend the night in their family home in Ardmore, the town before Haverford on the Main Line.

This home turned out to be no mere residence, but a veritable mansion. Their hospitality, too, was extraordinary. A member of the family was about to be married; relatives were arriving from distant parts. Food fit for the most educated tastes was being served at every meal. Lady Luck, I reflected, seemed particularly well disposed towards me!

The following morning, as I was sitting in the living room preparatory to leaving, the dowager of the clan entered and took a chair next to mine. Her smiling manner hinted at good news for me.

"I have a nephew," she began, "who is being sent by his firm to Mexico City. He will be leaving tomorrow by car. As he is traveling alone, I'm sure he would appreciate company. Do you think you might like to go with him?"

A three-thousand-mile ride! Lady Luck was taking a most welcome interest in my case. Bob Watson, the nephew, not only took me along, but appointed me his extra driver, thereby paying all my travel expenses from his expense account. When we reached Mexico City, he put me up in his home. Thus my money, which I found had less purchasing power than I'd imagined, lasted me the entire summer.

Bob, and later his wife, Dorothy, when she joined us, were the kindest of friends to me. Our Mexican adventure was as new and fascinating for them as it was for me. Together we shared its daily lessons, rewards, and comic twists as we reported our new experiences to one another in the evenings.

Recalling my impromptu system for learning Greek, I was resolved now to learn Spanish the same way. The day Bob and I crossed the border at Nuevo Laredo, I told myself with deep concentration, "You're a Mexican." Hours later, having carefully rehearsed my words, I entered a restaurant and asked for something to drink, taking pains to get the accent as correctly as I could. An American tourist lady was standing nearby. Hearing me speak, she promptly boosted my confidence by exclaiming in astonishment, "Why, you're a Mexican!"

In one week, by following what was, I realized, a definite principle for self-education, I was speaking Spanish well enough to carry on protracted, if halting, conversations on a wide variety of subjects with people who knew no English. By the end of two and a half months my Spanish was fairly fluent.

The principle, I discovered, is to put oneself completely in tune with whatever subject one wants to master. Inborn talent, though helpful, is not nearly so important as deep concentration. Anyone can do well if he will attune himself sensitively with his subject, and resolutely exclude from his mind any thought of the task's foreignness to him. I have tested this principle many times since then—in learning to write music, to play musical instruments, to paint, to understand some of the deeper aspects of numerous subjects both abstract and practical, to attract money when I needed it, to found a successful community, and to receive helpful answers on countless matters in meditation. Always, the system has taken me far deeper into my subject than intellectual study alone could have done. Friends also, to whom I have taught this principle, have had remarkable success with it.

The principle has many ramifications, one of which is my theory on attracting luck. For a strong, positive affirmation of success is more effective when it is sensitively attuned to one's goal, and protected from the thought of possible failure.

This innocence of the chances of failure is, I think, largely responsible for the phenomenon that is popularly known as "beginners' luck."

An English girl of my acquaintance in Mexico City once told me, "A few weeks ago Mummy and I accompanied Daddy to the racetrack. He goes often, but for us it was the first time. He spent most of the afternoon making fun of our 'system' for betting. We'd choose a horse, you see, because we liked the cute white spot on its nose, or because it had a nice name. Daddy's system was more scientific. But would you believe it? He usually lost, and we won every time!"

If my theory is valid, a beginner's temporary advantage over more seasoned players is that, not knowing the obstacles he is up against, his expectations are more confident. Of course, ignorance of those obstacles also *limits* his success. It takes sensitive awareness of all aspects of a subject, including its difficulties, to achieve genuine mastery.

I had an opportunity during my stay in Mexico to test the mind's power in another way also. Near the end of summer I succumbed to a debilitating combination of diseases: streptococcal infection, tonsillitis, and dysentery. It was several days before I was even strong enough to go see a doctor. When at last I did so, he sent me straight to a hospital. "You'd better reconcile yourself," he told me, "to staying there *at least* two weeks." Worried that I couldn't afford such a long stay, I made a few discreet inquiries, and found that my fears were amply justified. To get money from America would have been difficult, though Dad had left emergency funds there for us boys. The most obvious solution was for me to get well at once.

"You're in perfect health," I told myself firmly, saturating my mind with the thought of well-being, and rigidly excluding from it the slightest indulgence in the thought of my illness. Within two days of my arrival I was out of the hospital, fully cured.

Years later a friend corroborated my belief in the mind's healing power. He had once worked as a physio-therapist in a polio sanitarium. While there, he had noticed that the poor patients, unable to afford a long stay, were more likely to recover than the wealthy ones. He had concluded that their strong desire to get well generated the energy their bodies needed to heal themselves.

My Mexican adventure proved on the whole exciting, interesting, and fun—even though, in its innocent exposure to a wide variety of experiences, it bore some resemblance (as Dad put it later) to the travels of Pinocchio. I didn't get from it, however, what I'd been seeking most keenly: a better way of life. I'd hoped if nothing else to find more laughter there, more human warmth, more inspiration. For a time I imagined I'd actually found them. But then it dawned on me that what I was experiencing was only my own joyous sense of adventure; the people around me, meanwhile, were engrossed in the same dull round of existence as those back home. Mexicans differed only superficially from Americans; in essence both were the same. They lived, worked, bred, and died; the imaginations of a rare few in either land soared above these mundane activities.

Worse still, from my own point of view, I found that I too was basically no different whether in Villa Obregon and Cuernavaca, or in Scarsdale. I experienced the same physical discomforts, the same need to eat and sleep, the same loneliness. I could appreciate more fully now Thoreau's statement with which he dismissed the common fancy that a person was wiser for having traveled abroad. "I have traveled a good deal," he wrote, "in Concord." He had, too. He knew more about his home town and its environs than any other man alive.

The important thing, I realized, is not what we see around us, but the mental attitude with which we look. Answers will not be found merely by transporting one's body from one clime to another. To those people who expect to find abroad what they have overlooked especially *in themselves,* Emerson's words are a classic rebuke: "Travel is a fool's paradise."

In college that fall I was discussing with a few friends a movie we'd seen—*The Razor's Edge,* a tale about a Westerner who traveled to India and, with the help of a wise man whom he met there, found enlightenment.

"Oh, if only I could go to India," cried a girl in our group fervently, *"and get lost!"*

Newly returned as I was from my Mexican experience, I had few illusions left about travel as a solution to the human predicament. "Whom would you lose?" I chuckled. "Certainly not yourself!"

Illness towards the summer's end, and disappointment at not finding what I had hoped to find in Mexico, left me for a time feeling a little dispirited. I continued my search for reality, but with less than my customary enthusiasm. It is a striking fact that, until my faith returned with all its former vitality, Lady Luck withheld from me further proofs of her favor.

CHAPTER 10

Intellectual Traps

A<small>N ANCIENT</small> Greek myth says that Icarus and his father, Daedalus, escaped from Crete on artificial wings fashioned by Daedalus out of wax and feathers. Icarus, over-confident with the joy of flying, ignored his father's advice not to soar too high. As he approached nearer and nearer to the sun, the wax on his wings melted, and Icarus plunged to his death in what has been known ever since as the Icarian Sea.

Many of the old Greek myths contain deep psychological and spiritual truths. In this one we find symbolized one of man's all-too-frequent mistakes: In his joy at discovering within himself some hitherto unsuspected power, he "flies too high," ignoring the advice of those who have learned from experience to value humility.

I had discovered that, by will power, faith, and sensitive attunement to certain things that I had wanted to accomplish, I could turn the tide of events to some degree in my favor. I could learn new languages. I could choose to be well, and I was well. I could walk confidently toward certain of life's closed doors, and they opened for me. In all these little successes there had been two key words: *sensitivity* and *attunement*. In learning Greek, I had tried to attune myself sensitively to the Greek consciousness; the important thing had been that attunement, not my mere *resolution* to learn the language. In the affirmation "I'm a Greek," *Greek*, not *I*, had been the operative word. But now, in my exuberance, I fairly flung myself into the breach. Partly, indeed, I was moved to enthusiasm by the sheer grandeur of my new insights. But because my enthusiasm was excessive, sensitivity and attunement often got lost in the dust cloud kicked up by my overly affirmative ego.

I wanted wisdom. Very well, then: I *was* wise! I wanted my works to inspire and guide people; I wanted to be a great writer. Very well, then: I *was* a great writer! How simple! All I had to do was some fine day produce the poems, plays, and novels that would demonstrate what was already, as far as I was concerned, a *fait accompli.*

The idea probably had a certain merit, but it was marred by the fact that I was reaching too far beyond my own present realities. In the strain involved there was tension; and in the tension, ego.

Faith, if exerted too far beyond a person's actual capabilities, becomes presumption. Above all it is best always to tie positive affirmations to the whispered guidance of God in the soul. Knowing nothing of such guidance, however, I supplied my own. That which I decreed to be wisdom *was* wisdom. That which I decreed to be greatness *was* greatness. It was not that my opinions were foolish. Many of them were, I believe, fairly sound. But their scope was circumscribed by my own pride. There was no room here for others' opinions. I had not yet learned to listen sensitively to the "truth which comes out of the mouths of babes." Yet I expected ready agreement with my opinions even from those whose age and experience of life gave them some right to consider *me* a babe. I would be no man's disciple. I would blaze my own trails. By vigorous mental affirmation I would bend destiny itself to my will.

Well, I was not the first young man, nor would I be the last, to imagine the popgun in his hand to be a cannon. At least my developing views on life were such that, in time, they refuted my very arrogance.

For my junior year I transferred to Brown University, in Providence, Rhode Island. New perceptions, I felt, would flourish better in a new environment. At Brown I continued my major in English literature, and took additional courses in art appreciation, philosophy, and geology. But my attitude toward formal education was growing increasingly cavalier. I didn't see of what possible use a degree would be to me in my chosen career as a writer. Nor did I have much patience with an accumulation of mere facts, when it was the *why* of things I was after. Even our philosophy course, which ought to have been at least relatively concerned with the *whys,* was devoted to categorizing the mere *opinions* of the men we were studying. When I found I wasn't expected to concern myself with the *validity* of their opinions, I took to reading poetry in the classroom in silent protest.

Intent on developing the identity I had selected for myself, I played the role, for all who cared to listen to me, of established author and philosopher. A few people actually did listen. For hours they and I sat together, engrossed in the adventure of philosophical thought. I got them to see that joy *has* to be the real purpose of life, that non-attachment is the surest key to joy, and that one

ought to live simply, seeking joy not in things, but in an ever-
expanding vision of reality. Truth can be found, I insisted, not in
the sordid aspects of life, as so many writers claim, but in the
heights of human aspiration.

Most of the writing of my student days has long since been con-
signed to fire and blessed oblivion. One piece, however, which escaped the holocaust expresses some of the views I was expounding
at that time. It may serve a useful purpose for me to quote it here,
unedited.

My countrymen, having begotten what is in many respects a monstrosity, go
about saying what had never before been said so strongly, that we must go with
the age if we would create great things. That it is necessary for them to repeat
what should normally be too obvious for repetition shows how slight is the hold
this century has on our hearts.

They have, moreover, misunderstood the true meaning of democracy, which
is not (as they suppose) to debase the noble man while singing the virtues of the
common man, but rather to tell the common man that he, too, can now become
noble. The object of democracy is to raise the lowly, and not to praise them for
being low. It is only with such a goal that it can have any real merit.

God's law is right and beautiful. No ugliness exists except man's injustice and
the symbols of it. It is not life in the raw we see when we pass through the
slums, not the naked truth that many "realists" would have us see, but the facts
and figures of our injustice, the distortion of life and the corruption of truth. If
we would claim to be realistic it is not reality we shall see from the squalid
depths of humanity, for our view will be premised on injustice and negation.
Goodness and beauty will appear bizarre, whereas misery, hatred and all the sad
children of man's misunderstanding will seem normal, and yet strange withal and
unfounded, as if one could see the separate leaves and branches of a tree and yet
could find no trunk. It is not from the hovel of a pauper that we can see all
truth, but from the dwelling place of a saint; for from his mountain, ugliness itself is seen, not as darkness, but as lack of light, and the squalor of cities will be
no longer foreign, but a native wrong, understood at the core as a symptom of
our own injustice.

The more closely we watch the outside as a means to understand the inside,
the farther off the inside withdraws from our understanding. The same with
people as with God.

My ideas were, I think, basically valid. But ideas alone do not
constitute wisdom. Truth must be lived. I'm afraid that, in endless
discussions about truth, the sweet taste of it still eluded me.

One day a friend and I were crossing campus on our way back
from a class. Lovingly he turned to me and remarked, "If ever I've
met a genius in my life, it is you."

For a moment I felt flattered. But as I reflected on his words,
shame swept over me like a wave. What had I actually done to deserve his praise? I had *talked!* I had been so busy talking that I hadn't
even had much time left over for writing. And his compliment had

been so sincere! It was one thing to have played the part of the author and philosopher to convince *myself*. It was quite another that my acting had convinced others. I felt like a hypocrite. Sick with self-disappointment, I withdrew from then on from most of my associates at Brown, and sought to express in literature the truths I had hitherto been treating so lightly as coffee shop conversation.

It didn't take me very long to realize that it is much easier to talk hit-or-miss philosophy over a coffee table than to transform basic concepts into meaningful writing. There are levels of understanding that come only when one has lived a truth deeply over a space of years. Initial insights may suggest almost the same words, yet the power of those words will be as nothing compared to the conviction ringing in them when their truths have been deeply lived.

St. Anthony, in the early part of the Christian era, was called from his desert hermitage by the bishop of Alexandria to speak in defense of the divinity of Jesus Christ. Arguments had been raging throughout Christendom as a result of the so-called Arian heresy, which denied Christ's oneness with God. St. Anthony gave no long, carefully reasoned homily in defense of his ideas. His words, however, charged as they were with the fervor of a lifetime of prayer and meditation, conveyed such a depth of power that, among his listeners, further argument ceased. All St. Anthony said was, "I have *seen* Him!"

Alas, *I* had *not* seen Him. Nor had I deeply lived a single truth. My painting was more a sketch than a finished work. Try as I would to express my ideas in writing, the moment I picked up a pen I found my mind growing strangely vague. Whatever I did write was more to develop my literary technique than to express what I really wanted to say. I described situations with which I wasn't familiar. I wrote about people whose living counterparts I had never met. To master my craft, I imitated the styles of others, hoping to find in their phrasing and choice of words secrets to clarity and beauty of self-expression that I might develop later into a style of my own.

I had the satisfaction of being praised by certain professors and professional men of letters. Some of them told me I would someday become a front-ranking writer. But at nineteen I was far from justifying their friendly expectations. Worst of all, in my own opinion, was the fact that I was saying almost nothing really worthwhile.

I worked on the psychological effects, in poetry, of different patterns of rhyme and rhythm. I studied the emotion-charged rhythms of Irish-English, which the great Irish playwright, John Millington

Synge, captured so beautifully. I wondered why modern English, by comparison, was so barren of deep feeling, and pondered how, without sounding studied and unnatural, to bring beauty to dramatic speech.

One of the dogmas I had been taught in English classes was that iambic pentameter, the blank verse form of Shakespearean drama, is the most natural poetic rhythm for speech in the English language. Shakespeare, of course, was trotted out as the ultimate proof of this dogma. But in *modern* English, blank verse sounded to me much too courtly. Maxwell Anderson, the Twentieth-Century American playwright, used it in several of his plays, and the best I could say of them was that they were brave attempts. I certainly didn't want to confine myself to the sterile formulae modern writers so often follow who try to render speech realistically. ("Ya wanna come?" "Yeah, yeah, *sure*." "Hey look, I'm not beggin' ya. Just take it or leave it." "Okay, okay, smart boy. Who says I don't wanna come?") Shakespeare, even when imitating common speech, idealized it. My problem was how to follow his example without sounding artificial. If literary language couldn't uplift, there seemed little point in calling it literature.

For my summer vacation in 1946 I went to Provincetown, on Cape Cod—a haven for artists and writers. There I rented a small room, turned an upside-down dresser drawer into a desk, and devoted myself to writing a one-act play. To make the few dollars I had stretch as far as possible, I ate the chef's special at a local diner for lunch every day. For forty-five cents I got a greasy beef stew with one or two soggy slices of potato in it, and, if I was lucky, two or three slices of carrot. After two months of this daily banquet, even the bargain price could no longer tempt me to endure such punishment another day. I went into the diner one afternoon, ordered the chef's special, watched a slice of potato disintegrate as I stabbed it half-heartedly with a spoon, then got up and walked out again, never to return.

Toward the end of the summer I spent a week on a distant beach, "far from the madding crowd." (How wonderful it would be, I thought, to be a real hermit!) My one-act play, which I finished on those dunes, didn't turn out badly, though I hadn't been able to shake off the hypnotic charm of Synge's English.

The summer itself was pleasant also, despite my penury. But above all what it did was show me that I was as much an outsider in artistic circles as in any other. Increasingly it was becoming clear that I would never find what I was seeking by *becoming* anything. To say, "I'm a writer," or even, "I'm a great writer," wasn't at all the answer. What I needed above all concerned the deeper question of *what I was already.*

CHAPTER 11

By-Paths

LIVING IN PROVIDENCE, a short train ride away from Boston, I often visited Rod and Betty. Rod lived in Wellesley Hills, a Boston suburb. Betty, a dear friend as well as my cousin, was a student at nearby Wellesley College.

Rod had enrolled at Boston University. He was as good-humored and intense about everything as ever. Together we devoted much time to what might, with some generosity, be described as the Indian practice of *neti, neti* ("not this, not that").* That is to say, we engaged in a running analysis, complete with droll commentary and merry exaggeration, on some of the follies to which mankind is addicted.

There was the living-to-impress-others dream: "I work on Wall Street. *(Pause)* Of course, you know what *that* means."

There was the "Protestant ethic," I'm-glad-I'm-not-happy-because-that-means-I'm-good dream: "I wouldn't *think* of telling you what you ought to do. All I ask is that you *(sigh)* let your conscience be your guide."

A favorite of ours was the if-you-want-to-be-sure-you're-right-just-follow-the-crowd dream: "You'd better march in step, son, if you want the whole column to move."

Rod was a wonderful mimic. He could make even normally reasonable statements sound ridiculous. He attained his height when imitating someone hopelessly inept trying to sound like a big shot.

We also discussed seriously the fulfillments we both wanted from life. The longer we talked, the longer our list of minuses kept growing, and the shorter that of the plusses. For Rod, these narrowing horizons meant his gradual loss of ambition to become a writer. For me, it meant a gradual redirection of ambition from worldly to divine attainments.

---

* By examining every human delusion dispassionately, abandoning each with the conclusion, "This, too, is unreal *(neti, neti),*" the seeker arrives at last at the vision of perfect Truth.

In those days, as I've mentioned earlier, students were not as preoccupied as they are nowadays with the search for meaning. For most of them the ideal was "Get to the top; become wealthy and important; marry; buy a big home, and populate it with a large family; let everyone see you enjoying life; better still, get them to *envy* you for enjoying it." Needless to say, the gradations of worldly ambition are many, by no means all of them crass. But youth in its quest for personal directions is seldom sensitive to the directions of others. If Rod and I were ungenerous, it was partly because we were still preoccupied with defining our own goals.

Not surprisingly, some of the people whose values we rejected reciprocated with a certain antagonism. Rod, in fact, almost invited their antagonism, by judging *them* along with their values. Ever tending to extremes in his reactions, he either praised people to the skies as "perfectly wonderful," or condemned them to the depths as "dreadful," or "ridiculous."

But judgment forms a barrier: In excluding others, it also encloses oneself. Rod, by his judgmental attitude, was gradually painting himself into a psychological corner. After all, if others didn't measure up to his ideals, it behooved him to prove that *he* did. The stricter his standards for others, the more impossible they became for himself. I remember a space of two or three months when, though supposedly working on a novel, he never progressed beyond typing "Page one, Chapter one," on an otherwise blank page. In time I suppose he had no choice but to abandon writing altogether. It was a pity, for his was, and still is, one of the most talented, intelligent, and deeply perceptive natures I have ever known.

I myself, though not as judgmental as Rod, could be cutting in my remarks. I justified this tendency by telling myself that I was only trying to get people to be more discriminating. But there is never a *good* excuse for unkindness. In one important respect, indeed, my fault was greater than Rod's, for whereas his judgments were directed at people he scarcely knew, my criticisms were reserved for my friends.

I once wrote a stinging letter to Betty, simply because I felt that she wasn't trying hard enough to develop her own very real spiritual potential. Occasionally even my mother came under fire from me. It was years, and many personal hurts, before I realized that no one has a right to impose on the free will of another human being. Respect for that freedom is, indeed, essential if one would counsel others wisely. Without due regard for another's right to be himself, one's perception of his needs will be insensitive, and

seldom wholly accurate. I, certainly, had all the insensitivity of im-
mature understanding. The hurts I gave others were never com-
pensated for by any notable acceptance, on their part, of my
advice.

Often on the path I have thought, How can I make amends for
the hurts I have given so many of my friends and loved ones?
And as often the answer comes back to me: By asking God to
bless them with *His* love.

Towards the end of my first year at Brown, Rod, having
dropped out of Boston University, came to live with me in a room
I had taken off campus. We cooked our own meals with the help
of a book that I had bought for its reassuring title, *You Can Cook If
You Can Read*. I'd always looked on cooking as a kind of magic. It
delighted me, therefore, to find in this book such quasi-ritualistic
advice as, "To ascertain if the spaghetti is done, throw a piece of it
at a wall. If it sticks there, it's ready to eat."

Rooming with Rod, I got an opportunity to observe on a new
level the truth, which I'd discovered during my last semester at
Haverford, that subjective attitudes can have objective consequences. Rod's tendency to judge others attracted antagonism not
only from people he knew, but, in some subtle way, from perfect
strangers. In restaurants, people sitting nearby would sometimes
snarl at him for no evident reason. One evening a passer-by pulled
a gun on him, warning him to mind his own business. Another
evening six men with knives chased him down a dark street; Rod
eluded them only by hiding in a doorway. Whenever he and I
went out together, all was peaceful. But Rod by himself continually
skirted disaster. Fortunately, no doubt because he really meant no
harm, he always got off without injury.

At this time Rod's life and mine were beginning to branch apart.
Rod shared some of my interest in spiritual matters, but not to the
extent of wanting to get involved in them himself. I, on the other
hand, was growing more and more keen to mold my life along
spiritual lines. We talked freely on most subjects, but on this one I
found it better to keep my thoughts to myself.

One day I was reading a book, when suddenly I had an inspiration that came, I felt, from some deeper-than-conscious level of my
mind. Stunned at the depth of my certitude, I told Rod, "I'm going
to be a religious teacher!"

"Don't be silly!" he snorted, not at all impressed.

Very well, I thought, *I'll say no more. But I know.*

The thought of being a religious teacher, however, in no way
inspired me to spend more time in church, where religion held no

appeal for me whatever. "Hel-*lo!*" our campus minister would sim-
per sweetly, almost embarrassingly self-conscious in his effort to
demonstrate his "Christian charity" to us when passing us in the
hallway. People, I thought, attended church chiefly because it was
the respectable and proper thing to do. Some of them, no doubt,
wanted to be good, but how many, I wondered, attended because
they *loved God?* Divine yearning seemed incompatible, somehow,
with going to church, carefully ordered as the services were, and
devoid of spontaneity. The ministers in their pulpits talked of politics and sin and social ills—and, endlessly, of money. But they
didn't talk of God. They didn't tell us to dedicate our lives to
Him. No hint passed their lips that the soul's only true Friend and
Lover dwells within, a truth which Jesus stated plainly. Socially
inconvenient Biblical teachings, such as Jesus' commandment,
"*Leave all,* and follow me," were either omitted altogether from
their homilies, or hemmed in with cautious qualifications that left
us, in the end, exactly where we were already, armed now with a
good excuse. My impression was that the ministers I listened to
hesitated to offend their wealthy parishioners, whom they viewed
as customers. As for direct, *inner* communion with God, no one
ever mentioned it. Communion was something one took at the altar rail, with priestly assistance.

One Sunday I attended a service in a little town north of Boston. The sermon title was "Drink to Forget." And what were we
supposed to forget? Well, the wicked Japs and their betrayal of us
at Pearl Harbor. The Nazis and their atrocities. There was nothing
here about righting our own wrongs, or seeing God in our enemies. Nothing even about forgiving them *their* wrongs. The sacrificial wine that was served later that morning was supposed to help
us forget all the bad things *others* had done to us. I could hardly
suppress a smile when that Lethe-inducing nectar turned out to be,
not wine, but grape juice!

If there was one subject that roused me to actual bitterness, it
was the utterly commonplace character of religion as I found it in
the churches. My bitterness was not because the demands this religion made were impossible, but because they were so unspeakably
trivial; not because its assertions were unbelievable, but because
they were carefully maintained at the safest, most timid level of
popular acceptability. Above all I was disturbed because the
churches struck me as primarily social institutions, not as light-
houses to guide people out of the darkness of spiritual ignorance. It
was almost as if they were trying to *reconcile* themselves to that
ignorance. With dances, third-class entertainments, and diluted

teachings they tried desperately to get people merely to come to church, while neglecting the commandment of Jesus, "Feed my sheep." Frank Laubach, the great Christian missionary, once launched a campaign to get more ministers simply to *mention* God in their sermons. His campaign suggests the deepest reason for my own disillusionment. Of all things in life, it was for spiritual under-standing that I longed most urgently. Yet, most notably, it was the churches that withheld such understanding from me. Instead, they offered me dead substitutes. For years I sought through other chan-nels the fulfillment I craved, because the ministers in their pulpits made a mockery of the very fulfillments promised in the Bible. To paraphrase the words of Jesus, I asked of them the bread of life, and they offered me a stone.*

Thus, hungry as I was for spiritual understanding, I saw no choice but to pursue my career as a writer, and looked to the arts for that kind of inspiration which, had I but known it, only God can supply. It was like walking into a void, for lack of any better place to go. An emptiness was growing in my heart, and I knew not how to fill it.

My college classes were becoming increasingly burdensome. In-tellectualism was not bringing me wisdom. It seemed to me almost unbearably trivial to be studying the Eighteenth-Century novel, when it was the meaning of life itself I was trying to fathom.

My parents had recently returned from Rumania. I sought their permission to take a leave of absence from college. Reluctantly they gave it. Thus, midway through my senior year, I left Brown University, never to return.

Thereafter for several months I lived with my parents. I struggled—gamely, perhaps, but without real hope—over a two-act play. It concerned nothing I really wanted to say. But then, the things I did want to say were the last I felt myself decently quali-fied to express.

Occasionally I went into New York City, and spent hours there walking about, gazing at the tragedy of worldly people's transition from loneliness to apathy. How bereft of joy they seemed, strug-gling for mere survival in those desolate canyons of concrete!

At other times I would stroll through the happier setting of Washington Square, almost in a kind of ecstasy, observing mothers with their babies, laughing children playing on the lawns, young people singing with guitars by the fountain, trees waving, the

---

* Matthew 7:9.

fountain spray playing colorfully in the sunlight. All seemed to be joined together in a kind of cosmic symphony, their many lives but one life, their countless ripples of laughter but one sea of joy.

The valleys and the peaks of life! What grand truth could bind them all together, making them one?

Back home one day I told Mother I wouldn't be going with her to church any more. This was one of the few times I have ever seen her weep. "It pains me so deeply," she cried, "to see you pulling away from God!" I wasn't aware of her promise, made before my birth, to give me, her first-born, to God. I would have loved in any case to reassure her, and was deeply touched by her concern for me. But what could I do? My duty above all was to be honest with myself.

A few days later Mother sought me out. Hopefully she quoted a statement that she had read somewhere that morning, to the effect that atheism sometimes presages a deep spiritual commitment. I was by no means the atheist she thought I was; nevertheless, it relieved me to see that she understood my rejection of her church as part, at least, of a sincere search for truth. I didn't explain my true feelings to her at the time, however, for fear of diluting the intensity of my search.

That summer I traveled up to the little town of Putney, Vermont, where my youngest brother Dick was in school. Dick was maturing into a fine young man; I loved him deeply. Something he'd told me had touched me particularly. One day he was driving to a house to pick up a group of friends. As his car was rolling slowly to a halt, it lightly touched a dog that was standing complacently before it. The dog wasn't hurt, but its owner, a small, older man, no physical match for Dick, was furious. Striding up to the car, he punched Dick in the jaw.

At that moment Dick's friends came out of the house. Dick, concerned that they might hurt the man if they knew what had happened, said nothing of the matter either to them or to him.

During my stay at Putney, a drama teacher there recommended the Dock Street theater in Charleston, South Carolina, as a good place to study stagecraft. For my twenty-first birthday Dad had given me five hundred dollars. (Dick's comment: "A pleasing precedent has been set!") I decided, albeit in rather a mood of desperation, that if I was going to be a playwright I might as well go to Charleston with this money, and gain direct experience in my craft at that theater.

CHAPTER 12

"Who Am I? What Is God?"

"ALL THE WORLD'S A STAGE," Jaques says in *As You Like It*. Few people realize how little their personalities represent them as they really are. Emerson wrote, in "The Over-Soul," "We know better than we do. We do not yet possess ourselves, and we know at the same time that we are much more. I feel the same truth how often in my trivial conversation with my neighbors, that somewhat higher in each of us overlooks this by-play, and Jove nods to Jove from behind each of us. Men descend to meet."

Every man in his soul is divine. He merely persuades himself, by concentration on his outer life, that he is a baker, banker, teacher, or preacher; that he is rude or sensitive, athletic or lazy, genial or solemn. He sees not that all these are but roles, reflections of the likes and dislikes, the desires and aversions that he has accumulated over incarnations. What has once been acquired can as surely once again be shed. The outer self changes endlessly. Only in his inner Self is man changeless and eternal.

Much of my life seems, in retrospect, almost as though it had been planned for me. Certainly my experiences up to this time in my narrative reflect, basically, the lessons I needed to learn. It was perhaps due to this same "suspicious Someone's" plan for me that I spent the better part of the next year working with the Dock Street Theater, in Charleston. The various roles I acted, quite unprofessionally, on its stage, taught me to stand back from myself mentally, to observe this peculiar specimen, Donald Walters, acting out his normal daily role as a young American male of somewhat cheerful disposition, an aspiring playwright, and a more or less perennial innocent abroad.

My associations at the Dock Street Theater helped me, in time, to see the shallowness of *all* role-playing, whether in or out of the theater. For most of the people I met there were always "on stage"; they based their very self-esteem on how well they could pretend.

A year spent with them added immeasurably to my yearning for values that were *true*.

I arrived in Charleston toward the end of June. The Dock Street Theater, I learned, had closed for the summer months, and was not scheduled to open again until September. I took a room in a small boarding house where I received lodging and three generous meals a day for only ten dollars a week. The atmosphere was pleasantly familial. Most of my fellow boarders were students at The Citadel, a nearby college for men. The friendship of congenial companions my own age threatened for a time my intentions of devoting myself to writing. Rationalizing the threat, I told myself that, as a budding writer, I needed to absorb all I could of local color. Aside from a few scattered poems, my "accomplishments" now were limited to a succession of parties, outings to the beach, and merry bull sessions where everything was discussed from politics to girls to local gossip.

Gradually I expanded my frontiers to a study of the way people lived on various levels of Charleston society. I went everywhere; met people in every walk of life, explored some of the dingiest "dives," and was a guest in several prominent homes.

Charleston was a small city of some 70,000 people. I found it possible to discover within its narrow boundaries a representative cross section of America. With the middle and upper social strata, and to a lesser degree with the lower, I was already somewhat familiar. But those lower strata which I now encountered were an eye-opener. I'm referring not to the poor, whose simple dignity often gives the lie to that condescending designation, "lower class," but to people, some of them actually wealthy, whose meanness of heart and narrow outlook condemned them to lives of criminal greed. Included among this type were the owners and operators of sordid speak-easies, which posed as fronts for still-more-illicit gambling rooms upstairs, and (one suspected) for other hush-hush activities as well. These people projected an almost visible aura of dishonesty, of cold brutality and evil. Some of them, as I say, were wealthy, but their riches had been acquired from feeding on human desperation.

Equally sordid were the lives of most of the people who frequented these places. For the customers, too, were out purely for what they could get for themselves. Their conversation reflected a hardness; their brittle laughter crackled like ice. Such people were the perennially homeless—in consciousness, if not in fact. They were men and women who wandered aimlessly from city to city, seeking transient jobs and still more transient pleasures; individuals whose character was fast losing distinction in the blur of alcoholic fumes; couples whose family lives were disintegrating under jackhammer blows of incessant bickering; lonely people who hoped blindly to find in this wilderness of human indifference just a glimpse of friendship.

Everywhere I saw desolation. This, I reflected, was the stuff of which countless plays and novels had been written. *Why* this preoccupation with negativity? Is great literature something merely to be endured? Who can possibly gain anything worthwhile from exposure to sterility and hopelessness?

Yet these, undeniably, were a part of life too. Their effect on me spiritually, moreover, proved to some extent wholesome. For the awareness they gave me of man's potential for self-degradation lent urgency to my own longing to explore a higher potential.

I took another stab, consequently, at attending church. I even enrolled in a church choir. But soon I discovered that this was only exchanging one kind of sterility for another. The church atmosphere was more wholesome, no doubt, but partly for that very reason it was also more smug, more resistant to any suggestion that some higher perfection might be attainable.

Civilized man prides himself on how far advanced his present state is beyond that of the primitive savage. He looks condescendingly on tribal cultures for their practice of endowing trees, wind, rain, and heavenly bodies with human personalities. Now that science has explained everything in prosaic terms, modern man considers himself wiser for the loss of his sense of awe. But I'm not so sure that he deserves congratulation. It strikes me rather that, dazzled by his own technology, he has only developed a new sort of superstition, one infinitely less interesting. Too pragmatic now to worship, he has forgotten how to commune. Instead of relating sensitively to the universe around him, he shuts it out of his life with concrete "jungles," air conditioning, and "muzak"; with self-promotion and noisy entertainments; and with an obsession with problems that are real for him only because he *gives* them reality. He is like a violin string without a sounding board. Life, when cut off from broader realities, becomes thin and meaningless.

Modern technology alienates us from the universe, and from one another. Worst of all, it alienates us from ourselves. It directs all our energies toward the mere manipulation of *things,* until we ourselves assume almost thing-like qualities. In how many modern plays and novels are men idealized for their ability to act with the precision, emotionlessness, and efficiency of a machine. We are taught to behave in this world like rude guests, gracelessly consuming our host's offerings without offering him a single word of thanks in return. Such is our approach to nature, to God, to life itself. We make ourselves petty, then imagine the universe petty also. We rob our own lives of meaning, then call life as a whole meaningless. Smug in our unknowing, we make a dogma of ignorance. And when, in this "civilized" smugness of ours, we approach the question of religion, we address God Himself as though he had better watch His manners if He would be worthy of a place on our altars.

After a month or so of paddling in the waters of Charleston's social life, I finally decided that I'd exposed myself quite enough to cross sections of a society whose members seemed at least as ignorant as I was. None of my new acquaintances had contributed anything positive to my search for meaning. And of "local color," I felt that I had seen altogether too many browns and greys.

My own "purism," of course, held a certain smugness of its own. Had I been less rigidly critical in my attitudes, I might have attracted more uplifting human associations. Or I might have discovered in the very people I was meeting qualities truer than I dreamed. On the other hand, to do myself justice, it was to a great extent with the very aim of overcoming such rigidity in my own nature that I had made it a practice to mix with so many different types of people.

Toward the end of the summer I moved out of my boarding house to a small apartment at 60 Tradd Street. Here I began writing a one-act comedy titled *Religion in the Park*. Bitter as well as funny, the play concerned a woman who wanted to live a religious life, and who eagerly sought instruction from a priest, only to have him discourage her every devotional sentiment with his careful emphasis on religious propriety. Meanwhile a passing tramp rekindled her fervor with tales of a saint who, he claimed, had cured him of lameness. Here at last was what she'd been seeking: religion *lived,* religion *experienced,* not couched in mere social customs and theoretical dogmas!

But, alas, in the end the tramp proved a fraud. An alcoholic, he had merely invented his tale in the hope of coaxing a few easy dollars into his pocket.

This woman's hope and subsequent disillusionment reflected my own spiritual longings, and the skepticism that continued to prevent my actual commitment to the religious life.

An interesting sidelight on that one-act play is that the "saint," according to the tramp's story, lived in California—the very state where I was later to meet my guru. Could I have been aware, on some deep level of my consciousness, that that was where my own destiny lay? Once as a child, while crossing the Atlantic, I had met a boy from California. I remember thinking as I heard the name, "*That* is where I must go someday." Years later, when first contemplating that trip to Mexico, I had considered briefly whether I might go to California instead. Then I had put aside the idea with the verdict, "It isn't yet time." Emerson's words come back to me now, more in question than in certainty: "We know better than we do." *Had* I known?

When the Dock Street Theater opened in September, I went there to seek affiliation with it, but was told that the only way I could do so officially was to enroll as a student in its drama school. Counting myself well out of the academic scene, I asked if I might not be given some other status. Finally the director permitted me, partly on the strength of my new play, to affiliate with them as an "unofficial" student. Under this arrangement I was able to study stagecraft in the evenings, and at the same time to devote my days to writing.

During the following months I acted in a variety of plays, mingled freely with teachers and official students, and served in a number of useful, if more or less nondescript, capacities. These activities gave me some understanding of the business of staging plays, particularly in a small community theater. As an actor, however, I'm afraid I was something of a disaster. "This isn't *me!*" I kept thinking. "How will I ever learn who I really am, if I keep on playing people I'm not?" From a standpoint of my intended profession as a playwright, however, the experience was worthwhile.

The daylight hours I spent by myself, at first writing, and then, increasingly, thinking, thinking over my old problems: What is the purpose of life? Who am I? Hasn't man a destiny higher than (I looked about me in desperation)—than *this*? Most important of all, what is true happiness? How can it be found?

During the time that I spent writing, I threw myself into the task of developing the techniques of my craft. Curiously perhaps, for a budding playwright, I wrote no plays at this time; I wanted to keep my mind flexible to pursue new directions in stagecraft as they presented themselves in the theater. Instead I wrote poetry, and sought—still—to develop a sense for poetic speech in drama. I also pondered the theater's potential for inspiring a far-reaching spiritual renaissance. To this end I studied the plays of the Spanish playwright, Federico García Lorca, to see whether his surrealistic style might be adapted to induce in people a more mystical awareness.

My probing thoughts, however, led one by one to a dead end. How much, after all, can the theater really accomplish? Did even

Shakespeare, great as he was, effect any deep-seated changes in the lives of man? None, surely, at any rate, compared with those which religion has inspired. I shuddered at this comparison, for I loved Shakespeare, and found little to attract me in the churches. But the conclusion, whether I liked it or not, was inescapable: Religion, for all its fashionable mediocrity, its sham, its devotion to the things of this world, remains the most powerfully beneficial influence on earth. Not art, not music, not literature, not science, politics, conquest, or technology: The one truly uplifting power in history, always, has been religion.

How was this possible? Puzzled, I decided to probe beneath the surface, to discover what deep-seated element religion contained that was vital and true.

Avoiding what I considered the trap of institutionalized religion, of "churchianity," I took to walking or sitting for hours on end by the ocean, pondering its immensity. I watched little fingers of water rushing in among the rocks and pebbles on the shore. Did the vastness of God find *personal* expression, similarly, in our own lives?

The juxtaposition of these thoughts with my daily contacts in and out of the theater filled me with distaste. How petty seemed man's desires compared to the impersonal vastness of infinity! The loftiest aspirations of most of the people around me seemed mean, their values to an incredible degree selfish and ignoble. Egos pitted themselves against other egos in childish rivalries. My fellow students insisted that such behavior laid bare the realities of human nature: So, in fact, had declared the modern dramas they admired, and, far from bemoaning these "realities," they gloried in them. Aspiring actors that they were, they prided themselves on pretending selfishness, "rugged egoism," indifference to the needs of others, and rudeness—until the pretense itself became their reality.

My associates of those days helped me spiritually more than I was capable of realizing at the time. The more they mocked me with their insistent claim, "This is life!" the more my heart cried, "It isn't! It *can't* be!" And as the urgency of my cry deepened me in my own search, I grew to understand that what they termed *life* was nothing but living death.

This isn't to say, however, that sordidness has no objective reality. God was trying to get me to see, rather, the depths to which man can sink, without Him.

One evening outside my apartment I met a fellow student walking in a daze, scarcely able to tread a straight line. At first I thought he must be drunk, but then I noticed dried blood on his forehead. Evidently there was something more serious amiss. I led him indoors. Between long pauses of mental confusion, he related the following story:

"I was sitting quietly on a park bench, enjoying the evening air. I remember hearing footsteps approaching behind me. The next thing I knew I was lying on the grass, slowly returning to consciousness. My coat and trousers were gone. So was my wallet.

"Minutes passed. Dazed as I was, I had no idea what to do. Then I saw a police car parked on the far side of the park. Relieved, I staggered over to it and explained my predicament. Naturally, I assumed they'd want to help me.

"Well, can you guess what they did? They arrested me for being indecently dressed! At the police station I was put into a jail cell without so much as a chance to protest.

"For some time I tried to get them at least to let me make a phone call. Finally they made that much of a concession. 'Just one call,' the sergeant said. I phoned a couple of friends of ours, who came over with fresh clothing.

"Now—would you believe it?—*our friends* are in jail, and *I'm* out!" Shaking his head incredulously, "I still don't understand how it all happened."

What had happened, I learned later, was that these friends, infuriated at the policemen's indifference, had cried, "You don't even seem to care that a crime has been committed!"

"You're under arrest!" bellowed the police sergeant.

Our friends resisted this further outrage, and were set upon by all the policemen in the room, beaten up, and thrown into jail. My injured friend, meanwhile, was released, presumably because he was decently dressed now, and told to go home and forget the whole thing. It was hardly fifteen minutes later that I met him wandering about, dazed and confused.

I returned with him immediately to the police station. As we entered, wild screams were issuing from a back room. Moments later a couple of policemen emerged, dragging a screaming black woman across the floor by her heels. They dumped her unceremoniously in front of the sergeant's desk, where she passed out. One of the men, evidently considering her silence disrespectful, fetched a rubber hose and beat her with it on the soles of her bare feet until she regained consciousness and started screaming again. Satisfied, they dragged her into the jail and flung her, still screaming, into a cell. The remainder of the time we were there I heard her moaning quietly.

Throughout this grim episode the rest of the policemen in the room, about fifteen of them, stood about, laughing. "I haven't had this much fun in *years!*" gloated one of them, rubbing his hands together.

Obviously, to reason with such brutes was impossible; I therefore tried getting information out of them. The sergeant finally gave me the name of some judge whose word he required, he said, "Before I can release those hoodlums." It was already late, but before the night ended I succeeded in getting the judge out of bed, and our friends out of jail.

From this utter mockery of justice I at least learned a salutary lesson. First, of course, I reacted with normal, human indignation at such brutality. But subsequent reflection convinced me that injustice of one kind or another is inevitable in this world. For aren't all of us to some extent lost in ignorance? Blind as I myself was, what right had I to blame others, simply because their blindness differed from my own? My first thought had been, "We need a revolution!" But then I realized that what was needed was a new kind of revolution: religious, not social.

Religion. Again that word! This time I was being pushed toward it by human injustice instead of pulled by my own longing for some higher good. I began now to wonder if evil weren't a conscious will in the universe. How else to account for its prevalence on earth? for the cruelty of man to man? the brutality of the Nazis? the terrors that millions suffer under communism? How else to explain the appalling twist of fate that causes the good intentions of many who embrace communism to result in human debasement, slavery, and death? What, outside of a renewed, widespread return to God—*a spiritual revolution*—could correct the almost unimaginable wrongs in this world?

I gave much thought at this time to communism as a force for evil. My parents had returned from Rumania with tales of Russian atrocities. Our Rumanian friends there were suffering under the new regime; some of them had been deported to slave labor camps in Russia. Surely, I thought, the common argument against communism, that it is inefficient, misses the point altogether. What is truly wrong with it is not that its top-heavy bureaucracy results in the production of fewer material conveniences, nor even that it denies men their political rights, but that it treats materialism* itself as a virtual religion. Denying the reality of God, it sets up matter in His place, and demands self-abnegation of its adherents much as

---

* Materialism, in this context, refers to the philosophical theory that all phenomena, including those of the mind, must be attributed to material agencies.

religions do everywhere. For committed communists, the shortage of material goods reveals, not the inefficiency of their system, but the measure of their willingness to sacrifice for "the cause." Believing in nothing higher than matter, they see spiritual values—truthfulness, compassion, love—as utterly meaningless. They feel morally justified, rather, in committing any atrocity, as long as it advances their own ideological ends. Their motto is, "In every circumstance, think only what is best for the cause."

Theirs might be called a religion of unconsciousness, of non-values. It does offer, however, a pseudo-moralistic rationale for the materialistic values of our age. For this reason, I'm afraid, its teachings will continue to spread, until men everywhere embrace another, truer kind of religion, one that places God, not matter, at the center of reality.

Pursuing these thoughts, I found myself for both objective and subjective reasons, for the sake of mankind generally as well as for my own personal development, drawn to the conclusion that what I wanted, what all men really needed, was God.

With ever more pressing urgency the question returned to me: *What IS God?*

One evening, taking a long walk into the gathering night, I deeply pondered this problem. I dismissed at the outset the popular notion that a venerable figure with flowing white beard, piercing eyes, and a terrible brow presides over the universe, with its billions of galaxies. But, I thought, what about the abstract alternatives that more thoughtful people have suggested—vague definitions such as "Cosmic Ground of Being," which leave one with little to do but close the book and see what is playing on the radio? No, I thought, the God I was seeking must be a *dynamic force,* one that could transform my life, else there was no point in seeking Him.

Well, then, I continued, if He *was* a force, might He possibly be a blind force, sort of like electricity? I'd heard Him so described. There would, of course, be little point in calling such a force God. But in any case, the argument didn't hold together. For if God was blind, whence sprang human intelligence?

Materialists I knew claimed that everything, including intelligence, evolved quite accidentally out of random combinations of electrons. According to them, the universe isn't marvelous at all. It only *seems* marvelous to us because, in the long struggle for survival, man happened to evolve a capacity for wonder as one of the conditioned responses of his emotional mechanism. But this proposition I had long discarded as absurd.

We all know the signs of exceptional intelligence in man: the bright, alert expression in the eyes, the prompt responses, the general air of competence. An intelligent person may pretend successfully to be stupid, but a stupid person can never successfully pretend to be intelligent. What then of the universe, revealing as it does so many signs of an extraordinary intelligence? The intricate organization of stars, atoms, and creatures, the amazingly exact laws on which the cosmos operates—could a mindless force have created these? Impossible! Only egotists, surely, in their desire to claim the highest intelligence for themselves and their kind, could overlook the evidence all around them of an intelligence far mightier than their own.

Continuing this line of reasoning, I thought, if the wonders of creation are the outward signs of a conscious, intelligent Creator, then surely one of the most wonderful of such signs is intelligence itself. Indeed, if human and animal consciousness manifest the *principle* of intelligence, and if God, as Universal Intelligence, *is* that principle, then human intelligence is a manifestation, however imperfect, of God!

Suddenly I felt I was very near to solving my problem. For surely, I reasoned, if God's intelligence is manifested through man, then the Lord cannot exist wholly outside His creation—like some heavenly traffic cop, I thought wryly, from a distance directing human lives here below. If to any degree we, in our intelligence, manifest His infinite intelligence, this can only mean that *we are a part of Him.*

What a staggering concept!

A further thought came: If our lives and consciousness are His manifestations, might it not be possible for us, by deepening our awareness of Him, *to manifest Him more perfectly?*

I recalled the days I had spent watching the ocean surf breaking into long, restless fingers among the rocks and pebbles on the shore. The width of each opening, I reflected, determined the size of the water's flow. Similarly, if the deepest reality of our lives is God, might it not be possible for us to chip away at the granite of our resistance, and thereby to *widen* our channels of receptivity to Him? And would not His infinite wisdom then, like the ocean, flow into us more abundantly?

If this was true, then, obviously, we should seek above all to develop ourselves, not in worldly ways—esthetically or intellectually or pragmatically—but spiritually, by developing that aspect of our nature which is closest to God, so that He might enter into and enlighten our consciousness. If we begin there, then perhaps the Divine Ocean will actually assist us to broaden our mental channels.

I realized now that religion is far more than a system of beliefs, and far more than a formalized effort to wheedle a little pity out of God by offering Him pleading, self-condemning prayers and propitiatory rites. If our link with Him lies in the fact that we manifest Him already, *then it is up to us to receive Him ever more perfectly, to express Him ever more fully.** And *this* is what religion is all about! True religion consists of *a growing awareness of our deep, spiritual relationship with God!* What I had seen thus far of religious practices, and turned away from in disappointment, was not religion *definitively practiced,* but the merest toddling first steps on a stairway to the stars! One might, I reflected, devote his entire life to such religion and still have an eternity of development to look forward to. What a thrilling prospect!

This, then, was my calling in life: I would seek God!

Dazed with the grandeur of my reflections, I hardly knew how or at what hour I found my way home again. "Home" at this time was a large, five-room apartment on South Battery which I shared with four of my fellow drama students. On my return there I found them seated, chatting in the kitchen. More or less automatically, I joined them for a cup of coffee. But my thoughts were far from that convivial gathering. So overwhelmed was I by my new insights that I could hardly speak.

"Look at Don! What's there to be so solemn about?" When they found that I couldn't, or wouldn't, participate in their merriment, their laughter assumed a note of mockery.

"Don keeps trying to solve the riddle of the universe! Yuk! Yuk! Yuk!"

"Ah, sweet mystery of life!" crooned another.

"Why, can't you see?" reasoned the fourth, addressing me. "It's all so simple! There's no riddle to be solved! Just get drunk when you like, have fun, shack up with a girl whenever you can, and forget all this craziness!"

"Yeah," reiterated the first, heavily. "Forget it."

To my state of mind just then my roommates sounded like yapping puppies. Of what use to me, such friends? I went quietly to my room.

A few days later I was discussing religion with another acquaintance.

"If you want spiritual teachings," he remarked suddenly, "you'll find all your answers in the *Bhagavad Gita*."

° "But as many as *received* him, to them gave he power to become the sons of God" (John 1:12).

"What's that?" Somehow I found this foreign name strangely appealing.

"It's a Hindu Scripture."

Hindu? And what was *that?* I knew nothing of Indian philosophy. This name, however, the *Bhagavad Gita,* lingered with me.

If religion was a matter of becoming more receptive to God, it was high time, I decided, that I got busy and did what I could to make myself receptive. But how? It wasn't that I had no idea how to improve myself. Rather, I saw so much room for improvement that I hardly knew where to begin.

There was the question of my psychological faults: intellectual pride, an overly critical nature. No one, myself included, was happy with these traits in me. But how was I to work on them? And for that matter, were they entirely unmixed evils? Was it wrong, for instance, to *think?* Was it wrong to stand honestly by the fruits of one's thinking, regardless of the opinions of others? And was it so wrong to be critical of attitudes that one's discrimination declared to be false? People who were more concerned for their own comfort than for my spiritual development condemned these traits in me outright. But to me it seemed that there were aspects of my very faults that must be deemed virtues. How was I to sift one from the other?

Contemplating my more socially admissible virtues, I saw that the very opposite was true: In some ways these assumed the nature of faults. My compassion for the sufferings of others, for example, prompted me to try to help them beyond my own capabilities. How else to account for my desire to help them through my writings, when I didn't even know what to write? Here again: How was I to sift truth from error?

Was there *any* way out of my psychological labyrinth?

Even on a physical level, the possibilities for self-improvement seemed bewilderingly complex. I read in a magazine advertisement the names of several famous people who had been vegetarians. *Vegetarians?* Was it really desirable, or even possible, to live without eating meat? Again, I read somewhere else that white flour is harmful to the health. *White flour?* Heretofore, a hamburger on a white bun, decorated with a thin sliver of tomato and a limp wisp of lettuce, had been my idea of a balanced meal. It seemed now that there were all sorts of opinions on even so basic a subject as diet.

Finally, bewildered by the sheer number of the choices before me, I decided that there could be but one way out of my imperfections: God. I must let *Him* guide my life. I must leave off seeking human solutions, and give up defining my search in terms of human relations.

And what of my plans to be a playwright? Well, what had I been writing, anyway? Could I, who knew nothing, say anything meaningful to anyone else? I had deluded myself for a time with the thought that perhaps, if I were vague enough, I might write works with cryptic messages that others would understand, even if I myself had no idea what those messages were. But now I realized that in this thought, common as it is among writers, I had not been honest. No, I must give up writing altogether. I must give up my plans to flood the world with my ignorance. Surely, out of very compassion for people I must leave off trying to help them. I must renounce their world, their interests, their attachments, their pursuits. I must seek God in the wilderness, in the mountains, in complete solitude.

I would become a hermit.

And what was it I hoped to find, once I made this renunciation? Peace of mind? Inner strength, perhaps? A little happiness?

Wistfully I thought: happiness! I recalled the pure happiness I had known as a child, and lost in the pseudo-sophistication of my youth. Would I ever find it again? Only, I thought, if I became simple once again, like a child. Only if I forsook over-intellectuality, and became utterly open to God's love.

I pursued this line of thinking for a time, when a new kind of doubt seized me: Was I losing my mind? Whoever had heard of anyone actually seeking God? Whoever had heard of anyone communing with Him? Was I completely lunatic, to be dreaming of blazing trails where none had ventured before? For I knew nothing as yet about the lives of saints. Vaguely I'd heard them described as people who lived close to God, but the mental image I'd formed of them was of no more than ordinarily good people who went about smiling at children, doing kind deeds, and murmuring, *"Pax vobiscum,"* or some such pious formula, whenever anybody got in their way. What demon of presumption was possessing me that I should be dreaming of actually *finding* God? Surely, I *must* be going mad!

Yet, if this *were* madness, was it not a more solacing condition than the world's vaunted "sanity"? For it was a madness that promised hope, in a world bereft of hope. It was a madness that promised peace, in a world of conflict and warfare. It was a madness that promised happiness, in a world of suffering, cynicism, and broken dreams.

I knew not how to take even my first steps toward God, but my longing for Him had by now become almost obsessive.

Where could I turn? To whom could I look for guidance? The religious people I had met, the monks and ministers, had seemed quite as lost in ignorance as I was.

It occurred to me that I might find in the Scriptures a wisdom those men had overlooked. At least I must *try*.

And what of my plans to become a hermit? That path, surely, I must follow also. Ah! but where? how? with what money to purchase life's essentials? with what practical knowledge to build, plant food, and otherwise fend for myself? Was I not, after all, a mere fool dreaming impractical dreams? Surely, if practical steps had to be taken, there must be a more pragmatic solution to my dilemma than drifting off to an existence for which I was utterly untrained.

At this point, Reason stepped onto the scene briskly to resolve my dilemma.

"There's nothing wrong with you," it asserted, "that vigorous, healthful country living can't cure. You've been spending too much time with jaded city people. Get out among simple, genuine, *good* country folk if you want to find peace of mind. Don't waste your life on impossible dreams. Get back to the land! It isn't God you want; it's a more natural way of life, in the harmony and simplicity of Nature."

Ease, in fact, not simplicity, was the heart of this message. For God is so mighty a challenge that the ego will cling to almost anything, rather than heed the call to utter self-surrender.

And, weakling that I was, I relented. I would heed Reason's counsel, I decided. I would go off to the country, commune with Nature, and live among more *natural* human beings.

CHAPTER 13

A Search for Guide-Maps

M Y DECISION TO SEEK peace of mind in an environment of bucolic simplicity coincided with the end of the school year, and the closing of the Dock Street Theater for the summer. I returned to New York.

Dad had recently been posted to Cairo, Egypt, as Esso's exploration manager there. Our home in Scarsdale was let, and mother had taken a house temporarily in White Plains, preparatory to departing for Cairo in August to join Dad. I stayed with her two or three weeks.

My plans for the summer were already set. I said nothing of them, however, to anyone, giving out only that I was going to upstate New York; my spiritual longings I kept a carefully guarded secret. But I put in effect immediately my plan to study the Scriptures. Borrowing Mother's copy of the Holy Bible, I began reading it from the beginning.

"In the beginning God created the heaven and the earth. . . . And God said, Let there be light: and there was light." Who is not familiar with these wonderful lines?

"And the LORD God planted a garden eastward in Eden; and there he put the man whom he had formed. . . . And the LORD God commanded the man, saying, Of every tree of the garden thou mayest freely eat: But of the tree of the knowledge of good and evil, thou shalt not eat of it: for in the day that thou eatest thereof thou shalt surely die."

But—what was this? How could God possibly want man to *remain* ignorant?

And so man ate the fruit, became wise, and was forced in consequence to live like a witless serf. What kind of teaching was this?

Chapter Five: Here I learned that Adam lived nine hundred and thirty years; his son, Seth, nine hundred and twelve years, and Seth's son, Enos, nine hundred and five years. Cainan, Enos's son, "lived seventy years, and begat Mahalaleel: and Cainan lived after he begat Mahalaleel eight hundred and forty years, and begat sons and daughters: And all the days of Cainan were nine hundred and ten years: and he died. And Mahalaleel lived sixty and five years, and begat Jared. . . . And Jared lived an hundred sixty and two years, and he begat Enoch. . . . And Enoch lived sixty and five years, and begat Methuselah. . . . And all the days of Methuselah were nine hundred sixty and nine years: and he died."

What in heaven's name did it all mean? Was some deep symbolism involved?* All this said nothing whatever to my present needs. Disappointed, I put the book down.

Over the years since then, a number of well-meaning Christians have sought to persuade me that God's truth can be found only in the Bible. If this were true, I cannot imagine that one who was seeking as sincerely as I was would have been turned away at the very threshold by what he read in the Good Book itself. It wasn't until I met my guru, and learned from *him* the teachings of the Bible, that I was able to return to it with a sense of real appreciation. For the time being, I'm afraid I simply bogged down in the "begats."

In Mother's library there was another book that captured my interest. This one contained brief excerpts from the major religions of the world. Perhaps here I would find the guidance I was seeking.

The selections from the Bible in this book proved more meaningful to me, but even so they seemed too anthropomorphic for my tastes, steeped as I was in the scientific view of reality. The Judaic, the Moslem, the Taoist, the Buddhist, the Zoroastrian—all, I found poetically beautiful and inspiring, but for me still there was something lacking. I was being asked to believe, but none of these Scriptures, as nearly as I could tell, was asking me to *experience*. Without actual experience of God, what was the good of mere belief? The farther I read, the more all of these Scriptures impressed me as—well, great, no doubt, but at last hopelessly beyond me. Perhaps it was simply a question of style. The standard language of Scripture, I reflected, was cryptic to the point of being incomprehensible.

And then I came upon excerpts from the Hindu teachings—a few pages only, but what a revelation! Here the emphasis was on cosmic realities. God was described as an Infinite Consciousness; man, as a manifestation of that consciousness. Why, this was the

* Later, when I read my guru's explanation of the story of Adam and Eve, I found its inner meaning profound and deeply inspiring.

very concept I myself had worked out on that long evening walk in Charleston! Man's highest duty, I read, is to attune himself with that divine consciousness: Again, this was what I had worked out! Man's ultimate goal, according to these writings, is to experience that divine reality *as his true Self.* But, how scientific! What infinite promise! Poetic symbolism abounded here, too, as in the other Scriptures, but here I found also explanations, crystal clear and logical. Best of all, I found advice: not only on the religious life generally, but more specifically, on *how to seek God.*

All this was exactly what I'd been seeking! I felt like a poor man who has just been given a priceless gift. Hastily I skimmed through these excerpts; then, realizing the awesome importance they held for me, I put the book aside, and resolved to wait for a later time when I would be free to read these teachings slowly and digest them. Casually I asked Mother if I might take the book upstate with me for the summer. "Of course," she replied, never suspecting the depth of my interest.

My Aunt Alleen, Mother's half-sister, visited us in White Plains during my stay there. Sensing the turmoil seething within me, she remarked to Mother one day, "I bet Don ends up in a theological seminary."

"Oh, not *Don!*" Mother's tone implied, "almost anyone else." The change in my life, when it came, caught her completely by surprise.

Two or three times during my stay in White Plains I took the train into New York City, and there contemplated anew the unending throng of tense, worried faces. How many human tragedies were written there in lines of desperation, of bitterness, of hidden grief! More keenly than ever I felt the bond of our common humanity. The worst criminal, I reflected, might have been I. For who was safe from ignorance? Doubtless even the drug addict felt justified in the attitudes that had drawn him into his web of confusion. What, then, of my own present attitudes? Did I dare trust them? How could anyone, at any given hour in his life, know *for a certainty* that his most well-intentioned behavior would advance him toward freedom, and not enmesh him in further bondage? My growing conviction that everything is a part of one Reality, while it gave me a deep sense of kinship with others, awakened in me at the same time a terrifying sense of my own vulnerability. I visualized myself drifting through skies of ignorance in which it was as much my potential to fall as to rise.

It was high time, surely, that I took my own life in hand. Too long had I been floating about haphazardly on seas of circumstance, vaguely hoping that my general direction would be toward the shores of truth. I must begin now to direct my life consciously.

One afternoon I was walking down Fifth Avenue. The heat was oppressive. A bar, cool and inviting, stood before me on a street corner. I stepped in and had a couple of refreshing beers. Though not intoxicated, I realized that my reflexes were not quite as keen as they had been when I came in. I'd never considered drinking a personal problem, nor had I seen anything wrong with drinking in moderation. But it occurred to me now that if anything could lessen my self-control even to this small degree, I would be wise to avoid it. On leaving that barroom I resolved never again to take another drink. Nor have I ever done so.

My trip upstate New York had been intended, originally, to help me find peace without effort, amid the beauties of Nature. But by the time I left White Plains my resolution to work on myself had stiffened markedly, encouraged by the brief excerpts I had read from the Indian Scriptures. Having given up drinking—and also, two or three months previously, smoking—I was beginning to feel an actual enthusiasm for self-discipline. I still hoped that more natural surroundings would contribute something to my peace of mind, but I had no illusions that all my answers would be found in a random assortment of hills and trees. God saw to it, as I shall explain later on, that *none* of my answers were found there.

As a start toward self-transformation, I decided to begin with vigorous physical discipline. In my initial enthusiasm, of course, I overdid it.

I set out on a one-speed bicycle, taking with me a knapsack that contained only Mother's book of Scriptural excerpts, a few clothes, and a poncho. I had no sleeping bag; absurd as it may seem, I knew nothing of proper camping procedures; I wasn't even aware that there *were* such things as sleeping bags.

My first night I spent in an open field, the poncho spread out underneath me as protection against the damp earth. At three in the morning I awoke, freezing cold, to find myself sloshing about in a puddle of water, collected by my poncho from the heavy dew. Further sleep proved impossible. After some time I got up, resignedly, and started bicycling again. Mile followed weary mile through deserted mountain terrain, scarcely a village in sight anywhere. Toward afternoon the seat of my bicycle felt so hard that, even though I tried softening it with a folded towel, I could hardly bear to sit down. After ten or twelve hours of ceaseless pedaling, my legs, unaccustomed to this strenuous effort, felt with every upgrade that they must shortly give out altogether. Towards later afternoon

I watched hopefully for signs of a village with an inn, for on one point I was resolved: I would not, if I could possibly help it, sleep in another field. But I saw not a house. Sixteen hours I pedaled that day, mostly uphill, on my one-speed bicycle; I covered well over a hundred miles.

The sun was low in the west when I met a hiker who informed me that there was a village two miles or so off the road I was on, and that that village had a guest house. With very nearly my last ounce of strength I pedaled there. In the center of the village I found a house in front of which stood the reassuring sign, "Rooms for Rent." Literally staggering inside, I collapsed in a chair by the front door.

"May I please have a room?"

"Oh, I'm *so* sorry. We've been meaning to take that sign down. We no longer rent rooms."

Despair seized me. "Is there no place nearby where I could spend the night?"

"Well, there's an inn down the road about a mile. I'm sure they'd have a room for you."

A whole mile! Even this short distance was too great for me, in my present state of exhaustion; I hardly had strength enough left to stand. "Please, do you think you might phone and ask them to come fetch me in their car?"

A ride was arranged. That night in bed I actually thought I might die. I didn't realize it at the time, but since early childhood I had had a minor heart condition. That entire night my heart pounded on the walls of my chest as though it would break them. I slept around the clock. Mercifully, by mid-morning my heartbeat had returned to normal. Feeling refreshed, though sore in every muscle, I was eager to continue my journey.

An important passage in the *Bhagavad Gita,* which unfortunately I had yet to read, counsels moderation in all things.° I had discovered the merits of this precept quite on my own! From now on, I

° But for earthly needs
  Religion is not his who too much fasts
  Or too much feasts, nor his who sleeps away
  An idle mind; nor his who wears to waste
  His strength in vigils. Nay, Arjuna! call
  That the true piety which most removes
  Earth-aches and ills, where one is moderate
  In eating and in resting, and in sport;
  Measured in wish and act; sleeping betimes,
  Waking betimes for duty.
           —*Bhagavad Gita,* in Sir Edwin Arnold's translation, *The Song Celestial*

decided, I'd better proceed on the pathway to perfection at a more measured pace. I must tighten the screw carefully, lest it split the wood.

And so I proceeded, this time more slowly, to the small mountain town of Indian Lake, where I rented a room and settled eagerly to my reward: a careful study of the few excerpts I had from the Indian Scriptures.

CHAPTER 14

Joy Is Inside!

"Perfect bliss
Grows only in the bosom tranquillised,
The spirit passionless, purged from offense,
Vowed to the Infinite. He who thus vows
His soul to the Supreme Soul, quitting sin,
Passes unhindered to the endless bliss
Of unity with Brahma."

R EADING THESE WORDS from the *Bhagavad Gita,* my imagination was deeply stirred. The task I faced, as I was learning from the excerpts before me, was to calm my thoughts and feelings, to make myself an open and empty receptacle for God's grace. If I did so, so these teachings stated, God would enter my life and fill it.

How different these simple precepts from the meandering theology that I had heard proclaimed from pulpits on Sunday mornings! Here I found no beggarly self-abasement—the weak man's masquerade of humility; no talk of the importance of entering a religious institution as a doorway to heaven; no effort to hold God at a distance with the diplomatic address of formal prayer; no hint at compromising one's spiritual commitment by concern over its social acceptability. What I read here was fresh, honest, and convincing. It gave me extraordinary hope.

One thing that had disturbed me about all the churches I'd visited was their sectarianism. "Ours is the one, the only true way" was a dogma implied even when it wasn't stated. Invariably it suggested that all other ways were false, that even if other groups loved the same God, *their* message, in some indiscernible manner, was "of the devil."

How different were the teachings I was reading now! All paths, according to them, lead by various routes to the same, infinite goal. "As a mother," one stated, "in nursing her sick children, gives rice and curry to one, sago and arrowroot to another, and bread and butter to a third, so the Lord has laid out different paths for different men, suitable to their natures."

How beautiful! How persuasive in its utter fairness!

Another point that had always troubled me in my contacts with the churches was their ministers' tendency to discourage questioning. "Have faith," they told me. But what sort of "faith" is it that refuses to submit itself to honest challenges? Could the motive behind such refusal be anything but what it seems on the surface: fear? Fear that one's beliefs are a house built on sand? Even in their efforts to be reasonable, those ministers wore blinders, for while they quoted Scripture to support their beliefs, they never admitted the possibility that those very quotations might have other meanings than those they ascribed to them. Even the closest disciples of Jesus were often scolded by him for mistaking his true meanings. Is it, then, wise and humble for us, who live so far from him in time, to insist that *we* understand him better? The Scriptures are intended to expand our understanding, not to suffocate it.

But then, as my guru later pointed out to me, one difference between recorded Scriptures and a living teacher is that the seeker's misunderstandings cannot be rebutted, patiently or sharply as the occasion demands, by the pages of a book.

The Indian teachings, unlike those ministers I had known, stressed the need for testing every Scriptural claim. Direct, personal experience of God, not dogmatic or uncritical belief, was the final test they proposed, but they also suggested intermediate tests by which the veriest beginner would know whether he was headed in the right direction, and not slipping off into one of life's innumerable detours.

I had already realized from my own experience that the difference between a right decision and a wrong one can be subtle. I was impressed therefore with teachings that can be verified not only after death, but here on earth, in this lifetime.*

These were the teachings for which I had longed. Yes, I vowed again, I would dedicate my life to seeking God! Too long had I delayed, too long vacillated with doubts, too long sought earthly, not divine, solutions to the deepest problems of life. Art? Science? New social structures? What could any of these things do to lift

---

* The Bible, too, stresses verification by actual experience. "Test the spirits," wrote St. John in his first epistle. Religionists who emphasize blind belief until death generally haven't tasted the fruits of the religious life themselves, because they haven't practiced it.

man high, or for very long? Without inner transformation, any outer improvement in the human lot would be like trying to strengthen a termite-ridden building with a fresh coat of paint.

One parable in the reading I was engaged in affected me especially. It was from the sayings of a great saint of the Nineteenth Century, Sri Ramakrishna. Not knowing who he was, I imagined the saying was taken from some ancient Scripture.

"How," Sri Ramakrishna asked, "does a man come to have dispassion? A wife once said to her husband, 'Dear, I am very anxious about my brother. For the past one week he has been thinking of becoming an ascetic, and is making preparations for it. He is trying to reduce gradually all his desires and wants.' The husband replied, 'Dear, be not at all anxious about your brother. He will never become a *sannyasin*. No one can become a *sannyasin* in that way.' 'How does one become a *sannyasin*, then?' asked the wife. 'It is done in this way!' the husband exclaimed. So saying, he tore into pieces his flowing dress, took a piece out of it, tied it round his loins, and told his wife that she and all others of her sex were thenceforth mothers to him. He left the house, never more to return." °

The courage of this man's renunciation stirred me to the depths. By contrast, how I had vacillated in my doubts!

All these excerpts were saying but one thing in essence: that perfection must be sought within the self, not in the outer world. Of the truth of this teaching God evidently had it in mind to give me abundant proof that summer.

Indian Lake is a beautiful place of pine trees and cool forest glades, of rolling hills and gently rippling water. "If I'm to relate more deeply to cosmic realities," I thought, "I could begin in no better place than right here." Indeed, the very scenery invited communion. I tried consciously to *feel* the thrill of a raindrop as it quivered on a pine needle; the exquisite freshness of the morning dew; the burst of sunlight through the clouds at sunset. Always I had loved Nature, and felt deeply drawn to her beauty in woods, lakes, flowers, and starry skies. But now, as I endeavored to intensify my sensitivity, *to enter directly* into the life all around me, I

° This story has to be understood in its own cultural context. Marital fidelity is highly regarded in India. The Hindu Scriptures state, however, that that which is otherwise a duty ceases to be such when it conflicts with a higher duty. The highest duty of mankind is to seek God. It is understood in India that one's spouse can and should be supportive in this search. Only if the desire for God is intense, and one's spouse, by his or her worldliness, poses an obstacle to that search, would it be permissible to break the marital tie without mutual consent.

discovered with a pang what an utter prisoner I was, locked in my own ego. I could see; I could not *feel*. Or, to the extent that I *could* feel, it was only with a small part of me, not with my whole being. I was like an eight-cylinder motor hitting on only one cylinder. Surely if even here, in these perfect surroundings, I could not rise out of myself and attune myself with greater realities, no mere *place* would ever accomplish such a transformation for me. Obviously, it was I, myself, who needed changing. Whether my outer environment was beautiful or ugly was not particularly significant. What mattered was what I made of my own inner "environment" of thoughts, feelings, and inspirations.

I now was spending some time every day in meditation. I didn't know how to go about it, but believed that if I could only calm my mind a little bit, I would at least be headed in the right direction. I prayed daily, too: something I hadn't had faith enough to do until now.

For my outer life God was, I suspect, saying to me with a friendly chuckle, "You expected to find a better type of humanity in the country? Take a look around you! Man is not better for *where* he lives. Dreams of outer perfection are a delusion. Happiness must be found inside or it will not be found anywhere!"

My first plan for a job at Indian Lake had been to work as a lumberjack. I asked my landlady what she thought of my chances of finding such employment.

"What!" she cried. "And get knifed in a drunken brawl? Those men aren't your type at all."

Well, I had to admit her description left something to be desired. But I wasn't to be put off so easily. For two days I trudged about in the woods, looking for a logging camp that was said to be in the vicinity. Perhaps it was God's will that I missed it; at any rate, all I encountered were swarms of deer flies. Covered with stings, I found myself more receptive the third day to my landlady's warnings. I decided to seek employment elsewhere.

That morning a local farmer agreed to hire me as a handyman. I'd had a little experience with farm work just after graduation from high school, and had enjoyed it then. But never before had I worked for such a man as this. My intention was to work quietly, thinking of God. But my employer had other, to him infinitely better, ideas: He wanted me to play the fool in his little kingdom. "What else is a handyman for?" he demanded rhetorically, when I remonstrated at being made the constant butt of his rustic jokes. Humor I didn't mind, but I drew the line at *witless* humor. There are few things so exasperating as meeting a gibe with a clever thrust, only to have it soar yards over the other person's head. When, after a few clever sallies, I lapsed resignedly into silence, the farmer teased, "C'mon, flannelmouth! I hired you to *work*. Don't stand there jabbering all day." And that, as I recall, was the high point of his comedy routine. My image of the genuine, innocent, *good* rustic was beginning to fade.

I soon left this worthy's employ. Putting peaceful Indian Lake resolutely behind me, I set off down the road on my bicycle in search of other work. Hours later I came to a mine owned by the Union Carbide Corporation. There the hiring clerk looked at me dubiously.

"We have work, all right," she said, "but it isn't your kind of work."

"What do you mean, not my kind of work? I can do anything!"

"Well, you won't like this job. You'll see. You won't last a week." With that encouragement I was hired.

The atmosphere of the sintering plant, where I was employed, was so thick with the dust of the ore they were mining that one couldn't even see across the room. At the end of every day my face and hands were completely black. Some idea was beginning to form in my mind of what the woman had meant.

But it wasn't the work itself that finally got to me. It was another of those simple, genuine, innocent, *good* rustics—a complete fool who, finding me too polite to tell him, as everyone else did, to go to hell, mistook me for an even greater fool than himself. All day, every day, he regaled me with lies about his heroic feats before, during, and after World War II. Then, taking my silence for credulity, he began preening himself on his own superior intelligence. Finally he informed me disdainfully that I was too stupid to be worthy of association with one of his own incomparable brilliance.

The hiring clerk didn't even trouble to remind me of her prediction, when I appeared after a week for my severance pay.

How, I wondered, would I ever become a hermit? A person needed money to buy food. Probably I'd have to find employment from time to time merely to stay alive. But if these were samples of the kind of work I'd find out in the country, I wasn't so sure that my spiritual losses wouldn't outweigh the gains. Perhaps, I thought, if I could find some place where the money I earned could be stretched farther. . . .

That was it! I would go to some part of the world where the cost of living was low: yes, to south America. I would work in this country first, and save up. It wouldn't cost much, surely, to get to South America; perhaps I could even work my way down there.

And there I'd find it possible to live a long time on my savings—years even, perhaps, meditating in some secluded jungle spot, or on a mountaintop. My problem, now, was how to earn as much money as possible in the shortest possible time.

At the mine, one of my co-workers had entertained me after work with tales of the huge earnings he'd accumulated one summer in tips as a bellhop at a resort hotel. The thought of milking people by doing special favors for them was odious to me, but perhaps, I thought, if I kept my goal firmly in mind, I would be able to suppress my distaste.

My next stop was the resort town of Lake George. Coming to a hotel, I approached the owner and asked if he was in need of a bellhop.

"Got one already." He eyed me speculatively. "Where you from?"

"Scarsdale."

"Oh, Scarsdale, eh?" His eyes flickered with interest. "Wouldn't hurt to have someone from Scarsdale working here." He paused. "Okay, you're on."

Well, by no stretch of the imagination could *this* fellow be called a rustic! He was first, last, and forever a shyster in the art of turning little fortunes into big ones. His guests received as little from him as possible in return for everything he could squeeze out of them. The janitor and cleaning woman were his first cousins, emigrants from Europe, but he treated them like serfs. When I saw him for what he was, it shamed me to be working for him. And it shamed me almost more to accept tips from the guests, whom it was my pleasure to serve. When one couple tried to tip me a second time for fetching something else from their car, I simply couldn't accept their offer. Hardly a week after my arrival I was off down the road again.

The time was approaching in any case for me to return to White Plains and help Mother make preparations for her voyage to Egypt.

My trip south held a certain hope also. A co-worker at the mine had suggested that I might get a job in the merchant marine, where the veriest beginner earned as much as $300 a month. This was good pay in those days. Better still, since I would be out at sea, receiving free board and lodging, I'd be able to save quite a lot of money quickly. I decided to try my luck before the mast.

The summer so far had proved a mixed bag: uplifting in the truths I had learned, but materially a fiasco. More and more I was coming to feel as though I had landed on the wrong planet. None of my experiences these past months had helped me to feel at home here.

Yet my desire to "drop out" seemed, from every practical standpoint, wildly unrealistic. I could not but admit to myself that my plans for becoming a hermit rested on the shakiest possible ground. I knew nothing of the practical skills I'd need to live alone in the wilderness. I had no idea how much money I'd actually require to remain in South America a long time. Worst of all, I knew so little of the spiritual path that I had no confidence in my ability to walk it alone. I didn't know how to meditate. I didn't know how to pray. I didn't know what to think about through the day when I wasn't meditating or praying. I was beginning to realize that, without guidance, I was as good as lost.

Yet I knew of no one whom I could trust to guide me out of the empty corridors of institutional religion into the free air of universal truth. I was contemplating a path that seemed, from every practical viewpoint, sheer folly. But I was doing so because I had ruled out every conceivable alternative.

The thought of living a so-called "normal," worldly life filled me with anguish, the more so because I felt so alone in my rejection of it. Most of my friends were getting married, and settling down into good jobs. The pressure on me—from them, and from society—to do likewise was, in a sense, constant. But to my mind, even a lifetime of starvation and suffering would be worth it, if only by so living I could find God.

And what did I hope to achieve in finding Him? There, my notions remained vague, though certainly I would have considered even peace of mind an incomparable blessing. But what mattered to me was that to know Him would be to know Reality, and that not knowing Him meant embracing falsehood and delusion. Wherever my path led, I knew I had but one valid choice: to offer my life to Him. Thereafter, it would be up to Him to lead me where He would.

CHAPTER 15

A Map Discovered

A s soon as possible after my return to White Plains I went to Bowling Green in New York City, and applied for a merchant mariner's card. This I received on August 24th with the classification "Ordinary seaman, messman, wiper." Thereafter I was told it was only a question of waiting for a ship that would give me a berth. My hope was to ship out as soon as possible.

Meanwhile I helped Mother pack. When her sailing date came, I accompanied her to the dock in New York and saw her off safely. Next I went down to Bowling Green to see if any ships had come in. No luck: "Come back in a few days." With most of the afternoon still before me, I went uptown to browse at Brentano's, the famous Fifth Avenue bookstore.

At Brentano's I got into a discussion on spiritual matters with a sales clerk, who showed me a few books by Thomas Merton, the young Protestant Christian who converted to Roman Catholicism, then went on to become a Trappist monk. I was intrigued, though I didn't feel personally attracted. It was the catholicity—which is to say, the *universality*—of India's teachings that had won my devotion.

From Brentano's I went up Fifth Avenue to another book store: Doubleday-Doran, as it was named then. Here I found an entire section of books on Indian philosophy—the first I had ever seen. Hungrily I feasted my gaze on the wide variety of titles: The *Upanishads,* the *Bhagavad Gita,* the *Ramayana,* the *Mahabharata,* books on yoga. I finished scanning these shelves, then turned back to go over them once again. This time, to my surprise, the first book I saw, standing face outward on the shelf, was one I hadn't even noticed the first time. The author's photograph on the cover affected me strangely. Never had I met anyone whose face radiated so much goodness, humility, and love. Eagerly I picked up the book and glanced again at its title: *Autobiography of a Yogi,* by Paramhansa Yogananda. The author lived in America—in California! Was this someone at last who could *help* me in my search? As I started to leaf through the book, these words caught my attention: "Dedicated to the memory of Luther Burbank, an American saint."

An American *saint*? But, how preposterous! How could anyone become a saint in this land of the "almighty dollar"? this materialistic desert? this. . . . I closed the book in dismay, returning it to its place on the shelf.

That day I bought my first book of Indian philosophy—not *Autobiography of a Yogi,* but Sir Edwin Arnold's beautiful translation of the *Bhagavad Gita.* Eagerly I took this treasure home with me to Scarsdale, where I had temporarily rented a private room. For the next couple of days I fairly devoured it, feeling as though I were soaring in vast skies of pure wisdom.

> By this sign is [the sage] known
> Being of equal grace to comrades, friends,
> Chance-comers, strangers, lovers, enemies,
> Aliens and kinsmen; loving all alike,
> Evil or good.

What wonderful words! Thrilled, I read on:

> Yea, knowing Me the source of all, by Me
>   all creatures wrought,
> The wise in spirit cleave to Me, into My
>   being brought. . . .
> And unto these—thus serving well, thus
>   loving ceaselessly—
> I give a mind of perfect mood, whereby they
>   draw to Me;
> And, all for love of them, within their darkened
>   souls I dwell,
> And, with bright rays of wisdom's lamp, their
>   ignorance dispell.

My own doubts, too, were being dispelled by these marvelous teachings. I knew now with complete certainty that this path was right for me.

The day after I finished my first reading of the *Bhagavad Gita,* I returned to New York, intending to visit Bowling Green and see if any ship had come in. I was walking down Seventh Avenue toward the subway, the entrance to which was on the far side of the next cross street, when I recalled the book I'd rejected so summarily on my last visit to the city: *Autobiography of a Yogi.* As I remembered that beautiful face on the cover, a strong urge from within prompted me to go buy it. I thrust the thought firmly out of my mind.

"That isn't what I'm looking for," I told myself. Chuckling, I added, "An American saint, indeed!" Resolutely I continued walking toward the subway.

"How can you know what the book's really like, if you won't even read it?" came the urge again, not with words, but with unmistakable meaning.

"No!" I repeated. I then offered reasons: "I've got to stop reading books; I'm too intellectual as it is. Besides, if I'm ever to become a hermit, I'm going to have to *save* money, not continually spend it!"

At that moment I reached the corner. I was proceeding toward the curb ahead of me when I felt as though an actual force were turning me left around the corner, and propelling me toward Fifth Avenue. I'd never experienced anything like it before. Amazed, I asked myself, "Is there something in this book that I'm *meant* to read?" Resisting no longer, I hastened eagerly in the direction of Doubleday-Doran's.

Entering the store, I made straight for the book and bought it. As I was turning to leave, I bumped into Doug Burch, that friend from my Scarsdale High School days who had introduced me to Nick's and Dixieland jazz. We exchanged news briefly. Doug began describing to me in glowing terms his plans for making a career in radio and advertising. The longer he talked, the more closely I hugged my increasingly precious new book to my heart. Imperceptibly, my doubts about it had already vanished. I felt as though Yogananda were sharing my dismay at the shining prospects Doug was describing, a way of life that, to me, spelled desolation. Holding the book, I felt suddenly as though this oriental yogi and I were old friends. The world and I were strangers, but here was one who knew me, and understood.

I waited until I reached my room in Scarsdale before opening the book. And then began the most thrilling literary adventure of my life.

Autobiography of a Yogi is the story of a young Indian's intense search for God. It describes a number of living saints that he met on his journey, including his great guru, Swami Sri Yukteswar. It also describes, more clearly than any other mystical work I have ever read, the author's own experiences with God, including the highest one possible, *samadhi,* or mystical union. In chapter after chapter I found moving testimony to God's *living* reality, not only in the abstraction of infinity, but in the hearts and lives of actual human beings. I read of how Yogananda's prayers even for little things had been answered, and of how, by placing himself unreservedly in God's hands, his unanticipated needs had always been met. I read of intense love for God such as I myself yearned to possess; of a relationship with the Lord more intimate, more dear than I had dared to imagine possible.

Until now I had supposed that a life of devotion might give one, at best, a little peace of mind. But here, suddenly, I discovered that the fruit of spiritual living is a joy beyond human imagination!

Until recently I had doubted the value of prayer, except perhaps as a means of uplifting *oneself*. But now I learned, and could not for a moment doubt, that God relates individually, *lovingly,* to every seeker.

Miracles abound in this book. Many of these, I confess, were quite beyond my powers of acceptance at the time. But instead of dismissing them, as I would certainly have done if I'd read of them in most other books, I suspended my incredulity. For the spirit of this story was so deeply honest, so transparently innocent of pride or impure motive that it was impossible for me to doubt that its author believed implicitly every word he had written. Never before had I encountered a spirit so clearly truthful, so filled with goodness and joy. Every page seemed radiant with light. Reading *Autobiography of a Yogi,* I alternated between tears and laughter: tears of pure joy; laughter of even greater joy! For three days I scarcely ate or slept. When I walked it was almost on tiptoe, as though in an ecstatic dream.

What this book described, finally, was the highest of sciences, Kriya Yoga, a technique that enables the seeker to advance rapidly on the path of meditation. I, who wanted so desperately to learn how to meditate, felt all the excitement of one who has found a treasure map, the treasure in this case being a divine one buried deep within my own self!

Autobiography of a Yogi is the greatest book I have ever read. One perusal of it was enough to change my entire life. From that time on my break with the past was complete. I resolved in the smallest detail of my life to follow Paramhansa Yogananda's teaching.

Finding that he recommended a vegetarian diet, I immediately renounced meat, fish, and fowl. He could have recommended a diet of bread and water and I'd have obeyed him without a qualm.

For, more than anything else, what this book gave me was the conviction that in Yogananda I had found my guru, my spiritual teacher for all time to come. A few days earlier I hadn't even known this strange word, *guru.* I hadn't known anything about yoga, or reincarnation, or karma, or almost any of the basic precepts of Indian philosophy. Now incredibly, I felt such deep, utter trust in another human being that, ignorant though I was of his philosophy, I was willing to follow him to the end of life. And while I had yet to meet him, I felt that he was the truest friend I had ever known.

The day after I became a vegetarian I was invited by friends of my family, Mr. and Mrs. Lloyd Gibson, to lunch at their home. To my combined amusement and dismay, the main dish consisted of chicken à la king. Not wanting to hurt my friends' feelings, I compromised by pushing the chicken bits to one side, and eating the vegetables in their chicken sauce.

George Calvert, on whose father's farm Bob and I had worked after my graduation from high school, had invited me for the following day to lunch at his parents' home, and to a polo game afterwards. This time I had no choice but to refuse the thick, juicy hamburger sandwich that his mother offered me. To make matters more awkward still, George had considerately provided me with a date! I must have seemed strange company indeed, eating hardly anything, and paying as little attention to the girl as politely possible, from the opposite end of the room. (Yogananda was a monk: I, too, would be a monk.) The polo game gave me an opportunity for a little surreptitious meditation, so I didn't view it as a total loss.

Later that day I met my brother Bob and Dean Bassett, a friend of ours, at Nielson's, an ice cream parlor in Scarsdale village. Dean had been voted "biggest wolf" in my senior high school class. He and Bob were discussing Dean's favorite subject: girls.

I listened in silence for a time. At last I protested, "Don't you see? Desire only enslaves one to the very things one desires!"

Bob and Dean gazed at each other quizzically. "What's wrong with him?" Dean asked.

It was years before I realized that comprehension, like a flower, must unfold at its own speed. Until a person is ready for a truth, not even the clearest logic will make it acceptable to him.

As soon as I finished reading *Autobiography of a Yogi,* my impulse was to jump onto the next bus bound for California. Not wanting to act impulsively, however, I waited a whole day! I even debated for several hours whether it might not be wiser for me to go to sea as I'd planned, and there to meditate a few months before making this important decision. But of course I knew already that it *was* the right decision. The following day I packed my bag and took an early train into New York City.

My godfather, Dr. Winthrop Haynes, had been sympathetically concerned for my future. He and his wife were like second parents to me; I didn't feel I could leave New York without bidding him farewell. On my way to the bus station, therefore, I stopped by his office at Rockefeller Center. Finding him not in, I left a note on his desk with the message, "I'm going to California to join a group of people who, I believe, can teach me what I want to know about God and about religion." This was the first intimation I had given anyone that God was my true goal in life.

I took the next westward-bound bus available. Thereafter, for four days and four nights, my home was a succession of buses.

My break with the past was so sudden, so complete that I sometimes ask myself whether some very special grace had not been needed to make it possible. I wonder what I'd have done, for instance, if Mother had still been in America. Would I have had the courage to take this drastic step? I'm not so sure. Very possibly she'd have detained me. And if so, would she have succeeded in deflecting me from my purpose? By this time, of course, the question has become academic, but wasn't it remarkable that I found the book that changed my life less than half a day after I'd put Mother on her ship to Cairo?

Strange indeed are God's ways! I was to see much of them in the years that followed, and never have they ceased to make me marvel.

CHAPTER 16

The Pilgrim Meets His Guide

I ARRIVED IN Los Angeles on the morning of Saturday, September 11, 1948, exhausted from my long journey. There I took advantage of the first opportunity I'd had in four days to shave and bathe, then continued by bus one hundred miles south to Encinitas, the little coastal town where, as I had read, Yogananda had his hermitage. In the fervor of first reading it had somehow eluded me that he had founded a world-wide organization. Perhaps I had subconsciously "tuned out" this information from my long-standing fear of religious institutionalism. In my mind, this little seaside hermitage was all that existed of his work.

I arrived in Encinitas late that afternoon, too tired to proceed at once to the hermitage. I booked into a hotel and fairly collapsed onto my bed, sleeping around the clock. The next morning I set out for the Self-Realization Fellowship hermitage, walking perhaps a mile past picturesque gardens, colorful with ice plant and bougainvillea. Many of the flowers I saw there were new to me. The vividness of their hues made a vigorous contrast to the more conservative flowers in the East—a contrast, I was to discover, that extended to numerous other aspects of life on the two coasts.

I approached the hermitage with bated breath. Yogananda, I recalled from his book, once visited a saint without sending prior notice that he was coming. He hadn't yet reached the saint's village when the man came out to welcome him. Did Yogananda, too, I asked myself, know I was coming? And would he, too, come out and greet me?

No such luck. I entered the grounds through an attractive gate, to find on both sides of the driveway a large, beautifully kept garden— trees to the left, a wide lawn to the right. At the far end of the driveway stood a lovely white stucco building with a red tile roof. I imagined disciples quietly going about inside, doing simple chores, their faces shining with inner peace. (Did *they* know I was coming?)

I rang the front doorbell. Minutes later a gentle-looking elderly lady appeared.

"May I help you?" she inquired politely.

"Is Paramhansa Yogananda in?"

My pronunciation of this unfamiliar name must have left something to be desired. The white palm beach suit I was wearing, moreover, didn't mark me as the normal visitor. I'd assumed, mistakenly, that palm beach was the accepted attire in southern California, as it was in Miami or Havana. My unusual appearance, together with my obvious unfamiliarity with Yogananda's name, must have given the impression that I was a serviceman of some sort.

"Oh, you've come to check the water?"

"No!" Gulping, I repeated, "Is Paramhansa Yogananda in?"

"Who? Oh, yes, I see. No, I'm afraid he's away for the weekend. Is there anything I can do for you?"

"Well, yes. No. I mean, I wanted to see *him*."

"He's lecturing today at the Hollywood church."

"You have a *church* there?" I'd always imagined that Hollywood consisted of nothing but movie studios. My astonishment must have struck my hostess as unseemly. After all, why *shouldn't* they have a church in a big city like Hollywood? Soon it became apparent to me that I wasn't making the best possible impression.

Well, I thought, perhaps it *did* seem a bit strange, my barging in here and asking to speak to the head of the organization, and—worse still—not even realizing that he *had* an organization. My hostess drew herself up a little stiffly.

"I want to join his work," I explained. "I want to live here."

"Have you studied his printed lessons?" she inquired, a bit coolly I thought.

"Lessons?" I echoed blankly. "I didn't know he had any lessons to be studied." My position seemed to be getting murkier by the minute.

"There's a full course of them. I'm afraid you couldn't join," she continued firmly, "until after you'd completed the lot."

"How long does that take?" My heart was sinking.

"About four years."

Four years! Why, this was out of the question! As I look back now on that meeting, I think she was probably only trying to temper what, to her, must have seemed my absurd presumption in assuming I had merely to appear on the scene to be welcomed joyously with cries of, "You've arrived!" In fact, the requirement for joining was not so strict as she made it out to be. But it is usual, and also quite proper, for the spiritual aspirant's sincerity to be tested.

It looked less than proper to me at the time, however. It was only later that I learned that my hostess had been Sister Gyanamata, Paramhansa Yogananda's most advanced woman disciple. She herself, it happened, because she had been married, had had to wait years before she could enter the hermitage. The mere *prospect* of a wait must not have seemed to her very much of a test.

Well, I reflected rebelliously, this wasn't *Yogananda's* verdict. Choking down my disappointment, I inquired how I might get to the Hollywood church. Sister Gyanamata gave me the address, and a telephone number. Soon I was on my way back to Los Angeles.

On the way there I alternated between bouts of heated indignation (at *her* presumption!) and desperate prayers for my acceptance. This was the first time in my life I had wanted anything so desperately. I couldn't, I simply *mustn't* be refused.

At one point, thinking again of my elderly hostess, my mind was about to wax indignant once more when suddenly I remembered her eyes. They had been very calm—even, I reflected with some astonishment, wise. Certainly there was far more to her than I'd realized. "Forgive me," I prayed, "for misjudging her. It was wrong of me in any case to think unkindly of her. She was only doing her duty. But I see now that she is a great soul. Forgive me."

A cloud seemed suddenly to lift inside me. I knew in my heart that I'd been accepted.

Arrived in Los Angeles, I checked my bag at the bus depot, and proceeded at once to 4860 Sunset Boulevard, where the church was located. It was about three o'clock in the afternoon. The morning service had long since ended, and, apart from a small scattering of people, the building was empty. A lady greeted me from behind a long table at the back of the room.

"May I help you?"

I explained my mission.

"Oh, I'm afraid you couldn't possibly see him today. His time is completely filled."

I was growing more desperate by the minute. "When *can* I see him?"

She consulted a small book before her on the table. "His appointments are fully booked for the next two and a half months."

Two and a half months! First I'd been told I couldn't join for four years. Now I was told I couldn't even *see* him for. . . .

"But I've come all the way from New York just for this!"

"Have you?" She smiled sympathetically. "How did you hear about him?"

"I read his autobiography a few days ago."

"So recently! And you came . . . just . . . like that?" She cooled a little. "Usually people write first. Didn't you write?"

Bleakly I confessed I hadn't even thought of doing so.

"Well, I'm sorry, but you can't see him for another two and a half months. In the meantime," she continued, brightening a little, "you can study his lessons, and attend the services here."

Morosely I wandered about the church, studying the furnishings, the architecture, the stained-glass windows. It was an attractive chapel, large enough to seat over one hundred people, and invitingly peaceful. An excellent place, I thought, for quiet meditation. But my own mind was hardly quiet or meditative. It was in turmoil.

"You *must* take me!" I prayed. "You *must!* This means my whole life to me!"

Two or three of the people sitting in the church were monks whose residence was the headquarters of Self-Realization Fellowship on Mt. Washington, in the Highland Park section of Los Angeles. I spoke to one of them. Norman his name was; tall and well-built, his eyes were yet gentle and kind. He talked a little about their way of life at Mt. Washington, and their relation, as disciples, to Paramhansa Yogananda. "We call him 'Master,' " he told me. From *Autobiography of a Yogi* I knew already that this appellation, which Yogananda used also in reference to his own guru, denoted reverence, not menial subservience.

How Norman's description of Mt. Washington attracted me! I simply *had* to become a part of this wonderful way of life. It was where I belonged. It was my home.

Norman pointed out two young men sitting quietly farther back in the church.

"They want to join, too," he remarked.

"How long have they been waiting?"

"Oh, not long. A few months."

Disconsolately I wandered about awhile longer. Finally it occurred to me—novel thought!—that perhaps I simply wasn't ready, and that for this reason the doors weren't opening for me. If this were true, I decided, I'd just go live in the hills near Hollywood, come to the services regularly, study the lessons, and—I sighed— wait. When I was ready, the Master would know it, and would summon me.

With this resolution in mind, and with no small disappointment in my heart, I made for the door.

No doubt I'd needed this lesson in humility. Perhaps things had always gone too easily for me. Perhaps I was too confident. At any rate, the moment I accepted the thought that I actually might not be spiritually ready, the situation changed dramatically. I had reached the door when the secretary—Mary Hammond, I later learned her name was—came up from behind me.

"Since you've come such a long way," she said, "I'll just ask Master if he'd be willing to see you today."

She returned a few minutes later.

"Master will see you next."

Shortly thereafter I was ushered into a small sitting room. The Master was standing there, speaking to a disciple in a white robe. As the young man was about to leave, he knelt to touch the Master's feet. This was, I knew from Yogananda's book, a traditional gesture of reverence among Indians; it is bestowed on parents and other elders as well as on one's guru. A moment later, the Master and I were alone.

What large, lustrous eyes now greeted me! What a compassionate smile! Never before had I seen such divine beauty in a human face. The Master seated himself on a chair, and motioned me to a sofa beside him.

"What may I do for you?" For the third time that day, these same, gentle words. But this time how fraught with meaning!

"I want to be your disciple!" The reply welled up irresistibly from my heart. Never had I expected to utter such words to another human being.

The Master smiled gently. There ensued a long discussion, interspersed by long silences, during which he held his eyes half open, half closed—"reading" me, as I well knew.

Over and over again in my heart I prayed desperately, "You *must* take me! I know that you know my thoughts. I can't say it outwardly; I'd only weep. But you must accept me. You *must!*"

Early in the conversation he told me, "I agreed to see you only because Divine Mother told me to. I want you to know that. It isn't because you've come from so far. Two weeks ago a lady flew here all the way from Sweden after reading my book, but I wouldn't see her. I do only what God tells me to do." He reiterated, "Divine Mother told me to see you."

"Divine Mother," as I already knew from reading his book, was the way he often referred to God, Who, he said, embraces both the male and female principles.

There followed some discussion of my past. He appeared pleased with my replies, and with my truthfulness. "I knew that already," he once remarked, indicating that he was only testing me to see if I would answer him truthfully. Again a long silence, while I prayed ardently to be accepted.

"I am taking fewer people now," he said.

I gulped. Was this remark intended to prepare me for a let-down?

I told him I simply could see nothing for myself in marriage, or in a worldly life. "I'm sure it's fine for many people," I said, "but I don't want it for myself."

He shook his head. "It isn't as fine for *anybody* as people like to make out. God, for everyone, is the *only* answer!" He went on to tell me a few stories of the disillusionments he had witnessed. Then again, silence.

At one point in our discussion he asked me how I had liked his book.

"Oh, it was wonderful!"

"That's because it has my vibrations in it," he replied simply.

Vibrations? I'd never thought of books as possessing "vibrations" before. But, clearly, I had found his book almost alive in its power to convey, not merely ideas, but new states of awareness.

Incongruously, even absurdly, it now occurred to me that he might be more willing to take me if he felt I could be of some practical use to his work. And what did I know? Only writing. But that, surely, was better than nothing. Perhaps he had a need for people with writing skills. To demonstrate my ability, I said:

"Sir, I found several split infinitives in your book." A twenty-two-year-old, literarily untried, but already a budding editor! I've never lived down this faux pas! But Master took it with a surprised, then a humorous, smile. The motive for my remark was transparent to him.

More silence.

More prayers.

"All right," he said at last. "You have good karma. You may join us."

"Oh, but I can wait!" I blurted out, hoping he wasn't taking me only because I hadn't yet found any other place to stay.

"No," he smiled. "You have good karma, otherwise I wouldn't accept you."

Gazing at me with deep love, he then said, "I give you my unconditional love."

Immortal promise! I couldn't begin to fathom the depth of meaning in those marvelous words.

"Will you give me your unconditional love?"

"Yes!"

"And will you also give me your unconditional obedience?"

Desperate though my desire was to be accepted by him, I

wanted to be utterly honest. "Suppose," I asked, "sometime, I think you're wrong?"

"I will never ask anything of you," he replied solemnly, "that God does not tell me to ask." He continued:

"When I met my master, Sri Yukteswar, he said to me, 'Allow me to discipline you.' 'Why, Sir?' I inquired. 'Because,' he answered, 'in the beginning of the spiritual path one's will is guided by whims and fancies. Mine was, too, until I met *my* guru, Lahiri Mahasaya. It was only when I attuned my will to his wisdom-guided will that I found true freedom.' In the same way, if you will tune your will to mine, you, too, will find freedom. To act only on the inspiration of whims and fancies is not freedom, but bondage. Only by doing God's will can you become truly free."

"I see," I replied thoughtfully. Then from my heart I said, "I give you my unconditional obedience!"

My guru continued: "When I met my master, he gave me his unconditional love as I have given you mine. He then asked me to love him in the same way, unconditionally. But I replied, 'Sir, what if I should ever find you less than a Christlike master? Could I still love you in the same way?' My master looked at me sternly. 'I don't want your love,' he said. 'It stinks!' "

"I understand, Sir," I assured him. He had struck at the heart of my greatest weakness: intellectual doubt. With deep feeling I said to him, "I give you my unconditional love!"

He went on to give me various instructions.

"Now, then, come kneel before me."

I did so. He made me repeat, in the name of God, Jesus Christ, and the others in our line of gurus, the vows of discipleship and of renunciation. Next he placed the forefinger of his right hand on my chest, over the heart. For at least two minutes his arm vibrated, almost violently. Incredibly, from that moment onward, my consciousness, in some all-penetrating manner, was transformed.

I left his interview room in a daze. Norman, on hearing the news of my acceptance, embraced me lovingly. It was unusual, to say the least, for a disciple to be accepted so soon. A few moments later, Master came out from behind the open curtain on the lecture platform. Smiling at us quietly, he said:

"We have a new brother."

PART II

CHAPTER 17

Mt. Washington Estates

Mt. washington, in the Highland Park district of Los Angeles, rises above that vast city like some guardian angel. Located not far from downtown, the mountain yet stands remote behind its succession of foothills. At the mountaintop the sound of traffic through the busy streets below is hushed to a quiet hum. Here in this tranquil spot, the problems of mankind appear more susceptible of harmonious solution. Though *in* the world, it seems a place not wholly *of* the world.

It is atop Mt. Washington, at 3880 San Rafael Avenue, that the determined visitor, after braving the steep, winding access road, arrives at the international headquarters of Self-Realization Fellowship.

At the turn of the Twentieth Century, Mt. Washington Estates, as this property is also known, was a fashionable hotel. Wealthy people desirous of escaping the strain and bustle of city life went there to relax, or to attend gala social events. Tournaments were held on the tennis courts; banquets and colorful balls in the spacious lobby. Guests were brought to the hotel by cable car up the steep mountainside from Marmion Way, a thousand feet below, where connection was made with a railroad from downtown Los Angeles.

The "city of angels" was much smaller then: some 100,000 inhabitants. In time, the increasing popularity of the automobile, and the city's inexorable engulfment of its surrounding orchards and farmland, induced Mt. Washington's fashionable clientele to seek their recreation farther afield. Mt. Washington Estates fell on hard times. The hotel closed its doors at last. Weeds began growing out of widening cracks on the once famous tennis courts. The hotel, like an indigent but still-proud aristocrat, continued to survey the world with resolute condescension from its twelve-acre domain. Its lofty mood, however, became increasingly difficult for it to sustain as, with the passing years, paint began peeling off the walls of the main building, the grounds lost their carefully tailored elegance, and on every side there appeared unmistakable signs of neglect. Alas, to such universal indifference are all brought who too pridefully oppose Time's all-leveling scythe. The busy world paid court to Mt. Washington no longer.

Unlike most once-fashionable resorts, however, pathetic in their memories of a heyday forever vanished, Mt. Washington's erstwhile glory was but the prelude to a far more glorious role.

Around the turn of the century, at the time when Mt. Washington had attained the height of its popularity as a resort, there was a young boy in India who, during periods of ecstatic meditation, caught glimpses of a mysterious mountaintop monastery in a distant land. The message conveyed by his enigmatic visions concerned the mission that, he knew, he was meant someday to fulfill. Mukunda Lal Ghosh, later known to the world as Paramhansa Yogananda, was the son of a senior executive in the Bengal-Nagpur Railway; as such, he faced the prospect of wealth and high worldly position when he grew up. But it was not this world that attracted him. From earliest childhood he had longed for God as intensely as others long for human love, or for worldly recognition. Mukunda's favorite pastime was visiting saints. *"Choto Mahasaya"* they often called him— "Little Sir," or, literally, "Little Great-Minded One." Treating him not as a child, but as their spiritual equal, many posed him deep questions, or sought his advice on spiritual matters.

Clearly this was no ordinary child, though in his autobiography Yogananda presents himself so unassumingly that the reader, unfamiliar with the intense preparation required for high yogic attainments, might draw the conclusion that anyone similarly placed might have had the young yogi's spiritual experiences.

Soon after graduation from high school, Mukunda met his guru,° the great Swami Sri Yukteswar of Serampore, Bengal. At the feet of this great master he attained, in the amazingly short space of six months, the high state of *samadhi,*† or unconditioned oneness with God. His guru kept him in the *ashram*§ another nine and a half years, while he trained him for his mission of yoga dissemination in the West. "The West," Sri Yukteswar explained, "is high in

---

° Spiritual teacher. The word *guru* is often applied, broadly, to any venerated teacher. On the spiritual path, however, it refers to the *sadguru* or *true* teacher— that enlightened sage who has been commissioned by God to lead the spiritually fit seeker out of darkness, and into the experience of Supreme Truth. While the seeker may have many lesser teachers, it is written that he can have only one such divinely appointed *guru*.

† See footnote, p. 196.

§ A place of retirement from worldly life for the purpose of pursuing spiritual practices.

material attainments, but lacking in spiritual understanding. It is God's will that you play a role in teaching mankind the value of balancing the material with an inner, spiritual life."

In 1917, Mukunda, now a monk with the name Swami Yogananda,* took the first outward step toward the fulfillment of his mission by founding a small school for boys in the village of Dihika, Bengal. In 1918 the Maharaja of Kasimbazar graciously gave him permission to transfer this fast-growing school to the Kasimbazar palace in Ranchi, Bihar. Here the school flourished. An institution offering education in the divine art of living along with the standard curriculum made an instant appeal to parents and children alike. In the first year, enrollment applications reached two thousand—far more than the existing facilities could absorb. By the end of two years, the young yogi-headmaster's educational theories were already beginning to have a serious impact on other educators.

Dear as Yogananda's Ranchi school was to him, however, there was another, broader mission for which the Lord was even now preparing him. In 1920 the youthful yogi was meditating one day when he had a vision: Thousands of Americans passed before him, gazing at him intently. It was, he knew, a divine message. The time had come for him to begin his lifework in the West.

The very next day he received an invitation to speak as India's delegate to an International Congress of Religious Liberals, being held that year in Boston, Massachusetts, under the auspices of the American Unitarian Association. "All doors are open for you," Sri Yukteswar told him, when he applied to his guru for instruction. "Your words on yoga shall be heard in the West." Thus commanded, he accepted the invitation.

---

* *Swami:* literally, *lord*—that is to say, one who has achieved mastery of himself. *Swami* is the title commonly given to *sannyasis* (renunciates), in affirmation of the truth that he alone is a true ruler in this world who is the ruler of himself. Renunciates, for the same reason, are often called *Maharaj* (Great King).

Ananda (divine bliss) usually forms part of the *sannyasi's* monastic name. Thus the name *Yogananda* means "Divine bliss through union (yoga) with God," or, also, "Divine bliss through the practice of yoga techniques for achieving union."

The custom of adding *ananda* to a *sannyasi's* name derives from the time of Swami Shankara, known also as Swami Shankaracharya, ancient reorganizer of the renunciate order in India. Shankaracharya rescued India from the atheistic misconstruction that Buddhists had come to place upon the sublime teachings of their founder. He explained that, while Truth is indeed beyond human conception (as implied by Lord Buddha, who consistently refused to speak of God), it nevertheless exists and can be experienced. The highest state of divine ecstasy is revealed as ineffable bliss—"beyond imagination of expectancy," as Yogananda described it. Swami Shankara's definition of God was *Satchidanandam*—"existence, consciousness, bliss." Paramhansa Yogananda translated this definition as "ever-existing, ever-conscious, *ever-new* Bliss."

In America he found many people hungry for India's spiritual teachings, and for the liberating techniques of yoga. Accordingly he stayed on in Boston, where for three years he taught and lectured. Gradually he accustomed himself to the American culture, and studied how he might reach past his listeners' preconceptions to their very hearts.

In 1923 he began a series of lectures and classes in major American cities. His success everywhere was extraordinary. Crowds flocked to him in unprecedented numbers, sometimes queuing up for blocks to get in. Unlike most other teachers from India, he never tried to impose his own country's cultural modes on Americans, but sought rather to show Americans how to spiritualize *their own* culture. Dynamically, and with contagious joy, he set out to persuade minds steeped in the virtues of "down-to-earth practicality" that the most practical course of all is to seek God.

His magnetism was irresistible. On January 25, 1927, in Washington, D.C., after a lecture attended by 5,000 people, the *Washington Post* reported, "The Swami has broken all records for sustained interest." For some time a famous photographer kept a life-size photograph of the Master on the street outside his shop. President Calvin Coolidge received Yogananda at the White House. On April 18, 1926, in New York's famous Carnegie Hall, the Master held a crowd of three thousand spellbound for an hour and a half, repeating with him the simple chant "O God Beautiful!" which he had translated from the original Hindi of Guru Nanak. That night many in his audience found themselves transported into a state of divine ecstasy.

In 1924 Swami Yogananda toured westward across the continent. As he taught and lectured, countless thousands found their lives transformed—not by his words alone, but by his magnetic love, and the sheer radiance of his inner joy.

Louise Royston, an elderly disciple who first met him during those early years, described him to me as a man so alive with divine joy that he sometimes actually came running out onto the lecture platform, his long hair streaming out behind him, his orange robe flapping about his body as if with kindred enthusiasm.

"How is everyone?" he would cry.

"Awake and ready!" came the eager response, in which he led them.

"How *feels* everyone?"

Again the shout: "Awake and ready!"

Only in such a charged atmosphere was he willing to talk about God, Whom he described as the most dynamic, joy-inspiring reality in the universe. Dry, theoretical lectures were not for him. He had not come to America to philosophize, but to awaken in people an ardent love for God, an urgent longing to *know* Him. The forceful, inspiring personality of this teacher from India utterly captivated his audiences.

Louise Royston told me a charming little story from Yogananda's 1927 visit to Washington, D.C. There Mme. Amelita Galli-Curci, the world-renowned prima donna, became his disciple. At this time Galli-Curci had reached the pinnacle of her own extraordinary fame. One evening, while singing before a packed concert hall, she spotted her guru seated in the balcony. Interrupting the performance, she pulled out a handkerchief and waved it eagerly in his direction. The Swami in his turn rose and waved back at her. The audience, finally, seeing whose presence it was that had interrupted the proceedings, broke into enthusiastic cheers and applause, sustaining the acclamation for several minutes.

One reason for the almost overwhelming response the Master received everywhere was that, unlike most public speakers, he never looked upon his audiences as nameless crowds even when they numbered many thousands. He was amazingly sensitive to each listener *as an individual.* Often he would address himself to the specific needs of a single member of his audience. I myself sometimes had the experience of finding him, during the course of a public lecture, addressing briefly some private difficulty of my own. When I thanked him mentally, he would glance smilingly at me before continuing his discourse.

Mr. Oliver Rogers (later, Brother Devananda), an older man who entered Mt. Washington as a monk a year or two after me, told the Master once in my presence:

"I heard you lecture twenty-five years ago at Symphony Hall, in Boston. Through the years since then I often wondered where you were. I suppose it was my karma that I had to seek God first in other ways, but the compelling inspiration behind my search was always that evening with you in Symphony Hall.

"It was strange, too," Mr. Rogers continued reflectively. "That huge hall was completely packed, yet through your entire lecture you kept your eyes fixed on me!"

"I remember," replied the Master quietly.

Above all, during every public lecture Swami Yogananda sought souls who were spiritually ready to devote their lives to God. As he often put it, "I prefer a soul to a crowd, though I love crowds of souls."

During his transcontinental tour in 1924, many would have been thrilled for Swami Yogananda to make his home in their cities. But to every such invitation he replied, "My soul calls me to Los Angeles." Years later, a guest at Mt. Washington asked him, "Which do you consider the most spiritual place in America?" "I have always considered Los Angeles the Benares* of America," the Master replied.

To Los Angeles he came. People flocked to his lectures in unprecedented numbers even for that city, noted as it is for its fascination with matters spiritual. Weeks passed in unceasing public service. And then he informed his delighted students that he planned to establish his headquarters there.

Numerous properties were shown him. None, however, corresponded to the visions he had received in India. He continued his search.

In January 1925 he was out driving one day with two or three students, including Arthur Cometer, a young man who, with Ralph, another student, had chauffeured the Master across America. They drove up winding Mt. Washington Drive. As they passed Mt. Washington Estates the Master cried out, "Stop the car!"

"You can't go in there," his companions protested. "That's private property!"

But Yogananda wasn't to be dissuaded. He entered the spacious grounds, and strolled about them in silence. At last, holding onto the railing above the tennis courts, he exclaimed quietly, "This place feels like home!"

As it turned out, the property had recently been put up for sale; there were others already who wanted to buy it. But Yogananda knew it was destined to be his. So certain was he, in fact, that he invited all his students in southern California to a dedication ceremony on the still-unpurchased land. During a speech that day he informed them, "This place is yours."

The price of the property was $65,000. The Master was on the very point of signing the purchase agreement when his hand froze

---

* Benares, or Varanasi as it is now officially named, is the holiest city of the Hindus. Thousands of years old—indeed, quite possibly the oldest continuously inhabited city in the world—Varanasi possesses an aura of timelessness and world detachment. Numerous ashrams and temples are found here. Devout pilgrims from all over India come to bathe in the sacred river Ganges. The aged and the infirm flock here, convinced that to die in Benares is a guarantee of salvation. Indeed their faith is founded, albeit symbolically, on a divine truth. For Hindus that take their mythology literally consider Benares the earthly abode of God in the form of Sri Viswanath, "Lord of the Universe." And truly, one who lives and dies in the *inner* abode of God, which is to say in His consciousness, is assured salvation.

into immobility. "God held my hand from signing," he told me years later, "because He wanted me to have the property for less money." A few days afterwards another real estate agent was found who agreed to negotiate terms. The seller consented to come down to $45,000, provided that the sum be paid in full at the time of purchase, and that that date be set no later than three months from the day Yogananda signed the agreement. The price, though excellent, represented a lot of money, particularly in those days, when the dollar had a much higher value than it does today. When Yogananda's students learned that he had been given only three months to raise the entire sum, their interest waned noticeably. One lady exclaimed in dismay, "Why, it would take you twenty years to raise that much money!"

"Twenty years," replied the Master, "for those who *think* twenty years. Twenty months for those who think twenty months. And *three* months for those who think three months!"

He acquired the money in three months. The story of how he did so illustrates wonderfully the power of faith.

There was a student of the Swami's, a Mrs. Ross Clark, whose husband some months previously had contracted double pneumonia. The man's doctors had said he couldn't live. "Oh yes he will live," declared the Master when Mrs. Clark turned to him for help. Going to her husband's bedside, he had sat there and prayed deeply. The man was cured. Thus it was that when Mrs. Clark learned of the Master's dilemma, she told him, "You saved my husband's life. I want to help you. Would you accept a loan of $25,000 without interest for three years?" *Would* he!

"Other money," he told me, "began pouring in from our centers around the country. Soon we had another $15,000, making $40,000 in all. But the final purchase date was approaching, and we still lacked $5,000 of the total price. I wrote Mrs. Clark again to see if she could help us with this amount. Regretfully she answered, 'I've done all I can.' I thanked her once more for the enormous help she had already given. But where was that help going to come from?

"At last just one day remained! The situation was desperate. If we didn't get those five thousand dollars by noon the next day, we would forfeit our option."

Master chuckled, "I think Divine Mother likes to keep my life interesting!

"I happened to be staying in the home of someone who was rich, but insincere. He could easily have helped us had he been so inclined, but he made no move to do so. I was battling with God,

'How do You plan to give me that money before noon tomorrow?'

" 'Everything will be all right,' said my host soothingly.

" 'Why do you say that?' I demanded. I knew the money would come, but God needs human instruments, and this man had shown no intention of serving in that capacity. He left the room.

"Just then a gust of wind* turned my face toward the telephone. There I saw the face of Miss Trask, a lady who had come to me twice for interviews. A voice said, 'Call her.' I did so at once, and explained my predicament to her.

"After a pause she said, 'Somebody just the other day returned a loan I made him years ago. I never expected to get it back. It was for $5,000! Yes, you may have it.'

"Silently I offered a prayer of thanks. 'Please,' I urged her, 'be at Mt. Washington Estates tomorrow before noon.'

"She promised to come. But by noon the next day she hadn't yet arrived! Several prospective buyers were waiting like wolves. One was telling everyone he planned to turn the place into a movie school. But the seller announced, 'We will wait the rest of the day.'

"Minutes later Miss Trask arrived. The drama was over. We paid the full purchase price, and Mt. Washington was ours!"

Thus was founded the international headquarters of Self-Realization Fellowship, the institution through which Paramhansa Yogananda disseminated his yoga teachings throughout the world.

When I came to the Master in 1948, Mt. Washington Estates was a monastery. At first, however, he had planned to make it a "how-to-live" school similar to his well-known institution in India. For his hopes for spiritualizing the West rested on all-round education for the young. But soon he realized that his educational dreams were premature for this country. First, the grown-ups would have to be converted to his ideals; only then would there be properly trained teachers, and enough parents willing to send their children to his schools. Soon, therefore, Mt. Washington became a residential center for adults desirous of devoting their lives to God.

In 1925, though many Americans derived inspiration from Yogananda's message, relatively few were ready to give their entire

---

* As I understood this story from Master, this was a spiritual, not a physical, manifestation. Wind is one of the manifestations of *Aum,* the Holy Ghost. We find a reference to it in Acts of the Apostles: "And when the day of Pentecost was fully come, they were all with one accord in one place. And suddenly there came a sound from heaven as of a rushing mighty wind, and it filled all the house where they were sitting. . . . And they were all filled with the Holy Ghost" (Acts 2:1,2,4). The visions that St. Bernadette Soubirous received of the Virgin Mary at Lourdes were also preceded by a gust of wind. Others couldn't feel it.

lives to the spiritual search. Even in India, so Lord Krishna stated in the *Bhagavad Gita,* "Out of a thousand, one seeks Me; and out of a thousand who seek, one fully knows Me."* Swami Shankaracharya once remarked, "Childhood is busy with play-things; youth is busy with romance and family; old age is busy with sickness and worries: Where is the man who is busy with God?" Here, in the materialistic West, few indeed were willing to spare the time for deep meditation. By ones they came. Many left; few remained. Yogananda might have compromised his high standards and made it easier for many more to stay, but he never did so. Still, by ones they *did* come, and among these were a growing number of deeply seeking souls. Slowly a monastic order developed, and in time achieved such a high spiritual caliber as I have seen nowhere else, not even in India.

For some years Swami Yogananda continued to tour the country, lecturing, teaching, and drawing to his work a gradually growing band of dedicated disciples. At last he felt guided by God to end these spiritual "campaigns," as he called them, and return to Mt. Washington to devote his time to training the souls he had sent there.

There began now for him and his little band a period of severe testing. During his previous years of public teaching, all the money he had sent home, it turned out, had been spent, and not always wisely. No doubt those in charge had imagined the supply would never run out. To replenish their depleted bank account the Master might have gone out campaigning again, but he felt that God wanted him at Mt. Washington now, and he obeyed the summons unflinchingly. He and his little group planted tomatoes on the hillside. For months their diet consisted of raw tomatoes, stewed tomatoes, fried tomatoes, baked tomatoes, tomato soup. With a little culinary imagination, they found, even this drastically limited fare could be pleasantly varied.

With the passing years, more and more students around the country realized that what the Master had given them was far more than an adjunct to the church teachings they had grown up with: It was a complete spiritual path in itself. He always encouraged his students to remain loyal to their own churches, if they so desired. But increasing numbers of them, as they practiced his teachings, began to feel that *his* work was all the church they needed. Thus his work developed, not by missionary tactics of conversion, but by his students' own, personal experience of the

---

* The *Bhagavad Gita,* VII:3.

efficacy of his teachings. More and more, those whose worldly responsibilities prevented them from entering his monastery began
uniting together in their own towns to form Self-Realization Fellowship centers. Lessons were compiled at Mt. Washington from his
teachings and writings,° and sent to devoted students around the
country, eventually reaching students throughout the world. By
1935 the work was firmly established and flourishing.

This was the year that Yogananda's guru, Swami Sri Yukteswar,
summoned him back to India. The now-famous disciple spent a
year there traveling about, addressing large audiences.

A visitor to Sri Yukteswar's Serampore ashram one day compared
Swami Yogananda to a certain other swami, well known in India.
The great Guru, though rarely one to bestow even the mildest
praise, replied now with quiet pride, "Yogananda is *much* greater."

During that year Sri Yukteswar bestowed on his beloved disciple
the highest of India's spiritual titles, *Paramhansa.*† It was hoped by
many Indians that Yogananda would remain in India now. But
God was already calling him inwardly back to America. His guru's
death was a further, outward, sign that God was releasing him to
go. Accordingly, in 1936, he returned to Mt. Washington. And
now a new phase of his mission began.

° Louise Royston, the disciple mentioned earlier in this chapter, was chiefly responsible for this labor of love.

† Literally, "Supreme Swan." The swan has been since ancient times a symbol of
divine enlightenment. The reason is threefold. First, like the swan, which is
equally at home on land and on water, the enlightened yogi is at home both in
this world and in the ocean of Spirit. Second, the swan is believed to have the
ability, when sipping a mixture of milk and water, to swallow only the milk;
presumably what it does is curdle it. Similarly, the *hansa,* or enlightened yogi, dis-
criminates clearly between the "milk" of divine reality and the "water" of delusion. Third, *hansa* (swan) in Sanskrit means also *han sa* ("I am He"): words
expressive of the blissful realization of a true master. Supreme among such
"*hansas*" is the *parama* (supreme) *hansa.* Already liberated, the *paramahansa* no
longer *needs* to combat earthly delusions with the sword of discrimination, for he
sees the Divine at all times effortlessly, everywhere.

Yogananda wrote his title *Paramhansa,* without the additional *a* in the middle.
This is how the word is commonly pronounced in India. According to Sanskrit
scholars, "paramhansa" is more properly written *paramahansa,* with an extra *a* in
the middle. Scholarly precision, however, doesn't always coincide with unschol-
arly comprehension.

In English, that middle *a* increases the problem of pronunciation to the point
where people pause there, and thus give emphasis to a letter that, in India, is
unpronounced. The average American or Englishman, in other words, and very
likely the average non-Indian, pronounces the word thus: "param*a*ahansa." The
correct pronunciation, however, is *paramhansa.*

For Westerners who want simply to know, with some degree of accuracy, how
to pronounce this, to us, difficult word, Sanskrit scholars accept the spelling
paramhansa.

In conjunction with his early visions of Mt. Washington, Yogananda had always seen two other buildings. The first was the main hall of his Ranchi school. The other had yet to be found. It was a beautiful hermitage somewhere by the sea.

Several times, while driving down the California coast to San Diego, he had felt attracted to a certain spot in the little town of Encinitas. Each time he had received the inner prompting: "Wait. Not yet." Obedient to the divine guidance, he had never pursued the matter further. But after his return from India a surprise awaited him. On the very spot that had attracted him on those drives, Mr. James J. Lynn, a wealthy disciple and highly advanced spiritually, had purchased and built the hermitage of his visions! Here it was that Paramhansaji,* as many people now began calling him, spent most of his time over the next several years writing books, including his spiritual classic, *Autobiography of a Yogi*.

His days now were an idyll of divine tranquillity. After years of traveling, of spiritual "campaigning," and of courageously meeting a never-ending series of challenges to his mission, he was able to enjoy for a time some of the fruits of his labors. The challenges he met now were in the more congenial realm of spiritual ideas.

In order to share this idyll with devoted students, he constructed in 1938 a small, beautiful place of worship on the grounds in Encinitas. "The Golden Lotus Temple," he named this building. Situated not far from the main hermitage, it overlooked the Pacific Ocean. Here the Master led group meditations, with the ocean to remind them of the vastness of Spirit, and shared with devotees some of the deep inspirations that were pouring daily through his pen. The Golden Lotus Temple attracted widespread public interest. Visitors sometimes compared it to the Taj Mahal. One person said of it, "It is like seeing paradise without dying!"

But the Master's idyll didn't last long. In 1939 World War II started in Europe. Its disruptive vibrations could not but affect the tranquillity of a work as attuned as Yogananda's was to serving the needs of mankind everywhere. In 1942, not long after America's entry into the war, The Golden Lotus Temple slipped into the sea. Its foundations had been undermined by soil erosion, caused by water seepage from the road outside the hermitage property. The loss of this famous structure received front-page Associated Press coverage in hundreds of newspapers across the nation. To Paramhansaji, however, the loss was not a tragedy, but a sign of God's will. The time had come for the next stage in his mission.

---

* *Ji* is a suffix commonly added to names in India as a mark of respect.

God's true lovers on earth seem to attract more than their share of trials. Perhaps the reason is so that the rest of us can learn from their example that adversity, if met with divine faith, proves invariably a blessing in the end. Hardship is but a shortcut—tunneled, so to speak, through mountains so as the more quickly to reach the fertile meadows beyond them. Paramhansaji declared that out of the destruction of his Golden Lotus Temple many other places of worship would come. To him, then, its loss meant that the time had come to expand his work, and to reach out more actively to others through the medium of his organization, which by this time was firmly established.

Within a year and two months of the loss of the Encinitas temple, two new places of worship were established. The first was in Hollywood, at 4860 Sunset Boulevard, dedicated in August 1942. The second was in San Diego, at 3072 First Avenue, dedicated in September 1943. The Master now began lecturing in these churches on alternate Sundays.

This increase in his public activities attracted an ever-larger number of lay disciples to the churches, in addition to those coming to live as renunciates at his Mt. Washington and Encinitas ashrams. It was now that an old dream, one that he had often described in lectures and in magazine articles, began to take definite shape.

One of the primary aims of his work had been, as he put it, "to spread a spirit of brotherhood among all people, and to aid in establishing, in many countries, self-sustaining colonies for plain living and high thinking." It was to the establishment of such a "world brotherhood colony," as he called it, that he now turned most of his energies.

The problem to which he addressed himself was similar to that which had first inspired his interest in child education. "Environment," he used to say, "is stronger than will power." The environment in which a child lives determines to a great extent his attitudes and behavior after he grows up. The environment an adult lives in, similarly, can make all the difference between success and failure in his efforts to transform old, unwanted habits. Paramhansaji urged people to live in harmonious environments, if possible. For single persons with a deep desire for God, he often suggested the monastic life. But although for students with worldly commitments he recommended regular attendance at Self-Realization Fellowship church or center services, he was sadly aware of the obstacle these people faced. Most modern environments, alas, even when outwardly harmonious, are not spiritually uplifting.

The solution he arrived at was to provide places in which *all* devotees, whether married or single, could live among divine influences: places where family, friends, job, and general environment all would conduce to spiritual development—in short, a spiritual village, or "world brotherhood colony." In the early 1940s he set himself to found one such community.

Encinitas was the site he chose for this project. Here he began accepting families. In lecture after lecture in the churches he urged people to combine their meditative efforts with the simpler, freer life-style of a spiritual community.

A number of the projects that he undertook during his lifetime might be considered guidelines for the future, in as much as their fulfillment depended on the preparedness of society as a whole, and not only on his own far-seeing vision and vigorous power of will. Society was not yet ready for them. Thus, although he dreamed of founding "how-to-live" schools in America, and actually tried to start one in 1925 at Mt. Washington, America simply wasn't spiritually developed enough yet to permit the fulfillment of his dream.

Everything he did, however, seems to have been done for a good reason. Indeed, what better way to indicate his wishes for the work in years, or even in generations, to come than to make a serious attempt to carry those wishes out during his own lifetime? Great men cannot hope to materialize all the inspirations of their genius during the short time allotted to them on earth. But how much clearer a demonstration of their intentions, for those who follow in their footsteps, if they can start something tangible, however inchoately, instead of merely talking about it. Such was Yogananda's "how-to-live" school at Mt. Washington. Such also was a Yoga University that he founded there in 1941, with a California State charter, only to bow later to public indifference. Such, too, was his "world brotherhood colony" in Encinitas.

For it was not possible for him to complete this project during his lifetime. America simply wasn't ready for it. The fact that he dropped it, however, cannot be viewed as a change of heart in view of the lifelong importance he attached to it. Rather, the practical demonstration of his interest must have been intended to inspire others to take up the plan later, when the fulfillment of it would be possible.

In 1946 his best-known book, *Autobiography of a Yogi,* was published. Its appearance marked the beginning of the last chapter of his life: the completion of his major literary works, and the arrival of a veritable flood of new disciples.

In the summer of 1948 he experienced a supreme state of ecstasy. God, in the form of the Divine Mother of the Universe, showed him the secrets of cosmic creation. It was as though, in lifting these last veils, She wanted to prepare him for his own departure from this stage of material appearances. "I sent you a few bad ones in the beginning," She told him during that ecstasy, "to test your love for Me. But now I am sending you angels. Whoever smites them, I shall smite." Indeed, it was within this period—from approximately 1946 onwards—that the majority of his destined disciples came. We may suppose that God had wanted his life during his earlier years to stand out more brilliantly than it might have, had all his energies been devoted to the personal training of hordes of followers. In the life of the great Sri Ramakrishna, too, most of the disciples came during the last years of that master's life. At any rate, now, in the closing chapters of Paramhansa Yogananda's life, a swelling throng of dedicated souls arrived. They helped to ensure the continuance of his work after his departure from this earth.

Within this period of time, too, he acquired several new properties: a retreat in the desert at Twenty-Nine Palms, California, where he went for periods of seclusion to work on completing his writings; a new church in Long Beach, California, and another one in Phoenix, Arizona; and a lake and temple in Pacific Palisades, California. He also developed the already-existing church property in Hollywood, adding an auditorium and an excellent vegetarian restaurant.

The lake and temple in Pacific Palisades were dedicated by him in 1950. This was his last and most beautiful center. The SRF Lake Shrine, as he called it, forms a natural bowl of steep hillside around a charming jewel of a lake. It contains a church, an outdoor temple, little shrines to each of the major religions of the world, and beautiful flower gardens. The Lake Shrine is enjoyed by many thousands of visitors every year.

Increasingly, during these last years of his life, he spent his time working on his writings. One of the major assignments that his guru had given him was to demonstrate the intrinsic compatibility of the Indian Scriptures, particularly the *Bhagavad Gita,* with the Old and New Testaments. At Twenty-Nine Palms he wrote commentaries on the *Bhagavad Gita,* Genesis, and Revelation. (The teachings of Revelation he said, are "pure yoga.") He had already completed detailed commentaries on the four Gospels of the Bible.

It was on March 7, 1952, that he left his body. It had been an incredibly fruitful life. By the time it ended, SRF centers flourished in many countries. Yogananda's disciples around the world numbered many tens of thousands. He had opened the West to India's teachings in a way that no other teacher has ever succeeded in doing. This was the first time that a great master from India had spent the greater part of his life in the West. It is largely as a result of his teaching and radiant personal example that there has been, in recent decades, such widespread and growing interest in India's spiritual teachings.

The headquarters for this vast movement was Mt. Washington Estates. Here it was that my own life of discipleship began.

Paramhansa Yogananda in the garden of his Encinitas Hermitage.

Mt. Washington Estates, headquarters of Self-Realization Fellowship.

The monks energizing on the tennis courts at Mt. Washington.

Master's usual everyday wear was a business suit. His desire was not to "Indianize" Americans, but to help them spiritualize their own culture.

The hermitage at Encinitas.

Paramhansa Yogananda in the late 1940s.

CHAPTER 18

First Impressions

R EV. BERNARD, THE disciple I'd met in Master's interview room at the Hollywood church, drove Norman and me to Mt. Washington. On our way we stopped by the bus terminal to pick up my bag. My first glimpse of Mt. Washington Estates as we entered was of tall palm trees that lined the entrance driveway on either side, waving gently in the slight breeze as though to extend a kindly greeting: "Welcome!" they seemed to murmur. "Welcome home!"

Norman showed me about the spacious grounds. We then went and stood quietly above the two tennis courts, which, Norman said, were used now for gentler, more *yogic* forms of exercise. In silence we gazed out over the city far below us.

Yes, I reflected, this *was* home! For how many years had I wandered: Rumania, Switzerland, England, America—and so many countries fleetingly in between. And always my feelings, if not my nationality, had stamped me as a foreigner. I had begun to wonder if I belonged *anywhere*. But now, suddenly, I knew that I did belong: *right here* in this ashram; *here* with my guru; *here,* with his spiritual family! (Yes, I decided happily, every one of these people was my family, too.) Gazing about me, I breathed deeply the peace that permeated this holy place.

Norman stood by my side, wordlessly sharing my elation. After a time we both faced the opposite direction, and looked up across an attractive lawn towards the large main building. Calmly self-contained, it seemed suggestive of an almost patrician benignity.

"Master's rooms are those on the top floor, to the right," Norman said, pointing to a series of third-storey windows at the eastern end of the building. "And that," he indicated a room that protruded outward above the main entrance, "is the sitting room where he receives guests.

"Women disciples live on the second floor," he continued, "and also on the third floor, to the left of Master's apartment. In addition, there's a sort of second-floor annex in the back, where a few live. Because we're renunciates, the men and women aren't allowed to mix with one another, so I can't take you up there. But come, I'll show you around the first floor. That part's more or less public."

He led me into a spacious lobby, simply and tastefully furnished. We passed through a door at the eastern end into three rooms that had been converted into a print shop. Proceeding towards the back of the building, we crossed over a narrow bridge that overlooked a small interior garden, and entered the main office. From here, Norman explained to me, books, printed lessons, and a continuous stream of correspondence went out to yoga students around the world.

We re-entered the lobby at the western end. Here, large, sliding doors opened into a chapel, where we found two nuns seated together at an organ, one of them playing selections from Handel's *Messiah,* the other one listening. They looked so relaxed and happy that I forgot the rule for a moment, and greeted them. The dignified, yet kindly, way they acknowledged my greeting, without in the least encouraging further conversation, impressed me.

I was impressed also by the tasteful simplicity of my new home. Everything looked restful, modest, harmonious. Leaving the chapel, I turned eagerly to Norman. "Where do the men live?"

"In the basement, most of them," he replied laconically.

"The basement!" I stared at him incredulously. Then suddenly we were both laughing. After all, I told myself, what did it matter? If humility was a virtue, anything that furthered it must be considered a blessing.

We went downstairs to the men's dining room, which, Norman explained, had once served as a storeroom. Windowless, it stood at the dark end of a dim hallway. The only light in the room came from a single light bulb. In a small adjoining room all the monks showered, brushed their teeth, and washed the dishes. Meals were brought down thrice daily from the main kitchen upstairs.

"Come," said Norman, "let me show you our rooms. You've been assigned the one next to mine."

We left by a downstairs exit and, proceeding down the front driveway, arrived at a cottage about fifty feet from the main building, set picturesquely amid spreading trees, fragrant flowers, and succulents. I was charmed with the unassuming simplicity of this little outbuilding. Here, Norman explained, the hotel guests decades earlier had waited to take the cable car down to Marmion Way. Recently, he went on, smiling, the waiting room had been "renovated, after a manner of speaking," and divided into sleeping quarters for two. His was the larger of the new rooms; mine was the smaller. Why, I marveled, had we, young neophytes that we were, been assigned such delightful quarters?

Understanding came moments later, as we entered the building. I tried to suppress a smile. Here, set so idyllically amid stately grounds, was a scene incongruously reminiscent of the hasty reconstruction that must have followed bombing raids during the war. Schoolboys, Norman explained, had done all the work. As I examined the consequences, I wondered whether the boys hadn't considered the windows and the window frames separate projects altogether. At any rate, the windows hung at odd angles, as though disdaining to have anything to do with mere *frames*. Months later, as if to atone for their stern aloofness, they extended a friendly invitation to the winds of winter to come in and make merry.

The walls, made of plasterboard, had been cut more or less according to whimsy. They did manage to touch the ceiling—shyly, I thought—here and there, but the gap between them and the floor was in no place less than two inches. The resulting periphery made a lair, conveniently dark, for spiders of every description.

But it was the floor that provided the *pièce de résistance*. It appeared to be composed of a cross between pumice and cement. This substance, I later learned, was the proud invention of Dr. Lloyd Kennell, the alternate minister at our church in San Diego. Dr. Kennell had boasted that his product would "outlast the Taj Mahal." But in fact it was already doing its best to prove the Biblical dictum "Dust thou art." Every footstep displaced a part of this miracle substance, which rose in little clouds to settle everywhere: on clothes, books, furniture. . . .

Not that the room held any furniture, except for a hard wooden bed which, Norman assured me, improved one's posture. The small closet had no door to protect clothes against the ubiquitous dust. With Norman's help I found an old, discarded quilt in the basement storeroom. Folded double, it made an adequate mattress. I also located an old dressing table, wobbly on its own legs, but fairly steady when propped into a corner. Next I found a small table, which acquitted itself admirably when leaned against a wall. For a chair an orange crate was pressed into service. And a few days later I came upon a large, threadbare carpet in the storeroom. Though the pattern was barely discernible, this important addition helped to hold down the dust from the fast-disintegrating floor. In place of a closet door, further search through the storeroom yielded a strip of monk's cloth, two feet wide, which I used to cover part of the opening. (Now at least I didn't have to *see* the dust as it settled on my clothes!) A light bulb dangled precariously at the end of a long, rather frayed wire in the center of the room. The bathroom was in the main building, which was kept locked at night. It wasn't until a year later that I was given curtains for the windows.

It no longer mystified me why the older monks preferred living in the basement. But I didn't mind at all. Quite the contrary, the disadvantages of my ramshackle quarters only added fuel to my leaping happiness. For I was so utterly thrilled to be here in the ashram of my guru that every fresh inconvenience only made me laugh the more delightedly.

I laughed often now. The pent-up agony of recent years found release in wave after fresh wave of happiness. Everything I had always longed for seemed mine now, in my new way of life.

"There must be many good people here," I remarked to Norman the day of my arrival.

He was astonished. "Why, they're *all* good!"

It was my turn to be astonished. Could it really be, I wondered, that in this mixed bag of a world a place existed where *everyone* was good? But Norman must be right, I concluded: This *had* to be such a place. For hadn't everyone come here to find God? And what higher virtue could there be than the desire to commune with the very Source of all virtue?

Thrilled though I was to be at Mt. Washington, my mind importuned me with innumerable questions, many of which I inflicted day after day on my poor brother disciples. (Surely another demonstration of their goodness was the unfailing patience with which they answered me!) My heart and soul were converted indeed, but my intellect lagged far behind. Reincarnation, karma, superconsciousness, divine ecstasy, the astral world, masters, gurus, breathing exercises, vegetarianism, health foods, *sabikalpa* and *nirbikalpa samadhi,* Christ Consciousness—huff! puff! For me these were all new and staggering concepts; a week or two before I hadn't even known they existed. It was part of the excitement of those early days for me to dive into these strange waters and play in them joyously. But confusion often assailed me also, and doubt—doubt not about what I was here for, but about some puzzling point in the teachings. At such times I would sit down, wherever I happened to be, and calm my mind. For I knew that soul-intuition, not intellect, was the key to real understanding.

My greatest help at this time, apart from Master himself, was Rev. Bernard. Bernard was the alternate minister at our Hollywood church. He had a brilliant mind, and a clear understanding of the teachings. Fortunately for me, he seemed to enjoy answering my questions. Less fortunately, I hadn't as many opportunities to be with him as my searching mind would have liked. I sought answers, alternatively, wherever I could find them.

One of the monks, a young man with the improbable name of Daniel Boone, was friendly and loquacious, and willingly shared with me not only the teachings he had received from Master, but anything else he might have stumbled upon during years of metaphysical reading. In fact, he suffered from what Master described as "metaphysical indigestion." I was too new on the path to realize that Boone's seeming strength was actually his greatest weakness. But the more I pondered his answers, the more I began to suspect them of fallibility.

"Did *Master* say that?" I would challenge him. Only if he answered, "Yes," would I accept without question whatever he told me.

A more reliable, if less erudite, aid was Norman. A veritable giant, Norman had a heart almost as big as his body. It was inspiring to me to see the intensity of his love for God. Not at all interested in the theoretical aspects of the path, he understood everything in terms of devotion. God was to him, simply, his Divine Friend. He required no intellectual explanations to clarify his perception of God's love for him, and of his for God.

"I don't know any of those things!" he would exclaim with a gentle smile whenever I raised some philosophical conundrum. "I just know that I love God." How I envied him his child-like devotion! (Even Master was moved by it.) And how I longed to be able to still my own questioning mind, that from habit demanded answers which it already knew full well were not the wisdom it craved. For love, I knew, was the answer, not knowledge. Love was the highest wisdom. More and more I struggled to progress on the fragrant pathway of devotion.

Another aid to me in those days was an older man by the name of Jean Haupt. Jean, true to his Germanic heritage, had extraordinary will power. He was determined to find God in the shortest possible time. Whenever he wasn't working, he meditated. One weekend his meditation lasted forty hours without a break. "It seemed more like forty minutes," he told me with a quiet smile.

I worked on the grounds with Jean and Norman, gardening, plastering, and doing whatever odd jobs were required. Jean, though fifty-five years old and little more than half Norman's size, could do more work than Norman and I combined. If Norman struggled too long over some heavy job, Jean would mutter impatiently, "Here let me do it!" Moments later the job would be done. I was as deeply impressed by his will power, and as anxious to emulate it, as by Norman's devotion.

The most attractive feature of my new quarters was a small basement, reached by a narrow set of steps at the far end of the room. Here the motor had once been housed that pulled cable cars up the steep mountainside. It seemed ideal for a meditation room. I carted out piles of rubble that had accumulated over decades of neglect, constructed a trap door for the opening to ensure virtual silence, and soon was devoting all my free time to meditating in this, my "Himalayan cave," as I thought of it. Over the ensuing months I put in a ceiling, painted the room a soothing blue, and found everything here that a young yogi could possibly desire in the way of silence, remoteness from the demands of daily life, and divine tranquillity.

My first evening at Mt. Washington, Rev. Bernard visited me in my room. "Master wants me to give you instruction in the art of meditation," he said. He taught me an ancient yoga technique of concentration, and added some general counsel.

"When you aren't practicing this concentration technique, try keeping your mind focused at the point between the eyebrows. We call this the Christ center, because when Christ Consciousness is attained one's awareness becomes centered here."

"Would it help," I asked him, "if I kept my mind focused there all day long as well?"

"Very much! When Master lived in his guru's ashram he practiced keeping his mind fixed there all the time.

"And another thing," Bernard added, "this is also the seat of the spiritual eye. The more deeply you concentrate your gaze at this point, the more you'll become aware of a round light forming there: a blue field with a bright, golden ring around it, and a silver-white, five-pointed star in the center."

"This isn't just a subjective experience?" I inquired, doubtfully. "Does *everybody* see it?"

"Everybody," he assured me, "provided the mind is calm enough. It's a universal reality, like the fact that we all have brains. Actually, the spiritual eye is the astral reflection of the medulla oblongata, at the base of the brain. I'll tell you more about that some other time.

"For now, suffice it to say that energy enters the body through the medulla, and that by the sensitive application of will one can actually *increase* this energy-inflow. The Christ center is the seat of will power, and also of concentration in the body. Notice how, whenever you concentrate deeply, or whenever you strongly will anything to happen, your mind gets drawn to that point automatically. You may even frown a little in the process, inadvertently. By concentration on the Christ center, the will increases. Consequently, the inflow of energy through the medulla oblongata increases also. And with this increased inflow, the spiritual eye forms naturally in the forehead.

"Through concentration on the spiritual eye, the consciousness gradually becomes attuned to the subtle rate of vibration of this light. At last one's consciousness, too, takes on the quality of light. That is what Jesus meant when he said, 'If thine eye be single, thy whole body shall be full of light.'* It is in this purified state of awareness that ecstasy comes."

After Bernard left me, I sat for awhile practicing the techniques I had learned. Later on I went out and stood above the tennis courts again. I gazed out, this time, over a vast carpet of twinkling lights. How lovely, in the night, was this huge, bustling city! I reflected that those myriad lights were manifestations of the same divine light which I would behold someday within myself, in deep meditation. But electricity, I told myself, lights only the pathways of this world. The divine luminescence lights pathways to Infinity.

"Lord," I prayed, "though I stumble countless times, I will never cease seeking Thee. Lead my footsteps ever onward toward Thy infinite light!"

---

* Matthew 6:22. Modern translators, unaware of the hidden significance of this passage, have changed the word *single* in the King James version to read "sound," or "clear." *The New English Bible* even changes *eye* to "eyes," thus: "If your eyes are sound." One wonders how often the Scriptures have been tampered with by scholars who, though intellectually learned, are steeped in spiritual ignorance.

CHAPTER 19

The First Days of a Neophyte

THE DAILY ROUTINE at Mt. Washington was fairly individual. Freedom was given us, as it is in most Indian ashrams, for private spiritual practice. We met regularly for work and for meals, and held occasional evening classes in the SRF printed lessons, following the classes with group meditation. Paramhansaji had expressed the wish that we meditate together more often. We lacked a leader, however, and group initiative without steady direction seldom travels a straight line. Rev. Bernard, whom Master had placed in charge of our daily activities, wouldn't assume responsibility for our spiritual life; *that* he viewed as Master's exclusive domain.

Indeed, I suspect Master himself didn't greatly mind our lack of organization. For while daily group meditations might have kept a few of the less dedicated monks more firmly on the path, it would also have interfered with the free time the rest had to devote themselves to longer private meditations. Master wanted our spiritual endeavors to spring from the depths of our own yearning for God, and not to follow mechanically, merely, the well-worn paths of established habit. To be sure, he stressed the importance of *regular* practice, but I think the clockwork regularity of Western monastic discipline must have struck him as rather too mechanical, too much a part of that most far-reaching Western delusion: the belief that perfection can be achieved through outward, not inward, reforms. At any rate, Master himself often took us out of any groove of routine into which we'd become too firmly settled. In his company, there was little danger that our mental grooves would become worn into ruts!

I myself was glad for the opportunity to develop a meditative routine of my own. Soon I was rising at four o'clock every morning—staggering out of bed, admittedly, with the indispensable aid of an alarm clock. After practicing Master's exercises for recharging the body with energy, I would meditate two or three hours. At seven o'clock I would enter the main building, where I showered and breakfasted before going out into the garden for work. At noon I would put food aside for myself in the men's dining room, then meditate half an hour in the main chapel upstairs. Evenings I would eat lightly (a heavy meal in the stomach, I soon discovered, makes it difficult to meditate deeply), study a bit, then go down to my "cave" to meditate two or three more hours before bed.

Soon I was looking forward to my times for meditation as eagerly as the worldly man looks forward to an evening's partying. Never had I dreamed there could be such a wealth of enjoyment within my own self!

In addition to techniques of meditation, Paramhansa Yogananda, as I've indicated, taught a series of energization exercises. He based these exercises on a little-known truth, which Rev. Bernard explained to me my first evening at Mt. Washington. Cosmic energy is drawn into the body through the medulla oblongata by the agency of the will. "The greater the will," the Master said, "the greater the flow of energy." Practicing these exercises gratefully morning and evening, I found them marvelously effective for banishing fatigue and for developing a radiant, lasting sense of well-being.

On Saturdays, no work was scheduled. This gave us time to do personal chores, and for longer private meditation. Usually I meditated late into the morning, then kept silence the rest of the day. Sometimes I fasted. In the evening I meditated again several hours.

Sundays we attended morning and evening services in our Hollywood church. There being only a pickup truck to get us there, we younger monks piled happily into the back of it for the trip, which took fifteen or twenty minutes. In winter, to harden ourselves against the cold, and develop *titiksha* (endurance), we sometimes bared our bodies from the waist up, joyously welcoming the invigorating air and laughing with youthful good spirits as we bounced along. ("You should learn *tumo*," Boone shouted to me one day as the wind whistled around us. "What's that?" "It's a Tibetan technique for overcoming cold." From then on, if ever Boone looked a little chilly, I would shout to him to "do mo' *tumo!*")

The Hollywood church was charming in its simplicity. Its color scheme, both inside and out, was blue, white, and gold—"Master's colors," Boone informed me. Little niches on either side of the sanctuary contained figurines depicting various leaders in the great world religions. Paramhansa Yogananda had named this a "Church of All Religions." His teachings stressed the underlying oneness of all faiths. Seats for about 115 people faced the small stage from which services were conducted. Before and after services, curtains were usually drawn shut across this stage. When they were parted, there stood revealed along the back wall an altar containing five niches, each with a picture of one of our line of gurus: Babaji, Lahiri Mahasaya, Swami Sri Yukteswar, Paramhansa Yogananda, and Jesus Christ.

Bernard, who was to conduct the service in the church the first Sunday after my arrival, showed me around beforehand. "Why," I asked him, "is the picture of Jesus Christ on our altar, too? Surely *he* isn't in our line of gurus. Do we include him just to appease the Christian denominations?"

Bernard smiled. "Master has told us it was Jesus himself who appeared to Babaji, and asked him to send this teaching of Self-Realization to the West. 'My followers,' Jesus asserted at that meeting, 'have forgotten the art of divine, *inner* communion. Outwardly they do good works, but they have lost sight of the most important of my teachings, to "seek the kingdom of God first." '*

"The work he sent through Master to the West is helping people to commune inwardly with God," continued Bernard. "Jesus, too, through people's practice of meditation, is becoming a living reality for them—a being with whom they can commune, instead of one whom they merely read about in the Bible. This was what Jesus meant when he said that he would come again. Master often speaks of this work as the Second Coming of Christ, for it teaches people how to fulfill the true promise of Jesus—not to return again outwardly, but in the souls of those who loved him and communed with him."

"That isn't what most Christians believe." I smiled wryly.

"True! But you may recall several Biblical accounts in which the apostles themselves were rebuked by Jesus for taking his words literally, when he meant them metaphorically. 'I have meat to eat that ye know not of'† he said, and they thought he must have a sandwich hidden on him somewhere! Jesus himself, moreover, placed his Second Coming *within the present lifetimes* of his listeners. 'Verily I say unto you,' he told them, 'This generation shall not pass, till all these things be fulfilled.'§ In those days, and many times since then, he *has* fulfilled his promise to appear to true devotees—not to fanatical adventists who waited for him on

° Matthew 6:33.
† John 4:32.
§ Matthew 24:34.

hilltops in flowing, white gowns, but to those who sought him humbly within their own souls."

"Tell me," I said, hesitating before taking this philosophical plunge, "why do we have pictures on our altar at all? If the state of consciousness we're seeking is formless and omnipresent, something we're supposed to commune with in our own selves, doesn't it hinder our development to have our attention diverted outwardly, to individuals?"

"No," Bernard replied. "You see, our masters *have* that state of consciousness. For us, it is difficult even to visualize such a state! By attuning ourselves to them, we begin to sense what it is they have, and to develop that same consciousness in ourselves. This is what is meant in the Bible by the words, 'As many as received him, to them gave he power to become the sons of God.' "°

"Then is it more important to try to tune in to Master's consciousness, in meditation, than to concentrate on what he says and does outwardly?"

"Very much so! I don't mean, of course, that his outward teachings don't hold vital lessons for us also. But the very gist of those teachings is to guide us into inner attunement. One might say that *attunement* is the essence of discipleship."

I wondered whether such an intensely personal relationship to one's guru might not cause emotional attachment to him, thereby limiting the disciple's consciousness instead of freeing it. Most important of all, I wondered, would attunement with Master threaten my attunement with God? Would it externalize my attention, instead of interiorizing it?

As time passed, and I got to know Master better, it became obvious to me that the attunement he encouraged in his disciples was impersonal. It was his practice to turn people's devotion resolutely away from himself, as a human being, and toward the omnipresent Divinity that was the sole object of his own devotion. Attunement with him, I found then, meant attunement not with his human personality, but with his universal state of awareness. Indeed, in the deeper sense there was no personality there for us to attune ourselves to. As he often put it, "I killed Yogananda long ago. No one dwells in this temple now but God."

At first, unaware as yet of how deeply impersonal his consciousness was, I saw him rather as a great and wise man. He sought to help me expand those mental horizons. Looking deeply into my eyes one day, he said, "If you *knew* my consciousness!"

° John 1:12.

If anyone betrayed toward him the slightest attachment, or the slightest presumption as a result of some favor received, Master invariably became more impersonal than usual toward that disciple. Those who were closest to him were, without exception, those whose relationship with him was a relationship primarily in God.

The day of our first meeting on September 12th, Master returned to Encinitas. I didn't see him until two weeks later, when he was scheduled to preach again at Hollywood Church.

The church that day was divinely peaceful. As we entered, music was sounding on the organ. The organist, Jane Brush (now Sahaja Mata), was playing her own arrangements of devotional chants that Master had written. I found her arrangements so sweet, so devotionally inspiring, that my heart soared upward in longing for God. Of all the renditions I have ever heard of Master's chants, none have moved me so deeply as hers.

After some twenty minutes, it was time for the service to begin. The curtains parted; and there stood Master, in his eyes a deep, penetrating gaze that seemed to bestow on each one present a special blessing. Then suddenly he was smiling, radiant with divine joy. We rose spontaneously to our feet. As had been his custom during his early "campaign" days, he demanded, "How is everybody?"

"Awake and ready!" we all shouted.

"How *feels* everybody?"

"Awake and ready!"

We sat down, inspired by his dynamic power. He led us in chanting and meditation, then gave a brief interpretation of selected passages from the Bible and the *Bhagavad Gita*. His sermon followed—an altogether delightful blend of wit, devotional inspiration, and wisdom. I had always supposed that deep truths must be spoken portentously, in measured cadences, almost in the style of Emerson's essays. Rev. Bernard had addressed us rather that way the Sunday before (indeed, his very conversation had that sort of ring to it!), and I had been suitably impressed. But Master now lectured in a manner so totally natural that, for several minutes, I was quite taken aback. Was *this* the way to convince people of the importance of divine truths? He made no attempt to impress us with the depth of his insights. Frequently, rather, he sent us into gales of merriment. Only gradually did I observe that his flashes of humor invariably preceded some very sound spiritual advice. Yogananda wore his wisdom without the slightest affectation, like a comfortable old jacket that one has been wearing for years.

"Behind every rosebush of pleasure," he cautioned us, "hides a rattlesnake of pain." He went on to urge us to seek our "pleasures" in God, and to ignore the fickle promises of this world.

"There are two kinds of poor people," he remarked—"those who wear cloth rags, and those who, though traveling in limousines, wear spiritual rags of selfishness and indifference to God. It is better to be poor physically, and have God in your heart, than to be materially rich without Him.

"Never say that you are a sinner," he went on to tell us. "You are a child of God! Gold, though covered over with mud for centuries, remains gold. Even so, the pure gold of the soul, though covered for eons of time with the mud of delusion, remains forever pure 'gold.' To call yourself a sinner is to identify yourself with your sins, instead of trying to overcome them. To call yourself a sinner is the greatest sin before God!"

He proceeded to discuss different levels of spiritual development: "I slept and dreamed life was beauty. I woke up, and found life was duty. But even in this, my dutiful ego, I dreamed myself separate from God. And then I awoke in Him, to realize that life truly *is* beauty! For the beauties we seek in this world can never be found except in Him. To experience them, we must first be dutiful to His will. Only then can we rise above self. We have not been sent here on earth to create a pleasure garden. This world is a battlefield! Our highest duty is to seek the Lord. 'Seek ye the kingdom of God first,' Jesus said, 'and all these things shall be added unto you'—nor be ye of doubtful mind!"

Finally, Master gave us this invaluable suggestion: "Never go to bed at night until you have convinced your mind that this world is God's dream."

Following the sermon, Bernard made a few announcements. He concluded by recommending *Autobiography of a Yogi* to newcomers. At this point Master interrupted him to say, "Many are coming from afar after reading the book. One recently read it in New York, and—Walter, please stand up."

I glanced around to see who this "Walter" might be who, like me, had read the book recently in New York. There was no one standing. Turning back to Master, I found him smiling at me! *Walter?!* "Ah, well," I thought philosophically, "a rose by any other name. . . ." Self-consciously I rose to my feet.

"Walter read the book in New York," Master continued affectionately, "and left everything to come here. Now he has become one of us."

Members, lay and renunciate alike, smiled at me in blessing.

"Walter" was the name Master called me ever thereafter. No one else used this name, until, after Master's earthly passing, I longed for every possible reminder of those precious years with him. I then asked my brothers and sisters on the path to call me by that name.

Master spent the next few days at Mt. Washington. During this period I saw him several times, though not privately. Indeed, such was my inner turmoil, as a result of the drastic change my life had undergone, that I doubt whether another private interview at this time would have helped me much. For Master's part, he probably was waiting for me to assimilate the instructions he had given me at our first meeting.

A few days before Master's return to Mt. Washington, Norman had talked me into joining him in what is known to health-faddists as the "Grape Cure," a diet of nothing but grapes and grape juice. A few weeks of this cure would, Norman assured me, purify my body, and help me to make rapid progress in the spiritual life. Master saw us that Monday morning.

"Devotion is the greatest purifier," he remarked, smiling.

"Is it your wish then, Sir, that we break this fast?" I inquired.

"Well, I don't want you to break your wills, now that you have set them this way. But your time would be better spent if you worked on developing devotion. A pure heart is the way to God, not a pure stomach!"

Heeding his counsel, I soon lost "heart" for the grape cure though I continued it another day or two so as, in his words, not to "break" my will. But it wasn't long before I took up the infinitely more rewarding, though also far more demanding, task of deepening my love for God, through chanting, and holding constantly to the thought of God's presence in my heart.

Mental habits, alas, are not always easy to change. Months were to pass before I could feel that I had made substantial progress against my years-old tendency to over-intellectualize. Master, seeing my desire, helped me from the start with constant encouragement and advice.

"Get devotion!" he would tell me. "You *must* have devotion. Remember what Jesus said"—here he paraphrased the words of the Gospel—" 'Thou dost not reveal Thyself unto the prudent and the wise, but unto babes.' "

Swami Sri Yukteswar, a saint of wisdom if ever there was one, and therefore, so one might think, a saint more likely than most to endorse intellectual attitudes, said that love alone determines a person's fitness for the spiritual path. In his book *The Holy Science* he wrote, "This heart's natural love is the principal thing to attain a holy life. . . . It is impossible for man to advance a step towards [salvation] without it." The present age, alas, perhaps even more than most, affords little encouragement for the development of that all-surrendering love of which the saints have ever spoken. "Mawkish sentimentalism" is the common judgment on deep feeling of any kind. An unfeeling heart is even admired by many, as evidence of a "scientific outlook." But the truth is that without love no one can penetrate deeply into the heart of things. For while emotions can and sometimes do cloud the mind, calm, pure love clarifies it, and makes possible the subtlest intuitions.

A certain visitor once requested a private interview with Master. On the appointed day he arrived armed with a long list of what he considered to be "profound," intellectual questions.

"Love God," Master said in answer to the first of them.

The man paused a moment uncomprehendingly, then shrugged his shoulders and posed his second question.

"Love God!" Master persisted.

Nonplussed, the visitor proceeded to the third "profound" item on his list.

"Love God!" came Master's reply once more, this time sternly. Without another word he rose, concluding the interview, and left the room. The intellectual guest never did grasp the relevance of Master's counsel to his questions. But Paramhansaji was telling him that until he developed love, the doors of true wisdom would remain closed to him.

Stern discipline from an all-compassionate master puzzles some devotees. The neophyte, when he first finds his guru "treating" him to a good scolding, may even ask himself, "Has he lost his temper?" But a true master lives on a plane far above such corrosive emotions. Sometimes, indeed, he may make a *show* of anger, but only to emphasize some counsel which, if delivered gently, might simply be ignored. A mother may be obliged, similarly, to scold her child if he won't heed her gentle admonishments.

Jean Haupt told me of one occasion when Master upbraided one of the nuns in his presence. "You'd have thought the roof would fly off!" Jean said, chuckling. "Master was pacing the floor, shouting. I was seated at one end of the room; the nun was at the other. Master, whenever he faced her, emphasized his meaning with a stern look. But when he turned his back to her, his face relaxed into an amused smile. He didn't stop shouting, but he winked at me before turning back fiercely in her direction."

Master disciplined only those who accepted his discipline.

Otherwise he was the soul of consideration. I remember him sometimes inquiring gently of new disciples to whom he'd offered mild correction, "You don't mind my saying that, do you?"

One of the traits that impressed me about him most deeply was his quality of universal respect. It was a respect born of the deepest concern for others' welfare. The veriest stranger was, I'm convinced, as dear to him as his own disciples were.

Debi Mukerjee, a young monk from India, told me of an example he had seen of the universality of Master's love. Master had invited him out for a drive one afternoon. They were on their way home, near sundown.

"Stop the car!" Master cried suddenly. They parked by the curb. He got out and walked back several doors to a small, rather shoddy-looking variety shop. There, to Debi's astonishment, he selected a number of items, none of them useful. "What on earth can he want with all that junk?" Debi marveled. At the front counter the owner, an elderly woman, added up the price. When Master paid it, she burst into tears.

"I very badly needed just this sum of money today!" she cried. "It's near closing time, and I'd almost given up hope of getting it. Bless you, Sir. God Himself must have sent you to me in my hour of need!"

Master's quiet smile alone betrayed his knowledge of her difficulty. He offered no word of explanation. The purchases, as Debi had suspected, served no practical purpose thereafter.

At first I found it a bit awkward living with a master who was, as I soon discovered, conscious of my inmost thoughts and feelings. Nor was space any barrier to his telepathic insight. Wherever his disciples happened to be, he could read them like a proverbial book.

Boone and Norman told me of how, a few weeks before my arrival, they had gone together by bus to Encinitas. Their conversation had been somewhat less than edifying, apparently.

"Master met us at the gate," Norman told me. "He looked stern. After quoting to us several of our more colorful remarks on the bus, he gave us a good scolding. 'You've come here to forget worldly things,' he said. 'Spend your time talking to God. When you mix with one another, talk of Him.' He ended up telling us not to mix with one another!"

James Coller, another disciple, visited us at about this time from Phoenix, Arizona, where Master had appointed him the minister of our church there. James, though deeply devoted to God and Guru, had a tendency to be a little immune to hermitage discipline.

"I was driving from Phoenix to Encinitas recently," James told us, "to see Master. It was late at night, and I was getting hungry. After some time I came to a restaurant that was still open, and went in eagerly. As bad luck would have it, all they served was hamburgers. What was I to do? I knew Master wanted us to be vegetarians, but still. . . . I mean, I was *really* hungry! 'Oh, well,' I decided finally, 'he won't know!' So I ate two hamburgers. After I reached Encinitas, I spoke with Master. At the end of our conversation, he remarked gently:

" 'By the way, James, when you're on the highway late at night, and you come to a place that serves nothing but hamburgers—better not eat anything.' "

Disconcerting though it sometimes was to live near someone who had free access into the hidden recesses of my mind, I became increasingly grateful, too, for his insight. For here at last, I realized, was one human being whose misunderstanding I need never fear. Master was my friend, ever quietly, firmly on my side, concerned only to help me toward the highest understanding, even when I erred. Almost incredibly, moreover, he was exactly the same to all, no matter what they did, nor how they treated him.

He once scolded Rev. Stanley, the minister at the SRF Lake Shrine.

"But please, Sir," Stanley pleaded, "you will forgive me, won't you?"

"Well," Master replied in astonishment, "what else can I do?"

I never knew him to hold a grudge.

There was a man who for years, out of intense jealousy, slandered Master. One day, less than a week before the end of Master's life, the two of them met at a formal gathering.

"Remember," Master said, gazing into the man's eyes with deep forgiveness, "I will always love you!" I saw the man later, gazing at Master with deep love and admiration.

Master's counsel to people, too, born as it was of that love, was always particular to their needs. Seeing me one day on the grounds, he advised me, "Do not get excited or impatient, Walter. Go with slow speed." Only one who knew my private thoughts in meditation could have perceived the galloping zeal with which I'd entered the spiritual path. It was not an attitude that I displayed outwardly.

Toward the end of September he invited me to Encinitas, where he said he would be spending the next week or so. There a small group of us meditated with him one evening in the peaceful salon of the hermitage, overlooking the Pacific Ocean. Sitting in his presence, I felt as though some powerful magnet were uplifting my entire being and concentrating it at the point between the eyebrows. The thought came to me, "No wonder the Indian Scriptures praise above all else the uplifting influence of a true guru!" Never, by my unaided efforts alone, could I have plunged into meditation so suddenly, or so deeply.

Soon thereafter Master invited me to Twenty-Nine Palms, where he said he was planning to go for a period of seclusion. Here it was that, over the years, I gained my most precious memories of him.

CHAPTER 20

Twenty-Nine Palms

"YOU MUST KEEP this place a secret," Bernard warned me as we drove out to Twenty-Nine Palms. "With the rapid growth of the work, Master needs a place where he can go to concentrate on his writings. Otherwise it's telephone calls and interviews all day long. He's even bought the property in his family name, Ghosh, to safeguard his privacy."

This was the first time I'd ever seen a desert. The vast wasteland of sand, sagebrush, Joshua trees, and tumbleweed held a strange fascination for me. It seemed a different dimension, as though time here had slipped imperceptibly into timelessness. The sky, pastel hues of blue, pink, and orange-yellow in the waning afternoon sunlight, looked almost ethereal. I gazed about me in wonder.

Bernard noted my expression. "I see the desert's magic is working on you already!" He added, "Master says the light here resembles the astral light."

The monks' retreat, at which we arrived soon afterward, was a small cottage on some fifteen acres of land. It was without electricity. A tall windmill creaked and clanked complainingly with every breeze, as it pumped water up from a well. A grove of blue-green smoke trees hid the cottage from the seldom-traveled sand road. Even with the windmill, which seemed determined to go public with news of how hard it was made to work, this seemed a perfect spot for seclusion and meditation. Over the coming years I was to spend many months in these tranquil surroundings.

Master's place was five miles up the road. Located in a more developed area, it had city water, and electricity, which he needed since he did much of his writing at night. His property nestled near the base of a range of low hills which, because of their barrenness, looked almost like mountains. Master's house had pale stucco walls, in the Spanish style typical of southern California.

Surrounding it were a profusion of plants and delicate Chinese elms. The entire property, enclosed by a low wire fence, was one or two acres in size.

My first visit to Twenty-Nine Palms was for a weekend. We visited Master at his place. My recollection of him on that occasion isn't so much of the things he *said,* as of what he *didn't* say. I didn't know it at the time, but he placed great importance on silence. Disciples working around him were permitted to speak only when necessary. "Silence," he told them, "is the altar of Spirit."

Master was seated out of doors by the garage; Bernard and I were standing nearby. Master asked Bernard to go into the house and fetch something. Suddenly, for the first time since my acceptance as a disciple, I found myself alone with my guru. It seemed an opportunity not to be missed: a chance to learn something—*anything!* Master, evidently, didn't see it in the same light. He made no move to speak. Finally I decided I'd better "break the ice."

I had learned from Bernard how to commune inwardly with *Aum,* the Cosmic Sound, which manifests itself to the yogi in deep meditation. "Sir," I inquired, "what does *Aum* sound like?"

Master gave a prolonged "Mmmmmmmmmmm." He then reverted comfortably to silence. To me, alas, his silence was anything but comfortable.

"How does one hear it?" I persisted, though I already knew the technique.

This time Master didn't even answer, but simply assumed the prescribed position. After holding it briefly, he returned his hands in silence to his lap.

Some months later I told him I was having trouble calming my breath in meditation. "That," he replied, "is because you used to talk a lot. The influence has carried over. Well," he added consolingly, "you were happy in that."

Silence is the altar of Spirit. As I grew into my new way of life I came to prize this maxim.

Soon after our first visit to Twenty-Nine Palms, Bernard drove Norman and me out there again. Master had devised a project for the two of us to work on, probably to give us an excuse to remain near him while he concentrated on his writings. He asked us to build him a small swimming pool behind the house, near his bedroom. It was not that he *wanted* a pool, particularly; in fact, once it was finished he never used it. But it did give Norman and me the opportunity to be with him for weeks at a time.

Soon we were busy shoveling out a deep hole in the sand. Master, taking an occasional break from his writing, would come out and work with us for fifteen minutes or so. Whenever he did so, I felt a deep blessing. But I hadn't yet adjusted to his habitual silence. One warm, sunny afternoon I noticed that he was panting slightly with the physical exertion, and remarked conversationally, "It's hot work, isn't it?"

"It is *good* work." Master gazed at me a moment sternly, then returned in silence to his digging.

Gradually, inspired by his example, I learned to speak less, and to listen more to God's soundless whispers in my soul.

Late one afternoon we were sitting with Master on a little porch outside the sitting room where he dictated his writings. After several minutes of silence, Master posed me an unexpected question.

"What keeps the earth from shooting out into space, away from the sun?"

Surprised, and not as yet familiar with the cryptic way he often taught us, I assumed he simply wanted information. "It's the sun's gravitational pull, Sir," I explained.

"Then what keeps the earth from being drawn back into the sun?"

"That's the earth's centrifugal force, pulling it constantly outward. If the sun's gravity weren't as strong as it is, we'd shoot off into space, out of the solar system altogether."

Master smiled significantly. Had he intended more than I realized? Some months later I recalled this conversation, and understood that he had been speaking metaphorically of God as the sun, drawing all things back to Himself, and of man as the earth, resisting with desires and petty self-interest the pull of divine love.

One hot day at noon Norman and I stood up from our digging and stretched, grateful that lunchtime had arrived. We enjoyed our work, but there was no denying that it was also tiring. Besides, we were famished. Briefly we surveyed the yawning pit at our feet.

"God, what a hole!" exclaimed Norman. We gazed out over the mounds of sand we'd deposited about the grounds with the wheelbarrow. The very sight of them, lumped there in mute testimony to our exertions, only reinforced our fatigue.

At that moment Master came out of doors.

"Those mounds don't look very attractive," he remarked. "I wonder if they couldn't be leveled out. Would one of you mind fetching a two-by-four?"

Armed with the board, we stood before him apprehensively and awaited further instructions.

"Each of you hold the two-by-four at one end," Master said. "Then—just come over to this mound here. Pull the sand back toward you by pressing down hard on the board, and moving it slowly back and forth between you."

Probably even this meager description suffices to convey some idea of how difficult the job was. By the time we'd leveled one mound, Norman and I were panting heavily. Well, we reflected, at least we'd demonstrated that the job could be done. Master, now that his curiosity was satisfied, would no doubt tell us to go and have our lunch.

"Very good," he commented approvingly. "I *thought* that method would work. Now then, why don't we try it just once more—on that mound over there?"

Adjusting our expectations accordingly, we started in a second time.

"Very good!" Master commented once again. Evidently not wishing to place obstacles in the way of the momentum we'd built up, he said, "Let's do just one more—this one over here."

And after that: "One more."

And then again: "Just one more."

I don't know how many mounds we leveled, but Norman, strong as he was, was beginning to moan softly under his breath. "Just one more," Master said again.

Suddenly, getting the joke at last, I stood up and laughed. Master smiled back at me.

"I was playing with you! Now—go and have your lunch."

Often, in his training of us, he would push our equanimity to the limit, to see which way we would break. If we rebelled, or if under the strain we grew upset, it meant we had failed the test. But if we responded with an extra spurt of energy, and affirmed a bright, positive attitude, we found his tests immeasurably strengthening.

In the foregoing test, Master helped Norman and me to learn to resist the thought of fatigue. Curiously, I found I was actually *less* tired after leveling those mounds than I had been beforehand. "The greater the will," as Master often said, "the greater the flow of energy."

One day Norman and I sat down to lunch, ravenous as usual. We reached for the tray that had been set before us, and gasped. It was practically empty! Two cups of tepid water, faintly flavored with chocolate, and a couple of dry sandwiches that someone had waved in the general proximity of a jar of peanut butter—and that was all.

"What a banquet!" cried Norman in dismay. We paused a moment. Then suddenly we were laughing. "What comes of itself,"

Master often said, "let it come." One of the keys he gave us to unshakable inner peace was an ability to accept life as it is. Our meager fare that day gave us adequate food for meditation, if not for our bodies!

Shortly after the test of the two-by-four, Master began inviting us indoors after hours to listen to him while he dictated his writings. The truths I learned during those sessions were invaluable. So also were some of the lessons I received, sometimes less weightily, during periods of relaxation when he wasn't dictating.

As I've indicated earlier, the concept I had formed of a sage during my college years was of one to whom everything was a Serious Matter. I myself had laughed frequently, but it was more often *at* folly than in innocent joy. Like most college-trained intellectuals, my notion of wisdom tended to be rather dry. But until the intellect is softened by heart qualities, it is like earth without water: weighty, but unfertile. Master was anxious to wean me from this addiction to an arid mental diet, even as I myself was anxious to be weaned.

One evening Norman and I were sitting with him in the kitchen. Master summoned one of the sisters, whom he asked to fetch a brown paper bag with something in it from his bedroom. When she returned, he switched off the lights. I heard him remove something from the bag, then chuckle playfully. Suddenly there was a metallic buzzing sound as sparks came leaping out of a toy pistol. Laughing with childlike glee, Master turned the lights back on. Next, from another toy pistol out of the bag, he shot a tiny parachute into the air. We watched it gravely as it descended to the floor. I was utterly astonished.

Master glanced at me merrily, though with a covert gaze of calm understanding. "How do you like them, Walter?"

I laughed, trying earnestly to enter into the spirit of this occasion. "They're fine, Sir!" My comment was almost an affirmation.

Looking at me deeply now, but with love, he quoted the words of Jesus: "Suffer little children to come unto me, for of such is the kingdom of God."[*]

One of the most amazing things about Master was the utter freedom of his spirit. In the deepest matters he maintained the simplicity and light-hearted innocence of a child. In severe trials he could find cause for joy. Yet even when he laughed he retained the calm, devotional outlook of one who beheld only God everywhere. Often in the veriest trifles he saw illustrated some deep truth.

[*] Luke 18:16.

There was a dog at Twenty-Nine Palms named Bojo, who belonged to a neighbor. Bojo had decided, since Master's retreat remained untenanted much of the time, that it belonged within his rightful domain. On our first arrival Bojo objected fiercely to Norman and me, growling and barking at us continually as we worked on the pool. It was Norman finally who won him over, with a combination of roughhouse and love: Whenever Bojo barked, Norman would tumble him onto his back, then pat him and throw sticks for him to fetch. Soon our canine neighbor began visiting us as a friend.

One day Master joined us out of doors for lunch. Bojo smelled the food and approached, sniffing hopefully.

"Look at that dog," Master remarked chuckling. He gave Bojo a little food from his plate. "Do you see how his forehead is wrinkled up? Though his thought is only for the food, in his one-pointed concentration his mind is focused on the spiritual eye!"

During dictation one evening, Master touched on the subject of reincarnation.

"Sir," I inquired, "have I been a yogi before?"

"Many times," he replied. "You would have to have been, to be here."

At this time Master began also revising his printed lessons. He was never able to get very far with them unfortunately; the task proved simply too big considering the many new writings he had in mind. The first evening he worked on this project, Dorothy Taylor, his secretary, read to him from the old first lesson. She arrived at a passage where Master had said one can't get answers to scientific questions by merely praying for them; the appropriate experiments must be conducted also. Spiritual truths, similarly, the lesson stated, require verification in the "laboratory" of yoga practice and of direct, inner contact with God.

"M-mmm," Master interrupted her, shaking his head. "That's not completely true. If one prayed deeply enough he *would* get answers, even to intricate scientific questions." He pondered the problem awhile.

"No," he concluded, "the point here concerns the need for verification by *appropriate* methods. In this sense, what has been written is valid, since prayer is effective in such matters only for those who already have some contact with God. I think I'll let it stand the way it is."

In this way, paragraph by paragraph, he would analyze what had been written before, clarify certain portions, and deepen the import of others. The insights I received from him in this way were priceless. Impressive to me, also, was his *manner* of teaching. Universal in outlook, never self-assertive, conscious of the relationship of everything he was considering to the broadest realities, he was, I realized more and more, a true guide to the Infinite.

I was struck also by the sheer, dynamic courage with which he taught. Some people, I knew, would be tempted to tone down the power of his words, as if, in making them bland, to make them more popularly acceptable. But the hallmark of greatness is extraordinary energy. Such energy is always challenging. I was amused, some months later, by an example of the tendency to want to tone down that sort of energy. I have mentioned how, in his early years in America, Master sometimes actually ran out onto the lecture platform, challenging his audiences to rise to his own level of divine enthusiasm. Even now, long since those "campaign" days, he began every Sunday service with the joyous demand, "How is everybody?" joining his congregation in the vibrant response, "Awake and ready!" Dr. Lloyd Kennell, our alternate minister in San Diego, a sincere and good man, couldn't match Master's energetic spirit. "I like to keep things on a more moderate level," he explained to me before commencing a service one Sunday morning. He went out onto the stage. "Good morning," he began. "I trust that everyone present this morning is feeling awake and ready?"

Master, more than any other teacher I have ever met, was able to stir people, to shake them with the unexpected, to charm them with a sudden funny story, or startle them into alertness with some novel piece of information. Like Jesus, he spoke with the ring of truth. Even newcomers found his conviction irresistible.

No one else would have dared it, but for his very first lesson Master dictated a passage in support of his claim that a close karmic bond exists between our own direct line of gurus and the great master Jesus.

"Babaji, Lahiri Mahasaya, and Sri Yukteswar," he announced, "were the three wise men who came to visit the Christ child in the manger. When Jesus was a grown man he returned their visit. The account of his trip to India was removed from the New Testament centuries later by sectarian followers, who feared its inclusion might lessen his stature in the eyes of the world."*

---

* The fact that the Bible says *nothing at all* about those missing eighteen years offers the strongest possible evidence that the account of them was later deleted. For it simply is not credible that all four of the apostles would have omitted every mention of so large a segment of their Master's brief life on earth. Even granting the possibility, which seems doubtful, that those eighteen years were too uneventful to record, any conscientious biographer—not to mention a *disciple*—

Master often talked to us of our line of gurus and of their special mission in this age. For he was the last in a line of direct spiritual succession. What he taught represented no radical new theory, no Eastern counterpart to our own interminable "scientific breakthroughs" in the West, but the purest, highest, and indeed oldest spiritual tradition in the world.

Babaji is the first in this direct line of gurus. A master of great age, he still lives in the Badrinarayan section of the Himalayas, where he remains accessible to a few highly advanced souls. In the latter half of the Nineteenth Century, Babaji, feeling that in the present scientific age mankind was better prepared to receive higher knowledge, directed his disciple, Shyama Charan Lahiri, to reintroduce to the world the long-hidden, highest science of yoga. Lahiri Mahasaya, as his disciples called him, named this exalted science *Kriya Yoga,* the meaning of which is, simply, "divine union through a certain technique, or spiritual act." Other techniques bear the same name, but, according to our own line of gurus, the Kriya Yoga of Lahiri Mahasaya is the most ancient and basic of all yoga techniques. Babaji explained that it was to this technique that Lord Krishna, India's greatest ancient prophet, was referring in the *Bhagavad Gita* when he said, "I related this imperishable yoga to Bibaswat; Bibaswat taught it to Manu [the ancient Hindu lawgiver]; Manu gave it to Ikshvaku [the renowned founder of the Solar dynasty]. In this way it was handed down in orderly succession to great sages until, after long stretches of time, knowledge of that yoga deteriorated in the world [because the generality of mankind lost touch with spiritual realities]."

Lahiri Mahasaya, like Babaji, was a great master of yoga—a *"yogavatar,"* Master called him, or "incarnation of yoga"—though also a householder with worldly responsibilities. Of the many disciples that he initiated, the chief was Swami Sri Yukteswar—modern India's *gyanavatar,*° or "incarnation of wisdom," as Yogananda designated him. Thus it was, through Sri Yukteswar, that Paramhansa Yogananda was sent to America with the high technique which, our gurus said, would give wise direction to the hitherto scattered, and potentially dangerous, development of modern Western civilization.

---

would not on any account have left them out altogether. At the very least he'd have said something like, "And Jesus grew up, and worked in his father's shop." The fact that nothing whatever is said suggests the later work of priests, whose religious convictions inspired them to delete, but prevented them from being brazen enough to add words of their own.

° *Gyana* (wisdom) in books is often spelled *Jnana.* Master once commented to me on the problems of transliteration from Sanskrit to Roman characters. He was going over some of his writings with me at Twenty-Nine Palms, after I'd been with

"In the divine plan," Yogananda stated on another occasion, "Jesus Christ was responsible for the evolution of the West, and Krishna (later, Babaji), for that of the East. It was intended that the West specialize in developing objectively, through logic and reason, and that the East specialize in inner, intuitive development. But in the cosmic plan the time has come to combine these two lines into one. East and West must unite."

During these evening dictations Master reviewed also the lessons on Kriya Yoga, and made certain changes in the way he had taught them previously. "This doesn't alter the technique itself," he explained, "but it will make it easier to understand."

I was avidly absorbing Master's every word: I hadn't yet been initiated into Kriya Yoga! Master paused suddenly.

"Say—Walter!" he exclaimed, "you haven't had Kriya initiation!"

"No, Sir." I was smiling smugly. He had already dictated enough for me to understand the technique.

"Well, in that case I shall have to initiate you right now." Interrupting his dictation, Master told us all to sit upright in meditative posture. "I am sending the divine light through your brain, baptizing you," he said from where he sat across the room. I felt immediately blessed; a divine current radiated through my brain from the Christ center. He went on to guide me in the practice of the technique.

"Don't practice it yet, however," he concluded. "I shall be giving a formal initiation at Christmas time. Wait until then."

Gradually, as weeks passed, I found my heart opening like a flower under the sunrays of Master's love. More and more I found myself able to appreciate what a blessing it was to be with him. During his dictation one evening he explained a method for attuning oneself to the Guru's subtle spiritual vibrations.

"Visualize the Guru," he said, "at the point between the eyebrows, the Christ center. This is the 'broadcasting station' in the body. Call to him deeply at this point. Then try to feel his response in your heart—the body's 'receiving set.' Intuitively you will feel his response here. When you do so, pray to him deeply, 'Introduce me to God.' "

---

him about a year, when we came upon this word, *gyana.* "*Jnana* is how scholars like to spell it," Master scoffed. "It isn't *pronounced J-nana.* And how else are you going to pronounce it if you find it spelled that way? This is just an example of scholars' pedantry. *Gyana* is the correct pronunciation. The *g-y* in English doesn't show it exactly, but at least it's much closer to the right way of saying it.

"Another transliteration that scholars prefer," Master continued, "is *v* in place of *b.* Instead of *Bibaswat,* they write *Vivaswat.* Why? The way *v* is pronounced in English makes this Sanskrit pronunciation wrong. Again, *b* isn't exact, but it's closer."

Sometimes also I visualized Master seated in diminutive form on the top of my head. Either way, as I meditated on him, I often felt a wave of peace or love descend over me, suffusing my entire being. Sometimes answers to questions came, and a clearer understanding of qualities that I was trying to develop, or to overcome. Sometimes, in a single meditation on Master, I would find myself freed of some delusion that had plagued me for months, perhaps even for years. On one such occasion, as I approached him afterward and knelt for his blessing, he commented softly, "Very good!"

Master occasionally came over to the monks' retreat at Twenty-Nine Palms. At such times he would walk about the grounds with us, or sit and talk. Sometimes we meditated together. After one such meditation I recorded his words:

"This is the kingdom of *Aum*. Listen! It is not enough just to hear it. You must *merge* yourself in that sound. *Aum is* the Divine Mother." He paused a few minutes. "Om Kali, Om Kali, Om Kali. Listen. . . ." He paused again. "Oh, how beautiful it is! Om Kali, Om Kali, Om Kali!"°

On another occasion I was sleeping at the monks' retreat. It was late at night. Suddenly I was awakened by the feeling that a divine presence was in the room. It was overwhelming, almost as though God Himself were there, blessing me. I sat up to meditate. As I did so, I caught a glimpse of Master walking outside in the moonlight. Inexpressibly grateful to him, I went outdoors and silently touched his feet.

Master had the amazing gift of universal friendship. Each of us felt in some way uniquely loved by him. At the same time, it was a completely impersonal relationship, one in which outward favors counted for little. Such always, as I have come to understand, is divine friendship. Yet I have been in ashrams where human personalities were so much the focus of attention that, almost within minutes of one's arrival, one knew who the important disciples were, what they did, what the Guru said about them. By contrast, during my first few months as a monk in SRF I doubt whether I

° *Om* is a common transliteration for *Aum*. I have written it thus here to indicate how it should sound when chanted. Technically, *Aum* is the more correct spelling. The three letters indicate the three distinct vibrations of cosmic manifestation: creation, preservation, and destruction. But for pronunciation this spelling is misleading, as the *a* is not pronounced long, as in *car,* but short. The resulting diphthong sounds rather like the letter *o* in English.

In Hindu mythology the three vibrations of cosmic manifestation are represented by Brahma, Vishnu, and Shiva. *Aum* is the vibration by which the Supreme Spirit brings all things into manifestation. It is the Holy Ghost of the Christian Trinity.

would have recognized more than one or two names in a "Who's
Who" of Master's closest disciples. We received simply no encouragement to be curious about them.

Thus it was that, when word came that fall that Faye Wright
(now Daya Mata, the third president of Self-Realization Fellowship)
had been taken seriously ill, her name, though high on the list of
Master's close disciples, meant nothing to me. I learned of her illness itself only as the explanation for why Master had suddenly
departed Twenty-Nine Palms for Los Angeles.

"It would be a serious loss to the work if she died," Bernard
assured me gravely.

"She was already gone," Master announced on his return from
Los Angeles. "Just see how karma works. The doctor, though summoned in plenty of time, diagnosed her case wrongly. When he
discovered his mistake, it was too late. She would certainly have
died. But God wanted her life spared for the work."

Master counseled us not to be preoccupied over matters that
didn't directly concern us. "Always remain in the Self," he advised
me once. "Come down only to eat or talk a little bit, if it's necessary. Then withdraw into the Self again." I didn't meet, or even
see, Daya Mata until I had been with Master almost a year.

My immediate concern at Twenty-Nine Palms was our job.
We'd dug the hole for the swimming pool. Other monks then
came out to help construct the wood forms. Bernard informed us
that the pouring of the concrete would have to be done continuously, to prevent seaming. We did the whole job by hand, mixing
and pouring with the aid of a small cement mixer. I shoveled the
sand; someone else added the gravel; others maneuvered wheelbar-
rows to the pouring sites. Twenty-three hours we labored, pausing
only occasionally to refresh ourselves with sandwiches and hot
drinks. But we chanted constantly to God as we worked, and the
hours passed joyously. At the end of it all I think we actually had
more energy than at the day's start. We were all smiling happily.

All of us, that is, but one. This man, after an hour or two of
half-hearted labor, had grumbled, "I didn't come here to shovel
cement!" Sitting down, he watched us for the remainder of the day,
reminding us occasionally that this wasn't what the spiritual path
was all about. Interestingly, at the end of that long day it was he
alone who felt exhausted.

The subject of this particular disciple's unwillingness came up a
few months later, in a discussion with Master. "He told me," I remarked, "that he can't obey you implicitly, Sir, because he feels he
must develop his own free will."

"But his will is not free!" Master replied wonderingly. "How can it be free, so long as he is bound by moods and desires? I don't *ask* anyone to follow me, but those who have done so have found true freedom.

"Sister," he continued, using the name by which he always referred to Sister Gyanamata, the elderly disciple whom I'd met on my first visit to Encinitas—"Sister used to run up and down all the time doing my bidding. One day a few of the others said to her, 'Why are you always doing what *he* says? You have your own will!' She answered, 'Well, but don't you think it's too late to change? And I must say, I have never been so happy in my life as I have been since coming here.' "

Master chuckled. "They never bothered her again!"

Already I, in my own little way, could endorse Sister Gyanamata's reply to those reluctant disciples. For the more I tuned my will to Master's, the happier I found I became.

"My will," Master often said, "is only to do God's will." The proof of his statement lay in the fact that the more perfectly we followed his will, the freer we ourselves felt, in God.

As Christmas approached, my heart was singing with a happiness I had never before dreamed possible. Christmas was an important holiday at Mt. Washington, the most sacred in our entire year. Master divided it into its two basic aspects: "spiritual Christmas," which we celebrated on Christmas Eve, and "social Christmas," celebrated the following day with traditional present-opening and a banquet. (Master later agreed to shift our "spiritual Christmas" back to the twenty-third, so that devotees wouldn't have to stay up all night afterwards, preparing food for the large Christmas Day banquet.)

On the 24th we gathered in the chapel at ten in the morning for an all-day meditation, to invite the infinite Christ to be born anew in the "mangers" of our hearts. I don't know how many have approached their first experience of this long meditation without trepidation. Few, I suspect, and among them certainly not I.

We took our seats, Master at the front of the room facing us. The doors were closed. From that moment on, save for a short break in the middle, no one was supposed to enter or leave the room except in case of emergency.

We began with a prayer to Jesus Christ and the other masters to bless us on this holy occasion. There followed some fifteen or twenty minutes of chanting.

Paramhansa Yogananda's "Cosmic Chants" consist of simple sentences repeated over and over again, each time with deeper concentration and devotion. I had been raised on the intricacies of Western classical music. It had taken me some time, as Master's disciple, to adjust fully to this rather stark form of musical expression. But by now I loved the chants. In their very simplicity I found beauty, and a power that surpassed that of most music I had ever heard. For these were "spiritualized" chants: Master had infused subtle blessings into them by singing each one until it elicited a divine response. As buildings and places develop vibrations according to the consciousness of the people frequenting them, so music also develops vibrations beyond those of actual sound. Chants that have been spiritualized, particularly by great saints, have a heightened power to inspire whoever sings them.

One chant we sang that day was "Cloud-colored Christ, come! O my Christ, O my Christ, Jesus Christ, come!" I found it marvelously effective for taking me deep into meditation. Periods of chanting alternated with increasingly longer periods of meditation. Sometimes, to alleviate any physical tension we might be feeling, Master asked us to stand as we chanted; for some of the more rhythmic chants he had us clap our hands. A couple of times he requested Jane Brush to play devotionally inspiring pieces on the organ.

At some time during that afternoon Master had a vision of the Divine Mother. In an ecstatic state he related Her wishes to many of those present. Some he told to give themselves unreservedly to God. Others he informed that the Cosmic Mother had blessed them specially. And then he spoke to Her directly, out loud so that we might hear one side, at least, of this blissful communion.

"Oh, You are so beautiful!" he repeated over and over. "Don't go!" he cried at last. "You say the material desires of these people are driving you away? Oh, come back! Please don't go!"

The meditation that day was so deep that the customary ten-minute recess halfway through it was omitted. The apprehension I had felt at the outset proved a delusion. "The soul loves to meditate," Master told us. It is the ego, in its attachment to body-consciousness, that resists entering the vastness within.

On Christmas Day we exchanged gifts in the traditional manner. Included with a more serious present that I gave Master was a "Slinky" toy, in memory of that incident of the toy pistols at Twenty-Nine Palms. In return, I received from him a four-color pencil—"To split infinitives with!" he told me, smiling.

This day had, for its main feature, an afternoon banquet at which Master presided. I helped to serve the curry dinner. Afterwards Master addressed us. The sweetness of his speech so charmed me that I felt as though I were living in heaven. Never had I thought such divine inspiration possible on this, our prosaic earth.

The following day Master gave Kriya Yoga initiation—primarily, if not entirely, to the renunciates. As I approached him for his blessing, I prayed mentally for his help in developing divine love. After he'd touched me at the Christ center, I opened my eyes to find him smiling at me blissfully.

Toward the end of the initiation ceremony, Master said, "Lots of angels have passed through this room today." And then these thrilling words of promise: "Of those present, there will be a few *siddha*s, and quite a few *jivan mukta*s."*

On New Year's Eve we gathered for a midnight meditation, again led by Master, in the main chapel. At one point during the proceedings he softly beat a large gong, then gradually increased and decreased the volume, in waves. "Imagine this as the sound of *Aum,*" he told us, "spreading outward to infinity."

At the same time, one hundred miles away in Encinitas, another group of disciples was meditating in the main room of the hermitage. They, too, heard the gong that Master was striking. One of the monks later told me, "It was as though someone were beating it in the hallway just outside the room."

The meditation that followed at Mt. Washington was enthralling.

Midnight came. Suddenly, waves of noise swept upward from the city below, and inward from the surrounding neighborhood: factory whistles, car horns, shouts. Countless celebrants were ushering in the New Year. A neighbor's door opened, and a voice screamed desperately into the night: "Happy New Year!"

How pathetic those festive tones, compared to the soul-joy we were experiencing in our little chapel! And how blessed, I reflected, how wonderfully happy I was to be in this holy place—at the feet of my divine guru! I prayed that the New Year would bring me an ever deepening awareness of God's love.

---

* A *jivan mukta* is one who has become freed of delusion, but who still has past karma to overcome. A *siddha* has become freed of all traces of past karma as well.

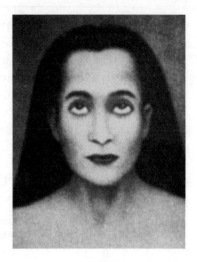

Jesus Christ   **Babaji**

Our Line of Gurus

"In the divine plan," Paramhansa Yogananda stated, "Jesus Christ was responsible for the evolution of the West, and Krishna (later Babaji), for that of the East. It was intended that the West specialize in developing objectively, through logic and reason, and that the East specialize in inner, intuitive develpment. But in the cosmic plan the time has come to combine these two lines into one. East and West must unite."

Jesus Christ *(above left)*. Master said to me once, at Twenty-Nine Palms, "What a pity that none of the pictures of Jesus Christ really look like him." This painting by Hoffman was the one he preferred, because it resembled the Galilean master better than most.

Babaji *(above right)*. Babaji is known as *Mahavatar,* or Great Incarnation.

Lahiri Mahasaya *(opposite page, upper left)*. Disciple of Babaji. Paramhansa Yogananda described him as a *Yogavatar,* or Incarnation of Yoga.

Swami Sri Yukteswar *(opposite page, upper right)*. Disciple of Lahiri Mahasaya. Paramhansa Yogananda described him as a *Gyanavatar,* or Incarnation of Wisdom.

Paramhansa Yogananda *(opposite page, bottom)*. Disciple of Sri Yuikteswar. Rajarsi Janakananda, Yogananda's foremost disciple, bestowed on his guru the title *Premavatar,* or Incarnation of Love.

Sri Krishna, India's ancient avatar, and first in our line of gurus, is shown on page 422.

Lahiri Mahasaya

Swami Sri Yukteswar

Paramhansa Yogananda

The monks' retreat at Twenty-Nine Palms.

The swimming pool at Master's retreat, Twenty-Nine Palms, built mostly by Norman and me.

Paramhansa Yogananda in the 1920s.

CHAPTER 21

Paramhansa Yogananda

ON JANUARY 5th, the disciples gathered at Mt. Washington to celebrate Paramhansa Yogananda's birthday. As the function began, we went up to him individually and knelt for his blessing. After a banquet, later, he spoke of his longing to see an awakening of divine love throughout the world. In a more personal vein he continued:

"I never dreamt, during my first years of teaching in this country, that such a fellow-feeling in God's love would be possible here. It exists only because you have lived up to the ideals that I have cherished, and which I lived for in the company of my great guru."

Friendship in God, surely, was the key to our relationship with him. It implied no easy-going relationship, such as worldly people enjoy with one another, but rather demanded of us the utmost. The friendship our guru extended to us was to our souls. To reciprocate in kind meant to strive ever to meet him on that divine level. Those who clung to the desire for ego-gratification could not coax from him a compromise in the pure quality of his friendship for us. If a disciple flattered him, Master would gaze at him quietly as if to say, "I will not desecrate the love I bear you by accepting this level of communication." Always he held out to us the highest ideal to which each of us might aspire. Such perfect love imposes the most demanding of all disciplines, for it asks nothing less of the disciple, ultimately, than the total gift of himself to God.

I used to pray to Master, "Teach me to love you as you love me." Chatting with a group of us one day in the main office, he looked at me penetratingly and said, "How can the little cup expect to hold the whole ocean of love? First it has to expand and become as big as the ocean!"

The Indian Scriptures state that when the soul releases its hold on egoism, it merges into the ocean of Spirit and becomes one with it. While most of us loved Master from varying degrees of ego-consciousness, his love for us was without limit, cosmic. To ordinary human beings, such love is inconceivable. "I killed Yogananda long ago," he said. "No one dwells in this temple now but God." His love for us was God's love, manifested through his human form.

"Whenever I look at you," Norman once wrote Master in a note, "I see only the Divine Mother."

"Then behave accordingly," Master replied calmly when next they met. This was no modest disclaimer, but only an impersonal acceptance of things as they were. Yogananda was the humblest man I ever knew, yet it was humility only in the sense that there was no ego in him at all, not in the sense that his manner was self-deprecating. Indeed, when someone once praised him for his humility, I recall his simple answer: "How can there be humility, when there is no consciousness of ego?" In essence, our relationship with him was not only a friendship *in* God, but *with* God, whose love alone permeated him. Always, with firm resolution, he turned toward the Divine all the love that we gave him. Whenever we touched his feet, in the manner customary among Indian disciples to their guru, he held his right hand reverently at his forehead, extending the fingers upward, to indicate that he directed our devotion to God. And if ever our affection for him displayed the slightest attachment, he would become distant and reserved until we had understood that it was God's love alone that he extended to us.

Daya Mata tells a story dating back to when she was a teenager, and new on the path. At first, in her association with Master, he had treated her lovingly, like a daughter. But once her feet were planted firmly on the path, he prepared to teach her the superior merits of impersonal love. To her now, feeling for him as she did the affection of a devoted daughter, he seemed all at once distant, even stern.

One evening in Encinitas, he addressed her with what seemed unusual aloofness. She went out onto the bluff behind the hermitage, and prayed deeply for understanding. At last she reached a firm resolution. "Divine Mother," she vowed, "from now on I will love only Thee. In beholding him, I will see Thee alone."

Suddenly she felt as though a great weight had been lifted from her. Later she went indoors and knelt before Master for his blessing, as she always did before retiring for the night. This time he greeted her gently with the words, "Very good!"

From then on he showed himself once more affectionate toward her. But now their relationship was on a far deeper level, for the disciple saw him now in that impersonal light in which he beheld himself.

For us who came years later, it was an inspiration to see between Daya Mata and Master a friendship truly divine. Such, too, was the friendship that he extended to each of us, though few, alas, ever came to appreciate so fully the extraordinary sensitivity of his gift. Each of us struggled in his own way to reconcile the apparent contradiction between this kindest, most considerate of friends, as he so often showed himself to be, and one who was willing on the other hand to subject us to painful lessons. For though we knew the lessons were for our good, too often it was a good that awaited us beyond the limits of our present understanding. Yet in fact the contradiction lay in ourselves: between the petty demands of our egos for comfort and reassurance, and our souls' uncompromising call to inner perfection. Master himself was completely self-integrated. Living in the impersonal Spirit made him in no way indifferent to human pain. Both levels, the human and the divine, were to him parts of a single reality—the human merely its limited, outward manifestation.

He once told us, "I prefer to work with love. I just wilt when I have to work in other ways." I myself noted, whenever he scolded me, the deep regret in his eyes at my lack of understanding, which had made his reprimand necessary. But he reassured us, "I scold only those who listen. I won't scold those who don't." It wasn't that he *couldn't* relate to us on a human level. Rather it was that, for those who wanted the most precious gift of all that he had to bestow—the knowledge of God—he knew he had to destroy all our attachments to ego.

With other people—and with us, too, when he chose to relax his discipline—he was, I think, as charming, warm-hearted, and utterly delightful a human being as ever lived. In the truest and best sense of the word he was a *noble* man. Because his self-integration was flawless, divine perfection reflected itself even in his casual behavior. To some, also, he showed complete approval and acceptance: to those who were able to relate to him purely in God.

To hear him talk informally with such disciples was deeply inspiring. I think what struck me most about his relationship with them was its quiet dignity, its foundation in the deepest mutual respect. When they laughed together, it was as though they shared some deep, inner joy, of which laughter was but a fleeting, outward expression, and by no means a necessary one. Manifestly, their deepest communion together was in silence.

The more I attuned myself to Master, the more deeply I came to appreciate the transcendent beauty of this inner friendship. It was a communion that needed no outward proximity to confirm it. Blessed with it, one even rejoiced when others endeavored to set themselves higher than oneself in the Guru's esteem. For one knew that egoic approval had nothing to do with that attunement.

In some ways it was, I think, his utter respect for others that impressed me about Master the most deeply. It always amazed me that one whose wisdom and power inspired so much awe in others could be at the same time so humbly respectful to every one. I had always considered respect to be something one gave only where it was due. And in a sense, of course, Master gave it in that spirit, too, but in his case it meant showing the deepest respect to *all,* because he saw them all as God's children. As Master said once to Dr. Lewis, his first disciple in America, "Remember, God loves you just as much as He loves me. He is our common Father."

Sometime during my second year at Mt. Washington a man came from India with a letter of introduction to Master. He asked permission to stay in the ashram two or three days. To everyone's inconvenience, those "two or three days" extended to many weeks. Soon after his arrival he sent Master a complaining note. The food, it seemed, was too Western for his tastes; would Paramhansaji kindly rectify the matter? Master quietly arranged for Indian-style food to be sent to him from his own kitchen.

I once saw Master chat with a group of Indians after a public performance in Pasadena. One man in the group was, as the saying goes, "feeling no pain." Affecting great familiarity in his drunkenness, he threw an arm around Master's shoulders and shouted playfully, as though the two of them were old drinking buddies. Debi, who was standing nearby, made some disparaging remark in Bengali.

"Don't," Master replied, shaking his head a little sternly. In his eyes this man, regardless of his temporary condition, deserved the respect due to a child of God.

A certain religious teacher in Los Angeles, a woman of considerable worldly means, once helped the Master's work financially, and behaved consequently as if she owned him. Master, as unbuyable a person as ever lived, continued to act only as God guided him from within. Gradually the woman developed toward him a sense of possessive jealousy, and on several occasions spoke venomously to him, and hurled such insults as would have made any ordinary man her enemy. But Master remained unalterably calm and respectful toward her. Never sharp in his replies, ever kind, he was like a fruit tree in bloom which, when an axe is laid to its roots, showers its attacker with sweet-smelling blossoms. The lady gradually developed the highest regard for him. She praised him to others, and often took her friends and students to visit his centers. All her anger and jealousy were converted into ungrudging esteem.

In Ranchi, India, I was told a touching story dating back to Master's return there in 1935. It seems an anniversary banquet was planned at his school. Someone was needed to preside over the function and give it official standing. The name of Gurudas Bannerji, a prominent judge, was recommended. Widely esteemed, this man was, as everyone agreed, the best possible choice. Master went to invite him.

What was his surprise, then, when the judge coldly refused to come. He knew all about India's so-called "holy men," he said; he was looking at a typical example of them right before him. They were insincere, after people's money, a drain on the community. He had no time to speak for their worthless causes.

Master, though astonished at this reception, remained unruffled. As he often told us, "Praise cannot make me any better, nor blame any worse. I am what I am before my conscience and God." After hearing the judge out he replied in a friendly tone, "Well, perhaps you'll reconsider. We should be greatly honored if you would come."

The principal of a local school agreed to preside in the judge's stead. When everyone had assembled that evening for the banquet, and the affair was about to begin, a car drove up. Out stepped the caustic judge. Because Gurudas Bannerji was such a prominent figure in those parts, the school principal readily offered up his own place to him.

Following the banquet, there were several preliminary reports. One dealt with the school's growth, and the number of students who had gone on after graduation to become monks and religious teachers. "If the present trend continues," the report read, "soon all of India will be full of our teachers spreading the ancient wisdom of our land."

It then came the judge's turn to speak. Rising, he said: "Today is one of the happiest days of my life. This morning your Swami Yogananda came to visit me. I felt great joy when I beheld him, but I decided to test him to see whether he was really as good a man as he looked. I addressed him as rudely as I knew how. Yet he remained so calm, and answered me so kindly, that I tell you in all sincerity he passed my test better than I would have dreamed possible. And I will tell you something more: Never mind the numbers of your graduates who are becoming monks. India has many monks. But if you can produce even one such man as this, not your school only, nor only our city, but our whole country will be glorified!"

One of my brother disciples, acting under the spell of a violent delusion, once wrote Master a long letter filled with scathing criticism for what he imagined to be Master's faults. The letter announced his intention of leaving the ashram immediately. He must have seen his error, subsequently, for he remained. One day, shortly after writing that letter, he was standing with a group of us when Master came downstairs. Seeing him, Master remarked, "You should take up writing. That was the best letter Satan ever wrote me." Master's voice, free of all resentment, held a note of genuine admiration.

But his humility didn't prevent him from giving a strong reply, sometimes, if he felt one might prove helpful. An orthodox minister once, incensed at the presence of a genuine "heathen" in this our most Christian land, and especially perturbed because the Master wouldn't endorse certain of his more narrow dogmas, shouted at him, "You will go to hell!"

Master, seeing the anger that was etched at that moment on the man's face, replied amiably, "Well I may get there by and by, but *you* are there already!"

Wonderful as Master's quality of universal respect was, it might be supposed that it entailed at least one disadvantage: an inability to see the funny side of what is often called the human comedy. The supposition would be unwarranted. The truth is, I have never known anyone with a keener sense of the ridiculous. Master's capacity for merriment, as we see from the foregoing story, was lively enough to remain undaunted even when faced with what might be termed the "ultimate denunciation." Under similar circumstances, most people would have been reduced to humorless indignation.

In the case of that fanatical minister, Master had a lesson to impart to him. But he never made fun of others if he thought it might inflict unnecessary pain on them. Herein, indeed, lay a fundamental difference between his sense of humor and most people's.

For that performance at Pasadena, which I mentioned earlier, our presumptuous guest from India had somehow managed to seize star billing as a Hindu dancer. As far as I know the only actual "dancing" he'd ever done was in the boxing ring, where he'd managed to achieve some sort of fame. But his large physique was impressive. When he announced that he intended to dance, it was taken by all that he meant business.

His performance that evening portrayed a deer being stalked by a hunter. Playing both roles himself, he alternately lumbered through his representation of the deer as it gamboled playfully about in forest glades, and stalked ferociously through tall grasses as the hunter. Presently it became evident that he wasn't keeping step with the music. This realization finally dawned on him, also, and only one explanation would do: Obviously, the orchestra wasn't following *him*. Indignantly instructing the players to cease and desist, he strode down to the footlights and apologized to the audience for their lack of musicianship.

"They aren't professionals," he explained solemnly. Thereafter, whenever his "playful gamboling" took him past where they sat, ranged against the back of the stage, he would wave his hands and exhort them in a fierce undertone to play better.

Master and I, seated together, were in paroxysms of mirth. Tears streamed down our cheeks, though we managed fairly well to keep from laughing aloud. "Don't!" squeaked Master unsteadily when I let slip a muffled guffaw.

Well, the hunter finally got his deer, but this wasn't the end by any means. The poor creature then had to be portrayed writhing about the stage in incredible agonies. After many minutes it sighed its last. There followed a little scattered applause—less, I'm sure, from a desire to congratulate the artist than as an expression of relief. But our relief was premature: The hunter was still alive! Leaping up now in this role, he flung the deer over his shoulders and began a sort of victory cakewalk. Already we knew he had no sense of timing. Now it appeared he also lacked a sense of *time*. At any rate, his performance gave every evidence of being planned to embrace eternity. Through tears of laughter, finally, we saw one of the musicians glance offstage and make a lowering motion with his hand. The curtain began to fall. The hunter, poised in yet another victory stance, saw it coming. Angrily he turned. The last we saw of him was his legs from the knees downward, striding purposefully off toward stage right to give the hapless stagehand a piece of his mind.

Master had laughed as heartily this evening as I ever saw him laugh. Yet he showed no inclination, afterward, to discomfit his guest. Such indeed is the nature of pure joy; though good-humored, it is always kindly. When the man complained later that evening of how he had been mistreated, Master's mood was gentle. Consolingly he said, "I understand." And he did, too. He understood all aspects of the matter. He could feel the man's indignation, and sympathize with it on its own level, though he knew it was founded on a delusion.

But then, it was his sympathy for all of us, in our multifarious delusions, that inspired his lifelong labor of teaching, counseling, and self-sacrifice on our behalf.

One day, in Chicago, a drunken stranger staggered up to Master and embraced him affectionately.

"Hello there, Jeshush Chrisht!"

Master smiled. Then, to give the man a taste of the infinitely better "spirits" he himself enjoyed, he looked deeply into the man's eyes.

"Shay," the fellow cried thickly, "whad're *you* drink'n'?"

"It has a lot of kick in it!" Master replied, his eyes twinkling. The man was sobered by this glance. "I left him wondering what had happened!" Master told us later.

It is particularly interesting that this man should have addressed Master as Jesus Christ, since the Master's olive-colored skin, black hair, and brown eyes didn't at all correspond to the popular, Nordic image of a blue-eyed, blond Jesus. Master, moreover, kept no beard.

A woman whom I once met at an SRF center meeting in New York described a similar reaction to that man's. "I bought a painting," she told me, "in a dusty old second-hand store. It was a portrait, but I didn't know who the subject was; I just knew his eyes inspired me. I used to think of him as Jesus Christ. Placing the painting on my mantelpiece, I prayed daily in front of it. Years later I came upon *Autobiography of a Yogi*. The moment I saw Master's photograph, I recognized him as the very man in that painting!"

Another woman, a member of our Hollywood congregation, told me, "I used to pray deeply to God to draw me closer to Him. One day I had a vision of someone I'd never seen before. A voice said, 'Christ is coming!' Shortly thereafter, a friend brought me to this church for the first time. Master was conducting the service. The moment I saw him, I said to my friend, 'Why, that's the very face I saw in my vision!'"

Another member of our Hollywood church told me, "Years before I knew anything about Master, my husband and I happened to catch a glimpse of him through a restaurant window. 'Look at that man!' I exclaimed. 'He must be the most spiritual human being I've ever seen!' Years later I met Master, and knew him immediately for that very man."

Even as a boy, the Master's magnetism was extraordinary. Dr. Nagendra Nath Das, a Calcutta physician and lifelong friend, visited Mt. Washington in July 1950. He told us, "Wherever Paramhansaji went, even as a boy, he attracted people. His father, a high railway official, often gave us travel passes. No matter where we traveled, within minutes after we'd got down from the train a group of boys would have gathered about us."

Part of the basis for Master's amazing charisma was the fact that, seeing his infinite Beloved in all human beings, he also awakened in them an inchoate faith in their own goodness. With the impersonality of true greatness, he never accepted the thought from others that he was essentially any different from them.

Bernard, upon whom Master had been urging some difficult undertaking, remonstrated one day, "Well, Sir, *you* can do it. You're a *master*."

"And what do you think *made* me a master?" the Guru demanded. "It was by *doing!* Don't cling to the thought of weakness if your desire is to become strong."

"There was a devotee," Master once told us, "who was sitting before the image of his guru, chanting and tossing flowers onto it as an expression of his devotion. His concentration became so deep that, suddenly, he beheld the whole universe contained within himself. 'Oh!' he cried, 'I have been putting flowers on another's image, and now I see that I, untouched by this body, am the Sustainer of the universe. I bow to myself!' And he began throwing the flowers onto his own head.

"Oh! when Master [Sri Yukteswar] told me that story I was so thrilled I went into *samadhi*.° That devotee wasn't speaking from ego. Rather he was rejoicing in the *death* of his ego."

This was the relationship that Master sought ever to establish with us: a relationship wherein we realized with our entire being that we, too, were That.

Leo Cocks, one of the young monks, for some time made a practice of taking photographs of Master every opportunity he could. The walls of his room ended up being almost papered with them.

"Why do you keep on taking photographs of this physical form?" Master demanded of him one day. "What is it but flesh and bones? Get to know me in meditation if you want to know who I really am!"

And once, when we were serving him, he remarked, "You all are so kind to me with your many attentions." Karle Frost, one of

---

° *Samadhi* (cosmic consciousness) is the state of infinite awareness that comes to the yogi once the hypnosis of ego has been broken. Christian saints have sometimes described this state as "mystical marriage," for in it the soul merges into God and becomes one with Him.

the disciples present, exclaimed, "Oh, no, Master. It is *you* who are kind to us!"

"God is helping God," Master replied with a sweet smile. "That is the nature of His cosmic drama."

The closer we drew to him spiritually, the less he sought to teach us by words. "I prefer to speak with the eyes," he once told me. He never wanted to *impose* his instruction on us from without. His method of teaching, rather, was to help us to dig wells of intuitive insight within ourselves. The closer we felt to him, the closer we came to knowing our own, true, Self: the God within.

CHAPTER 22

Renunciation

M Y SUDDEN CONVERSION to this totally unheralded way of life had the effect on my earthly family that a grenade might have if hurled unexpectedly into someone's home during a leisurely Sunday breakfast. My parents believed strongly in giving us children the freedom to follow our own lights, but even so, their concern for my happiness made them anything but indifferent to what struck them as a sudden plunge into insanity. Nor did I help matters much when, in my zeal of conversion, I endeavored to persuade them that my choice was the only sane one.

Some weeks after my arrival at Mt. Washington, I received a letter from Father Kernan, the associate minister at our Church of St. James the Less, in Scarsdale. Was I, he inquired sympathetically, in some emotional or spiritual difficulty? And was there anything I might like from him in the way of help or advice? I was touched by his considerateness, but replied that, if he really wanted to understand why I'd left the church, he might read *Autobiography of a Yogi*. Some months later he remarked to Mother, "We don't ask enough of people like Donald."

Next, some military officer came out (I don't recall his connection with my family), offered to help if he could, decided he couldn't, and left—presumably to report that at least I wasn't starving to death. Some time after that, Sue and Bud Clewell, relatives in Westwood Village (a suburb of Los Angeles), visited me with pleas that I not estrange myself from the family. My brother Bob wrote from New York to suggest that I might like to join him in some housing-development scheme. Dick, my youngest brother, wrote from Williams College, "Couldn't you have found what you wanted in one of the monastic orders of your own church?"

Bernard told me one day of his own experience—not with relatives in his case, but with erstwhile companions. "Shortly after I moved to Encinitas," he said, "a group of my old friends arrived, determined to kidnap and hold me forcibly until I agreed to give up this 'wild-eyed fanaticism'—in other words, to become, like them, a devotee of the dollar! Fortunately I wasn't around to receive them: Master had sent me that morning on some urgent errand to Mt. Washington. My friends, thwarted, soon abandoned their plan."

Whether by coercion or by love, it is not unusual for people who want to dedicate their lives to high ideals to encounter opposition from well-meaning friends and relatives. For between selfless idealism and worldliness there exists a fundamental incompatibility. Worldliness lives in the constant expectation of personal rewards and benefits, of desires satisfied, of value *received*. Idealism scorns personal benefit, renounces selfish desires, and views life rather in terms of value *given*. It finds its highest benefit in the very act of sacrifice, and considers that to be true gain which worldliness views only as loss. "Fanaticism," is the verdict commonly pronounced by worldly people on any but the most pallid expressions of idealism. And if, out of unconscious shame, that verdict isn't forthcoming, "ulterior motives" is the next charge. All the while, however, worldliness feels vaguely uneasy in the presence of selfless dedication, as though sensing in it some hidden threat to all that it holds dear. For the soul knows that its true home lies not in this world, but in infinity.

Perfect representatives of either side are, of course, rare. Worldliness and renunciation are qualities which people *manifest* in varying degrees, but no single human quality ever suffices to define an individual. Worldly people may even, on one side of their natures, applaud heroic self-sacrifice in others. And many, of course, are no strangers to self-sacrifice themselves; in fact—strange twist of human nature!—it is the worldly man, frequently, who most sternly censures the renunciate who falls from his ideals. And of course the renunciate, for his part, must do constant battle against worldly self-interest in himself.

But the fact remains that between worldliness and renunciation, considered as abstractions, there is not and can never be the slightest compatibility. As the Bible puts it, "Whosoever will be a friend of the world is the enemy of God."*

The renunciate's worldly friends and relatives would always prefer to see him keep his feet in both boats. Indeed, he, too, may legitimately show them love as children of God. But if he dwells *pleasurably* on the thought, "These are *my* people," or if he looks on

---

* James 4:4.

their worldliness with sympathetic favor, he places himself in real danger of losing his vocation. For one who stands in two boats may end up falling between them and drowning. Many a renunciate has abandoned his high ideals because he tried to reconcile in his own mind these two opposite worlds.

In the Biblical story of the Jews' exodus from Egypt lies a deep spiritual allegory. Only those Jews who had been born in the wilderness, out of captivity, were permitted to enter the Promised Land. With man, similarly, only those mental qualities which are born in the "wilderness" of meditative silence—qualities such as humility, devotion, and soul-joy, the gifts of divine grace—can be brought over into the "Promised Land" of divine union. Pride, anger, greed, lust—the offspring, in short, of man's bondage to ego—must die before God-consciousness can be attained. ("Blessed are the pure in heart," Jesus said, "for they *shall see God.*"*) Even a wise, discriminating ego—symbolized in this story by Moses†— though capable of leading one out of worldly captivity, and of shepherding one through the long process of spiritual purification, must eventually offer itself up into the infinite light. Moses was permitted to behold the Promised Land from afar, but he had to die before his people could enter and live there. As Jesus put it, "He who will lose his life [who will, in other words, offer it up] for my sake shall save it."§

The worldly person asks first of life, "What do *I* want?" The devotee asks only, "What does God want?" Renunciation is an inner state of consciousness, not an outward act. All those, whether married or single, who love God and want to know Him must reconcile themselves to living for Him alone. The pathway of the heart is too narrow for both the ego and God to walk it together; one of them must step aside and make way for the other. "Living for God," Yogananda said, "is martyrdom": martyrdom of the ego; martyrdom of self-will and selfishness; martyrdom of all that worldliness clings to so desperately. But the true devotee comes in time to see that this isn't martyrdom at all, since its end is joyous freedom in the only *true* Self: God. We are sons of the Infinite! Anything that binds us to a limited existence desecrates this divine image within us. Renunciation is no abject self-deprivation, but a glorious affirmation of the universe of joy that is our birthright.

---

* Matthew 5:8.
† Symbolism apart, Paramhansa Yogananda once told me that Moses was a true master.
§ Luke 9:24.

As St. John of the Cross put it:

> In order to arrive at having pleasure in everything,
>   Desire pleasure in nothing.
> In order to arrive at possessing everything,
>   Desire to possess nothing.
> In order to arrive at being everything,
>   Desire to be nothing.
> In order to arrive at the knowledge of everything,
>   Desire to know nothing.°

The essence of renunciation is to relinquish the clinging attitude of a beggar towards things, places, people, experiences—in short, the limitations of this world—and to offer oneself constantly at the feet of Infinity.

In the beginning of the spiritual life, especially, Yogananda told us, it is better to mix little or not at all with worldly people. For it is essential that one's heart be strengthened, in preparation for making this heroic gift to God of every desire, every thought, every feeling. No weakling could ever make so total a self-offering. Cowards quickly fall by the wayside. None who enter the spiritual path for its superficial glamour alone can survive tests that have no other purpose than to assault the devotee's every natural inclination. The more completely one can identify himself with the consciousness of complete self-surrender, the more likely he is to succeed in his spiritual search.

This is as true for householders as for monks and nuns. Outward renunciation merely helps to affirm the inner resolve, necessary for all devotees, to seek God alone.

In the Self-Realization Fellowship monasteries, Paramhansa Yogananda taught us boldly to claim our new identity as sons of God, rejecting all consciousness of worldly ties.

"Sir," I began one day, "my father...."

"You have no father!" Master peremptorily reminded me. "God is your Father."†

° This poem, incidentally, shows also the close correlation that exists between the mystical experiences of great Christian saints and those of great yogis. St. John's expressions—"possessing everything, being everything," etc.—are no mere metaphor. He is describing, quite literally, the state known to yogis as *samadhi,* or cosmic consciousness. In Chapter 33 many more such Christian corroborations are presented of the ancient yogic teachings.

† "While he yet talked to the people, behold, his mother and his brethren stood without, desiring to speak with him. Then one said unto him, Behold, thy mother and thy brethren stand without, desiring to speak with thee. But he answered and said unto him that told him, Who is my mother? and who are my brethren? And he stretched forth his hand toward his disciples, and said, Behold my mother and my brethren! For whosoever shall do the will of my Father

"I'm sorry, Sir. I meant, my *earthly* father."

"That's better," the Master replied, approvingly.

"Milk will not float on water," he often reminded us, "but mingles with it. Similarly, as long as your devotion is still 'liquid'— that is to say, untried—it may be diluted by worldly influences. You should therefore avoid such influences as much as possible. Only when the 'milk' of your consciousness has been churned into the 'butter' of divine realization will it float easily on the water of this world, and remain unaffected by it."

"The mind of the worldly man," he once said, "is like a sieve, riddled with desires, distractions and worries. It is impossible for a person in such a state of mind to gather and hold the milk of peace."

Master was compassionate toward those who were weak, and never sought to impose on any of us ideals that were beyond our reach. Rather, he took each of us as we were, and tried to guide us from that point onward. Thus, even in the monasteries, disciples sometimes mistook his kindness and encouragement for leniency, and never realized how drastic was the inner revolution to which he was actually calling them. He would be satisfied with nothing less than the total destruction of our mental limitations. The more we gave to God of ourselves, the more he, encouraged by our willingness, demanded of us. I always smiled when I met people who defined his love for them in terms of the little things he had given them or done for them, outwardly. The real definition of his love for us lay not in what he gave to us, except spiritually, but in what he took from us. His real purpose was not to tidy up our little mud puddles of delusion and make them more comfortable to sit in. It was to take us out of those mud puddles altogether. If, in the process, this meant subjecting us to temporary pain, he flinched no more from that task than a conscientious doctor would in trying to cure his patients of serious physical ailments.

On the subject of renunciation, especially, there was often in Master's manner a certain sternness, as though to impress on us that the staunchness of our dedication to God was, for each one of us, a matter of spiritual life or death.

Daya Mata tells the story of how, as a girl, she once asked Master whether he thought she ought to go out and find work to support her needy mother. Instead of the sympathetic reply she expected, Master cried, "Go on! Get out of here this minute!"

---

which is in heaven, the same is my brother, and sister, and mother" (Matthew 12:46–50).

"Master," she begged him tearfully, "I don't want to leave here. This is my entire life!"

"That's better," he replied, very gently. "You have given your life to God, renouncing all worldly ties. The responsibility for your mother is His now."

On Yogananda's invitation, the mother came to live at Mt. Washington. She remained there as a dedicated nun until her death some forty years later.

Soon after that scolding, Master began referring to Daya Mata affectionately as his "nest egg." For it was from her arrival that he dated the beginning of his monastic order.

Nothing won Master's approval so much as the willingness to renounce all for God. But renunciation, to him, meant an inner act of the heart; outward symbols he viewed more tentatively, as potential distractions to sincerity. In Phoenix, Arizona, a raggedly dressed, unkempt man once boasted to him, "I'm a renunciate." Yogananda replied, "But you are bound again—by your attachment to disorder!" For this present age, prejudiced as it is against many aspects of the spiritual life, he counseled only moderate adoption of the outward symbols of renunciation. Perhaps he felt that more extreme austerities might attract too much attention to themselves, and thus feed the very ego which the renunciate was striving to overcome. Much, for example, as he loved St. Francis of Assisi, and referred to him affectionately as his "patron saint," he often said, "St. Francis loved Lady Poverty, but I prefer Lady Simplicity." Renunciation, to him, was not a matter of where one's body is, nor of how it is clothed, but of inner, mental purity. "Make your heart a hermitage," he counseled us. It was not so much that he rejected outward forms; some of them, indeed, he favored. But his concern was that we use them to *internalize* our devotion.

Monasteries, like any human institution, have a tendency to involve their members outwardly in communal affairs. To some extent, of course, this is necessary, but Yogananda urged us even in our monastic life to remain somewhat apart from others.

"Don't mix with others too closely," he recommended to us one evening. "The desire for outward companionship is a reflection of the soul's inward desire for companionship with God. But the more you seek to satisfy that desire outwardly, the more you will lose touch with the inner, divine Companion, and the more restless and dissatisfied you will become."

Frequently he held up to us examples of saints who had remained aloof even from fellow devotees. "Seclusion," he told us, "is the price of greatness." Though mental withdrawal may not make one popular with less dedicated devotees (Daya Mata, who lived that way through her early training, soon found herself dubbed "the half-baked saint"), it is a shortcut to God.

Disciples seeking Master's help in overcoming delusion received loving encouragement and sympathetic counsel from him in return.

"If the sex drive were taken away from you," he told a group of monks one evening, "you would see that you had lost your greatest friend. You would lose all interest in life. Sex was given to make you strong. If a boxer were to fight only weaklings, he too, in time, would grow weak. It is by fighting strong men that he develops strength. The same is true in your struggle with the sex instinct. The more you master it, the more you will find yourself becoming a lion of happiness."

The three greatest human delusions, he used to say, are sex, wine (by which he meant intoxicants of all kinds), and money. I once asked him to help me overcome attachment to good food. He smiled gaily.

"Don't worry about those little things. When ecstasy comes, everything goes!"

But where the principal delusions were concerned he was very serious, and worked with infinite patience to help us overcome them.

The desire for money he contrasted with the joys of non-attachment and simple living. "Renounce attachment to all things," he told us, "even to the fruits of your action. Don't work with the thought of what you might get out of it. What comes of itself, let it come. Work to serve God, and for the supreme satisfaction of pleasing Him."

Related to the desire for money is the ambition for worldly power and recognition. "Realize," Master said, "that God's is the only power in the universe. In all your actions, see Him alone as the Doer; seek to please only Him." He added, "Worldly power, fame, and riches are like prostitutes: loyal to no one. Only God will stand by you loyally forever."

The desire for "wine" Master related to the soul's deep-seated longing to escape pain and suffering, and to reclaim its lost inheritance of bliss in God. "Pseudo-ecstasy," he labeled all intoxicants— even the "intoxicant" of too much sleep. He urged his students to escape the delusions of worldly life, not by dulling their minds to its sorrows, but by rising above them in the higher "intoxication" of soul-joy. "Meditate," he urged us. "The more you taste God's joy within you, the less taste you will have for those mere masquerades of ecstasy."

In fact, I knew a disciple who at one time had been an alcoholic. He took Kriya Yoga initiation from Master, and thereafter practiced the technique—quite literally!—with a bottle of whiskey in one hand, and his prayer beads in the other. In time he found so much enjoyment in Kriya Yoga practice that one day, halfway through his meditation, he set the bottle disdainfully aside, and never touched it again.

In sex-desire Master saw not merely the physical, procreative instinct, but the soul's longing for union with God manifested in the need for a human mate. It was to this unitive urge that he usually addressed himself when referring to the sex instinct. Romanticists in his audiences sometimes objected to the cheerful irreverence with which he often treated the "tender passion." But Yogananda was particularly not interested in feeding people's illusions: It was his goal to demolish them.

"Marriage," he once told a church congregation, "is seldom the beautiful thing it is commonly pictured to be. I smile when I think of the usual movie plot. The hero is so handsome, and the heroine so lovely, and after all kinds of troubles they finally get married and (so we are supposed to believe) live 'happily ever after.' And then I think, 'Yes, with rolling pins and black eyes!' But of course, the producers hurriedly finish the story before it can get to that part!"

"Remember," he advised us once, "it is the Divine Mother who tests you through sex. And it is She also who blesses, when you pass Her test." He counseled his male disciples to look upon women as living embodiments of the Divine Mother. "They are disarmed," he said, "when you view them in that light." I was never present when he counseled women disciples in these matters, but I think his suggestions must have been based on encouraging in them similar attitudes of respect—perhaps to see reflected in men the Heavenly Father, or the Cosmic Teacher. For only by deep, divine respect for one another can men and women win final release from the magnetic attraction that draws them to seek fulfillment in outer, not in inner, *divine* union.

In the monastery, as I have mentioned earlier, Master permitted the monks and nuns no social communication with one another. When the necessities of work demanded contact between them, he counseled them not to look at one another, especially avoiding communication with the eyes, and to keep their conversation as brief and impersonal as possible. So strict was he that he even discouraged many of the normally accepted courtesies that men and women extend to one another. I remember one day, when Master and I were standing out of doors near the entrance to his Twenty-Nine Palms retreat, a young nun came to the door from the car, laden with packages. Observing that she was having difficulty in opening the door, I went over and opened it for her.

"You should not have done that," Master told me, after she had gone inside. "Keep your distance," he added, "and they will always respect you."

It is only when one strives to *overcome* delusion that one discovers its primal power. "As soon as the first thought of sex arises," Master said, "that is the time to catch it." Worldly people scoff at what they consider such exaggerated precautions. "It's absurd," I've heard them exclaim, "to suggest that every time I look at a member of the opposite sex I'm going to feel tempted!" But basic attraction, which may find outward expression sooner or later toward the "right" person, and which in any case can distract the heart from one-pointed devotion to God, begins long before the stirrings of any noticeable attraction to one human being. Its root lies in an instinctive pleasure in the mere abstraction "man," or, "woman." It affects all ages. A woman once told me that her little daughter, while still a toddler, had a special giggle that she affected only in the presence of little boys. It was to this deep, instinctive, and generally not specifically directed response that Yogananda was most particularly referring when he spoke of tracing temptation to its "first thought." Years of introspection have taught me that if one can catch this subtle first response—so rarely even noticed by most people—and immediately impersonalize it, the thought of such attraction virtually vanishes from the mind. But even then one must be careful. "One is not safe from delusion," Yogananda said, "until he has attained the highest, *nirbikalpa, samadhi.*"

Rejection of the world is only the negative side of devotion. Master's usual emphasis was positive. "Nothing can touch you," he told us, "if you inwardly love God." Nevertheless, there is a beauty in the act of utter self-offering to God that makes renunciation, even in its more limited, negative aspect, one of the most heroic and noble callings possible to man.

Bernard told me of one occasion when a visitor from India came to see Paramhansa Yogananda. The man was received by Sister Gyanamata, and had the poor grace to treat her condescendingly—as though, in serving her guru, she were only Master's servant. Later, inspired by his interview with Master, he apologized to her.

"In India," he said, "we are taught to respect all women as wives and mothers. Forgive me, please, that I failed to pay you that respect earlier." Smilingly he concluded, "I offer it to you now."

Sister Gyanamata, in her usual impersonal manner, replied, "At least half the people in the world are women. Most of them sooner or later become mothers. There is nothing in either fact that merits any special respect. But you may, if you wish, pay respect to the fact that in this life I have become a renunciate."

The visitor could only bow. For renunciation of egoic desires and attachments is, ultimately, the stepping stone for all people, whether married or single, to rediscovery of that divine image within, which alone gives man importance in the greater scheme of things.

CHAPTER 23

God Protects His Devotees

Norman entered the dining room one day at lunchtime looking stunned.

"This morning," he announced shakily, "I was driving the big flat-bed truck down Mt. Washington. As I came to the steepest part of the hill, I stepped on the brake to slow down for that hairpin turn at the bottom, but my foot went right to the floor! I pumped frantically; nothing happened. By this time the truck was going so fast I couldn't shift down. In moments I knew I'd be hurtling to my death over the edge of that steep embankment. Desperately I prayed to Master: 'Is this what you want?'

"Suddenly the truck slowed to a complete stop! The brakes still weren't working, but I was able to park safely in gear and curb the front wheel.

"What a blessing," Norman concluded, "to have a God-realized master for a guru!"

As disciples of a great yogi, we often found that we had only to call Master mentally for misfortune to be speedily averted.

A year before Norman's miraculous escape, Jerry Torgerson, another disciple, hitchhiked into Los Angeles. This mode of travel was contrary to Master's advice, but Jerry, like many other young Americans, had been practically raised on hitchhiking; more than Master's casual proscription was needed, evidently, to get him to change his habits.

"Three guys picked me up," he told us. "We were riding along, when suddenly—how, I couldn't say—I *knew* they were criminals. 'I want to get out right here,' I told them. But they wouldn't stop. After some distance we left the main road, and drove through open countryside to a secluded house. One of the men got out; the other two stayed in the car with me. I didn't know what they had in mind, but I can tell you I was plenty scared. I started praying to Master for help.

"Well, the first guy went and knocked at the front door. No answer. He went around the house, knocking and calling at every door and window. Still no answer. By this time the two men in the car were getting worried. 'Let's get outa here!' they called out nervously. The first fellow came back, just as nervous as they were. We all drove back to the main road, and there they let me out. The moment I'd slammed the door behind me, they rushed off at high speed.

"I never did find out what they had in mind, but I had the strong impression that they were planning to use me in some crime.

"I said nothing to anyone about all this. After church the following Sunday, I went up to Master for his blessing. The moment he saw me, he scolded, 'You see, Jerry? I *told* you not to hitchhike! I had to close the ears of all the people in that house so they wouldn't hear that man when he called to them.' "

Some months later, Joe Carbone and Henry Schaufelberger (now Brothers Bimalananda and Anandamoy) were plastering the lotus tower that forms the archway entrance to the SRF church grounds in Hollywood. Joe was mixing and carrying the plaster. Henry, at a height of about twenty feet, was troweling it onto the wall. The ladder Joe was using was set at too steep an angle. On one climb, as he reached up to grasp the top rung, he missed it. The heavy hod on his shoulder began pulling him backward; he could no longer grasp the rung with either hand. A twenty-foot drop with all that weight on his shoulder might very well have killed him. Realizing that it was now too late to save himself, Joe thought urgently of Master; aloud, he chanted, "Om!"

Both men later testified as to what happened next. As Joe was chanting, some invisible force pushed him slowly back upright. A moment later he was able to grasp the rung again. Gasping with relief, he completed his climb.

Andy Anderson, the foreman on this job, was a professional carpenter and builder who had been hired from outside to oversee our work. He knew nothing of our philosophy, and often chuckled at the thought of working with "all these yogis!" But there was no doubt in his voice when he told me of how he had witnessed an uncanny instance of protection:

"Why you guys don't all get killed on this job beats me. You just aren't careful enough. I was standing right over there one day, when someone on a scaffold dropped a long two-by-four—without even looking below him! Another of you yogis was standing underneath, for all I could tell not even minding his *own* business! The two-by-four struck the ground at such an angle that it couldn't possibly have missed him as it fell over. It might've killed him.

"'Look out!' I hollered. Just then that two-by-four—leaning in *his* direction, mind you—stood back upright and, so help me, *fell over in the opposite direction!* I *know* I wasn't just seeing things."

Andy ended up becoming a lay-disciple himself.

James Coller told us of another hitchhiking incident, one in which he and another monk gave a man a ride. The two monks were in the front seat. "When we picked this man up," James said, "there was no room for him in front, so he sat in the back. Some minutes later, as we were driving along, I suddenly heard a voice in my inner ear: 'Look out! He has a knife!' I turned around quickly. The man was leaning forward, a fiendish expression on his face. His hand was upraised, holding a knife; he was on the very point of striking the boy beside me, who was gazing ahead unsuspectingly.

"'Put that knife down!' I commanded sternly. The man was so astonished he obeyed me. I stopped the car. He got out without a word."

In the almost thirty years that I have been on this path, I cannot recall to mind a single instance where a disciple of Paramhansa Yogananda has failed to find protection in time of real need. Considering the length of time involved, and the thousands of disciples I have known during this period, this is quite an amazing record.

The most striking of these cases occurred among those whose lives were placed unreservedly in the Guru's care. Dr. Lewis told of an episode similar to Norman's, when, on a cold winter night in Massachusetts, he had been out driving. With him were two fellow disciples, Mrs. Laura Elliott and Mrs. Alice Hasey (Sister Yogmata). Suddenly, as they approached a narrow bridge, they found their way blocked by another car that had skidded sidewise across the icy road. A crash seemed inevitable.

"At that moment," Dr. Lewis said, "we felt as if a giant hand were being pressed down on the hood of the car. We slowed instantly to a stop, our car still safely on the road."

Señor J. M. Cuaron, the leader of the SRF center in Mexico City, related the following incident to me.

"I was badly in need of a job, but for a long time could find none anywhere. Then one day an excellent offer came from a company in Matamoros. Taking that job would mean moving away from Mexico City. I therefore wrote Master to request his permission to put the SRF center in someone else's charge. My letter was just a formality. I was sure Master would congratulate me on my good luck. Imagine my surprise, then, when he replied *by telegram:*

'No. Absolutely not. Under no circumstances whatever accept that job.' I'll admit I was a bit upset. But even so, I obeyed him.

"One month later the news came out in the papers: The company that had offered me that job was exposed for fraud. Its officers were sent to prison, including the man who had taken the post I'd been offered. He hadn't been aware of the firm's dishonesty, just as I wouldn't have been. But because of the position he held, he was imprisoned. It was only by Master's grace that I was spared that calamity!"

Tests there must be in life, of course. They come especially on the spiritual path, for if devotees are to escape the coils of *maya* (delusion), they must be taught the lessons they need to develop in wisdom. Master didn't shrink from giving us whatever tests we needed to grow. For example, although on that occasion he saved Señor Cuaron from ignominious arrest, he never helped him to find the employment he so badly wanted. Señor Cuaron in fact had enough money to live on simply, as became a world-renouncing yogi. Master saw no good reason, evidently, to help him return to his former levels of opulence.

But our tests were always blessings; outright misfortune Master spared us. And where a test was not required for a disciple's spiritual growth, Master often removed it from his path altogether.

I remember how he "de-jinxed" a student—not a close disciple—who was having trouble earning money. It was Jean Haupt's brother, Richard. Not long after Master's intercession, the man became quite well-to-do.

In 1955 I went to Switzerland on a lecture tour. There I met a lady from Czechoslovakia who told me a story concerning Professor Novicky, the late leader of a small SRF group in Prague.

"One day," she said, "after Yogananda's passing, a stranger came to Professor Novicky and requested instruction in yoga. The professor didn't know what to do. Normally he kept his spiritual activities a secret, so as not to expose himself to persecution. If this man was a genuine seeker, the professor would want to help him. But if he was a government spy, any admission of interest in yoga might result in a prison sentence. Our friend prayed for guidance. Suddenly, standing behind the self-proclaimed 'devotee,' Paramhansa Yogananda appeared. Slowly the Master shook his head, then vanished. Professor Novicky told the man he had come to the wrong place for information. Sometime later, he learned that the man was indeed a government spy.

"I am free to tell this story now," my informant continued, "for the good professor died recently, of natural causes."

In January 1959 my own life was spared in a remarkable manner. The incident took place in India. I was preparing for a religious gathering in Dakshineswar, outside Calcutta, at which Daya Mata was to be the principal speaker. Part of my task was to set up the loud-speaker equipment. With both hands I grasped the microphone boom, to move it. Suddenly 230 volts of electricity shot through my body, lifting me right off the ground. Involuntarily I cried out. Such high voltage tightens the muscles, making it impossible to release anything one is holding. Unable as I'd have been to let go of the metal boom, I would certainly have been killed. But just at that moment, inexplicably, the fuse blew. The function was delayed half an hour till we located another fuse, but my life was spared. The only ill effect I suffered was a slight tremor in the heart that lasted two or three days.

Death must, of course, come to everyone sooner or later. But I have been struck by its beauty and dignity when it has visited disciples of this path.

A regular visitor to our Hollywood church died of a stroke. His wife later told me, "In his final moments, my husband whispered to me lovingly, 'Don't feel badly, dear. I am so happy! And I see a bright, bright light all around me.' "

Another church member, who had known the Master since his early years in America, exclaimed at the end of her life, "Swamiji is here!" Her face was radiant; she smiled blissfully.

And Sister Gyanamata's last words were, "Such joy! Too much joy! Too much joy!"

Disciples who have died of cancer or other painful diseases have gone peacefully, with a smile on their lips.

People often point to the sufferings of humanity as proof either that God doesn't exist, or that He doesn't care for His human children. Paramhansa Yogananda's answer to that charge was that people don't care enough about God to tune in to His help. Indeed, by their indifference they create the very problems which, later, they lay accusingly at His door. If in daylight one moves about with closed eyes, he may bump against something and hurt himself. By closing one's eyes to light, one creates his own darkness. By closing one's heart to love, one creates his own fear, hatred, or apathy. By closing one's soul to joy, one creates his own misery.

In case after case I have seen fulfilled Yogananda's promise that faithful devotees of his path would be protected. "For those who stay in tune to the end," he added, "I, or one of the other masters, will be there to usher them into the divine kingdom." Truly, the words of the great Swami Shankaracharya have found justification in Paramhansa Yogananda's life: "No known comparison exists in the three worlds for a true guru."

It is perhaps the greatest sign of God's aid to His devotees that, when the soul yearns deeply for Him, He sends to it the supreme blessing of a God-awakened master to guide it along the highway to Infinity.

CHAPTER 24

True Teaching Is Individual

O NE SOMETIMES HEARS the lament, "There are too many denominations in Christendom." Yet I dare say that even if there were only one, there would still be as many different forms of Christianity as there are Christians. For every man's understanding is conditioned by his own special experiences, his aspirations, his outlook on life—in short, by what he *is*. He might recite the Nicene Creed in church every Sunday, yet attach meanings to it that would surprise some of his fellow worshipers. In reciting the Lord's Prayer, children have been heard to say, "Give us this day our jelly bread," and, "Lead us not into Penn Station." We smile at their innocence. But are we so sure that we ourselves really *know* all that is intended in the Lord's Prayer, or in the Credo?

The same problem confronts us in our efforts to understand one another. Even the people to whom we feel closest remain closed books to us on certain levels of their being. What, then, of a God-realized master? Is it worthwhile even *trying* to comprehend his vast nature?

Whenever fellow disciples spoke to me of trying to "understand" Master, I would marvel. It struck me as rather like trying to understand the universe! But the task that Infinity has placed squarely in our laps is, "Understand thyself—*know* thyself." To study the life of a master with the purpose, not of understanding *him,* but of obtaining deeper insight into *one's own* true nature, into *one's own* potential for divine unfoldment: This is wise use of the faculty of discrimination.

Master himself was, to each one of us, like a flawless mirror. He held up to our inner gaze, not his opinions of us, but the subtle reactions of our own higher natures. His perfect self-transcendence never ceased to amaze me. In another person's company he actually, in a sense, *became* that person. I don't mean that in our company he assumed our weaknesses, our pettiness, our moods of anger or despondency. What he showed us, rather, was the silent watcher deep within our own selves.

An amazing feature of my own relationship with him was that I could never clearly remember what he looked like. I needed a photograph to bring his image clearly to mind. Even among photographs of him, I have never seen any two alike. When he is shown posing with someone else, in some subtle way he actually looks like that person. Shown with Señor Portes Gil, the President of Mexico, he *looks* like Señor Gil. Posed with Amelita Galli-Curci, the great opera singer, he looks strangely like her. Photographed with Goodwin J. Knight, Lieutenant Governor of California, he appears almost to be Mr. Knight's alter ego.* Standing with any disciple, he seems to *become* that disciple. One wonders how a single face could display such a wide variety of expressions. But of course it was not his face that changed, but the consciousness behind it. Master went a step beyond seeing the god in each of us: He *became* that god, in order that we might see our own divine potential for ourselves, and understand better how the Lord wanted to express Himself through our lives.

Ah, Master! If only I had comprehended as clearly then as I do now the magnificence of your gift to us! But I suppose, had I done so, by this time I would be making the same lament. For evolution never ceases, until at last it embraces eternity.

In his training of us Master's teaching was individual also. It was not that he *altered* his basic teachings to suit our personal needs. It was his emphasis rather that varied. To some he stressed attitudes of service; to others, deep inwardness. To one he emphasized the need for greater joy; to another, for less levity. His emphasis was to a great extent too subtle to be phrased in words. He conveyed it by some intonation of the voice, by the expression in his eyes, by a tilt of the head. What he said to one person he might never say to anyone else. In a very real sense he was, to each of us, our very own, *personal,* divine friend.

In our work, one might have expected him to honor that basic principle of every well-run institution: "Make the best use of individual talent." But to Master this practice would have meant *using* his disciples. His true concern, always, was for our spiritual needs. Sometimes he would actually take us away from some important assignment—one, perhaps, for which no one else could be found—

---

* These three photographs may be seen in two publications of Self-Realization Fellowship: the Golden Anniversary booklet, and *Paramahansa Yogananda, in Memoriam* (p. 81).

simply to help us spiritually. Sometimes, too, he placed people in positions for which they weren't qualified, with a view to prompting them, in their struggle to meet his expectations, to develop needed spiritual qualities. At other times he gave us work we disliked—not particularly because we would be good for that work (I recall a job of carpentry that he put me on once: For every time my hammer hit the nail, there must have been nine others that it missed), but because the work would be good for *us*. Perhaps it was that we needed to learn some spiritual quality—for example, to overcome unwillingness.

Sometimes he would not place people in positions for which they were eminently qualified, simply because they no longer needed those particular experiences to grow spiritually. One might have thought, for instance, that he would have called upon all his most advanced disciples to help him in the ministry. In fact he did say that he appointed as ministers only those who in former lives had developed the requisite spiritual qualifications. But along with those qualifications was the still-more-pressing question of what we ourselves needed, to grow. Speaking to me once of Rajarsi Janakananda, his most highly advanced disciple, he said, "He was leading a center in Kansas City years ago, but I asked him to give it up. Service in that capacity was no longer necessary for his spiritual development."

Sister Gyanamata, his most advanced woman disciple, and a person of deep wisdom, could have rendered enormous assistance by giving lectures, teaching classes, and writing articles for the SRF magazine. But Master never asked her to serve in any such role. That kind of work simply wasn't necessary for her spiritual growth. In fact, I once tried to get her, along with several other advanced disciples, to write articles for *Self-Realization Magazine*. My effort was in response to Master's request that I try to make this bimonthly publication more attractive and helpful to the general reader, with "short, practical articles," as he put it, "on the techniques and principles of right living—articles designed to help people on all levels: physically, mentally, and spiritually." I was trying to enlist as many as possible in this cause, and naturally thought that, the more spiritually developed the writer, the better the article would be. But to my surprise, neither Sister Gyanamata nor any of the others I hoped most to hear from responded to my appeal. Indeed, this was my first confrontation with the truth that a master's training is individual. My first, instinctive response ("Don't they *want* to do Master's will?") conflicted with my awareness that they must know a great deal more about his will than I did. I was forced at last to conclude that, while Master wanted the magazine improved, he didn't necessarily want every hand on deck to improve it. It was not only a question of *what* he wanted, but of *whom* he wanted it from.

My own deep-seated desire had always been to share joy with others. Having suffered spiritually myself, I felt deeply the spiritual sufferings of others, and longed to do all I could to help assuage their sufferings. Master responded to this deep inner longing of mine, and trained me from the beginning for public service.

In January 1949 he put me into office work, answering letters. I typed them in my room, since at that time there was no separate office for the monks. At first my letters tended to be too long.

"I once knew a lady novelist," Master told me one day, by way of advice, "who ended her letters, 'If I'd had more time, this letter would have been shorter.' " He corrected me at other times, too, on the best ways of presenting our teachings to others.

Not long after he'd made me a letter writer, he asked me to study the complete set of the SRF lessons. His stated reason for doing so amused me: "I want your suggestions for their improvement." His real purpose, I knew, was to get me to study the lessons as deeply as possible.

Soon thereafter he also made me the official examiner. This job meant reviewing and grading students' answers to the tests which, in those days, were sent out at the end of each step of the lessons.

By these means Master sought to give me a thorough grounding in his teachings.

In March 1949 he asked me to write articles for our bimonthly magazine. I began writing under the pen name Robert Ford. My first endeavor, "You Can Change Your Personality," was featured in the May-June issue of that year.

One evening Master sent for two or three of us, and talked at length about his work in India. A strong intuition awakened within me that Master would someday send me to that country. Eagerly I jotted down everything he said. A few days later I saw him standing upstairs on his private porch.

"I have plans for you, Walter," he remarked with a quiet smile.

Certain as to his meaning, I was delighted. But after I'd left him, the thought came, "To go to India would mean leaving Master!" The enormity of this threatened loss threw me into a deep depression. "Master is my India!" I cried silently. "What could I possibly find there that I haven't already, right here?"

Gradually my mood left me. As I grew calmer, I reflected that Master surely would want nothing of me but what was spiritually for my best. Two days later I saw him again. By this time I had banished my depression.

"No more moods, now," Master said gently when we met. "Otherwise, how will you be able to help people?"

Every year for the next three years he made plans to go to India, and to take me with him. Each time the trip was postponed. It was his death, finally, that canceled it the third time. But I did get sent to India eventually, in 1958, and there spent the better part of four years.

Sometime in February or March 1949, Master instructed me to stand outside the Hollywood church after the Sunday morning services, and shake hands with people as they left. In his lessons he states that people exchange magnetism when shaking hands. Thus, what Master wanted me to do was not merely greet people, but act as his channel of blessings to others. The first time I tried it, I felt so drained of energy I actually became dizzy. I suppose what happened was that people unconsciously drew from me, in the consciousness that I was serving as Master's representative.

"Master," I said later, "I don't believe I'm ready for this job." I explained what had occurred.

"That is because you are thinking of yourself," he replied. "Think of God, and you will find *His* energy flowing through you."

His suggestion worked. By holding to the thought of God, I discovered that I felt actually more uplifted after shaking hands with the congregation than beforehand.

"When this 'I' shall die," Master wrote once, in a rhymed couplet, "then shall I know who am I."

One of my office jobs was to send weekly advertisements to the newspapers to announce which minister would be speaking at which church the next Sunday, and what his sermon topic would be. Master had been lecturing fortnightly in our San Diego church, alternating weekly between there and Hollywood. Of recent months, however, he had taken to going to San Diego only occasionally. The church members there, ever anxious to see him, were instructed to check the church page of the *San Diego Union* every Saturday. Whenever Master came, the church was full to overflowing.

One week in May I was instructed to send in the announcement that Master would appear there the following Sunday. It had been at least two months since the last time. I smiled to think how delighted the congregation would be.

Saturday morning Bernard came to my room with horrifying

news. "Master can't go to San Diego after all. He wants you to speak in his stead."

"*Me!* But . . . but I've never lectured before in my life!"

"He also wants you," Bernard continued with appalling detachment, "to give a Kriya Yoga initiation afterwards."

"What! Why, I've only attended one initiation!"

"Two," Bernard corrected me. "Master also initiated you last October at Twenty-Nine Palms—remember?"

"All right, two. What difference does that make? I mean—well, of course I'll obey him, but. . . . Oh, those poor people!"

"You'll only have to initiate one of them," Bernard consoled me. "Here's money for the bus. You'd better leave immediately."

In Encinitas, several hours later, Rev. Michael (now Brother Bhaktananda) reviewed for me the outlines of the Kriya initiation ceremony. I worked hard on my sermon, also. With a sinking heart I drove down to San Diego the next morning. In a little room behind the church I prayed desperately for help and guidance. As the time for the service approached, I went and sat in a chair in the center of the stage, as was the custom in those days. Through the closed curtains I could distinctly hear the murmurs of a large and eagerly waiting crowd.

The dreaded moment arrived. I stood up. The curtains parted. My worse fears were realized: The church was completely packed. People were standing in the aisles. Others craned their necks to peer in through the windows. I could feel their shock as an almost physical wave. Instead of their long-awaited guru, here facing them was an unknown and rather lost-looking boy of twenty-two, asking them if they were—still?—awake and ready. I felt so sorry for them in their disappointment that I forgot the awkwardness of my own position. If everyone there had walked out, I would have understood. But regular meditation, I supposed, had made them gracious. No one left.

The Kriya initiation that afternoon frightened me even more than the service had. Michelle Evans, the lady I initiated, looked as terrified as I was—infected, as she later admitted, by my own fear. But Master's blessings, powerfully felt, soon dispelled all anxiety. The ceremony went smoothly. I returned to Mt. Washington that afternoon bowed, perhaps, but unbloodied.

Later, Master received compliments on my lecture. "Most of all," he reported, pleased, "they liked your humility." I reflected that, under the circumstances, humility had been virtually unavoidable!

From this time onward, Master had me lecture regularly in the San Diego and Hollywood churches. He referred to me publicly as

"Reverend Walter," though the actual formalities of ordination weren't completed until a year later.

"Your desire to be happy," he often told us, "must include others' happiness." I had always known in my heart that I would be called upon someday to serve others through teaching and lecturing. But whether out of the humility that Master sometimes praised in me, or from darker motives of unwillingness, it was, I'm afraid, not a few years before I could bring myself to believe that my lectures really did anyone any good.

Master, however, made it clear that he expected me to take this responsibility seriously. "Sir," I once pleaded with him, "I don't want to be a lecturer!"

"You'd better learn to like it," he replied pleasantly. "That is what you will have to do."

At informal gatherings of the monks he would usually direct his conversation to me—as if to get me to absorb his philosophy to my depths. At such times I would think, "It's because I'm so superficial that he won't let me close my eyes and meditate in his presence." That was what I wanted to do. But Master was responding to more deep-seated tendencies in my nature—and was subtly emphasizing that the work of absorbing his philosophy, and of sharing it with others, was what I myself needed, to grow.

CHAPTER 25

Work vs. Meditation

"MASTER ONCE TAUGHT ME a good lesson on the attitude we should hold toward our work." Mrs. Vera Brown (now Meera Mata), an advanced older disciple whom Master had made responsible for training some of the newer ones, was sharing with me a few of her experiences with our guru.

" 'You work too hard,' Master told me one day. 'You *must* work less. If you don't, you will ruin your health.'

" 'Very well,' I thought, 'I'll try not doing so much.'

"Two or three days later, much to my surprise, Master gave me *more* work to do!"

Mrs. Brown's eyes twinkled. " 'Okay, Master,' I thought, 'you must know what you're doing.' I took on my new duties. But all the time I kept wondering, 'How am I going to reconcile all this extra work with his instructions to me to work *less*?'

"Well, a couple of days after that Master again told me, sternly this time, 'You *must not* work so hard. In this lifetime you've done enough work for several incarnations.'

"What was I to do? Again I tried cutting down my activities, only to find Master, after two or three days, giving me more work than ever!

"We repeated this little act several times. Every time that Master told me to work *less,* he soon added duties that forced me to work *more.* I figured he must know what he was doing, and that it was up to me to try and understand what that was.

"Well, finally one day I looked at Master. 'Sir,' I said, 'instead of our using the word *work* in our life here, why don't we substitute the word *service*?'

"Master laughed. 'It has been a good show,' he said. 'All your life you've been thinking, *work! work! work!* That very thought was exhausting you. But just see how differently you feel when you think of work as a divine service! When you act to please God you can do *twice* as much, and never feel tired!' "

Mrs. Brown, whose frail body never seemed to run out of energy no matter how much she did, laughed merrily. "You see, the very thought of pleasing God fills us with *His* energy. Master tells us it's our unwillingness that cuts off that flow of energy."

"True," I replied thoughtfully, "as often as I've put that principle to practice, I've found it works marvelously. But," I continued, "there's another obstacle I run into: that of being *too* willing. What can one do about that?"

"How can one be too willing!"

"Well, what I mean is, I become over-enthusiastic about what I'm doing. As a result, I lose my inner peace, and fall into the old consciousness of hard work, which ends in exhaustion."

"I see." Mrs. Brown nodded sympathetically. "That's right. Without inner peace we lose the consciousness of God's presence. And if we can't feel Him within us, we can't really feel His energy." Again she laughed happily. "Master taught me a good lesson on that subject, too.

"He was cooking one day in his kitchen. I was there in the room with him. For lack of anything better to do, I decided I'd clean up after him. The moment he emptied one pan, I washed it. Whenever he spilled anything, I cleaned up the mess.

"Well, he started dirtying pans and more pans, spilling food and more food. I was working faster and faster to keep up with him. In my whole life I'd *never* seen such sloppy cooking! At last I just gave up. It occurred to me that I might as well wait till he was finished before I did any more.

"As I sat down to watch him, I noticed him smile; but he said nothing. Presently, I saw he wasn't messing things up any more. Finally it dawned on me that he'd only been teaching me the difference between calm, God-reminding activity, and the sort of restlessness that one indulges in just for activity's sake. I'd been working in a spirit of busy-ness. Master's way of showing me my mistake was to lead me to its own logical conclusion!"

The spiritual path would, one suspects, be relatively easy to understand if it involved only meditation, ecstatic visions, and blissful expansions of consciousness. Why, one asks, must it be complicated by mundane activities like ditch digging and letter writing and cleaning up kitchens? One may sympathize, on one level at least, with that reluctant disciple the day we completed the swimming pool at Twenty-Nine Palms who grumbled, "I didn't come here to pour *cement!*" Many a sincere devotee, too, has probably wondered what pouring cement (or digging ditches, or writing letters, or cleaning up kitchens) has to do with finding God.

The answer is, quite simply: *nothing!* Not in itself, anyway. Master once told the story of a man who placed a hundred-dollar bill in the collection plate at church, then was upset because God didn't answer his prayer. Laughingly Master commented, "God already *was* that hundred-dollar bill—whether in or out of the collection plate! Why should He care where it was placed?" The realm of *maya* (cosmic delusion) resembles the surface of an ocean: However high the waves get whipped up by the storm, the over-all ocean level remains the same. God doesn't *need* anything that we can give Him. He already *is* everything! The one thing He wants from us, Master said, is our love.

The purpose, then, of spiritual work is not really to do things for God, but rather to do the most important thing of all for ourselves: to purify our own hearts. No work for God is more or less important than any other. *The Bhagavad Gita* states that He accepts even a flower or a leaf as an offering, if it is tendered with devotion. The important thing is to reach the point where *all* our love, *all* our energy flows naturally toward Him.

Meditation, too, is a kind of work. True, it differs from such labor as digging ditches, but then, so also does mental planning, and who will say that planning is less truly work than the physical execution of plans? Even in the animal kingdom, mental ability is often more highly regarded than brute force. (Witness a group of dogs playing together. Usually it's the brightest one the others follow, not the largest.) Meditation is the most refined and exalted of all mental activities. From it have come the greatest inspirations. If one could meditate deeply all day there would be no need for those seeking divine communion to dig ditches or do any other work.

The criterion, of course, is that word *deeply.*

When Mrinalini Mata, already a disciple when still a young schoolgirl, met Master at the breakfast table one day, he remarked to her, "You didn't meditate this morning."

"Sir," she protested, "I meditated a whole hour!"

Master, quite unimpressed, replied, "You should have meditated half an hour." He had seen that in sitting longer, when not in a mood that day to meditate with intensity, she had actually done less *effective* meditation.

Intensity is everything: intensity of *awareness*. Superconsciousness cannot be attained by half-hearted efforts. "You must be calmly active, and actively calm," Master said. "Be intensely aware of everything you are doing." Work, on the spiritual path, is a means of helping one to channel his energies constantly, *dynamically*, toward God.

"Make every minute count," Master said. "The minutes are more important than the years." People who put their whole concentration into working for God find they can also meditate more deeply.

"When you work for God, not self," Master told us one day, "that is just as good as meditation. Then work helps your meditation, and meditation helps your work. You need the balance. With only meditation you become lazy, and the senses become strong. With only work, the mind becomes restless, and you forget God."

Master taught us to consider any work holy that we did to please God. To keep his minister-disciples from imagining their work of teaching and counseling to be more spiritual than that of disciples who served in the gardens, he gave them manual labor to do also. On that weekend when Master first sent me to San Diego to lecture, I received a valuable lesson from Carl Swenson (later, Brother Sarolananda), a fellow disciple in Encinitas. "Look at my hands!" I lamented. "They're all seamed with cement. People will think I didn't bother to wash them."

"What do you mean?" protested Carl. "They are your badge of honor."

Master taught us not only to offer our work moment by moment to God, but also to see God acting through us as the real Doer. "I slept," he said once, "and dreamt I was working. I woke up, and saw God was working." Action in this spirit wasn't intended to make us automatons. I remember thinking, halfway through a sermon one Sunday morning, "If God really *is* the Doer, why not mentally remove myself from the scene altogether, and wait for *Him* to speak through me?" There followed two minutes of silence! Friends in the audience thought I'd frozen from nervousness. But to me this pause was simply an interesting experiment. Finally I concluded that God had no intention of speaking for me; it was I who had to do the work. His was simply the inspiration for my words, to the extent that I was able to draw on that inspiration.

To see God, then, as the Doer means recognizing that it is *His* energy and inspiration by which we live. It means not taking personal credit for anything we do. This attitude keeps one humble, and also vastly increases one's powers of accomplishment.

Master instructed me to pray to God and our gurus before every lecture, and ask them to use me as their instrument, that I might express what *they* wanted me to say. Humility, alas, is not easy to acquire. After working some months on developing it, I awoke one morning to the realization that I was becoming proud of my humility! In working to develop devotion, too, I discovered that I was becoming pleased with myself for feeling it. (Master's comment: "If you love yourself, how can you love God?") The real secret of humility, I gradually came to realize, is honesty. To see everything in its true proportion to other things reduces the chances that one will take anything too seriously, least of all oneself.

As Sister Gyanamata once remarked to Bernard, when he had thanked her for spiritual help that she had lovingly given him over several years: "It is the nature of a fig tree to bear figs." Her words revealed the humility of perfect detachment—that is to say, again, her complete self-honesty.

Master, in his effort to break us of half-hearted willingness— what he called "one-horse power consciousness"—urged us always to keep a positive outlook, to affirm possibilities rather than weaken them with too many so-called "reasonable" objections.

I remember his greeting to me one day: "How are you, Walter?"

"Well," I began. . . .

"That's good!" he interposed promptly, nipping in the bud what he saw was only a mild case of "vapors."

Never supportive of us in our moods, he urged us to banish them firmly with vigorous, positive affirmations. "I suffer when you have moods," he said once, "for then I see that Satan gets ahold of you."

One young disciple, a girl of seventeen, was somewhat inclined to be moody. "If you want to be unhappy," Master once said to her, "no one in the world can make you happy. And if you determine to be happy, no one in the world will be able to make you unhappy." Daya Mata once told me, "Master wouldn't even allow us around him when we had moods."

Moods weren't often my specific problem, but I remember one that ambushed me one day, and the helpful method I discovered for combatting it.

It was in February or March, 1949. Master had been away from Mt. Washington several weeks, and I hadn't seen him in all that time. I was beginning to feel his absence keenly. Finally he returned. The next day word was sent down to me to get someone to carry a five-gallon bottle of drinking water up to his kitchen. Eagerly I appropriated the job to myself. Arriving upstairs with the bottle, I could hear Master dictating a letter in his sitting room.

Hoping to attract his attention, I rattled the bottle and made as much noise as I felt I decently could for a job that called for a minimum of tumult. Master paid no attention.

"He doesn't care that I miss him!" I thought, plunging suddenly into a violent depression. "I'm just a worker to him, not a disciple!" I rushed on to brood over the unfeeling nature of this world, where nobody really cares for anybody else. Moments later I made an abrupt about-face: "No, Master cares, but he sees I'm such a hopeless case that he might as well give up pouring water into a bottomless pit!" On and on my mind churned. I tried reasoning with myself: "Look here, he's obviously busy. Why should he drop everything just for you?"

"Yeah?" retorted my recalcitrant mind. "I imagine he said, 'Look out, here comes that worthless disciple, Walter! Quick, let me dictate a letter as an excuse not to have to call him in here.' "

Clearly, reason wasn't going to pull me out of this mental whirlpool. Indeed, reason's tendency is to support any feeling that happens to be uppermost in the mind.

"Do you *like* being moody?" I demanded of my mental citizens.

"No!" came the chorus—unanimously, except for one or two grumblers in the background.

"Very well, then, boys, if reason won't do it, let's see if changing our level of consciousness will do the trick."

I went down to my meditation "cave," and there plunged my mind deeply at the Christ center between the eyebrows. Five minutes was all it took. By the end of that time my mood was so positive that I no longer needed to affirm anything. "But *of course* he's busy!" I thought. "Hasn't he often told us that our real communion with him is *inside,* in meditation? And what if all his disciples tried selfishly to take up his time? He wouldn't have any time left over to complete his writings, which will help thousands."

"Sir," someone once asked Master, "what causes moods?"

"Moods," he replied, "are caused by past over-indulgence in sense pleasures, and consequent over-satiety and disgust. If you indulge your moods," he added warningly, "you will reinforce the mind's swing back toward sense pleasures again. For that is how the law of duality works: moving constantly back and forth, like a pendulum, between opposite states of awareness. If you remove energy from one end of the pendulum's swing, by not giving in to moods, you will find the hold that the senses have on you at the opposite end weakening as well."

I learned in another way, too, how important it is not to indulge one's mental tendencies too freely. For some time during my first year at Mt. Washington I was disturbed by periods of almost obsessive sleepiness during meditation. I no sooner sat for meditation than the nodding began. One day I felt particularly joyous inside, and was looking forward eagerly to that evening's meditation. But to my immense disgust, the moment I started to meditate drowsiness descended on me once again like a thick fog. I was furious.

"Since you insist so much on sleeping," I scolded my mind, "I'm not going to let you sleep at all!"

I stayed up all that night—typing letters, walking about the grounds, drinking tea—*anything* to beat down my insistent craving for sleep. When daylight came, I went out and worked hard in the garden. By the following evening my mind had become so submissive—terrified, I imagine, lest it be abused with sleeplessness a second night!—that my meditative drowsiness ceased completely, never to bother me again for many months.

I worked as hard at meditation as I did during the day at my various jobs. ("*Too* hard," Master once told me. "In meditation, you should emphasize relaxation more.") I soon learned that the adage "Don't put all your eggs in one basket" is as true for spiritual as for mundane expectations.

During my Saturday meditations I had been going deeper and deeper into inner stillness. "Just a *little* more effort," I began to think, "and surely I'll slip into full superconsciousness." One Saturday morning I entered my cave with the determination not to stop meditating until this goal had been achieved. For nine hours I sat, continuously applying all the will power I could summon. In the end, exhausted, I had to admit defeat. If I'd stopped short of exhaustion I might have avoided discouragement, and salvaged enough confidence to keep on trying over successive Saturdays. But as it was, though I continued to meditate regularly, months passed before I could again make a really deep effort It was from this very failure, in fact, that my obsession with drowsiness began.

Yet there were compensations, even now: at times deep joy during moments of inner stillness, and increasing devotion, and blissful inner sounds—one, particularly, that resembled wind in the trees. Master urged us not to talk about our meditative experiences, so I prefer to keep the most precious of them locked in my heart.

I worked hard to develop devotion, chanting and praying daily for the grace of intense love for God. Master one day smiled at me lovingly. "Keep on with your devotion," he said. "See how dry your life is when you depend on intellect."

His help was available to anyone who called to him mentally in meditation. Here he was the guide, ever subtly inspiring us, according to the measure of our receptivity, to make the right kind of spiritual effort. Sometimes, too, when we met him during the course of the day, he would admonish us on some point concerning our meditations. Indeed, he watched over us in all ways. It never ceased to amaze me that, with so many disciples to look after, he could be so perfectly aware of each of our needs.

"I go through your souls every day," he told us. "If I see something in you that needs correcting, I tell you about it. Otherwise, I say nothing." On another occasion he said, "I have lived the lives of each one of you. Many times I go so deep at night into a person that when I wake up in the morning I think I *am* that person! It can be a terrible experience, if he happens to be someone full of moods and desires."

Mrs. Michelle Evans, that lady I initiated into Kriya Yoga in San Diego, told me, "I used to drink—not much, but the way most people do—you know, to be sociable. When I met Master, he told me to give it up. So for awhile I took nothing alcoholic at all. But then I got to thinking, 'Surely beer doesn't count, does it? nor wine? I mean, they really aren't in the same class with whiskey and brandy, are they?' So I went back to drinking those two occasionally. It gave me less explaining to do whenever we had guests.

"Well, the next time I saw Master in San Diego, he looked at me sorta penetratingly and said, 'I meant *all* alcoholic beverages!' Well! Since then, what choice have I got? Any time I slipped, he'd know about it!"

Jan Savage, a young boy of nine who had come to Mt. Washington with his mother, was meditating one day with Daniel Boone when he had a vision of Jesus Christ. Thrilled, he told Boone about it afterwards.

"It could be your imagination," Boone said. "Better say nothing more till you ask Master about it."

Master, who was away at that time, returned to give the service the following Sunday. Afterwards Jan joined the line of devotees that always waited to come forward for Master's blessings. As he approached, Master reached out and tousled his hair affectionately.

"So!" he cried. "Little Jan had a vision of Jesus Christ. That's very good. That was a true vision!"

Boone told me in February of an experience he too had had after keeping his mind steadfastly on Master for two days. He was given a kind of ecstasy in which he was quite unable to feel his body, even while moving about and performing his daily duties in the print shop. "I had to pray finally that I'd be able to feel my body again," he said. "I was afraid I might hurt it on the machinery."

Well, I thought, *that* was for me! More eager for the experience itself, I'm afraid, than for humble attunement with my guru, I kept my mind on Master one-pointedly. He was in Encinitas at the time, but after two or three days returned to Mt. Washington. I met him by the front porch as he arrived.

"What sort of mischief are you up to, Walter?" He smiled significantly.

"None, Sir." Mischief? It didn't seem like mischief to me.

"Are you *sure* you aren't up to some kind of mischief?"

I began to understand what he meant, but was reluctant to accept his definition of what I'd been doing. As he went indoors, he smiled lovingly. Thinking the matter over, I had to admit to myself that, while my practice had been right, my intentions had not been.

"Don't seek experiences in meditation," Master told us. "The path to God not is not a circus."

More moving was the experience of another disciple, Rev. Michael, who, feeling deep love for Master, would often repeat the words mentally, "I love you, Guru."

One day, to his joy, Master responded to his silent offering. The two happened to meet in the hermitage garden at Encinitas. With a gaze of deep tenderness, the Guru said, "I love you, too."

Master responded instantly to sincere love. One day, missing him intensely, I went down to see him in Encinitas where he was staying at the time. Shortly after my arrival he passed a group of us on his way back from a drive. Seeing me, he invited me to ride up with him to the hermitage. "I have missed you," he told me lovingly. How rare is it, I thought, for one's unexpressed feelings to be caught so sensitively.

Master's help was with us not only in our inner, spiritual struggles, but in our work as well. One day Norman and I were replastering the wall of a garage by the main entrance to the Mt. Washington grounds. The plaster was old, and was setting up fast. Though we kept on adding water, we had all we could do to complete each batch before it hardened completely.

Halfway through the job Master, on his way out for a drive, saw us and stopped the car. Calling us over to him, he chatted with us for about half an hour. We were delighted, of course. Yet in the back of our minds there lingered the slight apprehension: What about that plaster? I'd just mixed a fresh batch of it and poured it onto the board. There it was, getting harder by the second.

By the time Master left us, Norman and I were both certain it would take a sledge hammer to break it up. But to our amazement, we found it as soft as it had been when I poured it. For the rest of that day the plaster gave us no more trouble.

Hard work was as important in our way of life as regular meditation. "You must be intensely active for God," Master said, "before you can attain the actionless state of union with Him." More than either work or meditation, however, he stressed the importance of devotion. "Without love for God," he taught, "no one can find Him."

Nightly I chanted Master's translation of a song by the great Bengali saint, Ram Proshad: "Will that day come to me when saying, 'Mother! Mother!' my eyes will flow with tears?" Gradually I found myself becoming inwardly transformed. I began to think I had some cause for self-congratulation, when one day word came to me that Master had been talking with a group of the monks in Encinitas. During the course of the conversation, he had remarked lovingly:

"Look how I have changed Walter!"

Self-Realization Fellowship Church in Hollywood, California, where Paramhansa Yogananda spoke regularly. I gave regular classes and services here from 1949 onwards. From 1955–1958 I served as the main minister of the church.

Interior of the Hollywood church. Master built two pulpits in the church, one on either side of the stage. The left pulpit, as seen from the audience, was originally planned for our own ministers, and the right one, for guest speakers. It was his plan to invite ministers from other churches to speak there, in keeping with his universal ideals, as expressed in the name "Church of All Religions." Although the pulpits were never used in the way Master planned, the concept is worthy of preservation.

In front of my cottage at Mt. Washington, in the autumn of 1949.

Master in front of the Encinitas Hermitage, probably during the early 1940s.

Master at a public gathering.

Master exemplified the androgynous balance of the perfect human being. He had the compassion and love of a mother, and the wisdom and will power of a father. In this picture we see exemplified the mother aspect of his nature.

Here I am on the lawn in front of Mt. Washington headquarters.

CHAPTER 26

The Ministry

"YOU MIGHT LIKE to know something of the history of our Holly-wood church," Master remarked to me one day, "now that you are lecturing there regularly."

"Naturally, Sir," I replied, "I'm eager to learn everything I can about our work."

"We built the church during the war. New construction wasn't allowed at that time, but we were able to build legally anyway. We bought an old church, and had it moved onto our property. The building was a mere shell," Master chuckled. "How the neighbors howled! But we fixed it up—stuccoing the walls, fixing the roof, painting everything beautifully, and putting in valuable stained-glass windows. Finally the building looked completely new." Master paused reminiscently.

"Finding those windows was a real blessing from God. I wanted stained glass, but everyone insisted, 'You can't get that. There's a war on!' Still, I knew we would get it.

"One morning God showed me in a vision where our windows were sitting, just waiting for us, in an old junk store. I went there. 'I'm sorry,' the owner said, 'we have no stained glass here.' But I knew better.

" 'Just look once,' I pleaded.

" 'I told you,' he said, losing patience, 'we haven't any!' Growling, he stalked away.

"I went over to an assistant standing nearby, and asked him if *he* knew of any stained glass in the place.

" 'Boss say no,' he replied, his body stooped with lifelong reluctance. 'Muss be no.'

" 'Here are five dollars,' I told him. 'I'll give them to you if you take me where I want to go.' At this he agreed. Together we went out into the backyard. There, gathering dust against a far wall, was an assortment of old doors and whatnot. But no sign of any stained-glass windows.

" 'You see?' the man said, lifting his head in an attitude of vindication. 'Boss say no. Muss be no!'

" 'Just pull those things away,' I requested. 'Let's have a look at what's behind them.'

" 'Boss say . . .' he began a third time. Then he remembered those five dollars. Willingness may not have been his strong point, but finally, groaning and moaning, he moved everything out into the yard. And there at last, right up against the wall, were our stained-glass windows!

"In the condition they were in they looked like nothing but junk. The glass panes were in place, but all were hanging loosely, and covered with filth. The owner let me have the lot of them for next to nothing. But we fixed them up carefully. Miss Darling° saved us thousands of dollars by framing and gold-leafing them herself. And now—well, you can see how beautiful they are. I've been told they are valuable."

"One would never suspect the church of having such a grey past!" I remarked, smiling. It looked like a charming jewel now, immaculate in its white, blue, and gold colors. Set well back from the road, it was fronted by a pleasant garden. Unquestionably it had become an asset to the neighborhood.

Master continued, "The church carpet came from God, also." This carpet, a soothing, dark blue, covered the entire floor of the church. I had long admired it. Master went on to explain, "I had wanted a beautiful carpet, because I think that if theaters can be designed beautifully to remind one of the beauties of this world, then God's places should be designed even more beautifully to remind one that He is the Source of all beauty. My wish was for a rich blue carpet like the one we used to have in our Encinitas temple. I sent people scouting everywhere. But no one found anything like it.

"I myself then telephoned the company that had sold us that first carpet. 'Oh, I'm sorry,' a voice said, 'the man you bought that one from went out of business.'

" 'Who is this speaking?' I inquired. It proved to be that man's former business partner. He was just about to hang up, when he paused.

" 'Say' he exclaimed, 'I've just remembered that we still we a piece of that very carpet you bought left in our warehouse. How much did you say you needed?'

° Now Durga Mata.

" 'A hundred and one yards,' I replied.

"He went and measured his remnant. It came to exactly one hundred and *two* yards!

"I have often said," Master concluded, "that out of the loss of our Encinitas temple came two more temples—this one in Hollywood, and our church in San Diego. Just the other day a visitor remarked to me, 'What a pity you lost your Encinitas temple!' I answered, 'It was the best thing that ever happened to me!' You see, it forced me to come out more into the world with these teachings. And look, even the carpet in our new church came out of that very carpet for the old one!"

By June 1949 I was conducting midweek services more or less regularly in the Hollywood church. Soon thereafter I also gave occasional Sunday services, both there and in San Diego.

A problem for any new speaker is how to avoid feeling nervous in front of an audience. My own problem was accentuated by the fact that I was so young, and looked even younger. The average age of my listeners was about forty. I could count on their knowing a great deal more about most things than I did.

Abie George, a disciple in Hollywood of whom we were all particularly fond, suggested a solution. Deeply devoted ("a beautiful soul," Master called him), Abie also had a colorful sense of humor, and a most unusual way of expressing it. "It's very simple," he explained with mock earnestness. "No, hey, I mean it," he persisted, laughingly forestalling my anticipated objections, "it really *is* simple. All as you gotta do is picture to yourself alla them there people in fronta you as a buncha cabbage heads. That's all! Just say to yourself, 'You uns out there are nothin' but a buncha cabbage heads!' Like that." I thanked him, dubiously.

James Coller, the minister of our church in Phoenix, offered another suggestion. "I was so nervous when I first started lecturing," he said, "that Master suggested I take a hot bath before my talks, to relax. One evening I was supposed to give an introductory lecture to a series of public classes. The announced subject was 'What Yoga Can Do for You.'

"Well, I took a long, hot bath beforehand! *Too* long," James added, chuckling, "and *too* hot. It sapped all my energy. I arrived for that lecture so limp I felt more like a steam-heated towel than a human being! After five minutes of speaking I found I'd covered everything could think of to say on the subject. It was probably the shortest lecture those people had ever attended!

"Next, Horace took up a collection. He's spastic, you know. After my five-minute lecture on what yoga can do for you, my only assistant went staggering from row to row with the collection plate, clutching at the backs of chairs for support."

This story, told with much laughter on James part, left us holding our sides in merriment. It hadn't seemed quite so funny to his audience, however. They got up and left without a word. Fortunately, the episode had a more gratifying sequel. One man, after leaving the room, returned, moved by James's obvious goodness and sincerity. This man later became a devoted follower of Master's work.

"Well, anyway," James concluded, addressing me, "you might try soaking yourself in hot water before your lectures." His story, I confessed, had left me somewhat less than reassured.

The solution I myself found to the problem of nervousness was to imagine the worst audience response possible, and accept it—in short, to be *willing* to appear a fool. "It is all God's dream anyway," I would remind myself before a lecture, "so what does it matter whether people accept me or reject me?"

Indifference to the fruits of my efforts proved a solution to the problem of nervousness, but it didn't help me in the far more important matter of communicating with my listeners. For, in telling myself it was all a dream,* I ended up not really caring whether I spoke well or not.

Only gradually did I become a conscientious speaker, as the awareness grew in me that the people I was speaking to were manifestations of God, and as I understood that it was *through* them, rather than by merely surviving the personal ordeal of appearing before them, that I was being asked to serve Him. Thus I was cured also of a temptation that is common to public speakers, to be satisfied if they can make their points convincing to *themselves*. For in seeing God manifested in the forms of my listeners, and in realizing that what I had to say was a service to Him *through* them, it became important to me to express myself in a way that would *reach* Him through them.

At first I used to pray before every lecture, "Lord, inspire me to say what *You* want said." Later I learned to ask Him also, "Help me sense what this particular audience needs to hear through me." Often, sensing needs different from those I had come prepared to speak about, I would give a completely different talk from the one I'd intended. Indeed, I learned in time to prepare minimally, if at

---

* The Hindu teaching that life is a dream is intended to inspire non-attachment, not irresponsibility. Even in a dream, after all, it is preferable to dream wisely. In the cosmic dream-delusion, man must act willingly as an instrument of God, the Divine Dreamer, before he can win the right to eternal wakefulness in Him.

all, for my lectures, for I found that an open mind enabled me to respond more sensitively to the unvoiced needs of my listeners. The results of this approach proved gratifying. Many people began thanking me after my lectures for answering their specific questions, or for dealing with problems that had been weighing on their minds. I always shared with them the real secret of my success: "God is the Doer." For it was in this thought above all that Master trained us.°

When I was first learning to lecture, Master gave me the following words of advice: "Before lecturing, meditate deeply. Then, holding that meditative calmness, think about what you intend to say. Write down your ideas. Include one or two funny stories; people are more receptive when they can enjoy a good laugh. Then finish with a story from the SRF lessons. After that, put the subject out of your mind. While speaking, keep mentally before you the salient points of your outline, but above all ask the Spirit to flow through you. In that way you will draw your inspiration from that inner Source, and will not speak from ego."

Most important of all to Master was the question of our attunement while lecturing, that we might share with our listeners not only our ideas, but our vibrations. Late one Thursday afternoon he spied Dr. Lewis out on the grounds in Encinitas, enjoying a stroll.

"Doctor," he called out, "aren't you giving the service this evening?"

"Yes, Sir," Dr. Lewis called back.

"Then what are you doing roaming about? You should be meditating!"

In time, I reached the point where I could actually *feel* a power flowing from my attunement with Master, and filling any room in which I might be lecturing. If anything I said touched my listeners, the credit was due to this power far more than to any words I uttered.

During Master's early years in the West, thousands came to his public lectures. But the churches he built were small, sweet in their simplicity. Smallness, he felt, was more conducive to worship; it permitted a sense of inwardness, of closeness to God. Master told us of a visit he had once paid to a large, well-known cathedral in the American Midwest. "I was admiring it," he said, "when I heard

---

° "Take no thought how or what ye shall speak: for it shall be given you in that same hour what ye shall speak. For it is not ye that speak, but the Spirit of your Father which speaketh in you" (Matthew 10:19,20).

God's voice saying, 'Would you rather have all this, without Me? Or'—here a vision appeared in which I saw myself seated on the ground under a tree, a handful of disciples gathered about me—'this, with Me?'

" 'Lord,' I prayed, 'only where Thou art do I want to be!' "

The Master often remarked that an emphasis on large, expensive places of worship, and on crowds of worshipers, necessitates too much concentration on money, and too little on humble, inward communion with God. "The church system has to be revised," he told us. "Outward pomp must be replaced by simplicity, and huge cathedrals by small temples where sincere devotees gather for meditation. The well-educated minister of a large, modern congregation may lecture eloquently, but if he never meditates, and has no inward realization of God's presence, what is the use of his eloquence? His D.D. degree in this case stands for nothing but 'Doctor of Delusion'!

"If I went to a restaurant that had a good name, but couldn't get any food there, what good would that place do me? I'd come away as hungry as I had entered. So what is the use of a famous church, if it is spiritually dead? What is the good of a hive without honey?"

He then told us, "You are on the eve of a great change. You will see the entire church movement undergoing a revolution. Churches will become places where real souls will go to commune with God."

Sometimes, with great merriment, he paraphrased a story from the novel *Heavenly Discourse,* by Charles E. Wood. His version of the tale went something like this: "When Billy Sunday, the famous evangelist, died and went to heaven, St. Peter wouldn't let him enter the Pearly Gates, but demanded, 'What did you do on earth to deserve admission here?' 'Why,' Billy Sunday protested, 'what about all those thousands I sent up here from my revival meetings?' 'You may have sent them,' retorted St. Peter, 'but they never arrived!' "

"In Milwaukee," Master told us, "I was once taken to a church where a choir sang especially for me. Afterwards one of the singers asked me, 'How did you like our singing?'

" 'It was all right,' I said.

" 'You mean you *didn't* like it?'

" 'I didn't say that,' I replied. 'But please don't press me further.' Well, he kept insisting, so at last I explained, 'As far as technique went, you were perfect. But you weren't thinking of the One for whom that sacred music was written. You were thinking of pleasing *me.* Next time you sing devotional music, think of God; don't sing to impress others.' "

Master's own services were rich with inspiration. They conveyed none of the orphaned feeling that one encounters in many churches, of a God living distantly in some unimaginable heaven, or of a Jesus Christ who left no more vital testimony to his continuing reality than the printed words in the Bible. In Master's presence, divine truths came thrillingly alive, made vibrant with the immediacy of his own God-realization.

"You are a good salesman!" an American businessman exclaimed once after one of his lectures. "That," Master replied, "is because I have sold myself on the truths I teach!"

Some of my most impressive memories of Master are of his public lectures. While they lacked the sweet intimacy of talks with the disciples at Mt. Washington, they rang with the spirit of a mission destined, he told us, to bring spiritual regeneration to the world.

I remember especially how stirred I was by a talk he gave at a garden party in Beverly Hills on July 31, 1949. Never had I imagined that the power of human speech could be so great; it was the most stirring lecture I have ever heard.

"This day," he thundered, punctuating every word, "marks the birth of a new era. My spoken words are registered in the ether, in the Spirit of God, and they shall move the West. . . . Self-Realization has come to unite all religions. . . . We must go on—not only those who are here, but thousands of youths must go North, South, East and West to cover the earth with little colonies, demonstrating that simplicity of living plus high thinking lead to the greatest happiness!"* I was moved to my core. It would not have surprised me had the heavens opened up and a host of angels come streaming out, eyes ablaze, to do his bidding. Deeply I vowed that day to do my utmost to make his words a reality.

Often during the years I was with Master he exhorted his audiences on the subject of this cherished dream of his: "world brotherhood colonies," or spiritual cooperative communities—not monasteries, merely, but places where people in every stage of life could devote themselves to living the divine life.

"Environment is stronger than will power," he told us. He saw "world brotherhood colonies" as environments that would foster spiritual attitudes: humility, trust, devotion, respect for others, friendly cooperation. For worldly people, too, who dream of a better way of life, small cooperative communities offer the best hope

---

* *Self-Realization Magazine,* November–December 1949, p. 36.

of demonstrating to society at large that mankind is capable of achieving heights that are so scornfully repudiated in this age of spiritual underachievers. Such communities would be places where cooperative attitudes were emphasized, rather than social and political "rights" and the present social and business norms of cut-throat competition.

"Gather together, those of you who share high ideals," Yogananda told his audiences. "Pool your resources. Buy land out in the country. A simple life will bring you inner freedom. Harmony with nature will bring you a happiness known to few city dwellers. In the company of other truth seekers it will be easier for you to meditate and think of God.

"What is the need for all the luxuries people surround themselves with? Most of what they have they are paying for on the installment plan. Their debts are a source of unending worry to them. Even people whose luxuries have been paid for are not free; attachment makes them slaves. They consider themselves freer for their possessions, and don't see how their possessions in turn possess them!"

He added: "The day will come when this colony idea will spread through the world like wildfire."

In the over-all plan for his work, Paramhansa Yogananda saw individual students first receiving the SRF lessons, and practicing Kriya Yoga in their own homes; then, in time, forming spiritual centers where they could meet once or twice weekly for group study and meditation. In areas where there was enough interest to warrant it, he wanted SRF churches, perhaps with full- or part-time ministers. And where there were enough sincere devotees to justify it, his dream was that they would buy land and live together, serving God, and sharing the spiritual life together on a full-time basis.

As I mentioned in Chapter 17, Master had wanted to start a model world brotherhood colony in Encinitas. He felt so deeply the importance of this communitarian dream that for some years it formed the nucleus of all his plans for the work. Indeed, ruler of his own mental processes though he was, even he on one occasion became caught up in a whirlwind of enthusiasm for this project. He told a congregation one Sunday morning, "I got so involved in thinking about world brotherhood colonies last night that my mind got away from me. But," he added, "I chanted a little, and it came back."

Another measure of his interest may be seen in the fact that the first edition of *Autobiography of a Yogi* ended with a ringing report of his hopes for founding such a colony. "Brotherhood," he wrote in that edition, quoting a discussion he had had with Dr. Lewis in Encinitas, "is an ideal better understood by example than precept! A small harmonious group here may inspire other ideal communities over the earth." He concluded, "Far into the night my dear friend—the first *Kriya Yogi* in America—discussed with me the need for world colonies founded on a spiritual basis."

Alas, he encountered an obstacle that has stood in the way of every spiritual reform since the days of Buddha: human nature. Marriage has always tended to be something of a closed corporation. The economic depression of the 1930s had had the effect on a generation of Americans of heightening this tendency by increasing their desire for worldly security. "Us four and no more" was the way Yogananda described their attitude. America wasn't yet ready for world brotherhood colonies.

A further difficulty lay in the fact that the core of his work already was his monastic disciples. It was they who set the tone for all the colonies. Householders couldn't match their spirit of self-abnegation and service. Families were crowded out of the communal garden, so to speak, by the more exuberant growth of the plants of renunciation. But Yogananda was too near the end of his mission to fulfill his "world brotherhood colony" dream elsewhere.

"Encinitas is gone!" he lamented toward the end of his life. It was not that the ashram was lost. What he meant was that his plans for founding a world brotherhood colony on those sacred grounds would not be fulfilled—at least not during his lifetime. He stopped accepting families into the ashrams, all of which he turned now into full-fledged monasteries. For in his renunciate disciples he found that spirit of selfless dedication which his mission needed for its ultimate success.

Nevertheless, the idea of world brotherhood colonies remained important to him. It was, as he had put it during that speech in Beverly Hills, "in the ether, in the Spirit of God." Kamala Silva, in her autobiography, *The Flawless Mirror,* * reports that as late as five months before he left his body he spoke to her glowingly of this dream of his. Master knew that, eventually, the dream must be fulfilled.

But even with regard to so basic a part of his mission as world brotherhood colonies, Master was completely without anxiety. He never saw the world as most people see it. To him, it was all God's play—endless shadows and light in a divine motion picture.

---

* p. 183. This beautiful book may be purchased from Crystal Clarity, Publishers, 14618 Tyler-Foote Road, Nevada City, CA 95959 (800) 424-1055.

I remember the evening that he recorded some of his chants for public release. Partway through that recording session I had to leave to give a class in Hollywood Church. When I returned, I found Master standing outside on the lawn, listening to one of the chants being played back to him: "What lightning flash glimmers in Thy face, Mother! Seeing Thee I am thrilled through and through." Again and again he had the recording repeated. Presently he began almost to dance, swaying to and fro ecstatically, his arms outstretched sidewise and waving to the rhythm of the music. He was blissfully engrossed in the beauty of Divine Mother, whom he perceived as wondrous Light spreading out to infinity. I was deeply moved.

Afterwards, as he was taking leave of our little group, he said quietly, "I see all of you as images of light. Everything—these trees, bushes, the grass you are standing on—all are made of that light. You have no idea how beautiful everything is!"

CHAPTER 27

Attunement

M ASTER WAS TO SPEAK one Sunday morning at Hollywood
Church, when Sue and Bud Clewell, my relatives in
Westwood Village, came to visit me. After the service, Master graciously invited the three of us to join him for lunch.

A small group of us were served on the stage behind the closed curtains, there being no room large enough in the church to accommodate us. This afternoon was my first opportunity to observe Master in the role of host. I found it a charming experience. His total lack of affectation, delightful wit, gentle courtesy, and warm, kindly laughter, which included everyone in his joy, would I think have enchanted any audience.

Among those present were Dr. and Mrs. Lewis. A lady who recently had become a member, glancing at them, inquired, "Master, Dr. Lewis was your first disciple in this country, wasn't he?"

Master's response was unexpectedly reserved. "That's what they say," he replied quietly. His tone of voice, even more than his words, made such a marked contrast to the affability he had been showing that the lady seemed quite taken aback. Noticing her surprise, Master explained more kindly, "I never speak of people as my disciples. God is the Guru: They are *His* disciples."

To Master, discipleship was too sacred a subject to be treated lightly, even in casual conversation.

Later, Sue and Bud confessed they had found Master charming. "But," Sue challenged me a little belligerently, "why do you have to call him 'Master'?" Warming to her subject, she continued, "This is a free country! Americans aren't slaves. And anyway, no one has a right to be the master of another human being!"

"Sue," I remonstrated, "it isn't our freedom we've given him. It's our bondage! I've never known anyone so respectful of the freedoms of others as Yogananda is. We call him 'Master' in the sense of teacher. He is a true master of the practices in which we

245

ourselves are struggling to excel. You might say that he is our teacher in the art of achieving *true* freedom."

"*True* freedom! How can you say that? You can vote, can't you? You can travel anywhere you want to, can't you? Isn't our American way of life proof enough that you're free already?"

"*Is* it?" I smiled. "Think how bound people are by their attachments and desires. They want a thousand things, most of which they'll never get, in the belief that they'll find happiness through them. In conditioning their happiness by mere material objects, they enslave themselves! Happiness isn't *things*, Sue. It's a state of mind."

Sue pondered my words a few minutes. "Well," she concluded, "I still think I'll be happier when we can afford a new sofa!"

(Poor Sue, *were* you happier? In the years after that, I wish I could say that I saw it in your eyes.)

Sue's objection to our loving appellation for our guru was by no means unusual. Perhaps if a master were to appear on the stage of life like some Nietzschean Zarathustra, making grand pronouncements on obscure themes that no one in his right mind had ever thought of before, people, mistaking their bewilderment for awe, might cry, "Ah, here indeed is a *master*." But masters usually live more or less prosaically. They get born in mangers. They teach familiar truths in simple ways. One might say they almost flaunt their ordinariness. Human nature doesn't take kindly to greatness in mere *people*. And it is in their perfect humanity, not in their rejection of all that it means to be human, that masters most truly reveal their greatness.

In this ideal they are both a challenge to us, and a reproach. Most people don't want challenges. Still less do they want reproaches. One who isn't willing to face the need for self-transformation cannot view gladly the accomplished fact of transformation in others. "I'm as good as anyone else," is the common saying. A true statement it would be, too, if it referred to the eternal, divine image in us. But people who talk like that are not thinking of their souls. Who, in his egoic humanity, can say honestly, "I'm as virtuous as anyone else, as intelligent, as artistic, as wise as good a leader"? The reiterated egalitarian dogma of our age blinds people to the single most obvious fact of human nature—the vast variety of its manifestations. Belief in complete outward equality is a kind of democratic romanticism, a preference for pleasing sentiments over the clear vision of reality that is earned in hard struggles on the battlefield of life. Only when we have banished from our consciousness the delusions that keep us bound to this phenomenal

world of relativities can we know ourselves truly equal, in God, to
the very angels.

"My thoughts are not your thoughts, neither are your ways my
ways, saith the Lord. For as the heavens are higher than the earth,
so are my ways higher than your ways, and my thoughts than
your thoughts."* People rarely see that the greatness of God's
ways, as expressed through the lives of His awakened children, lies
in a transcendent view of mundane realities, and not in a rigid
denial of these realities. From the thought "Nothing is divine," man
must grow to the realization "All things are divine."

Our "bondage" to Master was a "bondage" purely of love. He,
far more than we, appreciated the sacredness of this relationship,
and treated it with the deepest dignity and respect. But where love
was missing on a disciple's part, the bond broke, or was never
formed. And then even disciples were known to lose sight of what
it meant to call their guru "Master."

"I didn't come here," they complained, "to pour *cement!*" No?
Why, then, did you come?

"Why, to meditate, of course, to attain *samadhi.*"

And did you imagine that *samadhi* would come in any other way
than by attunement with your guru?

"Well, no. After all that's why I came here. But what has attunement got to do with pouring cement? It's in my meditations that I
need his help."

O blind ones, can't you see that self-transformation is a *total* process? that what the Master gives us spiritually must be perceived
on *every* level of our existence? that no real difference exists between God in the form of cement and God in the form of blissful
visions? God is equally present in everything!

Rare, alas, is that disciple who feels no inner resistance, born of
his own egotism, to complete acceptance of his guru. "I want to
express my own creativity!" is a complaint frequently thought, less
frequently expressed. Or, "I know Master has the greatest thing of
all to give me, but I have something worthwhile to give him, too.
I'm a good organizer!" O foolish devotee, don't you see that man
has *nothing* to express that he can call truly his own? that his ideas,
his opinions, his so-called "inspirations"—all, *all* but reflect currents
of consciousness that are equally available to everyone? Only by
attunement to God's will can we truly express *ourselves.* Through
each of us the Divine has a unique song to sing; it isn't that we
should not *try* to be creative. Indeed, unless we ourselves act God

* Isaiah 55:8,9.

can't act through us. (The whole of the *Bhagavad Gita* is an exhortation to action.) But we must learn to *listen,* to accept, to absorb; herein lies the true and deepest secret of creativity.

For disciples, the surest way to express themselves creatively is to attune themselves to their guru's wishes. His entire task is to speed them on the path of self-unfoldment. *Are* you a good organizer? Then seek inwardly, from your guru, the inspiration you need for organizing. If you say, "This, at least, is something I know better than he does," you close the door that he has been so painstakingly prying open for you to the infinite source of all true inspiration, within yourself.

It is folly in any case, and a sure invitation to vainglory, to dwell on the thought that the understanding of one's guru is imperfect, even in trivial matters. For therein lies the seed of pride; it begins with the thought, "Wise as he is—look! In this particular matter *I* am wiser than he!"

As a matter of fact, our own Master often demonstrated an undreamed-of proficiency in subjects far outside the realm of his own direct, human experience. For example, though he had never studied medicine, he won the respect of many doctors for his familiarity with the esoterica of their profession.

In India once, not satisfied with the work of a certain well-known artist, whom he had commissioned to do a portrait of Lahiri Mahasaya, he painted a better portrait of that master himself. And this was his first attempt at painting!

The wife of Señor Cuaron, our center leader in Mexico City, told me in Spanish when I visited them in 1954, "I once had a private interview with Master. I knew he spoke no Spanish, and as you can see, I don't speak English. Yet we conversed for an hour, and I understood him perfectly." My assumption has always been that, for that one hour, he spoke with her in Spanish.

There were times when I myself felt that Master had erred in some matter, or had not sufficiently grasped some point. There was even a time, as you will see in a later chapter, when my questioning took the form of more serious doubts. But always I found, in time, that he was the one who was right. His actions, unusual though they sometimes were, and in appearance not always reasonable, were based on sure intuitions that, incredibly, always worked out for the best. Whenever his plans went awry it was, I think, usually because of our want of attunement in carrying them out.

A small example may suffice. Schooled as I had been in the importance of esthetic values, I was mildly disappointed by the Gothic arches on our church altars, which I was told Master had designed himself. To my eyes they looked somewhat stark and uninspired, though by no means offensively so. But one day I got to see his original sketch. It was exquisite. The subtle oriental sweep of his arches had been missed altogether by our carpenters.

Had we listened more sensitively to the subtle nuances of his guidance, and not run about—"like chickens with their heads cut off" as Master himself put it—trying frenziedly to do his will, nor tried so *reasonably* to obstruct it, I almost think we could have changed the world. Certainly we would all have radically transformed ourselves.

Now that Master had, albeit reluctantly, abandoned his dream of founding a world brotherhood colony in Encinitas, and had turned his mind to organizing the existing communities along more strictly monastic lines, the thought was in the air: "Organize!" I don't recall that Master himself said much about organizing at this time. At least, he never did so in my presence. But for whatever reason, many disciples were caught up in this thought.

There were several of the monks who, instead of saying merely, "*Now* we must organize," waxed critical of the fact that things hadn't been organized long before. New as I was in the work, I looked up to these men as my superiors on the path. It didn't occur to me that they were actually being negative. When they referred darkly to ways in which things were, according to them, being mismanaged, my reaction was to feel distress that Master should have been so badly served by the "mismanagers."

Master's way was, if possible, to let the disciples play out their fantasies, that they might learn from them. I was never really brought fully into the present picture, but one day Boone came charging into my room to announce grandly, "Master has appointed a committee. He wants you and me to be on it."

"A committee? What does he want us to do?"

"We're to organize the work," Boone replied, straightening up self-importantly.

"What aspects of it?"

"All aspects of it—everything!" Boone swept an arm outward in an expansive gesture.

"Well," I said dubiously, "if Master says so. But I don't really know much about the work. I can't imagine how he expects me to help organize it!"

"Oh, you won't have to do much. Just lend a hand whenever we ask for it."

It turned out I didn't really have to do anything. For some

weeks various members of the committee met by twos and threes, informally, to discuss everything they felt needed changing. There was much talk, some complaining, and little action. Gradually, complaints assumed the dominant role. The main office, Boone informed me indignantly, was obstructing the committee's work, and thereby, of course, Master's will. I felt incompetent to offer positive suggestions, but shared my fellow members' indignation. It amazed me that disciples should so stubbornly refuse to cooperate with their guru's wishes.

One day Boone dashed into my room in a burst of anger "Miss Sahly completely refuses to obey the committee's latest directive!"

Why, this was unthinkable! I rose to my feet. "We must go speak to her!" Together we strode over to the main office. I told Miss Sahly (now Shraddha Mata) that in refusing to cooperate with the committee she was disobeying Master, that the matter in question was a committee decision, and that, for the welfare of the work, she must absolutely accept it.

"You young hotheads!" Master cried when he learned about the episode. "What do you mean bursting in there and shouting like that?" He proceeded to give me, in particular, the best tongue-lashing I ever heard him give anyone.

I was aghast. I had pictured myself bravely striking blows in his cause, only to find myself fighting on the wrong side! Miss Sahly, it turned out, was a highly respected disciple of many years' standing, and a member of the Board of Directors. Master, moreover, had never told her, nor anyone else, that our committee had any special powers. (Nor, I suddenly realized, had I ever heard from him directly that we had any!)

Running out of things to say about our office invasion but finding himself still in fine voice, Master started in on the committee itself. He called it "do-nothing, negative, a complete farce." Most of the monks, including the other committee members, were present. Master's entire tirade, however, was directed at me.

But Master, I thought, *I took hardly any part in the committee's activities!* Outwardly, however, I said nothing; after all, I *was* at least nominally a committee member. But I couldn't help feeling a little resentment at what I considered my undeserved humiliation. Later, I reflected that my reaction only proved all the more my need for criticism.

"Sir," I pleaded earnestly that evening, "please scold me more often."

"I understand." He looked at me keenly. "But what you need is more devotion."

It was true. In heeding the negative criticisms of my older brothers I had fallen—from what had seemed to me good motives—into judgmental attitudes, which are forever inimical to love.

Soon afterwards I approached Master. "I'm sorry, Sir," I said.

"That's the way!" Master smiled lovingly. From then on the incident was closed between us.

Master always discouraged negativity, even in a good cause. A couple of years later a certain man tried by trickery to hurt the work in one of our churches. Mr. Jacot, a loyal and devoted member, uncovered the man's schemes and denounced him publicly. Master expressed his gratitude to Mr. Jacot afterwards for having saved us from a perilous situation. After thanking him, however, he gently scolded him for the means he had employed. "It is not good," he said, "regardless of one's intentions, to create wrong vibrations through anger and harsh words. The good that you have accomplished would have been greater had you employed peaceful means."

Negativity, from whatever motive, creates its own momentum. Unfortunately Mr. Jacot failed, even after Master's admonishment, to see the need for curbing righteous anger in defense of a good cause. Thus he gradually developed a judgmental mood that ultimately separated him from the work.

On another occasion, perhaps a year after our committee episode, I was invited by a certain Masonic lodge, to which one of our members belonged, to appear in a tableau that was to be presented on the occasion of their installation of officers. Master told me to go. The affair went smoothly enough until the time came for the installation ceremony itself. And then smoldering rivalries burst into flame. Half the lodge members walked out in angry protest. The ceremony ended in emotional ashes.

"How did it go?" Master inquired of me the following day.

"Not too well," I replied.

"It was a fiasco, wasn't it?"

"Completely, Sir, I'm afraid!"

"Well," he concluded, "don't say anything about it."

His wish that I say nothing at first surprised, and then impressed me. It surprised me because, no matter what I might say, the Masons would never get wind of my remarks. Nor did their internal problems at all affect us. But then I realized that what Master was warning me about was the power of negativity itself.

"Avoid speaking negative things," he said to us one evening. "Why look at the drains, when there is beauty all around? You could take me into the most perfect room in the world, and still, if I wanted to, I would be able to find faults in it. But why should I want to? Why not enjoy its beauty?"

Again he told us, "Don't speak of the faults of the organization. If I wanted to list them I could start now and never stop! But if we concentrate on the bad side, we lose sight of the good. Doctors say that millions of terrible germs pass through our bodies. But because we aren't aware of them they are far less likely to affect us than if we sensed their presence, and worried about it. So should it be here. For there is a great deal of good in this organization. But when we look at the negative side long enough, we ourselves take on negative qualities. When we concentrate on the good, we take on goodness."

It was several days after the committee episode that I first met Daya Mata (then Faye Wright). I had entered the main office after working-hours to deliver something. A youthful-looking woman of radiant countenance entered the room, her firm step suggesting boundless energy. I had no idea who she was, but sensed in her a deep attunement with Master. Seeing me, she paused, then addressed me pleasantly.

"You're Donald, aren't you? I'm Faye. I've heard about you." She smiled. "My, that was quite a stir you boys created with that committee of yours!"

I felt acutely embarrassed. As far as I was concerned, that committee was a dead issue. But she, not knowing how I stood on the matter, decided to help me to understand it better. As we conversed, I found myself thinking, "So this is an example of those disciples who were supposed to be 'obstructing' Master's wishes. I'd a thousand times rather be like her than like any of those complainers!" Her calm self-possession, kindliness, and transparent devotion to Master impressed me deeply. From now on, I resolved, I would look upon her as my model in the ideal spirit of discipleship that I was striving to acquire.

"We must learn to give up self-will if we want to please Master. And that," she added significantly, "is what we are trying to do."

Simple teaching, simply expressed! But it rang true. What, I thought, reflecting on her words, was the use of building this, of organizing that, of doing even the most laudable work, if *Master* was not pleased? For his job was to express God's will for each of us. To please him was, quite simply, to please God.

Let others do the important, outward things, I decided. For me only one thing would matter from now on: to do Master's will, *to please him*. I was immeasurably grateful to this senior disciple for her advice.

Ironically, it was very soon afterward—almost as if in response to my determination to court obscurity—that Master singled me out for responsibility. He put me in charge of the monks at Mt. Washington. By this time I had been with him one year—not long enough surely, I thought, for such a heavy responsibility. "He's testing me," I decided. But this time he must have made the appointment seriously, for I held this position for the remainder of my years at Mt. Washington.

Several weeks passed. Then one day I was standing with Herbert Freed, one of the ministers, outside the entrance to the basement. We were talking with Master, who was on the point of going out for a drive. Herbert was to leave that afternoon to become the minister of our church in Phoenix, Arizona, and Master was giving him last-minute instructions. After a pause, Master continued quietly:

"You have a great work to do."

Turning to Herbert, I smiled my felicitations.

"It is you I'm talking to, Walter," Master corrected me. He said no more on the subject; moments later his car drove away. To what sort of work had he been referring?

Thereafter, in one context or another, he often repeated this prediction. "You must do so-and-so, Walter," he would say, "because you have a great work to do." Or, "You have a great work to do, therefore. . . ." Two years after Master's *mahasamadhi,* Rajarsi Janakananda, his chief disciple, was blessing a group of us one evening in Encinitas. He paused when I came up to him, then said softly, "Master has a great work to do through you, Walter. And he will give you the strength to do it."

What was this "great work" they were referring to? Neither of them ever told me. But Master's words were, in their cumulative effect at least, the most insistent he ever addressed to me. They returned often to my mind through the ensuing years, demanding comprehension. Clearly, I reflected, they had been meant as a command, not as a compliment. They seemed intended to invest me with a sense of personal responsibility for some aspect of his mission, and also, perhaps, to inspire me not to shirk that responsibility. Clearly, too in the context of his remarks on several of those occasions, mine was to be a public work, one in which I would have to stand on my own feet, and one therefore, perhaps, not closely connected with normal institutional activities.

Instinctively I feared such responsibility. I wanted to be in tune with Master, and not to dance the wild jig of outward success and acclaim, fraught as it is with temptation. We are here, Daya Mata had said, to please Master. Couldn't I, I prayed, just please him from the background—the *safe* ground—where no lure of outward importance could intrude?

"I don't *want* to do a great work!" I wrote to Rajarsi the day after he had spoken those words to me. "I just want to serve Master unnoticed." (Rajarsi's reply was to come and bless me again, smiling quietly.)

But when, one time, I resisted Master's efforts to draw me into teaching activities, his response was brusque.

"Living for God," he said sternly, "is martyrdom!"

CHAPTER 28

Reincarnation

A BOATLOAD OF FISHERMEN in Encinitas had had a bad day. After hours of work, and very little to show for it, they were ready to go home. Paramhansa Yogananda happened to be out strolling on the beach when they brought their boat in.

"You are giving up?" he inquired.

"Yeah," they replied, sadly. "No fish."

"Why don't you try just once more?" the Master suggested.

Something in his manner made them heed his advice. Going out once more, they got a large haul.

And thus was added another puzzling item to a growing legend in the local community of Encinitas about the strange, kindly Swami around whom things seemed somehow always to happen for the best.

To me this story, which I heard indirectly from some of the townsfolk there, illustrates a basic truth of human life, one that Master often emphasized: No matter how many times a person fails, he should never accept failure as the final judgment of Destiny. As children of the Infinite, we have a right to God's infinite bounty. Failure is *never* His will for us. It is merely a temporary condition that we impose on ourselves through some flaw in our attunement with cosmic law. By repeated efforts to succeed, we gradually refine that attunement. "Try just once more," Master said. If our basic intentions are lawful, failure simply means we haven't yet succeeded. Life, in other words, gives us our failures as stepping stones to success.

In the case of the fishermen, Master's blessings proved a necessary additive, but only in the sense that they helped attune those men's efforts more quickly to what they were already on the way to accomplishing. Had the men themselves not been ready for his blessing, he would not have given it, which is another way of saying they would not have attracted it. The *sensitivity* with which one "tries just once more," rather than the mere act of repetition, is the real key to success. There are some people who succeed quickly, where others struggle unsuccessfully for years. *Attunement* is the secret. Genius depends far more on attunement than on hard work or intellectual brilliance. And of all existing sorts of attunement, the highest is to be aware that it is God's power that acts through us.

In that episode which I related in the last chapter, of the famous artist whose portrait of Lahiri Mahasaya failed to win Yogananda's approval, Paramhansaji asked him, "How long did it take you to master your art?"

"Twenty years," the man replied.

"Twenty years," Master exclaimed, "to convince yourself you could paint?"

This wasn't at all the comment the artist was expecting. Taken aback, he spluttered furiously, "I'd like to see you do as well in twice that length of time!"

"Give me one week," the Master replied calmly. Taking paintbrush in hand, he made several false starts, attuning himself more sensitively each time to the Source of all true inspiration. By the end of a week he had completed a portrait which, the artist himself was forced to concede, was better than his own.

The story of the fishermen is also a symbol of God's everlasting willingness to give men the "one more" chance they need to catch all they desire from the ocean of His abundance. By extension, this story suggests that God's forgiveness—call it, rather, His loving expectation of us—is eternal. The teachings of India claim that the soul, too, has an eternity of opportunities before it to achieve perfection. A man ought never to abandon hope, even if failure dog him all his life. Through repeated incarnations he can—indeed, he *must*—succeed, eventually.

On the subject of reincarnation, Indian philosophy seems at odds with Christian teachings. But in fact this doctrine is denied only in the prevailing *interpretations* of the Bible, and not in the Bible itself. Reincarnation is not an *un-Christian* teaching. Nor, for that matter, is it an un-Jewish one. It was taught by some of the great early Christian Fathers, including Origen (A.D. 185–254),* who claimed to have received it in an unbroken tradition "from apostolic times." Indeed, it was not until five centuries after Christ, in 553 A.D., at the Second Council of Constantinople, that this doctrine was finally removed

---

* The Encyclopedia Britannica calls Origen "the most prominent of all the Church Fathers with the possible exception of Augustine." Origen wrote, of reincarnation, "Is it not reasonable that souls should be introduced into bodies in accordance with their merits and previous deeds?"

from Christian dogma. The anathema that was pronounced against it was a consequence of political maneuverings, not of theological purism. Scholars have recently discovered that Pope Vigilius, although present in Constantinople at that time, took no part in pronouncing the anathema, and in fact boycotted the Council altogether.

Numerous Biblical passages* support belief in reincarnation. This doctrine may be found, subsequent to Biblical times, in Jewish as well as in Christian traditions. Rabbi Manasseh ben Israel (1604–1657 A.D.), Jewish theologian and statesman, wrote, "The belief or the doctrine of the transmigration of souls is a firm and infallible dogma accepted by the whole assemblage of our church [sic] with one accord, so that there is none to be found who dare to deny it. . . . The truth of it has been incontestably demonstrated by the Zohar, and all the books of the Kabalists." And while modern Jews generally reject this doctrine, rabbis familiar with the spiritual traditions of Judaism do not endorse their rejection. Reincarnation is endorsed in the *Shulhan Oruch,* which is the major book of laws in the Torah. A student for the rabbinate in Israel has sent me several supportive quotations from this book, including these words from the Sha'ar Hatsiyune, letter 6vav: "That soul will be sent time and time again to this world until he does what God wants

---

* "Then Job arose, and rent his mantle, and shaved his head, and fell down upon the ground, and worshiped. And said, Naked came I out of my mother's womb, and naked shall I return thither [i.e., into another womb]" (Job 1:20,21).

"But thou, Bethlehem Ephratah, though thou be little among the thousands of Judah, yet out of thee shall he come forth unto me that is to be ruler in Israel; whose goings forth have been from of old, from everlasting" (Micah 5:2).

"For all the prophets and the law prophesied until John. And if ye will receive it, this is Elias, which was for to come. He that hath ears to hear, let him hear" (Matthew 11:13–15).

"And as they came down from the mountain, Jesus charged them, saying, Tell the vision [of his transfiguration, in which he had revealed himself as the Messiah] to no man, until the Son of man be risen again from the dead. And his disciples asked him, saying, Why then say the scribes that Elias must first come? And Jesus answered and said unto them, Elias truly shall first come, and restore all things. But I say unto you, That Elias is come already, and they knew him not but have done unto him whatsoever they listed. Likewise shall also the Son of man suffer of them. Then the disciples understood that he spake unto them of John the Baptist" (Matthew 17:9–13).

"Him that overcometh will I make a pillar in the temple of my God, *and he shall go no more out*" (Revelation 3:12).

The above passages present a small selection, merely, out of many in the Bible that demonstrate support for the doctrine of reincarnation. Christian traditionalists would be wise to question some of the *sources* for their own traditions. Do those sources derive from great saints, who knew God? Or are they merely the deductions of rationalists, whose theological conclusions were founded on reason, not on actual spiritual experience?

him to do." The student said that his rabbi, after reading this letter, could no longer deny the doctrine of reincarnation.

Rabbi Abraham Yehoshua, a Hasidic master who died in 1825, spoke of ten lives that he had lived previously, concluding, "And so I was sent forth again and again in order to perfect my love. If I succeed this time, I shall never return again."*

Among famous Westerners who have subscribed to this doctrine, the German philosopher Schopenhauer wrote: "Were an Asiatic to ask me for a definition of Europe, I should be forced to answer him: It is that part of the world which is haunted by the incredible delusion that man was created out of nothing, and that his present birth is his first entrance into life."† Voltaire wrote, "It is not more surprising to be born twice than once." And the British philosopher Hume stated that reincarnation is "the only system to which Philosophy can hearken."

According to the doctrine of reincarnation, life on earth is a school containing many grades. The ultimate goal of human experience is graduation from limited, egoic awareness into cosmic consciousness. Stepping stones to this unconditioned awareness are the removal of all confining attachments and desires, the expansion of love, and a growing realization that God is the one underlying Reality of the universe.

The "plot" of the cosmic drama of creation embraces not only biological evolution, but individual, egoic evolution as well. For the ego to achieve ultimate perfection, many lifetimes are needed.

Egoic development begins, just as the outward life forms it assumes do, at the lowest levels of conscious identity. It moves upwards automatically at first, through plant, insect, and animal forms, until at last it reaches the human level.§ Thereafter evolution ceases to be automatic, for in man's more highly developed brain and nervous system the ego experiences for the first time the ability to exercise discrimination, and thus develops a certain amount of free will. Spiritual evolution from this time onward becomes speeded up, or delayed, or temporarily reversed, according to the caliber of the individual's own efforts.

The results of self-effort are regulated by the law of karma. (Newton's law of action and reaction is a material manifestation of this spiritual law.) According to karmic law, every action, even of

---

* Martin Buber, *Tales of the Hasidim*, New York, Schocken Books, 1948, p. 118.
† *Parerga and Paralipomena.*
§ The Hindu Scriptures state that to reach the human level requires from five to eight million incarnations in lower life forms.

thought, engenders its own balancing reaction. For creation, being nothing but a dream of the Creator, can maintain its appearance of separateness from Him only by the illusion of duality. That is to say, the Spirit, One and Indivisible, in creating sets a part of its consciousness into motion—like waves on the surface of the sea,° or like the tines of a tuning fork that, to produce sound, move in opposite directions from a state of rest. Because the natural position of the tines is in the middle, no movement in either direction from that point is complete in itself; it *must* be balanced by an equal and opposite movement.

Karma means, simply, *action. Any* action implies movement from a point of rest in the Spirit. And such movement inevitably results, sooner or later, in an equal and opposite movement: *a reaction in kind.* Hatred given, that is to say, results in hatred received. Love given attracts love. Gradually, as the ego develops in wisdom, it learns to allow actions to flow through it without feeling in any sense personally involved with them. The fruits of its actions too, then, cease to affect it. The sage, who represents the pinnacle of spiritual evolution, rests unshaken in the calm center of his being, blissful in the realization that he and the unmoving, Infinite Spirit are One.

Spiritually speaking, karma has different levels of manifestation depending on how clearly it expresses the divine consciousness. Love, for example, is a more spiritual karma than hatred, since it reinforces the awareness of life's essential oneness. Hatred increases the delusion of separateness from God, and from other people. To tell the truth is a more spiritual karma than to tell lies, because truthfulness helps to develop a refined awareness of *what really is*— of the Divine Reality behind all appearances.

Karma, then, may be described as the system of rewards and punishments by which the ego learns ultimately to manifest its innate divine nature. Suffering is the karmic result of action that is, in some way, out of tune with that true nature. Fulfillment is the reward for living, to some degree at least, in harmony with that nature. To learn these lessons thoroughly requires many more opportunities for error and self-correction than can be gained in only one lifetime. Often, indeed, more than one incarnation is needed to learn even *one* important lesson.

Reincarnation explains wonderfully the enormous inequities of health, intelligence, talent, and opportunity in human life. It is, as

---

° "And the Spirit of God moved upon the face of the waters. And God said, Let there be light: and there was light" (Genesis 1:2,3).

Hume stated, "the only system to which Philosophy can hearken."

People often object, "If everyone reincarnates why is it that no one remembers having lived before?" The simple answer is that many do remember! In the West, of course, children claiming such memories soon learn, from the scoldings of their elders, to keep their thoughts to themselves. But even so, a number of well-documented cases have received considerable publicity.* Because of my own relatively well-known interest in such things, a number of people through the years have related to me their own experiences with past-life recall.

One such lady told me that she had once played a piece on the piano for a four-year-old boy, a student of hers. Matter-of-factly the child announced, "I know that piece. I used to play it on my violin." Knowing that he had studied only the piano, she questioned him. The boy demonstrated correctly the difficult finger positions and arm movements for playing the violin. "He's never seen a violin before," insisted his mother later. "He's never even heard violin music!"

One of the most interesting accounts of this nature ever to come to my attention was sent to me years ago by a friend in Cuba, where it had been reprinted in the newspapers from an article that appeared first in France. According to the account, a young French girl, the child of devout Catholic parents, had been using recognizably Indian words, such as "rupee," as soon as she was old enough to speak. Two words that she used repeatedly were, "Wardha," and "Bapu." Her parents, intrigued, began reading books on India. Wardha, they learned, was the village where Mahatma Gandhi had established his ashram. And "Bapu" was the familiar nickname by which he was known to his intimate friends and disciples. The child claimed that in her last life she had lived in Wardha with Bapu.

One day someone presented her parents with a copy of *Autobiography of a Yogi,* in the latter part of which Yogananda describes his visit, in 1936, to Mahatma Gandhi in Wardha. The moment the child saw Yogananda's photograph on the jacket, she cried gleefully, "Oh, that's Yogananda! He came to Wardha. He was very beautiful!"

People who believe they live only once are compelled to compromise

---

* Books on the subject include *Twenty Cases Suggestive of Reincarnation,* by Dr. Ian Stevenson; *Many Mansions,* by Dr. Gina Cerminara; *Here and Hereafter,* by Ruth Montgomery; and *Reincarnation in the Twentieth Century,* edited by Martin Ebon. There are many others.

their hopes of perfection. Orthodox believers may try to conduct their lives in such a way as to avoid hellfire after death, but most I think, even so, are inclined to ask themselves pragmatically, "How bad can I be and get away with it?"

Belief in the principle of rebirth helps one to view progress joyously, without fear and self-doubt.

"Is there any end to evolution?" a visitor once asked Paramhansa Yogananda.

"No end," the Master replied. "Progress goes on until you achieve endlessness."

At Mt. Washington, reincarnation was a normal part of our way of thinking. We took it quite in stride if ever Master told us, as he sometimes did, about our own or someone else's past lives.

Looking at Jan Savage, aged nine, one day he exclaimed laughingly, "Little Jan is no child. He's still an old man!"

I once told him I had always wanted to live alone. His reply was, "That is because you have done it before. Most of those who are with me have lived alone many times in the past." He made such remarks so casually that it rarely occurred to me to ask him for more information. A few others expressed deeper interest, however, and sometimes Master responded to them quite explicitly.

A few years after Dr. Lewis lost his mother, Master, knowing Doctor's devotion to her, informed him, "She has been reborn. If you go to . . ." he mentioned some address in New England, "you will find her there." Dr. Lewis made the journey.

"It was uncanny," he told me later. "The child was only three years old, but in many of her mannerisms she seemed exactly like my mother. I observed, too, that she took an instantaneous liking to me. It was almost as though she recognized me."

Mrs. Vera Brown visited a theater one evening with Master and a few of the disciples. A little girl in the row ahead of them captured her interest. "I couldn't take my eyes off her," she later told me. "There was something about that child that just fascinated me. I guess it was because she looked so old and wise for her age, and at the same time so sad. Afterwards Master said to me, 'You were interested in that little girl, weren't you?' 'Yes, Sir,' I answered. 'I don't know why, but I found myself watching her the whole time we were there.'

" 'In her last life,' Master said, 'she died in a German concentration camp. That is why she looks so sad. But her tragic experiences there, and the compassion she developed as a result of them, have made her a saint. That was the wisdom you saw in her that attracted you so.' "

One day Master was given a newborn baby to hold. "I almost dropped it," he told friends later. "Suddenly I saw in that little, seemingly innocent form, the brought-over consciousness of a murderer."

Discussions on reincarnation sometimes became intensely interesting. One day I asked Master, "Did Judas have any spiritual realization?"

"He had some bad karma, of course," Master replied, "but all the same, he was a prophet."

"He *was?*" This variation on the common theme of Judas's villainy astonished me.

"Oh, yes," Master asserted emphatically. "He had to be, to be one of the twelve. But he had to go through two thousand years of suffering for his treachery. He was liberated finally in this century, in India. Jesus appeared to a certain master there and asked him to free him. I knew Judas in this life," Master added.

"You did!" Eagerly I pursued the matter. "What was he like?"

"Always very quiet and by himself. He still had a little attachment to money. One day another disciple began poking fun at him for this tendency. But the Master shook his head. 'Don't,' he said quietly. 'Leave him alone.' "

In 1936 Master visited Stonehenge in England. To his secretary, Richard Wright (Daya Mata's brother), he remarked quietly, "I lived here myself thirty-five hundred years ago."

Sometimes he intrigued us with references, always casual, to the past lives of certain well-known public figures. "Winston Churchill," he told us, "was Napoleon. Napoleon wanted to conquer England. Churchill, as England's Prime Minister, has fulfilled that ambition. Napoleon wanted to destroy England. As Churchill he has had to preside over the disintegration of the British Empire. Napoleon was sent into exile, then returned again to power. Churchill, similarly, was sent out of politics, then after some time came back to power again."

It is an interesting fact that Churchill, as a young man, found inspiration in the military exploits of Napoleon.

"Hitler," Master continued, "was Alexander the Great." An interesting point of comparison here is that, in warfare, both Hitler and Alexander employed the strategy of lightning attack—*blitzkrieg,* as Hitler called it. In the Orient, of course, where Alexander's conquests were responsible for the destruction of great civilizations, his appellation, "the Great," is quoted sarcastically.

Master had hoped to reawaken in Hitler Alexander's well-known interest in the teachings of India, and thereby to steer the dictator's ambitions toward more spiritual goals. He actually attempted to see Hitler in 1935, but his request for an interview was denied.

Mussolini, Master said, was Mark Antony. Kaiser Wilhelm was Julius Caesar. Stalin was Genghis Khan.

"Who was Franklin Roosevelt?" I inquired.

"I've never told anybody," Master replied with a wry smile. "I was afraid I'd get into trouble!"

Abraham Lincoln, he informed us, had been a yogi in the Himalayas who died with a desire to help bring about racial equality. His birth as Lincoln was for the purpose of fulfilling that desire. "He has come back again in this century," Master said, "as Charles Lindbergh."

It is interesting to note that the public acclaim that was denied Lincoln, though so richly deserved, came almost effortlessly to Lindbergh. Interestingly, too, after Lindbergh's death a Hawaiian friend of his, Joseph Kahaleuahi, exclaimed, "This is not a small man. This man is like a President."° Charles Lindbergh was noted for his interest in Indian philosophy. Perhaps (one wonders), having fulfilled his desire, as a yogi, to work for racial equality, and having rejected, as Lindbergh, the acclaim that was his karmic reward for Lincoln's success, he will once again in his next life become a yogi.

Of more saintly people, Master said that Therese Neumann, the Catholic stigmatist of Konnersreuth, Germany, was Mary Magdalene. "That," he explained to us, "is why she was granted those visions of Christ's crucifixion."

"Lahiri Mahasaya," he once told me at Twenty-Nine Palms, "was the greatest saint of his time. In a previous life he was King Janaka.† Babaji initiated him in that golden palace because he had lived in a palace before."

According to another disciple, Master told someone that Lahiri Mahasaya was also the great medieval mystic, Kabir.

"Babaji," Master told us, "is an incarnation of India's greatest prophet, Krishna."

Master then revealed to us that he himself had been Krishna's closest friend and disciple, Arjuna. ("Prince of devotees," the *Bhagavad Gita* calls him.) We found it easy to believe that he was that mighty warrior. Master's incredible will power, his innate gift of leadership and his enormous physical strength, when he chose to exert it, all pointed to one with the tendencies of an all-conquering

---

° *Reader's Digest,* December 1974, p. 258.

† Janaka, though a king, was also one of the great masters of ancient India.

hero. Speaking of that incarnation, Master told me, "That is why, in this life, I am so close to Babaji."

Master knew the value of offsetting abstract teachings with these interesting sidelights on reality. The barriers to memory raised between lifetimes to the average person melt away before the man of wisdom. But of course Master's real interest, and ours, lay in our attainment of divine enlightenment. We found that familiarity with the law of reincarnation helped us to deepen our determination to escape the monotonous round of death and rebirth.

It also provided us with occasional insight into our present spiritual difficulties.

Henry Schaufelberger and Ed Harding (another, older, disciple), were distressed for a time at the discovery of a deep-seated, apparently irrational animosity between them.

"That is because you were enemies in a former life," Master explained to Henry, who approached him one day for guidance in the matter. This knowledge helped both the men to understand their problem, and overcome it.

The doctrine of reincarnation is, as I have said, closely related to the law of karma. Sometimes people object, "But what can I learn from suffering, if I don't remember what I did in the past that brought on this suffering?" The answer is that both the act and the karmic consequence thereof reflect overtly a mental *tendency* that one still carries with him. It is primarily with this tendency that the karmic law deals.

If, for example, out of mercenary greed, I once cheated someone out of his inheritance, and in this life suffer the consequence of that act by losing an inheritance of my own, both my own act and my getting cheated will reflect the underlying fact of my greed. I may have forgotten what it was that I did, but if now I decide that cheating is something that shouldn't happen to anybody, *and resolve never, on my part, to cheat anybody,* I will have untied one knot, at least, in my own tendency toward greed. There may still be other knots of greed for me to untie. A whole series of other acts, in fact, may have sprung out of that single tendency, each in its own way reinforcing it. If I am wise, therefore, the loss of that inheritance will not only make me reflect on the fact that cheating is wrong; it will inspire me also to trace this question of dishonesty back to its root cause, in greed. I'll conclude that greed itself is a fault, and try to discover and uproot the seeds of this fault in myself. If I am successful in this effort, a nullifying force-field of non-attachment will be set up that will minimize the karmic consequences of any other greedy acts in the past.

The power of karma depends in great measure on the intensity of thought associated with it.

Suppose I have overcome greed, and acquired non-attachment, *before* I lose that inheritance. In this case, the money I lose may be returned to me unexpectedly. In any case I won't suffer as much.

Patanjali, the ancient exponent of yoga, states in his *Yoga Sutras* that when avarice is fully overcome, one attracts to himself everything in life that he needs. As Patanjali quaintly put it, "Jewels will come to one in abundance."*

It should be understood that the karmic law is quite impersonal. We can learn from our karma if we've a will to. But it is quite possible *not* to will to. An unwise reaction, for example, to a stolen inheritance would be to try to "get even" with the world by cheating others. One who takes this course will only reinforce the tendency which attracted his misfortune in the first place. Thus he will sow the seeds of still greater suffering in the future.

Dr. Lewis once asked Master why a certain acquaintance had been born with a club foot. "That," Master replied, "is because in his last life he kicked his mother."

Having a club foot in this life probably didn't stir that man to any noble resolution not to kick his present mother. But it must have acted on that tendency indirectly. His mother, after all, as the source of his physical existence, represented to him in a very special way the sacredness of life. When he kicked her, he expressed contempt, in effect, for life itself. His club foot in this incarnation may well have made him, at least in his own eyes, an object of contempt. An unwise reaction to such a self-image would be to hate life more than ever—a tendency that might be continued for many lives, until in sheer desperation he decided to reform. But if he reacted wisely to this self-image, he might tell himself what a blessing it would be to have a perfect body. Automatically, from such a reaction, would come a respect for life that would make it unlikely that he would treat any future mother so contemptuously.

One benefit of the doctrine of reincarnation is that it helps one to remain humble, concerned rather with attuning himself to God's all-ruling will than with imposing his own petty desires on the universe. A belief in reincarnation helps one to accept more easily that least popular, but most important of ancient injunctions, "Change thyself."

I once had an interesting dream; indeed, it has always seemed to me more than a dream. I saw myself in another life, deeply devoted

* *Yoga Sutras* II:37.

to a particular friend. He took advantage of my devotion, and treated me with an unkindness that fluctuated between condescension and outright contempt. In time I developed deep feelings of bitterness toward him. As I approached the end of that incarnation, I realized that if I died with this attitude, my bitterness would act as a magnet that would draw us both back into similar, but reversed, circumstances, giving me the opportunity to treat him as unkindly as he had me. And if I treated him so, ensuing bitterness on *his* part might very possibly reverse our positions once more. Perhaps only a succession of such "return engagements," of gradually diminishing intensity, would enable us at last to work out our love-hate relationship—rather in the way that echoes gradually die out in a valley.

"Why take so long?" I asked myself. "Isn't it possible to escape this web right now? Whatever the lessons my friend needs to learn, surely *I*, at least, can free myself." Then, from the depths of my heart, I cried, "I forgive him!" At that moment, with an expansion of ineffable relief, I awoke. In that simple act of forgiveness I felt that I had freed myself of some actual karmic burden.

All human life, so the Scriptures of India tell us, is a dream. Its ultimate goal is to help us to learn well our lessons, to overcome our attachments to material limitations, and to realize that all things, seemingly separate and real in themselves, are but manifestations of the one light of God. The highest lesson of all is to learn to love God. The best karma of all is the ability to love Him.

"Sir," Norman once said, rather morosely, to Master, "I don't believe I have very good karma."

"Remember this," Master replied with deep earnestness, "it takes very, *very*, VERY good karma even to *want* to know God!"

Through love of God, and only through that love, may one win final release from physical rebirth, and the right to advance to higher spheres of existence. Victory comes not by hating this world, but by beholding God's presence in it everywhere, by paying reverence to the veriest fool as though to a holy shrine.

"You must be very joyous and happy," Master said, "because this is God's dream, and the little man and the big man are all nothing but the Dreamer's consciousness."

CHAPTER 29

Gardens—Mundane and Spiritual

I T WAS, AS I RECALL, sometime during August or September 1949 that Paramhansa Yogananda acquired his last and most beautiful ashram property: twelve acres shaped by Nature into a steep-sided bowl surrounding a miniature lake. This "SRF Lake Shrine," as Master named it, nestles serenely in the arms of a broad curve formed by Sunset Boulevard as, leaving the town of Pacific Palisades, it makes its final sweep down to the ocean. The property is one of the loveliest I have seen in a lifetime of world travel.

Soon after Master obtained this property, he invited the monks out to see it. Walking its grounds, we were wonderstruck at their beauty. Happily Master predicted, "This will be a showcase for the work!" Later on he had us don bathing suits and enter the water with him.

"I am sending the divine light all through this lake," he said. Afterward he told us, "This is holy water now. Whoever comes here in future will receive a divine blessing."

Even today, nearly thirty years after that event, merely to enter those grounds is to feel their spiritual power. Often I have reflected that people in distant lands go on pilgrimages for blessings like these. Holy shrines in India, Palestine, and elsewhere owe their sanctity, as this one does in modern California, to the blessings of God-known saints. But in many of those more ancient shrines, throngs of people, eager for mere worldly boons, have diluted the spiritual vibrations. At the SRF Lake Shrine the original vibrations are still powerfully felt, as they are indeed in all Yogananda's ashrams. For not only do those places have his blessings (at Mt. Washington he once told us, "I have meditated on every spot on these grounds"), but since his passing they have been inhabited continuously by sincere devotees.

Soon after acquiring the Lake Shrine, we began the task of preparing it for a public opening one year later. An abundance of trees, shrubs, and flowers were brought in and planted on the steep hillsides. Statues of leading figures in the great world religions were placed in picturesque spots about the grounds, to emphasize Yogananda's teaching of the basic oneness of all religions. ("Where do you want the Buddha to sit?" we inquired one day. Master was standing nearby, directing operations. "The Buddha," he replied with a quiet smile, "prefers to remain standing.")

In the early months of preparation, swarms of gnats proved an extreme nuisance. The fascination they demonstrated for our eyes, ears, and nostrils was anything but flattering. "Master," I exclaimed in exasperation one day, "what irony! Why must this beautiful setting be spoiled by these flies?"

Calmly Master replied, "That is the Lord's way of keeping us ever moving toward Him."

Happily, the Lord found other ways to accomplish this objective. The gnats proved only a temporary pest.

One day we were moving a delicate but rather heavy tropical plant into position on the hillside. Our handling evidently was too rough, for Master cried out, "Be careful what you are doing. Can't you *feel?* It's alive!"

His sensitivity to all things living inspired sensitivity from them in return. Not only people and animals, but even plants seemed to respond to his feelings for them. His gardens flourished. Tropical mangoes and bananas grew at Mt. Washington, where the climate is not conducive to their survival. Shraddha Mata (Miss Sahly) tells of one day watching what she calls a "rose devotee" that kept turning in its vase to face Master as he moved about the room. "Plants," Master explained, "have a degree of consciousness." Above all, like every sentient being, they respond to love.

Master even felt with certain plants a mysterious personal identity. One day, pointing to an avocado tree by a walkway at Mt. Washington, he told us, "Originally I planted two trees here, one on either side of the path. We had a certain student living here in those days who was deeply devoted. Speaking of him once, I told a few others, 'One of us will leave this work, and one of these trees also will die. This tree stands for me; that one for him. The tree that dies will signal which one of us will leave.'

"Well, his tree died. Soon afterwards he left. He had been *very* devoted, too. But—his devotion fled. The delusion that took him away was the desire for—money." Master paused momentarily before naming that delusion, to give us time mentally to fill in the blank with our own karmic obstacles, and thus remind ourselves what we needed to work on for our own spiritual welfare.

A pine tree in the eastern part of the grounds at Mt. Washington was dying. In the summer of 1949 Jean Haupt cut it down. Master grieved over the loss of his arboreal friend. "You will see," he remarked quietly to Daya Mata. "The end of that tree marks the beginning of the end of my own life." Strangely worded though his prophecy was, it was to prove true.

Sometimes in his training of us he likened us, too, to plants. Of a certain monk who had been resisting his spiritual counsel, he exclaimed, "What a job one takes on when he tries to improve people! He has to go into their minds and see what it is they are thinking. The rose in the vase looks beautiful; one forgets all the care that went into growing it. But if it takes such care to produce a rose, how much more care is needed to develop a perfect human being!"

Like a divine gardener, Master labored unceasingly for our spiritual development. It took patience, love, courage, and considerably greater faith in us than most of us had in ourselves. For where we saw only our own egos struggling to shed their imperfections, he saw our souls struggling to reclaim their divine birthright in God. Some of his disciples justified his faith in them better than others did, but he extended to all the same vision of their ultimate perfectibility.

I soon learned that one of the most important things on the path, especially for the newcomer, is the wise selection of associates. For even in a spiritual environment there may be a few gossips and grumblers, a few devotees who meditate too little, while others can't seem to get it into their minds that it is *they* who need changing, not the rest of the world. On the other side, in every truly spiritual organization there are also those who, by their example of selfless service, constant cheerfulness, inward focus, and spiritual fervor inspire in others a constant renewal of dedication.

At Mt. Washington I found such inspiration in numerous disciples. Even today I recall them with gratitude. I think of Mrs. Merck (later, Sister Karuna). Well into her eighties, she worked hours every day in the garden. "Ya," she would say sweetly in a thick Swedish accent, "I lahv de flowers. Dey are my shildren!"

I think of Mrs. Royston, also elderly. She it was who told me of Master, years earlier, running joyously out onto the lecture platform. Her steadfast loyalty and unfailing good spirits epitomized Master's frequent instruction to us: "Be ever even-minded and cheerful."

I think of Mrs. Wright, Daya Mata's mother—at once firm and compassionate. "Great Mother," Master used to call her.

I think of Mrs. Brown, whose joyful loyalty to Master was as much a delight as it was an inspiration. Her joy, by no means callow, was rooted in great inner determination and strength. Mrs. Brown had to contend with prolonged physical suffering; yet she gladly ignored pain to serve others. To me, as no doubt to many others, she was truly like a mother.

Miss Sahly was the older nun whom I upbraided like a "young hothead" during that lamentable episode of the committee. As I got to know her better, I found in her a deep, steadfast devotion, one that brooked no nonsense. It reminded me rather of the efficient professional nurse she had once been. But I found her inwardly warm and sympathetic. Her outward sternness helped me never to forget that the divine quest, though joyful, is at the same time a very serious matter.

Miss Darling, though sometimes a little sharp-tongued (in this respect, astrology fans would call her "a true Scorpio"), impressed me with the intensity of her energy, and with the complete dedication with which she approached everything she did. Master once described to us how, years earlier, she and two of the monks had repainted the main building at Mt. Washington.

"The men," he said, "though larger and much stronger than she, waved their paint brushes lackadaisically to and fro as if making graceful peace offerings to the building. But Miss Darling fairly attacked the walls! Tirelessly her brush flew, back and forth, back and forth, never stopping to think how difficult the job was. That," Master concluded joyously, "is the kind of spirit it takes to find God!"

At Twenty-Nine Palms he once told me, "The day Miss Darling came here (to Mt. Washington), I said to her quietly, 'You have come.' I knew she belonged with us."

Of the nuns, Daya Mata was the one I got the opportunity to know best, and also the one from whom I drew the greatest inspiration. I found her always fair-minded, gracious to all, humble, childlike in her spontaneity. What inspired me most about her was her utter devotion to God and Guru. She had no desire that I ever observed except to do Master's will.

"Is everything all right?" she would ask me when we met in her office to discuss official matters. Ever ready to help us spiritually if she could, she would set organizational problems resolutely aside, even when they were pressing, if at any time she sensed that we needed counseling or encouragement. Into every office discussion she would weave subtle threads of devotional insight and guidance. From her I learned that work and meditation belong not in separate compartments from one another; that rather, when the thought of God is held uppermost, they blend together and become one.

"I feel that you have been close to Master in past lives," she told me once. Our own relationship was more like that of brother and older sister than of junior monk and superior. This relationship, too, as we both realized, was rooted in past lives. I could never express in words the depth of my gratitude for her constant friendship and guidance. It is one of the most precious gifts God has given me in this life.

Of the younger nuns I saw very little. Among the monks, few, it turned out, had been in the work as long as the older nuns. ("The spiritual path is harder for men," Master conceded. "But," he added, comfortingly, "those who get there become very great.")

Rev. Michael (Brother Bhaktananda) was one of the monks who inspired me. Deeply humble ("He has no ego," Master once said of him), and devoted to God: I almost envied him the unaffected simplicity with which he could sum up the entire spiritual path with the statement, "Devotion is the *only* thing."

Joe Carbone (Brother Bimalananda) was another inspiration— and Henry Schaufelberger (Brother Anandamoy), too, who came a year after me. Both men combined sweetness with calm insight in a way that I found deeply appealing.

Many others there were, besides. I felt it an immeasurable blessing to be living in their midst.

"Of the disciples," Master told a small group of us in the main office one evening, "the first in realization is Saint Lynn. Next comes Mr. Black, and then Sister." James J. Lynn, whom Master always referred to as Saint Lynn, later received from Master the title and name Rajarsi (royal sage) Janakananda.° Mr. Black was the leader of the SRF center in Detroit, Michigan, and now also leads a spiritual retreat upstate in Vanderbilt, called Song of the Morning Ranch.

At Twenty-Nine Palms in October 1949 Master said to me, "Those who are with me"—he must have meant, *in tune with me*— "I never have any trouble with. Just a glance with the eyes is enough. It is much better when I can teach that way." He added, "They are saints from before, most of them."

Another time he told me, "Many of the disciples will find

° *Janakananda* means "*ananda* (divine bliss) through an ideal balance of outward responsibility and inward spiritual attainment that was perfectly exemplified in ancient times in the life of the royal sage King Janaka."

freedom in this life." Looking out the window, he saw Mrs.
Royston working in the garden. "Even she," he added with an affectionate smile. In a lighter vein he continued, "You know, she
was even homelier when she first came here!" He went on to
praise her highly for her many years of selfless service and
devotion.

To a group of us at Twenty-Nine Palms he once said, "Horace
is very nearly there. God is satisfied with his devotion." Horace, as
the reader may recall, was the spastic devotee who helped James
Coller on the occasion of that disastrous yoga lecture in Phoenix.

James, who was present on this occasion, tried to reconcile
Master's praise of Horace with his brother disciple as he knew
him. "Sir," he said, "it must be a very simple kind of devotion,
isn't it?"

"Ah," Master replied with a beatific smile, "that is the kind God
likes! 'He does not reveal Himself unto the prudent and the wise,
but unto babes.' "

About James himself Master said several times, "He will be liberated in this life." Once, recalling James's difficulty with organizational discipline, he added jokingly, "I don't know *how!* But God
says so, so it must be true."

The disciple who was the most generous with his anecdotes
about Master was Dr. Lewis, the first Kriya Yogi in America, and
by now highly advanced on the spiritual path. We would sit for
hours with Doctor while he regaled us with stories, some of them
amusing, some serious, all of them instructive. They helped us to
see how the relationship between guru and disciple evolves gradually into one of divine friendship in God.

Toward the end of October of that year Dr. Lewis and several
other disciples, including Mrs. Lewis and Norman, accompanied
Master to San Francisco to meet India's Prime Minister, Jawaharlal
Nehru. Doctor returned to Mt. Washington with tales of their journey, then went on to share with us other reminiscences of his
years of association with Master.

"Master," Doctor reported, "asked me to join him in practicing
the energization exercises on the hotel porch in San Francisco."
Doctor laughed quietly. "I nearly died of embarrassment! But what
good reason can there be, after all, to feel embarrassed about doing
a good thing? My self-consciousness had no worthier basis than the
fact that our exercises aren't known to most people! Master decided to cure me of this false notion.

"As we were exercising, a policeman walked by on his beat.
Master, affecting a guilty conscience, stepped hastily behind a

pillar, continuing the exercises there. The policeman glanced at us suspiciously. I was praying for a miracle that would dematerialize me on the spot! But Master went right on exercising as though nothing had happened.

"Minutes later the policeman returned. Again Master ducked behind the pillar. This time the man, his suspicions thoroughly aroused, came over to us.

" 'What's going on here?' he demanded. He probably suspected that we were a pair of criminals planning a crime.

" 'Oh, *nothing*, Officer!' Master assured him with an exaggerated air of innocence. 'Nothing at all. We're just exercising. See?' To demonstrate his utter sincerity, he repeated a few movements, then smiled as if in hopeful expectation of a reprieve.

" 'Well,' the officer muttered, 'see that you don't get into trouble.' With massive dignity, he moved on. By this time I was laughing so hard inside that my embarrassment was completely forgotten."

Master and his little group had visited a Chinese restaurant in San Francisco. The "vegetarian" meal they'd requested had been served with bits of chicken in it. A lady in the group, a prominent member of another religious organization, had stormed angrily into the kitchen and denounced the staff for this "outrage."

"Master," Doctor told us, "considered an uncontrolled temper a 'sin' far worse than the relatively minor one of eating chicken. 'It's not important enough to make a fuss over,' he remarked to the rest of us. Pushing the bits of meat to one side, he calmly ate the rest of his meal."

That night Master and the Lewises had adjoining hotel rooms. "Master kept the door open between us," Doctor said. "I knew he didn't really want us to sleep that night. He himself never sleeps, you know. Not, at least the way you and I do; he's always in superconsciousness. And he wants to break *us*, too, of too much dependence on subconsciousness—'counterfeit *samadhi*,' he calls it. So I guess he saw here an opportunity for us to spend a few hours sharing spiritual friendship and inspiration with him. We don't get many chances for that any more, now that the work has become worldwide.

"The problem was, Mrs. Lewis and I were both tired—she especially so. We'd been traveling all day. 'We're going to sleep,' she announced in a tone of finality. That, as far as she was concerned, was that.

"But Master had other ideas.

"Mrs. Lewis and I went to bed. Master, with apparent submissiveness, lay down on his bed. I was just getting relaxed, and Mrs.

Lewis was beginning to drift peacefully off to sleep, when suddenly Master, as though with infinite relevance, said:

" 'Sub gum.'

"Nothing more. Sub gum was the name of one of those Chinese dishes we'd eaten earlier that day. I smiled to myself. But Mrs. Lewis muttered grimly, 'He's *not* going to make me get up!' A few minutes passed. We were just drifting off again. Suddenly, in marveling tones:

" 'Sub gum *duff!'* Master pronounced the words carefully, like a child playing with unaccustomed sounds.

"Desperately Mrs. Lewis whispered, 'We're sleeping!' She turned for help to the wall.

"More minutes passed. Then, very slowly:

" *'Super* sub gum duff!' The words this time were spoken earnestly, like a child in the process of making some important discovery.

"By this time I was chuckling to myself. But though sleep was beginning to seem to both of us rather an 'impossible dream,' Mrs. Lewis was still hanging on fervently to her resolution.

"More minutes passed. And then the great discovery:

" 'Super SUBMARINE sub gum duff!'

"Further resistance was impossible! Howling with merriment, we rose from the bed. For the remainder of the night sleep was forgotten. We talked and laughed with Master. Gradually the conversation shifted to serious matters. We ended up speaking only of God, then meditating. With his blessings we felt no further need for sleep that night.

"I was telling you," Dr. Lewis continued, "that Master never sleeps. I've found this to be true even when he snores! One day, many years ago, he was lying in his room, apparently asleep, and snoring quite loudly. I tip-toed stealthily into the room and tied a string to his big toe, doing my best to make sure he felt nothing. He was still snoring peacefully as I crept back to the door. I was about to tie the string onto the doorknob when he stopped snoring long enough to say, 'Aha!' "

Dr. Lewis, finding us keenly receptive to his good humor this evening, related another anecdote. "Master and I were standing on a sidewalk one day many years ago," he said. "when a man riding by on his bicycle noticed Master's long hair, and stuck his tongue out at him derisively. About two feet further on he came to a large mud puddle. Right in the middle of that puddle the front wheel of his bicycle came off. He went sprawling!"

Gradually, Doctor's reminiscences grew more serious. "Late in

October, 1941," he said, "Master visited us at our summer residence on Plymouth Bay, in Massachusetts. The ocean is extremely cold there at that time of year. Master, however, on his very first night insisted on going out for a moonlight swim. As he was wading out into the water, we stood shivering and watched him from the shore. Pretty soon he was waist deep. 'By now,' I thought, 'he *must* be feeling the cold!'

"Suddenly I saw a blue light form all around him. My son, standing beside me with his wife, saw it too. Later, when Master returned from his swim, we told him what we'd seen.

"Smiling, Master admitted, 'I had to go deep in the Spirit to escape the cold!'

"I saw that blue light around him on another occasion," Dr. Lewis continued, reverting once more to a humorous mood. "This happened years later. We were crossing the Mexican border into California. Master had bought mangoes for everyone; the car was fairly reeking with them! I was certain they'd be confiscated at the border; as you may know, the California customs are strict about that sort of thing. But when the inspector came up to examine our car, he said absolutely nothing!

" 'How did we manage that one?' another passenger asked me as we drove on merrily into California.

" 'I'm sure I couldn't explain the mechanics of it,' I replied. 'All I know is, as we passed the frontier I saw blue light all around us!' "

Doctor's reminiscences took him back to his early days with Master. "In the early spring of 1923 Master told me, 'Be careful of your health next summer.' Caught up as I was in the bustle of an extremely busy life, I forgot his warning. In midsummer, however, I got my reminder with a vengeance. A severe gastrointestinal pain seized me. Days passed; my agony only increased. At last I prayed urgently to Master.

"It was, as I recall, a Wednesday in July when he came to my rescue. I had gone to my summer home in Plymouth. By this time my endurance had reached a low ebb. Very early that morning— it must have been two or three o'clock—I heard Master's voice in the driveway: 'Doctor! Doctor!'

"What a relief just to hear his voice! He had commandeered a car and come all the way from New York in answer to my prayer. Entering the house with two students, he drew me aside. In that wonderful, unruffled way of his he promised me that I would be all right. He then gave me a marvelous yogic remedy for use in such cases. My condition improved immediately; soon I'd recovered altogether.

"During those early years in Boston there was a man who'd been condemned to death for a crime that I, and many others, felt he hadn't committed. The day before his scheduled execution I happened to be with Master, and mentioned this case to him. Master became very pensive. Silently he retired to a corner of the room, and sat there quietly. After some time he returned to our circle with a smile, and resumed conversation. He never mentioned the condemned man. The following morning, however, the news came out in the papers: At the eleventh hour, the governor had issued a pardon.

"You know, we weren't as familiar in those days with Master's methods as you all are now. We didn't know the wonderful things he could do. For that matter, we didn't know what *any* master can do. By now, people have had years to get to know him better. It was more difficult then for us to have the kind of faith you all have in him. In that episode of the condemned man, for instance, Master never told us he'd done anything to help him. He rarely speaks of the wonderful things he does. It's just that, when things keep on happening around him, you begin to wonder. On that occasion, it was only after the reprieve that I began to suspect strongly that Master had had a hand in the matter.

"You see, he doesn't want to amaze us with miracles. Love is the force by which he seeks to draw us to God. When I first met him in 1920, he said to me, 'Will you always love me as I love you?'

" 'Yes,' I said. I could *feel* his love, you see. 'Yes,' I said, 'I will.'

"But delusion is strong. Sometimes when he talked of the communities we would have someday, and the beautiful buildings, and I saw him living in that little room in Boston, almost in poverty, doubts would assail me. 'When, Sir?' I would ask him. 'When will such big things be possible?' But Master remained serenely confident. 'You'll see, Doctor,' he said. 'You'll see.'

"One day a man came to my dental office and told me lie after lie against Master. He spoke quite plausibly. Worse still, I hadn't any facts to contradict him with. I wouldn't believe his assertions, but I admit that, inside, I was a little shaken. The man left. Minutes passed. Suddenly I heard footsteps outside, approaching my office resolutely. The door opened. Master marched in. Striding right up to me, he gazed into my eyes. 'Do you still love me, Doctor?' he demanded. He proceeded to repeat word for word all that my earlier visitor had said to me.

"Master, I learned later, had been riding a streetcar four or five miles from my office at that time. He had gotten off at the next stop, and walked all that way with the sole purpose of helping me.

"Master inquired, in conclusion, if a certain person didn't owe me a sizeable sum of money. 'Yes,' I said, 'he does.'

" 'If you go there now, you will get it from him.' I went there, and the man repaid me immediately.

"In how many ways Master has helped me and my family!" Doctor concluded, gratitude shining in his eyes. "When my mother suffered a severe stroke, he prolonged her life. When my daughter, Brenda, then still a child, was stricken with convulsions, Master cured her.

"I was visiting Master at that time. The news reached me by telephone. As soon as Master learned what had happened, he stepped behind a screen. Moments later he reappeared, his face radiant. 'Don't worry, Doctor, she will be all right. And she will never have another seizure.' One worry, with illnesses of this type, is that there may be future recurrences. But in Brenda's case there have been none."

As we left Dr. Lewis late that evening, we thanked him from our hearts for so generously sharing with us his unique experiences.

During the fall of 1949 Master asked me, in company with several other monks, to demonstrate the yoga postures before Swami Premananda, an Indian disciple visiting Mt. Washington from Washington, D. C., where he served as the minister of an SRF church. I was at best a mediocre Hatha Yogi. Many of the postures I couldn't contort myself into at all. In Master's presence that evening, however, I found myself suddenly capable of assuming even difficult poses with ease. Indeed, from that day forth I was generally accepted as SRF's Hatha Yoga "expert." I posed for the photographs that illustrated the poses in a series of articles in *Self-Realization Magazine.* If ever anyone was needed to demonstrate the postures, I was the one selected. Master often had me serve lunch for him when he had guests, and afterwards demonstrate the postures to them. Would that all expertise might be acquired so effortlessly!

One day Master, while sitting, chatting with the monks in our dining room, looked at me pensively. "Why don't you grow a beard, Walter?"

"Do you *mean* it, Sir?" I was astonished. Beards were rarely seen in those days. A couple of the other monks, in fact, later tried growing them, and Master vetoed their plans with the remark, "I don't want my boys looking like wild men!" (Perhaps his feeling was that one "wild man" in the crowd was enough!)

"Try it," he said.

I was grateful when, soon afterward, he invited me to spend a few weeks with him at Twenty-Nine Palms. Lecturing in Hollywood Church with a slowly emerging stubble had threatened to saddle me with the reputation of being Hollywood's first hobo-minister. But, "wild" or not, by the time the beard had filled out I did, at least look somewhat older and more mature.

At Twenty-Nine Palms Master told me privately of his plans to take me to India with him the following summer. Naturally, I was delighted. "I'm sure I could learn Bengali," I said. "I already speak several languages."

"You'll learn it *very* easily," he assured me. He went on to tell me a few Bengali words: *hath* (hand), *chok* (eyes), *mukh* (mouth), *nak* (nose), *kan* (ears). As it turned out, nine years were to pass before I got my first real opportunity to use those words. But I remembered them easily all that time. I had only to recall the day he'd spoken them to me and I could hear his voice again, mentally, as though he were speaking them in my ear.

This was the first indication I had that he might have bestowed on me a blessing far greater than the mere ability to contort my body into a variety of unusual positions: the gift to be able to recall the words he spoke to me exactly as he'd uttered them. How else, I asked myself, could I recall his words, tone and all, even when he spoke them in a foreign language?

One day at Twenty-Nine Palms he told me the story of Lahiri Mahasaya's meeting with Babaji. In Hindi he quoted Babaji's words: "Lahiri, *tu agaya* (you have come)." Simple words to be sure, but to have heard them once only in passing and still to be able to recall them clearly enough to confirm them in India nearly a decade later, argues a talent greater, I think, than I possessed naturally.

One day he sang us a song in Bengali: *"Mukti dete pari; bhakti dete pari koi?"* Though in this case, too, I heard the words once only, they stayed with me until I went to India in 1958, and there verified their accuracy.

The interesting thing is that this power, if such it really was, existed only where Master's words were concerned. The speech of others continued to be recalled in the more or less shadowy fashion that is, I suppose, usual in such cases.

At about this time in my life Master began asking me to jot down his words. He intimated strongly that he wanted me someday to write about him. For long hours he would reminisce with me about his life, his experiences in establishing the work, his hopes and plans for its future. He told me countless stories, some of them to illustrate points he was making; others, I suppose, simply because they were interesting, or helped in some general way to round out my understanding of the path. Many of his meanings reached me not only through the medium of words and stories, but by a kind of osmosis, a subtle impression gathered from a facial expression, or from the tone of his voice, or by some even subtler transferral of consciousness.

Often he talked about various disciples.

"Sir," I inquired one day, "what about the young man whom you initiated in Brindaban, during that episode in your book, 'Two Penniless Boys in Brindaban'? Have you ever heard from him again?"

"No," Master replied. "Inwardly, however, he has kept in touch."

"Then it isn't necessary to have outward contact with the Guru?"

"There must be at least one outward contact with him." Master was referring, of course, to a *meaningful* contact, such as that which is made at the time of initiation.

From other things that he said, and from the fact that he sometimes had disciples initiate people into Kriya Yoga in his stead even while he was alive, I understood that this link with him would be forged by contact with successive generations of those disciples who were in tune with him.

One day I asked him, "What are the most important qualities on the spiritual path?"

"Deep sincerity," Master replied, "and devotion. It isn't the number of years one spends on the path that counts, but how deeply one tries to find God. Jesus said, 'The last shall be first, and the first last.'*

"I once met a lady in the state of Washington. She was eighty years old, and all her life she'd been an atheist. By God's grace, at our meeting she became converted to this path. Thereafter she sought God intensely. For the better part of every day, whenever she wasn't meditating, she would play a recording of my poem 'God! God! God!' She lived only a few years longer, but in that short time she attained liberation."

Master also told me stories about several more recondite aspects of the path. "There was a young man in India who died," he said.

* Matthew 20:16.

"His body was lying ready for cremation; the funeral pyre was about to be lit. Just at that moment an old yogi came running out of a nearby forest. 'Don't light the fire!' he shouted. 'I need that young body.' He fell to the ground, dead. A moment later the young man leapt up off the pyre; before anybody could stop him, he ran off into the forest. The family could only cremate that old man!"

"Sir," I asked Master one evening, "what about Swami Pranabananda's prediction, in *Autobiography of a Yogi,* that he would be reborn shortly after his death, and go to the Himalayas to live with Babaji?"

"He *was* reborn. At the age of six he left home." Master smiled reflectively. "His renunciation at that young age caused quite a stir in his village!"

As Christmas approached, St. Lynn visited Mt. Washington. This was my first opportunity to meet Master's foremost disciple and spiritual heir. I found him gentle, soft-spoken, and remarkably humble. He seemed completely dispassionate, ever centered in the Self within. As Master introduced each of us to him, St. Lynn smiled sweetly, but said little. In time I discovered that he took almost no interest in small talk. A self-made man of considerable worldly means, he referred hardly ever to his outer life. For all we heard from him personally, he might have been a man of few achievements. Virtually his sole topics of conversation were God, Guru, and meditation. Silently he would come up to us whenever we met him, and bless us. Perhaps then he would offer us a few words of spiritual encouragement or advice. His mind was always focused inwardly on God. To be with him seemed to me like standing before a window onto infinity.

After Master's passing, Rajarsi Janakananda, as we knew him then, seemed almost to *become* Master. His eyes, by some subtle transformation, were Master's eyes. So perfect was his attunement that our guru's very thoughts became his thoughts. Master used to say of himself, "I killed Yogananda long ago." Rajarsi Janakananda, similarly, had attained that state of consciousness where nothing of the ego remained. It was as if, through him, God and Guru spoke to us directly.

During the Christmas meditation that year Master led us in singing his chant "Do not dry the ocean of my love with the fires of my desires, with the fires of my restlessness." Over and over we sang it. "Christ is here," he told us. "Sing it to him." Later he added, "Because you have sung this chant today, whenever in future you feel delusion pressing in all around you, sing it again, thinking of this occasion, and Christ and Guru will come down themselves to save you. Mark my words, for they are true."

As he had done the year before, Master spoke to us for some time from the depths of his divine communion. He blessed St. Lynn, Dr. Lewis, Daya Mata, and several others, telling them how greatly pleased God was with them.

"Walter," he continued, "you must try *hard,* for God will bless you very much." His words thrilled me so deeply that I'm afraid my meditation the rest of that day was more on them than on God.

On Christmas Day we enjoyed our traditional banquet. Master spoke afterward, intimately and lovingly as he had done the year before. During his talk he said, "The ladies in the office gave Faye a Christmas present. They addressed it to, 'Our boss who never bosses.' " Smiling his pleasure at this beloved disciple, he went on to speak fondly of the garden of souls that was growing up around him.

Before the banquet, place cards had been set out on the tables; the affair had been planned as a restricted family gathering. But at the last moment, numbers of guests had arrived uninvited. Room was courteously made for them, some of the renunciates offering their own seats.

In the office afterwards, a few of us were discussing with Master the inconvenience that had been caused by the sudden influx of people. A monk expressed his distress at their presumption. But I had been fortunate to observe another aspect of the episode.

"Sir," I said, "the disciples were vying with one another for the privilege of giving up their seats."

"Ah!" Master smiled blissfully. "Those are the things that please me!"

SRF Lake Shrine Chapel, Pacific Palisades, California.

Outdoor temple at the Lake Shrine.

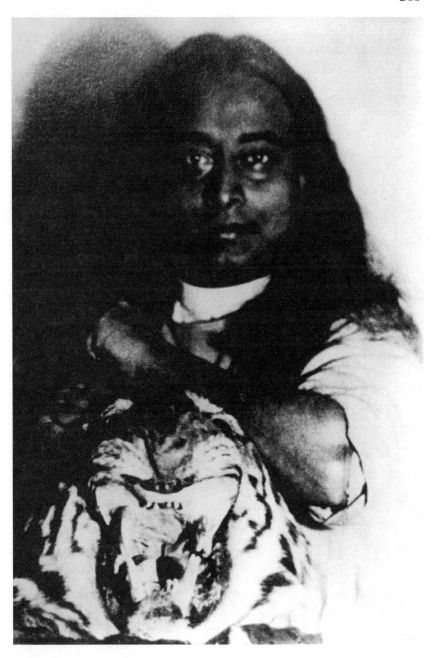

Master with a tiger skin. Advanced yogis sometimes meditate sitting on a tiger skin, a practice which they say heightens the sense of determination and self-control.

Christmas at Mt. Washington, 1949. St. Lynn (Rajarsi Janakananda), Master, and Dr. Lewis are seated at the table. Mrs. Lewis is standing behind St. Lynn. I am standing in the background.

Master with St. Lynn just after the disciple's initiation into *sannyas,* or monkhood. On this occasion Master gave him the name Rajarsi Janakananda.

Rajarsi told us, "Master said of me, 'You and I are one light in two bodies.' "

Paramhansa Yogananda

CHAPTER 30

A Divine Test

I N A VISION WHEN he was a boy, Paramhansa Yogananda saw himself standing in the marketplace of a town in the foothills of the Himalayas. The day was hot, and the dusty marketplace was crowded with squalid stalls, harassed shoppers, and whining beggars. Dogs ran everywhere. Monkeys stole down from the rooftops to snatch at food in the stalls. Donkeys brayed complainingly. People were bustling to and fro, laden with purchases, their brows furrowed with anxiety and desire.

No one looked happy.

But now and again some member of that milling throng paused before the entranced boy, and gazed high into the distance behind him. After a time, into each gazer's eyes, came a look of intense wistfulness. Then, with a deep sigh, he muttered, "Oh, but it's much too high for me." Lowering his eyes, he returned to the milling throng.

After this sequence had repeated itself several times, Yogananda turned to see what it was behind him that held such a strong appeal for these people. And there towering above the town he beheld a lofty mountain, verdant, serene; the absolute contrast it seemed to everything in this dusty hubbub of festering ambitions. At the mountaintop there was a large garden, inexpressibly beautiful. Its lawns were green-gold, its flowers many-hued. The boy yearned to climb up the mountain and enter that heavenly garden.

But as he reflected on the difficulty of the climb, in his mind the same words formed themselves: "It's much too high for me!" Then, weighing these words, he rejected them scornfully. "It may be too high for me to reach the top in a single leap," he thought, "but at least I can put one foot in front of the other!" Even to fail in the attempt would, he decided, be infinitely preferable to continued existence in this hot, dusty showcase of human misery.

Step by step he set out, filled with determination. Ultimately he reached the mountaintop, and entered the beautiful garden.

For Master this vision symbolized a common predicament of everyone with high ideals. Indeed, all men I imagine must fret at least sometimes at the restrictions their bodies place upon them, at the constant demand of those bodies for sustenance and protection. Man longs instinctively for a life free from competition and worry, free from hatred and violence. Few, alas, even suspect that such a state can be found—not outwardly, but within their own selves, on high pinnacles of spiritual achievement. And of those who do suspect, most turn away with the sigh, "But it's much too high for me!" How very few, alas, take up the path in earnest! "Out of a thousand," Krishna says in the *Bhagavad Gita,* "one seeks Me."

Yet the path is not really so difficult, *if one will but take it one step at a time.* As Jesus put it, "Sufficient unto the day is the evil thereof."* And as Paramhansa Yogananda often told us, "A saint is a sinner who never gave up."

The spiritual path requires courage, and dedication, and the absolute conviction that God alone will satisfy the soul's yearning for true happiness. Those who take up the path for what Yogananda called its glamour, expecting only blissful visions and a soft, mossy trail strewn with rose blossoms of divine consolation, become discouraged when they find how often God neglects the moss and roses in favor of thorns. But for those who cling to their purpose with devotion, taking the path calmly one day at a time, no test is ever too great. Obstructions then are seen to be blessings, for they give one the strength he needs to reach the heights.

I got an opportunity to learn something about spiritual obstructions during the early months of 1950. My period of testing began with weeks of exceptional inspiration. Encouraged, as it were, by a short, comparatively easy stretch on the journey, I had been running forward with eager expectations, only to be brought up with a jolt at the foot of a cliff.

For some time after the Christmas holidays, my meditations were blissful. I recall telling Jean Haupt one day, "If for the rest of my life I never get anything more, spiritually, than this, I shall be content." Dangerous words! God doesn't allow His devotees to enjoy for very long the luxury of over-confidence.

After a month or so of increasing inner joy, subtle delusions began to enter my mind. First came pride, in the feeling that this joy separated me from others—not, I believe, in the sense of making me think myself better than they, but in the equally false sense of holding me aloof from outward interests, however innocent.

---

* Matthew 6:34.

This state of consciousness masqueraded as wisdom, but in fact was born of my spiritual inexperience. For the devotee should learn to see God outside himself as well as inside—outside especially in wholesome activities and in beautiful things. The world we live in is God's world, after all. To reject it is, in a sense, to reject Him. Pride follows such rejection, and with pride, the temptation to take personal credit for whatever inspirations one feels.

Even as I congratulated myself on my growing inner freedom, I felt increasingly uneasy over my spiritual condition. I could see there was something seriously the matter with me, and that I was not responding as I ought to the blessings I'd been receiving. But where had I erred? My discrimination wasn't developed enough to supply the answer.

It took time for me to realize that I'd been grasping at my blessings too eagerly, as though it were I who had attracted them by my efforts alone. I had been flying by my own strength, forgetful that, to soar high, the devotee must allow himself to be lifted on the breezes of God's grace.

From pride there developed increasing tension in my spiritual efforts. And then, realizing that what I needed was to become more humble, more inwardly receptive, I began trying too urgently, too almost presumptuously, to offer myself up to God's will. I *grasped* at His guidance, as I had been grasping at joy.

"What do You want of me, Lord?" I prayed. "I'll do *anything* for You!" I tried imagining the demands He might make of me, then pictured myself following them to the last letter. In my over-anxiety His imagined demands gradually multiplied, until their sheer number defied comprehension. "Don't sit here. Don't go there. Don't eat this. Don't say that." I fell a prey to what the Roman Catholics call "scrupulosity." No longer could I feel joy in my self-offering. Scarcely even comprehending that I was playing this drama entirely in my own mind, I began to look upon God as almost a tyrant: His demands seemed so hopelessly unreasonable! I failed to reflect that He'd never actually made any of them!

"Walter is so confused!" Master exclaimed one afternoon to Mrs. Brown. Several more times that day he shook his head wonderingly. "Walter is so *confused!*" Then, as if to reassure himself, he added, "But—he will get there."

At about this time, Master went for seclusion to Twenty-Nine Palms to complete his commentary on the *Bhagavad Gita*. He took me with him. "I asked Divine Mother whom I should take," he told me, "and your face, Walter, kept popping up." Weeks in Master's company would, I hoped, banish the turmoil that had been building up within me.

It was wonderful to listen to him as he worked on his writings. The ease with which inspiration came to him was extraordinary. He would simply look up into the spiritual eye, then speak with hardly a pause, while his secretary, Dorothy Taylor, raced to keep up with him on the typewriter. The deepest insights poured from his lips effortlessly.

I got to spend several days at Master's place, listening to him dictate. But after that he instructed me to stay at the monks' retreat and go through the old SRF magazines, clipping out his *Gita* commentaries and "editing" them.

Editing? I knew this particular assignment had already been given to another, senior disciple. "How carefully do you want me to edit, Sir?"

"Just edit," he replied vaguely, gazing reflectively out the window. Then with greater immediacy he added, "Work like lightning. There is no time to be wasted. But"—here he gazed at me sternly—"don't change a word."

Edit, like lightning, and not change a word? To my spiritual confusion was now added the problem that I hadn't the remotest idea what he wanted of me in my work.

Master instructed me to remain in seclusion and devote myself "with all possible speed" to my job of "editing." Since I'd gone to the desert with high hopes of spending every day with him, it was particularly distressing now to find myself left completely alone. Unaccustomed to complete solitude, I felt abandoned utterly. Intense moods began to assail me. At times I fell into bleak despair, actually sinking onto the bed and staring helplessly at the ceiling. Every evening I told myself, "This simply *can't* go on another day!" But it did go on, day after day, for three long months. Each day seemed worse than the day before it.

It was as though two opposing forces were battling each other within me. Bravely I tried to give strength to the good side, by meditating several hours daily, but the very effort of meditation only deepened my sense of hopelessness. During the daylight hours I tried losing myself in work. My despair, however, at not even knowing what I was supposed to be doing made such absorption difficult. This "editing" job seemed like the labors of Sisyphus.

Master once told an audience, "I used to think Satan was only a human invention, but now I know, and add my testimony to that of others who lived before me, that Satan is a reality. He is a universal, conscious force whose sole aim is to keep all beings bound to the wheel of delusion." What I felt now was that God and Satan, warring inside me, were beating *me* up in their efforts to get at

Saturday [February] 18th, 1950

Dear Walter,   29 🌴 s [Palms]

I am sending all magazines. (1) Cut out first all of *Bhagavad Gita* articles—gather them on the side; paste only on one side; don't destroy any
writing (though different) on back of *Gita* articles.

(2) Keep editing in pencil the *Omar Khayyam* articles—put together in a book
form, pasting only the back as the pages in a book are.

(3) Have you got glue or paper or knife? If not, write and make a list and
Jane will bring them to you.

(4) Later you have to cut out all Bible articles and make a book—about the
Second Coming of Christ.

(5) Save all the magazines—what is left of them after the *Gita, Omar* and
Bible articles are taken out.

(6) Hand over Radio article and write Bernard to write them henceforth as
you are busy editing.

(7) Get up early, meditate a little, exercise and run or walk briskly; then
start from 8 A.M. to 6 P.M. <u>Every two hours</u> run for 5 minutes and <u>medi-
tate 15 minutes before lunch</u>—including lunch must be finished in 1 hour).

(over)

Work—9 hours a day with deep concentration—meditate two hours deeply at night after dining at 6:30. Sleep 7 hours. Be sure to walk briskly or run for 5 minutes every 2 hours. This will keep strain out. After dinner at night walk on the road and not in jungly brush—for one hour 6 to 7. Then eat and meditate two hours. Adjust routine whatever possible. Not necessary to walk at night. You can work from 7:30 A.M.—if you like. You should take 1/2 hours walk in the morning after quick meditation and breadfast covering (1/2 hour).

Q. Have you got a regular lamp—with strong light for use at night? Perhaps it needs a wick. Write what you need done about lamp. Write to Jane.
Q. Have you finished pasting *Omar Khayyam*?
Q. How much you have edited? Thorough but fast editing is necessary or nothing will be done. Time is scant.

With blessing,
P Yogananda

P.S. Do all work with the thought of God. PY

[Twenty-nine Palms, 1950]

Dear Walter,
(1) Please write Virginia Wright—what you need for food:
    (a) milk
    (b) bread
    (c) butter
    (d) Vegetables and fruits I am sending.
    (e) Sending $5 for everything
(2) Please report how much work you do daily—Please work fast—there is much to do—use kitchen knife and scissors to making cut
    (a) *Omar Khayyam*
    (b) Then *Bhagavad Gita*

I must have them soon—please be day and night busy. Must work fast.
(2) Give Virginia Miss Wright—Radio Script
(3) Write Bernard, he has

                                                                (over)

to prepare Radio Script as you are busy editing now.

Meditate deeply at night and every 2 hours and run around hermitage for 5 to 10 minutes. Keep exercised and body fit for God realization.

Do not procrastinate or act carelessly. Hurry with discretion.

Boundless Blessings through my Self,
P Yogananda

P.S. Have you Butane gas? If not tell Miss Wright. Water plants early morning if not watered.

PY

one another! It was not that I had the slightest wish to return to a worldly life. That desire, with God's grace, has never for a moment entered my heart since I first set foot on the spiritual path. What was happening, rather, was that, while I longed for inner peace, I found myself unaccountably terrified of going deep in meditation, where alone true peace can be found.

The reader may see in my psychological ferment at that time ample explanation for my feelings of helplessness, without this additional plea that forces greater than myself were belaboring me. The rational mind, dependent as it is on sensory evidence, would always prefer to reach its conclusions without the intrusion of supra-sensory causes, which it considers super-natural, which is to say, unreal. Moreover, it is a notorious weakness of irrational minds to leap eagerly to supernatural explanations for predicaments that they would otherwise be obliged to accept as their own responsibility. Nonetheless, this much is surely true—that every mental state reflects broader realities of consciousness. Our merriment, for example, demonstrates the already existing potential for merriment of the human race; our very consciousness, the potential for consciousness in the universe. Living beings *manifest* consciousness, even as a light bulb manifests energy. Consciousness is a cosmic fact. Man only tunes in to, and expresses, limited aspects of it. His thoughts are never solitary cries flung into a cosmic void. Like birds, rather, riding on a high wind, they are supported and further influenced by whatever stream of consciousness they enter. Depending on which aspects of cosmic reality man himself tunes in to, he is drawn downward or upward on the scale of spiritual evolution—down toward matter, by what is known as the satanic force, or up toward infinity, by God's love.

There are beings, both in this world and the next, that act more or less consciously as agents of these divine and satanic forces. Angels, we call those in the first group, and demons, those in the second.

A year or so before the period I am describing, I had an experience with one in the latter group. The episode sounds almost like a page out of some medieval romance.

I was new on the path, and naively eager for whatever information I could gather regarding it. Boone informed me one day that, according to Master, the stories of possession in the Bible were factual. He went on to describe a strange experience he himself had once had with a demonic entity that had tried to possess him. Intrigued rather than frightened, I decided that it would be interesting to test the truth of Boone's claim myself.

One night, not long afterward, I dreamed that I was at a party.

The thought suddenly came to me with striking certainty, "It's time for me to go meet a disembodied spirit." I left my friends and passed through an empty, well-lit room toward an open door on the far side of it. I can still see clearly in my mind's eye the bare floor boards and walls, the shining bulb dangling from the ceiling. The next room was dark; here, I knew, I was to meet the disincarnate entity. Momentarily I was afraid, and reached out to switch on the light. "Don't be a coward," I scolded myself. "How will you learn what this is all about if you can't even face it?" And so, leaving the room in darkness, I stood in the center of it and cried, "Come!"

Now comes the "gothic" part of the story. The following day Jean Haupt told me that he had been awakened at about this time of the night by a loud, ferocious pounding on his door.

"Wh-what is it?" he quailed.

A deep, rough voice loudly demanded, "Who's in there?"

"J-Jean."

"Who?"

"Jean Haupt." By now he was thoroughly frightened.

"I don't want you. I want Don Walters!" Whoever or whatever it was stormed noisily out of the main building.

It must have been shortly thereafter that my own strange experience began.

"Come!" I cried. As I did so, the floor beneath me began to heave like the waves on a lake. An instant later I felt myself being drawn up out of my body, and through the window into a sort of mist. A peculiar aspect of *Aum,* not at all pleasant, resounded loudly all around me. Evidently this was not to be a spiritually uplifting experience! Discrimination, however, was not my strong point that night.

"How interesting!" I thought, going along with events to see where they'd lead.

Presently some powerful force seemed to pit itself against me, as though determined to rob me of consciousness. At this point I struggled to resist, but the other will was strong; I wasn't at all sure I would win. I therefore decided to play it safe.

"Master!" I cried, urgently.

Instantly the experience ended. The sound ceased. Back once more in my body, I sat up in bed, fully awake.

Later that day I asked Master if that had been a true experience.

"Yes, it was. Such things happen sometimes on the path." He added, "Don't be afraid of them."

How, I thought, could one be afraid after such a demonstration of my guru's omniscient protection?

The worst of my ordeal at Twenty-Nine Palms, however, was that while it lasted I wasn't even able to call on Master with my accustomed faith in him. Suddenly, without any conscious intention on my part, I found myself plunged into violent doubts. It wasn't that I doubted Master's goodness, or his spiritual greatness, or even my commitment to him as my guru. But the thought suddenly forced itself upon me insidiously: "He lacks wisdom." It was an idea over which I had no control. If Master had told me, "The sun is shining in Los Angeles," this doubting serpent inside me would have sneered, "I'll bet it's raining!" There was no question of my *entertaining* these doubts. I would have done anything to be rid of them. They made me utterly miserable.

They began with the commentaries I was supposed to be editing. I found them in bad shape. I didn't realize it at the time, but Master's practice during the early years of his mission had been simply to write an article, then turn it over to his editors and printers and never glance at it again. Even I, who knew no Sanskrit, could see plainly in their inconsistencies that the Sanskrit names as printed showed a woeful lack of familiarity with that language. I didn't realize that the editors had simply not been conscientious enough to catch blatant typographical errors—that in fact they'd added not a few eccentricities of their own.

Worse still, in his commentaries Master would sometimes write, "This means so and so," then turn around—almost, to my mind, as though correcting himself—and say, "But on the other hand, it also means. . ." and go on to suggest an interpretation which—again, to my way of thinking—bore little relation to the first one. "Can't he make up his mind?" I marveled. "How is it possible for the same passage to have *both* meanings?"

It was only gradually, over years, that I came to appreciate the subtlety of this way of thinking. I also learned that this kind of Scriptural commentary is traditional in India. Indeed, I see now that it is a far more sophisticated approach, philosophically speaking, than ours, with our preference for limiting every truth to one definition of it—as though a definition and the truth it represents were one and the same thing. Reality has many dimensions. The more central a truth, indeed, the more clear its relation to the entire wheel of experience.

My dilemma of doubt illustrates more or less typically the problem of every devotee. Before he can attain divine freedom, he must weed out every obstructing tendency that he has carried over from the past. Mere intellectual affirmation of victory is not enough: He must also face his delusions in stern hand-to-hand combat. Each seeker has his own special, self-created combination of delusions to overcome. But overcome them he must, if he is to advance on the path.

"You are doubting now," Master told me one day, "because you doubted in the past." (Out of shame, incidentally, I hadn't consulted him about my dilemma. But he'd known what was on my mind.)

In time I realized that one of the reasons Master wanted me to teach others was that, having entertained doubts myself in past lives, and having already, to a great extent, conquered them in this one, I needed to reinforce my growing faith by expressing it outwardly, and by helping others to resolve *their* doubts. By helping them to find faith, I would also pay off my own karmic debt for ever having doubted God myself.

When I had been at the monks' retreat about a month, Master summoned Henry from Mt. Washington to work on certain projects at his retreat. Henry commuted from our place daily. After some time, Jerry Torgerson came out and stayed with us also. Jerry, too, of course, worked at Master's place. Later, others came out on weekends. They, too, worked—where else?—at Master's place. It provided additional anguish for me to see these crowds going over to be with Master, while I labored alone, hopelessly, over my incomprehensible task of editing. But Master insisted that I stick to it.

"How much have you edited?" he wrote me in a note that Henry brought back one day. "*Thorough* but *fast* editing is necessary or nothing will be done. Time is scant."

Henry's presence was a great blessing for me. During the weeks we spent together out there we became fast friends, our mutual attunement developing until it often happened that one of us only thought something, and the other spoke it. What rare good fortune, I reflected, to find even one such friend in a lifetime.

As it turned out, the other monks didn't get to spend much time with Master either, since their work was out of doors, and he stayed mostly indoors, deeply concentrated on finishing his commentaries. Nor was he indifferent to my welfare. Rather he tried in various ways to reassure me. But it was his way never to intrude on our free will to the point where it would mean fighting our important battles for us. That would have deprived us of the opportunity to develop our own strength.

So the weeks passed. In April Mother and Dad visited Mt. Washington. Dad was being posted from Egypt to Bordeaux, France, where eventually he made an important oil discovery at

Parentis. Master permitted me to go and receive them. "But you must return after four days," he wrote me, "after seeing your parents—designated by your real Parent, God." Then, referring to his commentaries, he added, "Only three chapters left. Soon we will get together."

My father, happy as he was to see me, was far from supportive of my new way of life. He shuddered to see my beard, deplored my abandonment of a promising writing career, and rejected my spiritual beliefs altogether. One day he said, "If I were to get the opinions of a few doctors on this teaching of yours about energizing the body by will power, would you accept their verdict?" It wasn't as though he were proposing to consult any of the numerous physicians who were already members of our work. Probably he didn't dream such an animal existed.

"Dad," I remonstrated, "doctors aren't omniscient!"

I attended the morning service with Mother and Dad at Hollywood Church that Sunday. The day before I had asked Rev. Bernard, who was scheduled to speak, "Do you think you might give a really scientific talk, to impress my father?" "Sure," he'd replied, confidently. Any correspondence, however, between Bernard's approach to science and Dad's was purely coincidental. Dad came away from church that day convinced that Bernard had taken complete leave of his senses, a judgment that probably, by extension, included the whole lot of us.

It might be conjectured that my parents' visit, coming as it did during my severe trial of faith, made the trial harder than ever for me. But in fact, their coming helped me to overcome it. For despite our philosophical differences, my parents and I loved one another deeply. The reality of this underlying bond helped me to see that love is a far better response than reason to that kind of doubt which is quick to condemn, but slow to investigate.

My parents were pleased, in the end, to see me happy in my new calling. Reflecting on my confusion and unhappiness during college and after it, Mother wrote Master a few weeks later to thank him for all the good he'd done me.

During my brief visit to Mt. Washington, I found that others of the monks, too, had been passing through inner trials. On my return to Twenty-Nine Palms I said to Master, "Sir, Jean is a little discouraged. Someone told him that, according to Sri Ramakrishna, grace is only a sport of God. He takes this to mean that a person could meditate for years and get nowhere, while God might reveal Himself to any drunkard, if He took a mere notion to."

"Ramakrishna would *never* have said that!" Master looked almost shocked. "That is what happens when people without realization try to interpret the saints' sayings. God is not a creature of whims! Of course, it may *look* like sport sometimes, to people who can't see the causal influences of past karma. But why would God go against His own law? He responds according to it. Tell Haupt I said this is a misunderstanding on his part."

"I will, Sir." I paused. "Master, won't you talk with him? He seems to be having a hard time lately."

"Well," Master answered quietly, "Satan is testing the organization. Haupt is not the only one."

"Is *that* what the trouble has been!"

"Yes." Sadly, Master continued, "Quite a few heads will fall."

"Will it go on for very long, Master?"

"Quite some time." After a pause, he went on, "It all started when that boy, Jan, left Encinitas. Then Smith left. Quite a few more heads will roll." Jan, the nine-year-old who had received a vision of Jesus, had left the work with his mother several months later. Rev. Smith had been the minister of our Long Beach chapel.

It would seem that, in the lives of great world teachers, a sort of housecleaning takes place toward the end of their missions. In this way their work is assured of being carried on as purely as possible after they leave this earth. Jesus Christ told his disciples, "The man who eats my flesh and drinks my blood has eternal life," and again, "The man who eats my body and drinks my blood shares my life, and I share his." He didn't trouble to explain that his words had a purely metaphorical significance. It was almost as if he were *inviting* people's misunderstanding, to find out who among his disciples were really in tune with him. The Bible goes on to say, "Many of his disciples, when they heard him say these things, commented, 'This is a hard teaching indeed; who could accept it?'" Their general reaction is reported next: "From that time many of his disciples withdrew, and walked no more with him." °
But the closest disciples of Jesus were in tune with him on an

---

° John 6:54–66. Paramhansa Yogananda explained that Jesus, in speaking of his body and blood, was referring to the omnipresent, eternal Spirit with which his consciousness was identified. By "body" he meant all vibratory creation, the Holy Ghost, or *Aum,* which the devotee must absorb into himself ("eat") until he feels inwardly identified with it. Christ's "blood" is the all-pervading Christ Consciousness, which, like blood which sustains the physical body, is the true "life" and sustenance of all creation. The meditating devotee must advance from oneness with *Aum* to oneness with Christ Consciousness, and thence to oneness with God the Father beyond creation. I asked Master once, "What stage must a person attain to become a true master?" He replied, "One becomes a master when he attains Christ Consciousness."

intuitive level. Nothing that he said outwardly could disturb the sublime certitude of that inner knowledge. Their intuitive understanding demonstrated their fitness to promulgate his message after he left his body.

In the struggle to edit Master's articles, it turned out that there was enough in them to correct even without changing their wording. Most of the mistakes were simply typographical errors, or the brainchildren of some editor with a quaint fetish for capitals. But these literary outcastes were so numerous that I could see no practical way of preparing the text for publication without first typing out all the articles afresh, double-spacing for surgery. Master, however, must not have realized in what very bad shape they were. When I suggested to him that I type them out, he said it would take too long.

When finally I submitted the fruits of my labors to the editorial department, however, having cluttered the margins with as many as six proofreading corrections to a line, it was obvious that my copy would be impossible to work from. The older disciple to whom Master had given the real responsibility for editing ordered that my work be thrown out altogether, and the whole job typed out, double spaced, from a fresh set of magazines. It was, as I had known all along, the only feasible thing to do.

One afternoon I overheard Master scolding Miss Taylor for not using my work. "If you gave me a million dollars," he cried, "I wouldn't go through what he did to get this job done! Not if you gave me a million dollars!"

That afternoon the senior editor happened to meet me in Master's garden. "My," she exclaimed, "that certainly was a lot of work you did!" Turning to go indoors, she added off-handedly, as if to the air, "Not that it did any good!"

Later that day, Master tried to comfort me for her seemingly unfeeling remark.

"But Sir," I pleaded, "she's quite right! It wouldn't have been possible for her to work from my copy."

"You are *defending* her!" Master's face expressed amazement. "But you did *good* work. All those capitals! They'd have made us a laughingstock."

I was touched by his anxiety to comfort me. But for me, the important thing was that I knew now, more deeply than ever before, that I belonged to him, and that the outward ups and downs of the path didn't really matter so long as I felt his love in my heart. Perhaps, I reflected, he had been keeping me at Twenty-Nine Palms only to help me face important defects in myself, and not for the sake of his book at all. At any rate I knew that my months of agony had matured me. Now, I felt grateful for them.

Several days later, before a group of the monks, Master looked at me kindly and said, "Walter was on his high horse. Now he is coming our way."

CHAPTER 31

The Bhagavad Gita

"A NEW SCRIPTURE has been born!" Master spoke ecstatically. His commentary on the *Bhagavad Gita* had been finished. In three months of unbroken dictation he had completed 1,500 pages. "I told Miss Taylor the pages numbered that many, but she carefully counted them to make sure I was right!"

Master and I were walking around the compound of his retreat. Having finished his manuscript, he had summoned me at last to help him with suggestions for the preliminary editing.

"A new Scripture has been born!" he repeated. "Millions will find God through this book. Not just thousands. Millions! I *know*. I have seen it."

My first task, now that I'd been brought out of seclusion, was to read the entire manuscript through and get an over-all feeling for it. I found the experience almost overwhelming. Never before had I read anything so deep, and at the same time so beautiful and uplifting. To think that only recently I had been questioning Master's wisdom! I kicked myself mentally for being such a chump. His book was filled with the deepest wisdom I had ever encountered. Unlike most philosophical works, moreover, it was fresh and alive, each page a sparkling rill of original insights. With the sure touch of a master teacher, profound truths were lightened occasionally with graceful humor, or with charming and instructive stories, or highlighted with brief touches of new, sometimes startling information. (I was intrigued to learn, for example, that advanced yogis sometimes reincarnate in several bodies at once, the more quickly to work out their past karma.) Best of all, the truths expressed in the book were constantly clarified, as Master himself said exultingly, with "illustration after illustration."

"I understand now," he told me, "why my master never let me read other *Gita* interpretations. Had I done so, my mind might have been influenced by the opinions they expressed. But this book came entirely from God. It is not philosophy, the mere *love* of wisdom: It *is* wisdom. To make sure I didn't write it to any degree from a level of opinion, I tuned in with Byasa's° consciousness before beginning my dictation. Everything I said was what he himself intended.

"There have been many other *Gita* commentaries," Master continued, "including several famous ones. But none have been so all-rounded in their approach as this one. Swami Shankara's, for example, deep though it was, was limited by the one-sided emphasis he placed on the purely spiritual nature of reality. Scriptures should deal with reality on *every* level. They should be helpful physically and mentally, not only spiritually, for these are levels that people have to contend with, and it is for ordinary people, not saints, that the Scriptures are written."

Again Master said, smiling blissfully, "A new Scripture has been born!

"It was God's will," he concluded, "that the *Gita* be fully explained only now. This was a main part of the mission with which Babaji commissioned me."

The *Bhagavad Gita* consists of a dialogue between Krishna and Arjuna, during which Sri Krishna relates deep, divine truths to his closest disciple. What, I thought, could be more fitting than for the task of interpreting this Scripture to be left to Arjuna himself, in a later incarnation? or for Sri Krishna, in his present form, to have commissioned the undertaking?

My three months of seclusion were over; there now followed two months of concentrated work with Master at his place. I spent many hours in his company, and much time also poring over his manuscript with Mrs. Nealey, an elderly lady—not a disciple, but a devotee and a trained editor—whom Master had invited to Twenty-Nine Palms to help with the editing.

"I don't like to have you working with her," he told me one day, "but just now the work demands it. While you are with her, though, never look into her eyes. That is where the attraction starts."

"Sir!" I remonstrated. "She's an old woman. How could there possibly be any attraction?"

"It makes no difference; that magnetism holds true for all ages." Master paused a moment, then added, "Already she feels a little attached to you—not in a bad way, and only very slightly—like a mother for her son. I don't want you to worry about it, but

---
° The ancient author of the *Bhagavad Gita.*

remember, that magnetism is subtle, so be careful."

It puzzled me at first why Master would want anyone to edit his writings for him. They were so manifestly inspired, and—well, I thought, didn't divine inspiration imply perfection on *every* level? Not necessarily, it seemed. Inspiration, Master explained, lies primarily in the vibrations and the ideas expressed.

Logical sentence structure, I gradually realized, like good plumbing, belongs to this physical plane of existence. It is a tool, merely, of thought and communication. Cerebration is slow and ponderous compared to the soul's transcendent intuitions. Many times it has happened that an important scientific discovery appeared full blown in the mind of its discoverer, only to require years of plodding work for him to present that intuitive insight clearly and convincingly to others.

Great masters usually submit to the laws governing this material universe, which they respect as a part of God's creation. But matter represents inertia, the *tamasic* ° quality in Nature. To saints whose consciousness has transcended matter, the material way of working must appear slow and cumbersome indeed. As Master told us, he preferred to work on a level of vibrations. ("That is how books are written in the astral world."†) In addition to this natural predilection for functioning on non-material levels of reality, great masters often deliberately leave to their disciples the task of translating their teachings onto the material plane, in order that they, too, may grow spiritually. As Master once said to me, "By helping me with editing, you yourself evolve." Master could cope easily and efficiently with mundane problems, including those of grammar and literary style, when he had a mind to. As he once told me, "I did edit one book myself: *Whispers from Eternity*." And this I considered not only one of his finest works, but one of the loveliest

---

° *Tamas,* the lowest of three *gunas,* or qualities, that infuse the entire universe. The other two are *rajas,* or *rajo guna,* the activating quality, and *sattwa,* the elevating, or spiritualizing, quality. The three *gunas* represent the progressive stages of manifestation outward from the oneness of Spirit.

† The universe in which souls find themselves after physical death. The astral is the second stage of manifestation outward from Spirit. In the order of cosmic creation, first comes the causal, or ideational universe, representing *sattwa guna.* At this stage of manifestation all things exist as ideas. The next phase is the astral, representing *rajo guna.* At this stage, primordial ideas have become clothed in energy. In the third phase, the physical energy takes on the appearance of solid substance. That this is an appearance, merely, has been demonstrated by modern physics in its discovery that matter *is* energy.

Shapes and colors exist in the astral world, as they do in the physical. There are planets, fields, lakes, mountains, and people. But all things there are seen as varied manifestations of light.

books of poetry ever written.* In editing his *Gita* commentaries, however, Master invited our suggestions, and seemed content to pursue much of his work on the basis of them.

On most days, after working on his manuscript, he would sit back and converse with me informally. Occasionally Mrs. Nealey would remain in the room with us and join the discussion. As usual, Master's teaching on these occasions often took the form of illustrative stories.

"God rarely wants miracles to be displayed publicly," he told us one day. He went on to relate the story of Sadhu Haridas, a famous miracle-worker in India in the Eighteenth Century, who, Master said, "remained buried underground for forty days. Afterwards, when his body was exhumed, a group of French physicians examined him, and pronounced him dead. Thereupon, to their amazement, he 'came back to life'!

"One day Sadhu Haridas was seated in a small rowboat with a missionary, who was trying to convert him to Christianity. 'Why should I follow your Jesus Christ?' demanded Haridas. 'What did he do that I couldn't do?'

" 'The powers he displayed were divine,' retorted the missionary. Glancing at the water surrounding them, he continued, 'He could walk on water.'

" 'Is *that* so special?' scoffed Haridas. Leaping out of the boat, he walked on the water ahead of it. Wherever he went, the boat followed him. The missionary, of course, was left speechless!

"But the maharaja of that state was a great soul. Seeing Sadhu Haridas from afar one day, he said, 'There is something about that man that I don't like.' His courtiers remonstrated, 'But he is a great saint. Look what he has done.' The maharaja replied, 'All the same, there is something about him I don't like.' He sensed that in concentrating on miracles Sadhu Haridas was forgetting God.

"And he was right. Not long afterwards, Haridas forsook his spiritual practices, married, and resumed a worldly life. Finally he saw his error and returned to his disciples. 'I am back,' he announced, simply.

"Years later he declared, 'I have done many wrong things, but now the Beloved is calling me.' Entering *samadhi,* he attained eternal freedom."

"Sir," Mrs. Nealey inquired, puzzled, "how did he rise again so quickly? When one falls from a high spiritual state, isn't the karmic punishment far greater than for a fallen neophyte?"

---

* I am referring to the 1929 and 1949 editions.

Master shook his head. "M-mmm. God is no tyrant. If one who is accustomed to drinking nectar takes to eating stale cheese, he soon grows dissatisfied with the change. He then throws the cheese away and cries for nectar again. God won't refuse him, if he realizes his mistake and longs sincerely once again for God's love.

"But you see," Master continued, "one shouldn't display spiritual powers publicly. Not many years ago there was a yogi in India who used to demonstrate before large gatherings an ability to swallow deadly poisons without suffering any ill effect. One day he forgot to prepare his mind in advance, and the poison began to take its toll. As he lay dying, he confessed, 'I know this is my punishment for displaying those powers before others.'

"A master may reveal more divine power, however, to his disciples." Master went on to speak of his guru, and of the miracles Sri Yukteswar had occasionally displayed.

"There was a loose tile on the roof of his ashram in Puri," Master recalled with a smile. "I wanted to fix it, because I was afraid it might fall down and hurt somebody. But my master showed not the slightest concern. 'Don't worry about it,' he told me nonchalantly. 'As long as I am alive, it will remain up there.' It stayed up there until the very day of his death, some twenty years later. On that day it fell down!"

One day we discussed the strictness of Sri Yukteswar's discipline in the training of his disciples. "He didn't want disciples," Master remarked. "Few could take his penetrating insight into their weaknesses—an insight which he never hesitated to reveal! But because I remained loyal to him, I found God. By converting me, he converted thousands."

"Master," I inquired, "might Sri Yukteswar's strictness have been due to his foreknowledge that he wouldn't be returning to this material plane of existence? Was it not that most of his real disciples were free already, and he was simply being careful not to assume responsibility for any new ones?"

"That's right," Master replied. "He had a few stragglers this time, that's all."

On other occasions Master told us that he himself had in fact attained liberation "many incarnations ago."

"Sir," I asked him one day, "how long have I been your disciple?"

"Well, it has been a long time, that's all I will say."

"But does it always take so long?"

"Oh, yes," Master replied. "Worldly desires take them away many times, until they learn their material lessons in this school of life."

In his *Gita* commentary, however, Master stresses that once the devotee sincerely longs for freedom it is only a matter of time before that desire is fulfilled. Compared to the vast number of incarnations that the soul wanders in delusion before it turns back toward its source in Infinity, the sincere longing for liberation is hardly a step away from freedom itself.

Talk turned one afternoon to Sri Yukteswar's book, *The Holy Science.* "I find much of it abstruse," I confessed.

"Do you?" Mrs. Nealey appeared surprised. "Why, I found it *very* easy to understand!"

Minutes later she left the room. Smilingly Master commented, "Even I, when I read that book, have to stop in places and think!"

Conversation turned occasionally to the ways of masters. "People always want miracles from them," Master remarked. "They don't see that in a master's humility lies his greatest 'miracle.' " He added, "The actions of true masters, though not easily understood by worldly people, are always wisdom-guided, never whimsical.

"A few years ago one so-called 'master' in India was planning to visit this country. He wrote asking me if he might visit Mt. Washington on his way to some religious congress in the Midwest. Well, we prepared an elaborate banquet for him and fifteen of his disciples. We were actually awaiting his arrival when a telegram came from Honolulu. He had traveled all that distance, then suddenly received the 'inspiration' to turn around and go home again." Master chuckled. "No *master* would behave that way!"

He went on to discuss a number of other prominent religious figures, some of them truly great, others perhaps less edifying than instructive in the examples they set.

"I met a great saint on my trip to India in 1935," Master said. "He is still alive. His name is Yogi Ramiah. He is a disciple of Ramana Maharshi, and a fully liberated soul. We walked hand in hand around the grounds at Ramanashram, drunk with God. Oh! If I had spent another half hour in his company, I could never have brought myself to leave India again!"

(In 1960 I myself spent four days with Yogi Ramiah—or Sri Rama Yogi, as he was then known. The visit marked a high point in my spiritual life.)

Master then spoke of his work in India, particularly of his Ranchi school.

"The trouble with training schoolboys," he said, "is that most of them, when they grow up, return to a worldly life. It does good in the long run, for society needs the uplifting influence of spiritual education, but when a great work like this is being started, it needs workers. From this standpoint, what we have here in America is much better. The people who come to us for training want to devote their entire lives to God. In this way these teachings can be spread more easily."

From time to time he talked of one or another of the disciples, always with a view to instructing me, through their examples, in the right attitudes of discipleship—not only for my sake, but to help me in teaching others.

"I was disciplining ———," Master said one afternoon, referring to one of the monks, "and a certain lady took pity on him. She felt I was being too hard on him. The young man, touched by her sympathy, was beginning to feel a little sorry for himself. But then I told him, 'You know, there is a saying in India: She who loves you more than your own mother is a witch! I am your mother. Wouldn't I know what was best for my own child?' After that he was all right."

Referring to that same lady, who was also a disciple, Master continued, "She has always been very obliging by nature; she would agree with almost anyone on practically any matter, simply out of good will. One day I said to her, 'If someone were to come up to you and say, "Yesterday I saw Yogananda dead drunk, staggering down Main Street," you would look wide-eyed and reply, "Is that so?" I know you wouldn't believe it. But don't you see that you must be courageous in your convictions? To "stand up" for what you believe in is a sign of loyalty.' "

Another day, referring again to the need for courage in one's convictions, Master said, "My earthly father, out of a touch of jealous attachment to me, attempted to criticize Master (Sri Yukteswar) to me one day for something trivial he had heard about him. I turned and faced him. 'Of all things!' I cried. 'The physical birth you gave me is something, but the spiritual birth my guru has given me is infinitely more precious! If ever I hear you say one more word against him, I shall disown you as my father!' After that he always spoke of Master very respectfully."

Referring to the need for attunement with the Guru, Master said one day, "Look at ———, and then look at Saint Lynn. I asked both of them to come and visit our colonies whenever they could, to maintain that spiritual contact. Saint Lynn has come out every opportunity he could get, and spent hours in meditation on the lawn in Encinitas. But ——— never came. He could easily have done so had he wanted to. He thinks he can get there by himself. But he will find out. He is spiritually advanced, but he is bogging down. He knows there is something the matter, but doesn't know what it is. Attunement with Guru, you see, must be on all levels."

Smiling, Master then discussed a certain student whose attunement with him, I gathered, had never been deep on *any* level. "Whenever I say anything to her, a few days pass, and then back comes a letter, *pages* long, explaining in how many ways I have misjudged her!"

Other monks came out on weekends, and sometimes for longer visits. To a group of us one day Master told of an amusing occurrence during his months of dictation. Jerry had taken a notion to cover the roof of Master's house with concrete. It was an outrageous idea, but Jerry, over Master's objections, had insisted that such a roof would endure forever. "I then told him to finish the job right away," Master continued, "but Jerry said, 'It will be all right. I know what I am doing.' " Master was laughing. "First he put tar paper down on the roof. Then he nailed chicken wire over it. At this point the roof was a complete sieve: Hundreds of nails were sticking through it. 'Hurry up!' I urged. But Jerry saw no reason to rush things.

"Well, presently a huge storm came. Pans were put out frantically in every room. Water was dripping everywhere. The house was like a shower bath!

"But there were two rooms in which no water fell: the dictation room, and my bedroom. The roof was as much a sieve over these two as over the rest of the house, but Divine Mother didn't want my work to be interrupted. Only at the very end of the storm one drop fell into a bucket in the dictation room, and another one on to my bare stomach in the bedroom while I lay relaxing on the bed. That was Divine Mother's way of playing a little joke on me!"

Jerry, who was present, said, "I'm sorry I'm so stubborn, Sir."

"Well, that's all right," Master spoke consolingly. "I attract stubborn people!"

"He has great love," Master said later of Jerry. "That is what changes people."

Looking at Henry one day, Master told us, "Henry dug the cesspool near this house. He kept digging, digging all day long without ever stopping to see how far he had gone. By evening, to his surprise, he found he had dug a deep hole. That," Master went on approvingly, "is the way to seek God—continuously digging, digging, without looking to see how far one has come. Then suddenly one day he will see: 'I am there!' "

One weekend Mrs. Harriet Grove, the leader of our center in

Gardena, California, came out uninvited with James Coller to see
Master. Not knowing where his retreat was, she found it by pure
intuition. ("Turn left here," she told James, who was driving.
"Turn right there." Then suddenly: "Stop! This is it." And so it
proved to be.)

"This is the afternoon," Master told her, "that I usually go out
for a ride in the car. But I knew you were coming, so I stayed
home."

"Master," James said that weekend, "I have such great longing
for God. Why should He take so long in coming?"

"Ah!" Master replied with a blissful smile, "that is what makes it
all the sweeter when He does come! Such is His romance with the
devotee."

"Sir," Debi said, anxious for a taste of such longing, "give me
the grace of devotion."

"You are saying, 'Give me the money, so I can buy what I
want.' But I say, No, first you have to *earn* the money. Then I will
give it to you so you can buy what you want."

In the evenings, Master exercised by walking slowly around his
retreat compound. Generally he asked me to accompany him. He
was so much withdrawn from body-consciousness on those occasions that he sometimes had to lean on my arm for support. He
would pause and sway back and forth, as if about to fall.

"I am in so many bodies," Master remarked once, returning
slowly to body-consciousness, "it is difficult for me to remember
which body I am supposed to keep moving."

Boone visited Twenty-Nine Palms for a short time. Accompanying Master and me one evening on our walk, he asked many questions concerning spiritual matters.

"You shouldn't talk to me when I am in this state," Master said.
The deepest wisdom, he was implying, is beyond words; it must
be experienced in silent, divine communion. But when he did
speak, his words those days were filled with such wisdom as has
rarely found expression in books. At such times he would remind
me, "Write down my words. I don't often speak from this level of
impersonal wisdom." More and more, from this time onward, he
was to speak not as a humble devotee of God, but as one whose
consciousness was saturated with the ultimate realization, *"Aham
Brahm asmi*—I am Spirit!"

One evening, Master was doing energization exercises by the
garage with Boone and me. Boone asked him about a certain
saint who had appeared to him once in Encinitas. "Who was he,
Master?"

"I don't know whom you're referring to," Master replied.

"It was out in the back garden, Sir."

"Well, so many have come there," Master said. "I often see them. Some have passed on; others are still on this earth."

"How wonderful, Sir!" I exclaimed.

"Wherever God is," Master replied, "there His saints come." He paused a minute or two while he did a few exercises. Then he added:

"Yesterday I wanted to know about the life of Sri Ramakrishna. I was meditating on my bed, and he materialized right beside me. We sat side by side, holding hands, for a long time."

"Did he tell you about his life?" I inquired.

"Well, in the interchange of vibration I got the whole picture."

One evening Master was walking around his compound with Boone and me. He was holding onto Boone's arm for support. After awhile he stopped.

"Hot!" he remarked, switching from Boone's arm to mine.

Boone at this time was going through a period of temptations that, alas, were to take him off the path.

During this time also, Master gave me much personal advice.

"Your life is to be one of intense activity," he told me one evening, "and meditation. Your work is lecturing and writing."

"But Sir," I protested, "you yourself have written so much already. How can more writing possibly be needed?"

"How can you say that?" My question surprised him. "*Much* yet remains to be written!"

Some months later I addressed him further on this subject. "Master," I said, "Mrs. Nealey has suggested to me that I write a book explaining how I was drawn onto the path—somewhat like Thomas Merton's *Seven Storey Mountain.* It might help many people, she says. Would you like me to write it?"

"Not yet," Master replied. As we discussed the idea further, he implied that he wanted me to write such a book someday.

"You have a great work to do," he emphasized one afternoon as we were taking a short walk on his retreat grounds. "You must be conscious of how your words and actions affect others." He was trying to get me to combine childlike simplicity with the dignity of one who is centered in the inner Self—a difficult combination it seemed to me at the time. My inclination was to speak boldly of my failings, and to present myself as having few virtues—all in the name of humility. This behavior, Master implied, was neither dignified nor necessary for the development of humility. To achieve perfection, one must dwell on the *thought* of perfection, while recognizing it as God's gift, not as one's own accomplishment. Master set out to correct this flaw in me.

"Sir," I asked him one day, "would you prefer that the other monks call me Walter?" They had been calling me Don.

"They should call you *Reverend* Walter." In dismay (we monks never addressed any of our own ministers as "Reverend"), I tried hastily to change the subject, but Master persisted: "It is not that one disciple is better than another, but in an army there have to be captains as well as privates. You must accept respect from others as proper to your position."

This was, I confess, one piece of advice that I found difficult to accept.

One day I was sitting in Master's dictation room, waiting while he worked on a few pages of his *Gita* manuscript. While he wrote, his whole mind gravely focused on the task at hand, I gazed at him and thought gratefully how wonderful it was to be his disciple. When he finished his work, he asked me to help him to his feet. Rising, he held my hands for a moment and gazed with joy into my eyes.

"Just a bulge of the ocean!" he said, softly.

In his *Gita* commentaries he had compared God to the ocean, and individual souls to its innumerable waves. "God is the Sole Reality manifesting through all beings," he said. I could see from his loving remark that he wanted my love to expand to embrace the Ocean of Spirit, of which his body was but a tiny expression.

CHAPTER 32

"I Am Spirit"

"Yet hard the wise Mahatma is to find,
That man who sayeth, "All is Vasudev!"*

THIS PASSAGE FROM Sir Edwin Arnold's translation of the *Bhagavad Gita* was often quoted by Master as an expression of the supreme truth, that God alone exists.

A beautiful story on this subject was told me in 1960 by Yogi Ramiah, the saint of whom Master had said that another half hour in his company would have made it impossible for him to leave India again:

Namdev (said Yogi Ramiah), a famous saint of Maharashtra, used to worship Krishna in his local temple with so much devotion that the Lord often appeared to him in vision. Namdev was revered by many devotees, who came great distances to sit at his feet.

In his village there was also another saint, a potter by profession. Like Namdev, this potter was widely reputed to have seen God. One day a large crowd assembled in the temple to celebrate an annual spiritual festival. Many of those present were devotees of Namdev. Partway through the proceedings, the potter, acting on some divine whim, decided to test the spiritual caliber of each of the assembled worshipers.

A potter tests the soundness of his wares by rapping on them with his knuckles. From the sound a pot emits he can tell whether or not it is cracked. With this practice in mind, Namdev's fellow saint went about the crowd, slapping the devotees. Because he was

---

* Vasudev: Krishna. In this context the reference is to God, the Supreme Spirit (*Bhagavad Gita* VII:19).

313

held in such high esteem by all, no one complained; it was assumed that his peculiar behavior was intended as some sort of spiritual lesson. But when the potter-saint slapped Namdev, Namdev was incensed. Wasn't he this man's spiritual equal?

"Why did you hit me?" he demanded.

Calmly the potter stood up and announced, "There appears to be a crack in this pot!"

Everyone laughed. Later, Namdev, stung to the quick, went into the temple and prayed, "Lord, You know I love You. Why did You allow me to be so humiliated before my own devotees?"

"But what can *I* do, Namdev," said the Lord. "There *is* a crack in that pot!"

"Lord!" cried Namdev, prostrating himself full-length on the floor, "I want to be worthy of You. Won't You show me the way to perfection?"

"For that you need a guru, Namdev."

"But I behold *You,* the Lord of the universe! Of what use would a guru be to me?"

"I can inspire you through visions," the Lord replied. "I can even instruct you. But I can't lead you out of delusion except through the medium of one who knows Me, for such is My law."

"Lord, won't You then at least tell me who my guru is?"

The Lord gave Namdev the name of a certain saint, and that of the village in which he lived. "He will be your guru," the Lord said. He added with a smile, "Don't be surprised if he seems a bit peculiar. That is just his way."

Namdev went to the village Krishna had named, and made inquiries as to the saint's whereabouts.

"That lunatic?" laughed the villagers. "Who would want anything to do with *him?*" It is a practice of some saints to disguise their spiritual greatness, you see, to protect themselves against curiosity seekers. But when Namdev pressed the villagers further, they replied off-handedly, "Oh, you'll probably find him somewhere around the temple. He usually spends his time there."

Namdev went there. No one was in the courtyard, but on entering the temple itself he found a wild-looking, disheveled old man sprawled carelessly on the floor. "Surely *this* can't be my guru," he thought anxiously.

A moment later, the question faded from his mind. For, to his horror, he noticed that the old man's feet were resting on a *Shiva Linga.*° Furious at this act of desecration, he strode over to the

---

° An emblem sacred to God in the aspect of Shiva, Destroyer of delusion. The *Shiva Linga,* usually considered an abstract representation of the male phallus, is

man and ordered him to shift his feet at once.

The old man opened his eyes drowsily. "You see, my son," he replied, "my difficulty is that I'm old. This body is no longer so easy for me to move. Would you do me the favor of moving my feet to some spot where there is no *Linga?*"

Namdev hastened to oblige. But as he was about to set the old man's feet down in a new spot, he saw, directly under them, another *Shiva Linga!* He shifted them again; a third *Linga* appeared. Yet again: a fourth one. Suddenly the realization dawned on him: This man was indeed his guru! Prostrating himself humbly before him, Namdev prayed for forgiveness.

"I was blind, Gurudeva!" * he cried. "Now I know who you are, and I understand what it is you've been trying to teach me."

With calm majesty, then, the old man rose to his feet. "God is everywhere, Namdev," he said. "Realize Him in yourself, and with transformed vision behold Him residing in all things!" The Guru struck Namdev gently on the chest over the heart. Breath left the disciple's body. Rooted to the temple floor, Namdev stood as if transfixed, unable to move a muscle. His consciousness, like rising waters in a lake, burst the frail dam of his body. Like fluid light it streamed outward in all directions, embracing temple precincts, the village, the whole of India! Nations, continents, oceans became absorbed by his expanding bliss. At last it included the entire world, solar systems, galaxies! In every speck of space he saw God alone: unending light, bliss infinite! Too deeply absorbed for mere amazement, he realized that all this was *he!*

From that day onward Namdev lived immersed in divine consciousness. He wandered about the countryside, intoxicated day and night with fathomless bliss.

One day, many months later, he happened to be in the vicinity

---

never literally thought of that way by devout Hindus. Western scholars have erred in claiming that the *Linga* symbolizes male sexuality, and that its worship signifies the worship of sex. In fact, Shiva, in classical mythology, is depicted as the Supreme Renunciate. To Hindus, the *Linga* represents, rather, the universal masculine *principle,* which in human nature manifests through such qualities as strength, determination, and wisdom—as distinct from their feminine counterparts: tenderness, adaptability, and love.

On a more esoteric level, the *Linga* represents also the human spine, through which the life force (*prana*) must flow upward to the brain for the yogi to achieve the state of divine union. The *Shiva Linga,* in fact, depicts in stone a state of expanding awareness that occurs as, in meditation, the life force begins withdrawing from the senses into the spine.

* "Divine Guru," a customary appellation of love and respect on the part of the disciple.

of his old village. Passing the temple where he had first worshiped
God, he entered and sat for meditation. Again the Lord appeared
to him in the form of Krishna, as of old.

"My child," He said, "for so many months you have neglected
Me—you, who never failed to worship here a single day! I have
missed you. Where have you been?"

"My Beloved," cried Namdev, smiling happily at the Lord's
playfulness, "how could I think of coming here to see you, when
everywhere I gaze I behold Your formless presence!"

Blissfully, then, the Lord replied, "Now there are no cracks in
that pot!"

The "crack" in Namdev's "pot" was his awareness of himself as
a unique being, distinct from all others. In cosmic fact, our egos
are nothing but vortices of conscious energy that, within the vast
ocean of consciousness, take on the appearance of a separate reality
of their own, like the swirls of water in a brook.

Before this world was formed, when its atoms drifted about in
infinite space, there were none of the distinctions of form and substance that man comes to look upon as reality. There were no
trees, mountains, or rivers, no animals, no people—only nebulous
gasses. Someday, so astronomers tell us, these forms will once
again become gasses. Considering their amorphous past and future,
material forms clearly are not real in any fundamental sense. They
exist, yes, but their reality is not what it seems.

In the last analysis, as unreal as all these forms are that we see
around us, so also are our egos. Spiritual evolution reaches its cul-
mination when our separate vortices of consciousness are dissolved
in infinite consciousness.

If human consciousness were, like weight, shape, and texture,
the mere product of a coalescence of material atoms, then consciousness, certainly, would be as impermanent as they, and would
die with the ultimate disintegration of our bodies. But matter itself,
according to modern physics, is the product of a subtler reality:
energy. This being the case, it would seem a contradiction in the
universal scheme of things for consciousness, the subtlest reality of
all, to be the outgrowth of the grossest, matter. Yogis are being
joined nowadays by a growing number of physicists whose claim is
just the opposite: that, as matter is a manifestation of energy, so
energy in its turn must be a manifestation of consciousness.

To our limited minds, definition and understanding are often
synonymous. The more specifically we can define a thing, the
more clearly, so we imagine, we have understood it. Infinite

consciousness—a state of being in which *all* definitions are perceived as unreal—means to us the total loss of everything we equate with understanding. If, we ask ourselves, our egos were dissolved, and our little awareness merged into cosmic consciousness, wouldn't this loss of self-awareness spell the death of *all* awareness as far as we ourselves were concerned?

How cumbersome are the ways of logic. The answer, of course, is, Yes, the loss of self-awareness *does* spell the death of awareness *as far as we ourselves are concerned.* For there remains no "we ourselves" to be concerned! But loss of egoic self-awareness in no way spells for us the loss of awareness itself.

Alfred Lord Tennyson, the great poet, wrote in his *Memoirs:* "A kind of waking trance—this for lack of a better word—I have frequently had, quite up from boyhood, when I have been all alone. This has come upon me through *repeating* my own name to myself silently, till all at once, as it were out of the intensity of the consciousness of individuality, individuality itself seemed to dissolve and fade away into boundless being, and this not a confused state but the clearest, the surest of the surest, utterly beyond words— where death was an almost laughable impossibility—the loss of personality (if so it were) seeming no extinction, but the only true life. . . . It is no nebulous ecstasy, but a state of transcendent wonder, associated with absolute clearness of mind."

Great yogis aver that with the complete loss of self-awareness, the seeker's consciousness merges into the ocean of infinite consciousness; *it, itself, becomes infinite.* Physical death alone cannot bring us to this state, for at death we shed only the physical body, but keep the astral body, and with it our egoic awareness. Only by meditation and self-transcendence in the vastness of superconsciousness can we win final release from the limitations imposed on us by our egos. In cosmic consciousness we discover our true Self to be infinite. This, and this only, is the actual meaning of that expression, so much abused nowadays: Self-realization.

One day at Twenty-Nine Palms, while Master was revising his *Bhagavad Gita* commentaries, he asked Dorothy Taylor to read sections of it to a group of monks from Mt. Washington. During her reading, Miss Taylor came to a passage that described the state of oneness with God. Once, Master had said, the devotee attains this divine state, he realizes that the Ocean of Spirit alone is real; God took on the appearance of his little ego, then, after a time, withdrew that wave into Himself again. In effect, the dream-child wakes up in cosmic consciousness to find himself God once more.

However, Master went on to explain, the saint who attains that exalted consciousness never says, "I am God," for he sees it was the vast Ocean that became his little wave of ego. The wave, in other words, would not claim, when referring to the little self, to be the Ocean.

At this juncture Debi, who was present, cried excitedly, "But Sir, if you are one with that Ocean, that means you are God!"

"Why *I?*" Master asked. "Say *'He.' He* is God."

"But still, Sir, you are one with Him, and He is the only reality. That means *you,* too, are God."

"But this body isn't God!"

"You aren't identified with your body, Sir, so one may still say that you are God."

"Well, in that case why do you say, 'You'? *You,* too, are that! In a discussion of this sort, it is less confusing if we say, 'He.' "

"But what's the difference?"

"The Scriptures say . . ." Master began.

"It's only your humility, Sir," Debi broke in, "that makes you distinguish between yourself and Him."

"How can there be humility, when there is no consciousness of ego?"

Triumphantly Debi cried, "But if you have no ego left, that means you *are* God!"

Master laughingly continued the earlier statement, which Debi had interrupted: "The Scriptures say, 'He who knows Brahma becomes Brahma.' "°

"There!" cried Debi. "You said it yourself!"

Master rejoined, still laughingly, "*I* didn't say it. It's the Scriptures that say so." Master, in other words, would not identify those words with the human body speaking them. It was in his overarching spirit that he saw himself one with the Infinite. But Debi was unable to make this mental leap from a pure expression of Infinity to Infinity Itself.

"You quoted those Scriptures, Sir," he reminded Master relentlessly. "That means you agree with them!"

Recognizing that the distinction was, perhaps, too subtle for many to grasp, Master concluded, "Well, he who says he *is* God, isn't God. And," he added with a smile, "he who says he isn't, isn't!"

And there the subject rested, amid general laughter.

Liberation from ego does not come with the first glimpses of cosmic consciousness. Present, at first, even in an expanded state of awareness, is the subtle memory, "I, the formless but nevertheless still real

° *Mundaka Upanishad.*

John Smith, am enjoying this state of consciousness." The body in this trance state is immobile; one's absorption in God at this point is called *sabikalpa samadhi:* qualified absorption, a condition that is still subject to change, for from it one returns to assume once again the limitations of ego. By repeated absorption in the trance state, however, ego's hold on the mind is gradually broken, until the realization dawns: "There is no John Smith to go back to. I am Spirit!" This is the supreme state: *nirbikalpa samadhi,* or unqualified absorption—a condition changeless and eternal. If from this state one returns to body-consciousness, it is no longer with the thought of separate existence from the ocean of Spirit. John Smith no longer exists: It is the eternal Spirit, now, which animates his body, eats through it, teaches through it, and carries on all the normal functions of a human being. This outward direction of energy on the part of one who has attained *nirbikalpa samadhi* is sometimes known also as *sahaja,* or effortless, *samadhi.*

Divine freedom comes only with the attainment of *nirbikalpa samadhi.* Until that stage the ego can still—and alas, sometimes does—draw the mind back down into delusion. With *nirbikalpa samadhi,* one becomes what is known as a *jivan mukta,* free even though living in a physical form. A *jivan mukta,* however, unimaginably high though his state is, is not yet *fully* emancipated. The subtle memory, "I am John Smith," has been destroyed; he can acquire no new karma, since the post of ego to which karma is tied has been broken. But there remains even now the memory of all those prior existences: John Smith in thousands, perhaps millions of incarnations; John Smith the one-time bandit, John Smith the disappointed musician, John Smith the betrayed lover, the beggar, the swaggering tyrant. All those old selves must be made over, their karma spiritualized, released into the Infinite.

"Very few saints on this earth have achieved final liberation," Master told me one day.

I marveled. "What about all those great saints in your autobiography? Are they all dead, leaving none to replace them?"

"Great though many of them certainly were, very few had final liberation—only Babaji, Lahiri Mahasaya, Sri Yukteswar, and a few others. But many had *nirbikalpa samadhi,* the highest state of consciousness. They were true Christs. Two of Lahiri Mahasaya's disciples attained full liberation: Swami Pranabananda ('the saint with two bodies') and Ram Gopal Muzumdar ('the sleepless saint')."

"What about Swami Keshabananda?"*

---

* An advanced disciple of Lahiri Mahasaya.

"Keshabananda was too much attached to miracles. Lahiri Mahasaya often scolded him for it."

"What about your father, Sir?"

"Oh, no! He was a great soul, but he was still attached to his sons."

"And Therese Neumann?"

"She has attained a high state, but isn't yet fully liberated."

"Was Badhuri Mahasaya, 'the levitating saint,' liberated?"

"He was a true master, but no, not he either. It is very difficult to reach complete liberation."

"And Trailanga Swami? I had the impression he was an *avatar*."°

"No, an *avatar* comes with a special mission. Trailanga Swami was a *jivan mukta*—a great master, simply not yet fully liberated."

"What about Mataji, the sister of Babaji. *She,* surely, is liberated, isn't she? Yet you wrote that she was 'almost' as spiritually advanced as her brother."

"Well then, that means she wasn't fully liberated yet." Master paused, then added, "But she must be by now."

"Sir, why can't a master dissolve all his karma the moment he attains oneness with God?"

"Well," Master replied, "in that state you don't really care whether you come back or not. It is just like a dream to you then. You are awake, merely watching the dream. You can go on for incarnations that way, or you can say, 'I am free,' and *be* free right away. It's all in the mind. As soon as you say you are free, then you're free."

Boone, who was present, had evidently missed the central point that the total freedom of which Master was speaking could be attained only *after* one had reached the highest *samadhi*. "But Sir," he objected, "if *I* said I was free, I wouldn't really *be* free, would I?"

"Oh, yes! That is, you would be if you said it in that *consciousness* of freedom. But you've answered your own question: You've said, 'I *wouldn't* be.' The trouble is, the mind is already poisoned with the very delusions it is trying to dispel; it lacks force." Master went on to tell a story to illustrate his point.

"A man who was being troubled by a demon searched the Scriptures for a method of disposing of such evil entities. Finding the remedy, he recited certain words over a handful of powder, which he then threw onto the demon.

" 'It won't work!' the demon laughed. 'I got into that powder

_____

° A "divine incarnation." The term is used to describe one who came into this birth already completely freed of all past karma.

before you said your incantations over it. How, then, could it hurt me?'

"The mind, you see, is like that powder—already infected with the very 'demon' of ignorance it is trying to dispel."

Another time, however, referring to that degree of mental freedom which is a prior condition for even a glimpse of *samadhi,* Master said, "It is only the thought that we are not free that keeps us from actually being free. Merely to break that thought would suffice to put us into *samadhi*! *Samadhi* is not something we have to *acquire.* We have it already!" Master added, "Dwell always on this thought: Eternally we have been with God. For a short time—for the fleeting breaths of a few incarnations—we are in delusion. Then again we are free in Him forever!"

When the soul attains final liberation, it becomes a *siddha* ("perfected being"), or *param mukta* ("supremely free soul"). Even in this state, individuality is not lost, but is retained in the form of memory. The karma of John Smith's many incarnations has been released into the Infinite, but the *memory* of them, now spiritualized, remains a fact throughout eternity. The soul, however, once it achieves this state of supreme liberation, rarely reactivates its own remembered individuality, and *never* does so except at the command of the Divine Will. When such a supremely free soul returns to this world, it comes only for the welfare of humanity. Such an incarnation is called an *avatar,* or "divine incarnation."

Such, Master told us, was Babaji, the first of our direct line of gurus. Such also were Lahiri Mahasaya—*yogavatar,* Master called him, or "incarnation of yoga"—and Swami Sri Yukteswar, whom Master identified as India's present-day *gyanavatar,* or "incarnation of wisdom."

"Sir," I asked Master one day at his desert retreat, "are *you* an *avatar?*"

With quiet simplicity he replied, "A work of this importance would have to be started by such a one."

An *avatar,* he told us, comes on earth with a divine mission, often for the general upliftment of mankind. The *siddha*'s effort, by contrast, has necessarily been to unite his own consciousness perfectly with God's. God, therefore, does not work through *siddhas* in the same way that He works through *avatars.* To *avatars* He gives the power to bring vast numbers of souls to freedom in Him. To *siddhas* He gives the power to liberate themselves and a few others.

"Master," I said once, "if Yogi Ramiah was fully liberated, did he, like his well-known guru, Ramana Maharshi, have disciples?"

"Oh, yes," Master answered. "He must have had. You must free others before you can become completely free yourself."

When I met Yogi Ramiah in 1960, and observed how very few disciples he had, I asked him why there weren't many more to absorb his divine wisdom. His reply was simple: "God has done what He wants to do with this body."

The lowest number that each soul must free before it can itself be raised to the state of *param mukta* is, I believe Master said, six.

Paramhansa Yogananda indicated that he had been sent into the world at a time of extraordinary spiritual need on earth. Debi once told me of a young Hindu friend of his who had come for a year of study in America, and who, on his way over by ship, had had a vision of Master. He had never heard of Yogananda before. Several months later Debi brought him to a Sunday service at Hollywood Church. When his friend saw Master, who was speaking that day, he recognized him immediately as the saint of his vision.

"Sir," Debi inquired later, "my friend has his own guru in India. Why was he granted that vision of you?"

"Because," Master replied, "this work is a special dispensation of God."

An *avatar,* unlike most saints who are still engaged in winning their own final freedom from *maya*'s coils, may appear engagingly human and life-affirming. In his humanity, however, he offers mankind new insights into what it really means to be a human being. For people commonly equate humanity with weakness, not with strength. "I'm only human," they say as an excuse for failure. They see not that their humanity gives them the best possible reason for success! In the presence of a master, the term "human failing" translates itself to mean "the failure to be *fully* human."

Though every great master is fully qualified to say, with Jesus, "I and my Father are one," many descend occasionally from that absolute state, as Jesus also did, to enjoy a loving "I-and-Thou" relationship with the Lord. The Indian Scriptures state that God created the universe "in order that He might enjoy Himself through many." The vast majority of His creatures, alas, have lost conscious touch with the infinite joy of their own being. The saints alone, in their joyous romance with the Lord, fulfill this deep and abiding purpose of His creation, by letting Him express His joy outwardly through their lives.

*Avatar*s and other masters will often go through years of *sadhana* ("spiritual practice") in their youth, as an example to others. If they didn't, their disciples might claim that meditation and self-effort are not necessary for God-attainment, or perhaps simply that such practices are not their "way."

"If you want God," Master used to say, "go after Him. It takes great determination and steadfast, deep effort. And remember, the minutes are more important than the years."

But a great aid on the path is the constant thought that one is free already. "Memorize my poem *'Samadhi,'*" he once told us. "Repeat it daily. Visualize yourselves in that infinite state; identify yourselves with it. For *that alone* is what you really are!"

CHAPTER 33

"Original Christianity"

H OW DOES THE CONCEPT of *samadhi* agree with Christian teachings? Most church-goers, certainly, get no hint on Sunday mornings that the Bible promises them anything like cosmic consciousness. The best they are encouraged to hope for is eternity in heaven after death, in a body much like the one they possess now.

No one, however, has a "corner" on Christ's teachings, or for that matter on any religion. The revelation that God gave to the world through Jesus Christ is the property of mankind, not of the churches alone.

The mass of Christian worshipers are often referred to as "the body of Christ." But in fact they are more like Christ's family. For a body is responsive to the brain, whereas few Christians are conscious enough of Christ's presence within them, or faithful enough to his teachings in the Bible, to give much thought to being *responsive* to him. A body, moreover, is coordinated by its brain, whereas Christians—even those who *want* to obey Christ—respond to his commandments by rushing off in hundreds of directions at once. *Family,* then, is certainly the apter metaphor. Even if family members revere their head, they respond to him variously according to their different temperaments and levels of understanding. A certain lack of coordination, which in a body might be a sign of functional disorder, is both natural and, to some extent, right in a family. At any rate it shows that its members have minds of their own.

The mass of Christians in the world are like the family of a great man, some of whose luster reflects on them by their association with him. But it is also notorious how many great men have been thoroughly *mis*understood by their relatives. To be the disciple of a great master gives one an incentive, certainly, to tune in to him, but it in no way *guarantees* such attunement. Jesus accused the Jews of misunderstanding Moses. He even chided his own close disciples for misunderstanding *him.* We must conclude, then, from his own statements that Christians have never had a *proprietary* claim on his full, or even his true, meaning. A disciple's understanding of his master's teachings depends on his own *capacity* for understanding, and not on his outward status as a member, or even as a leader, of any church.

Many times progress in human understanding has occurred when one civilization has been exposed to the different insights of another. Religion, today, stands at the threshold of such an opportunity. The energetic influx of teachings from the East has already had a strong impact on Western churches, making them rethink their position on several basic issues. Among other things, it has reminded them of dormant traditions of their own. The practice of meditation, for example, once a vital part of Christian observance—particularly in the Eastern Church—is being revived owing to the emphasis given it by teachers from India.

Nor has the influence of Oriental teachings on the churches been limited to reminders of forgotten Christian traditions: It has also shown many Biblical teachings in a wholly new light. For truth, like a diamond, is many-faceted. The teachings of Moses and Jesus Christ have been given certain emphases in the West, but other perfectly legitimate emphases are possible, and would reflect truths that have been cherished for centuries elsewhere in the world. Exposure to those unfamiliar traditions might prove enormously beneficial to Westerners who desire deeper insight into their own religious teachings.

A visitor once asked Paramhansa Yogananda, "You call your temples 'churches of all religions.' Why, then, do you place such special emphasis on Christianity?"

"It was the wish of Babaji that I do so," the Master replied. "He asked me to interpret the Christian Bible and the *Bhagavad Gita,* or Hindu Bible, and to show that their teachings are basically one. It was with this mission that I was sent to the West."

Many Westerners in this materialistic age doubt the truth of Christ's teachings. Indeed, many even doubt that he ever lived. Paramhansa Yogananda, by his example as much as by his teachings, turned agnostics into believing Christians again. For his mission wasn't to convert people to Hinduism, but to revitalize Christianity. What he taught, he said, was "the original Christianity of Christ."

One day in Boston, Massachusetts, he received a letter criticizing him for "sponsoring" Jesus in the West. "Don't you know that he never lived?" the writer demanded. "He was a myth invented to deceive people." The letter was left unsigned.

Yogananda prayed to be led to the writer. About a week later he visited the Boston Public Library. There, seeing a stranger seated on a bench under one of the windows, he went over and sat next to him.

"Why did you write me that letter?" he inquired.

The man started in amazement. "Wh-what do you mean? What letter?"

"The one in which you claimed that Jesus Christ was only a myth."

"But—how on earth did you know I wrote that?"

"I have ways," the Master replied. "And I wanted you to know that the power by which I have found you enables me also to know for certain that Jesus Christ did live, and that he was all that the Bible claims. He was a true Christ."

Another time in Boston Yogananda received another remarkable corroboration of his experiences of the reality of Jesus Christ. In meditation he saw Krishna and Jesus walking together on a sea of golden light. To convince himself (as he put it), though more probably to convince skeptics, including sectarian believers who couldn't imagine Jesus and Krishna sharing the same wave, Yogananda asked for objective verification of his vision.

A divine voice replied, "The fragrance of a lotus will remain in the room."

"All that day," Yogananda told us, "a lotus aroma, unknown in the West, lingered on in the room. Many visited me that day. 'What is that wonderful fragrance?' they asked. I knew then I had received proof positive that what I had seen was true."

In St. Louis one day Master visited a Roman Catholic monastery. The abbot had been shown to him in meditation to be a great saint. The other monks were horrified to see this orange-robed "heathen" in their midst. But when the abbot arrived on the scene, he hastened over to Paramhansaji and embraced him lovingly. "Man of God," he cried, "I am happy you have come!"

The saints alone are the true custodians of religion. For only they draw their understanding from the direct *experience* of truth, and not from superficial reason or book learning. The true saints of one religion bow to the divinity manifest in the true saints of other religions. When Paramhansa Yogananda visited Therese Neumann, the great Catholic stigmatist in Bavaria, Germany, she sent word, "Though the bishop has asked me to see no one without his permission, I will receive the man of God from India."

Far from undermining the faith of Christians in their own

Scriptures, Yogananda gave many of them renewed faith. One day a Catholic monk, inspired by an interview with him, begged in his prayers that he be vouchsafed a vision of Jesus. The next day he hurried to Yogananda, tears in his eyes. "Last night," he cried, "for the first time in my life, I saw Him!"

Oliver Wendell Holmes said, "To have doubted one's own first principles is the mark of a civilized man." By contrast, to hold any belief dogmatically is like saying, "This much I will have of truth, and no more." Dogmatism is the death of true understanding. Again and again throughout history it has stood in the way of progress, and even of common sense. Consider a few examples:

In 1728 potatoes were introduced into Scotland. The clergy declared them an outrage, unfit for Christian consumption, because no mention is made of them in the Bible. Again, when umbrellas were first invented, clergymen in many lands denounced them as the work of the Devil: for doesn't the Bible clearly state, "Your Father which is in heaven sendeth rain on the just and on the unjust" (Matthew 5:45)? Nor is bigotry a monopoly of the West; as Yogananda often remarked, "Ignorance, East and West, is fifty-fifty." In a pilgrim's guide to South Indian temples I discovered this little jewel of unreason: "Whosoever dares to spit on the temple grounds will be born for three successive incarnations as a tithiri bird." ("What," I asked an Indian friend of mine, "is a tithiri bird?" "Oh, a despicable creature," he replied vaguely.)

"Other sheep I have," Jesus said, "which are not of this fold" (John 10:16). Might it have been of devotees of those other great religions that he was speaking? We read in the tenth chapter of the Book of Acts: "God has no favorites, but in every nation he who reveres Him and acts righteously is accepted by Him" (Acts 10:34,35).

Christian fundamentalists, who insist that all authority rests in the Bible, quarrel endlessly over what the Bible really means. Luther and Zwingli, leaders of the Protestant Reformation, taught entirely on the basis of Scriptural, as opposed to Church, authority. Yet the two disagreed on basic Scriptural precepts. Their meeting at the Marburg Colloquy in 1529, summoned to resolve these differences, resulted in a doctrinal clash between them. The meeting ended in failure.

It need surprise no one that the Bible means different things to different people. For is it not obvious that it cannot hold authority *beyond a person's own ability to understand it?* Jesus said, "Therefore I speak to them in parables: because they seeing see not; and hearing they hear not, neither do they understand" (Matthew 13:13).

Even after *explaining* his parable of the sower, he said, "Who hath ears to hear, let him hear" (Matthew 13:43).

And what is it that determines one's ability to understand? Far more important than native intelligence is his actual, inner experience of divine truths. How else are they to be recognized? A certain American Indian in the Nineteenth Century, lacking experience with modern machinery, felt convinced that a steam locomotive was operated by a horse cleverly concealed where the boiler appeared to be. And many clergymen, lacking personal experience of God's love, are equally convinced that He is a God of wrath and vengeance. Jean Danielou, the French cardinal-theologian, wrote, "That which saves is not religious experience, but faith in the word of God." True faith, however, without *some* kind of experience, *some* kind of inner grace, simply is not possible. Reason alone cannot banish doubt. Only the breath of God's love in the soul can awaken true (as opposed to fanatical) faith in His word. The deeper the awareness—that is to say, the deeper the *experience*—of that love, the deeper the faith.

As St. Anselm put it: "Who does not experience will not know. For just as experiencing a thing far exceeds the mere hearing of it, so the knowledge of him who experiences is beyond the knowledge of him who hears."

The tendency of spiritually unaware theologians and ministers has been to take literally what was meant metaphorically, and to define Reality in terms of their own limited, human experience of life. Greatly needed in Christendom is a more mystical approach.

In Calcutta I once met a Christian missionary who had just visited the Holy Land. A few months previously I had visited Galilee myself, and felt blessed even now by the experience I had had of Christ's presence there. Imagining that in this blessing the missionary and I shared a common bond, I exclaimed, "Wasn't it wonderful! Jesus seemed so real I almost expected to see him come walking down out of the hills." The man stared at me a moment as though I were mad. Then he muttered, "It's a beautiful country. Wonderful *history*." Communion with Christ, obviously, had nothing to do with what he saw as his mission to India.

The Roman Catholics, in their long tradition, have experienced the problems that can arise from individual interpretations of the holy Scriptures. Their solution has been to insist that their Church be the final authority in such matters. Christ himself, they claim, gave it that authority when he said, "Thou art Peter, and upon this rock I will build my church" (Matthew 16:18). But their argument, though wisely motivated, is fatally flawed. For how do we know that Christ actually *intended* to delegate such authority to them? We have only their word for it, supported by their insistence that, having such authority, they *must* have interpreted Christ's meaning correctly. It is a perfect argument in a circle!

Paramhansa Yogananda's explanation of that same Bible passage was altogether different. Jesus, he said, was referring to the inner "church" of divine consciousness. He saw that he would be able to "build" this "church" in Peter, after his disciple recognized Jesus as the living Christ and thereby demonstrated that his spiritual life was founded on the bedrock of divine perception. Jesus' words—here, as everywhere else—had an individual, not an institutional, significance.

Yet in one important sense the Roman Catholic Church is perfectly right: Authority of *some* kind is very much needed in spiritual matters, lest the Scriptures be misinterpreted in such ways as to reinforce people's ignorance. It should, however, be the right kind of authority, and not the sort that the blind exert in leading the blind. *The only valid authority on spiritual matters is true spiritual experience.* For such experience we must look not to the commentaries of learned scholars and theologians, but to the saints. I repeat, therefore: *The saints alone are the true custodians of religion.*

"The words of the saints," wrote St. Gregory of Sinai, "never disagree, if they are carefully examined; all alike speak the truth, wisely changing their judgments on these subjects when necessary."

Because it is necessary for the same fundamental truths to be presented variously, according to the varying needs of the times, St. Simeon the New Theologian wrote, "A man who does not desire to link himself to the latest of the saints (in time), in all love and humility, owing to a certain distrust, will never be linked with the preceding saints, and will not be admitted to their succession even though he thinks he possesses all possible faith and love for God and for all His saints." Because all who know God drink from the same lake, to reject *any* expression of Him is to that extent to reject God Himself.

Yogananda once prayed to Jesus Christ for reassurance that he was interpreting his words in the Gospels correctly. Jesus appeared to him in a vision; the Holy Grail passed from his lips to Yogananda's. Jesus then, so Yogananda later told us, spoke these words of heavenly assurance: "The cup from which I drink, thou dost drink."

To return, then, to the question of Christian corroboration of the concept of *samadhi,* it is to the saints that we look first.

"The soul, when purified," wrote St. Catherine of Genoa, "abides entirely in God; its being is God."

"The soul must wholly lose all human knowledge and all human feelings," wrote St. John of the Cross, "in order to receive in fullness divine knowledge and divine feelings."

St. Catherine of Sienna stated that Christ had told her in a vision, "I am That I am; thou art that which is not." In other words, the little vortex of her ego had no abiding reality of its own.

St. Veronica Giuliani, the Seventeenth-Century Capuchin nun, concerning her experience of the supreme ecstasy of mystical union, wrote in her *Diary* that she had received a conviction, far deeper than any intellectual concept or belief, that *"outside God nothing has any existence at all."*

The great St. Teresa of Avila wrote that, in this state, "the soul is entirely transformed into the likeness of its Creator—it seems more God than soul."

Blessed Henry Suso, describing the enlightened soul, wrote: "In such a person God is the very essence, the life, energy, and vital force. The man himself is a mere instrument, a medium of God."

St. Anselm wrote, "Not all of that joy shall enter into those who rejoice; but they who rejoice shall wholly enter into that joy."

Do not these quotations suggest persuasively that state of oneness with God which is known to Indian yogis as *samadhi?* There are Christian writers (Dom Denys Rutledge, for example, in his pretentious book *In Search of a Yogi*) who claim that to the Christian an absorption of the ego into God would be undesirable. But is this a *Christian,* or merely a perfectly normal, human reaction? Similar, in fact, is an objection one sometimes hears from worldly people to the joys of heaven: "How can heaven be all that wonderful, when it makes no provision for sex enjoyment?" (They forget that, as children, they lived without sex perfectly happily.) But what do such ego-centered writers make of Jesus' own words, "Whosoever will save his life shall lose it: and whosoever will lose his life for my sake shall find it" (Matthew 16:25)? Paul Tillich, the great Protestant theologian, writing from the more expanded vision of a wise man, stated, "Endless living in finitude would be hell. . . . This has nothing to do with Christianity."*

Let us see what Christian saints have said further on the subject of *infinity* as a definition of divine awareness.

Meister Eckhart, the great mystic, said of souls that are merged in God, "By grace they are *God with God.*"

"I, *who am infinite,*" wrote St. Catherine of Sienna, "seek infinite works—that is, an infinite perfection of love."

° From his lecture "Symbols of Eternal Life."

St. Bernard wrote, "Just as a little drop of water mixed with a lot of wine seems entirely to lose its own identity, while it takes on the taste of wine and its color . . . so it will inevitably happen that in saints every human affection will then, in some ineffable manner, melt away from self and be entirely transfused into the will of God."

"A man who has attained the final degree of perfection," wrote St. Simeon the New Theologian, "is dead and yet not dead, but infinitely more alive in God. . . . He is inactive and at rest, as one who has come to the end of all action of his own. He is without thought, since he has become one with Him who is above all thought." How closely these words resemble Paramhansa Yogananda's description, in *Autobiography of a Yogi,* of his first glimpse of cosmic consciousness: "The flesh was as though dead, yet in my intense awareness I knew that never before had I been fully alive."

Of St. Simeon's experience of *samadhi,* his disciple, Nicetas Stathos, wrote: "Once, while offering up a pure prayer to God to be drawn into intimate converse with Him, he had a vision: Behold, the atmosphere began to shine through his soul, and though he was inside his cell, it seemed to him that he was lifted up high beyond its confines. It was then the first watch of the night. As this light from above began to shine like an aurora, the building and everything else disappeared, and he no longer believed himself to be in the house at all. Quite outside himself, as he gazed with his whole soul at this light that had appeared to him, it increased bit by bit, making the atmosphere more brilliant, and he felt himself taken, with his whole body, away from the things of earth."

Saints, keenly aware of how impossible it would be to describe the Indescribable, usually speak of it more or less vaguely. A few, however, have tried to suggest their experience in words.

"Divine darkness," wrote St. Dionysius, "is the unapproachable light in which God is professed to live."

And Basil the Great wrote, "Utterly inexpressible and indescribable is Divine beauty, blazing like lightning. . . . If we name the brightness of dawn, or the clearness of moonlight, or the brilliance of sunshine, none of it is worthy to be compared with the glory of True Light, and is farther removed therefrom than are the deepest night and the most terrible darkness from the clear light of midday."

The Bible, too, describes God in many passages as a great Light. The thirty-sixth Psalm states, "For with thee is the fountain of life: in thy light shall we see light."

St. Paul wrote, "For God, who commanded the light to shine out of darkness, hath shined in our hearts, to give the light of the

knowledge of the glory of God in the face of Jesus Christ"
(2 Corinthians 4:6).

Christ is spoken of in the Bible as "the only begotten son of
God." Does this make us sons of God in a different sense from
Jesus? Or has the term "the only begotten" a subtle, mystical
meaning? On one side of this argument we have the judgment of
orthodox theologians, but on the other that of great saints. Theologians, that is to say, contend that we are *radically* different from
Jesus. But the great saints put it as a difference, rather, in the *degree*
of Self-awareness. They say that we are sons by "adoption," as St.
Paul put it, only until the Divine Life courses in our veins. But
when that point is reached, to quote Meister Eckhart, "between the
only begotten son and the soul there is no distinction."

"The disciple is not above his master," Jesus said, "but every one that
is perfect shall be as his master" (Luke 6:40). And, "Be ye therefore
perfect, *even as your Father which is in heaven is perfect*" (Matthew 5:48).

"If we are [God's] children," St. Paul wrote, "we share His treasures, and all that Christ claims as his will belong to all of us as
well!" (Romans 8:17) Later in the same chapter Paul speaks of
Christ in relation to his followers as "the eldest of a family of
many brothers."

In what way is Jesus Christ the "only begotten son of God"?
Not as a man, certainly. Nor yet as a limited soul. The very word
Christ is a title meaning "The Anointed of God." Christ is part of
the infinite Trinity,* an aspect of God Himself. Jesus was called

---

* Paramhansa Yogananda explained the Christian Trinity (God the Father, Son,
and Holy Ghost) in a cosmic sense. God the Father, he said, is the Infinite Consciousness from which all things were manifested. God's consciousness was one
and undivided ("Hear O Israel, the Lord our God, the Lord is One"); apart from
that consciousness there was no substance out of which the universe could have
been made. The universe is His dream. To produce the dream, the Creator had
to set a portion of His consciousness into motion. You, I, our earth, the sun and
galaxies, our thoughts and inspirations, our very longing to be one with Him
again—*all* are products of the vibrations of His consciousness, separate manifestations of the vast *primal* vibration of *Aum,* the Holy Ghost.

The Son of the Trinity represents the underlying presence in all vibratory creation of the calm, unmoving consciousness of the Creator, so called because it
reflects the Father's consciousness. Vibratory creation itself is also known as the
Divine Mother. The devotee must commune first with *Aum,* or the Divine
Mother. Uniting his consciousness with that, he must proceed to realize his oneness with the Son. Only after achieving union with the Son can he proceed toward oneness with the Father beyond creation.

The Hindu Scriptures name this eternal Trinity, *Sat Tat Aum. Sat* stands for
the Spirit, the Supreme Truth, which is God the Father. *Tat* is the *Kutastha
Chaitanya,* the Christ Consciousness which underlies all creation. And *Aum* is the
Word, the Holy Ghost, called also the Comforter in the Bible.

"the Christ" because his consciousness was identified with God's presence in all creation. The Christ is the *"only begotten* son" because Christ Consciousness is omnipresent. It is not personal at all in an egoic sense. "I move my hand," said Meister Eckhart, "and Christ moves, who *is* my hand."

"God," St. Paul wrote, "created all things by Jesus Christ" (Ephesians 3:9). How could God have created the vast universe, with its billions of galaxies, with the help of a single, infinitesimal ego? That kind of thinking was possible only in the days of our civilization's innocence, when people regarded God Himself as a bearded old Gentleman seated on a golden throne somewhere up in the sky.

"Is it not written in your law, I said, Ye are gods?" (John 10:34) Thus Jesus answered the Jews, when they accused him of blasphemy for telling them, "I and my Father are one." He didn't say, "My Father says so, and you'd better believe it or you'll go to hell!" He said, *"You* are that, too," and went on to explain that the only difference between them and him was that he had been "sanctified" by the Father, a fulfillment they had yet to achieve.

Jesus himself distinguished between his human self and the omnipresent Christ Consciousness with which he was inwardly identified. In both cases he used the pronoun "I," but the meaning differed according to his emphasis.° Speaking impersonally, he said, "I am the way, the truth, and the life: no man cometh unto the Father, but by me" (John 14:6). And again impersonally, "The Father judgeth no man, but hath committed all judgment unto the Son" (John 5:22). His reference here to the Son is to the Christ Consciousness with which his own consciousness was fully identified. But when someone addressed him as "Good Master," he replied, reflecting then that person's consciousness of him as a man, "Why callest thou *me* good? There is none good but one, that is, God" (Matthew 19:17).

It was in his over-arching spirit that Jesus could say, "Before Abraham was, *I am*" (John 8:58). It was from a consciousness of omnipresence that he said, "Where two or three are gathered together in my name, there am I in the midst of them" (Matthew 18:20). It was of his infinite Self, not his physical body, that he spoke when he said, "Whoso eateth my flesh, and drinketh my blood, hath eternal life" (John 6:54). It was to rebuke teachers who drew the devotion of their students to themselves, instead of directing it to the

---

°In the Hindu Scriptures, too, this pronoun is frequently used to describe both the infinite consciousness of a master and limited, ego-consciousness.

Infinite Christ, that he said, "All that ever came before me are thieves and robbers" (John 10:8). Had he been referring to the prophets before him *in time,* as many imagine, he would not have said also, "Think not that I am come to destroy the law, or the prophets: I am not come to destroy, but to fulfil" (Matthew 5:17).

"Thou art *That,*" say the Indian Scriptures. Christians who cannot imagine a higher destiny than eternal confinement in a little body would do well to meditate on the parable of the mustard seed, which Jesus likened to the kingdom of heaven. The mustard seed, Jesus said, though tiny, grows eventually to become a tree, "so that the birds of the air come and lodge in its branches" (Matthew 13:32). Even so, the soul in communion with the Lord expands to embrace the infinity of consciousness that is God.

And Christians who imagine themselves *inherently* sinful, rather than sinning due to delusion, would do well to meditate on the parable of the prodigal son, whose *true* home was in God; and (if they aspire to heaven) on these words of Jesus, "No man hath ascended up to heaven, but he that came down from heaven" (John 3:13).

Sectarian Christians have a difficult time explaining the Second Coming as an objective event in history in the light of these words of Jesus, "When you are persecuted in one town, take refuge in another; I tell you this: *before you have gone through all the towns of Israel* the Son of man will have come" (Matthew 10:23). And again these words, when Jesus was discussing his Second Coming: "Verily I say unto you, This generation shall not pass, till all these things be fulfilled" (Matthew 24:34). And how could "all the tribes of the earth see the Son of man coming in the clouds of heaven with power and great glory" (Matthew 24:30)? There would have to be millions of Christs on as many clouds for all the nations to see him! But to great saints and yogis Christ's statements are perfectly clear. He meant that, in clouds of divine vision, he would come again into the souls of men anywhere, at any time, whose hearts were pure, receptive to his grace.

As Jesus put it, "Blessed are the pure in heart, for they shall see God" (Matthew 5:8).

CHAPTER 34

Kriya Yoga

"**B**LESSED ARE THE PURE in heart, for they shall see God." The truth in these simple words has been acclaimed equally by great saints of East and West. It is a truth which every devotee would do well to ponder, for in all religions it is a common delusion to believe that mere affiliation with a body of worshipers will be one's passport to salvation. Yet Jesus didn't say, "Blessed are my followers, for they shall see God." His message was universal: By the yardstick of inner purity alone is a person's closeness to God determined.

What *is* purity of heart? Jesus in effect defined it elsewhere as the capacity to love God with all one's heart, soul, mind, and strength.° And why is this capacity called purity? Simply because we *belong* in God; worldliness is foreign to our essential nature.

How, then, can one achieve such purity? Is self-effort the answer? Is grace? St. Paul said, "By grace are ye saved through faith; and that not of yourselves: it is the gift of God: Not of works, lest any man should boast."† Fundamentalist Christians often quote this passage as an argument against self-effort of any kind, and particularly against the practices of yoga. But the Book of Revelation states, "And, behold, I come quickly, and my reward is with me, *to give every man according as his work shall be.*"§ Do these Scriptures contradict one another? Not at all.

St. Paul didn't mean that self-effort is futile, but only that God is above bargaining. Outward "works," in other words, in God's name—such as building schools and hospitals—will not *in themselves* win His favor. Love alone can win Him. For like attracts like, and God *is* Love. But as for those inner efforts—trust, for example, and

---

° Mark 12:30.
† Ephesians 2:8,9.
§ Revelation 22:12; italics mine.

love—which lift the soul Godward, these are essential, else the Scriptures were written in vain. It is to this internal "work" that the Book of Revelation is referring above.*

To develop love for God, the first prerequisite is that no other desire hinder its free flow. This, then, is our first spiritual "work": to give up every desire that conflicts with our devotion. We need not *destroy* our desires so much as rechannel their energies Godward.

And it is in this true labor of love that the techniques of yoga serve most effectively. Wrong desires, it need hardly be added, could never be transmuted by technique alone. But just as the techniques of running are useful to those with a desire to be good runners, so the techniques of yoga can help devotees to control their physical energies, and to redirect them toward God. Yoga practice by itself won't give us God, but it *can* help us very much in our efforts to *give ourselves* to Him. The yoga science, in other words, helps us to *cooperate* with divine grace.

Take a simple example. Devotees naturally want to love God. Many, however, have no clear notion of how to go about loving Him. Too often their efforts are merely cerebral, and end in frustration. Yet Jesus hinted at a *technique* when he said, "Blessed are the pure in heart." For, as everyone who has loved deeply knows, it is in the *heart* that love is felt—not in the physical heart, literally, but in the *heart center,* or spinal nerve plexus just behind the heart. Christian saints have stressed again and again "the love of the *heart.*" And yogis claim that love is developed more easily if, instead of merely *thinking* love, one will direct the thought of love upwards from the heart center, through the spine to the brain.

Take another example. Devotees attempting inward communion with God often find their efforts thwarted by restless thoughts. But long ago yogis found a technique for overcoming this obstacle. The breath, they discovered, is intimately related to the mental processes. A restless mind accompanies a restless breath. By simple, effective techniques for calming the breath, they found they could free the mind more easily for divine contemplation.

Thus, by its practical application of laws governing man's physical body and nervous system, the science of yoga helps one to become more *receptive* to the flow of divine grace, much as technical

---

* In *The New English Bible,* St. Paul's words, "By grace are ye saved through faith," are rendered, "For it is by his grace you are saved, through trusting him." These words, *through trusting him,* help to emphasize the point that the *right kind* of self-effort *is* needed. For trust implies an active gift, and not mere passive acceptance.

proficiency at the piano makes possible the uninterrupted flow of musical inspiration. And divine communion, as St. Paul said, comes not by "pleasing" God, overtly, but only by making oneself fully receptive to His love. That love of its very nature *wants* to give itself.

I referred to the ego in Chapter 32 as a vortex of consciousness that separates itself from the ocean of awareness by its own centripetal force. Once this vortex is dissolved, I said, self-awareness flows outward to embrace infinity. But now I should explain that it vastly over-simplifies matters to speak of the ego as but a single vortex. The fact is, egoic awareness gives rise to countless millions of subsidiary eddies: vortices of likes and dislikes, resulting in desires, which in turn lead to ego-motivated activities. Every such vortex draws energy to itself, and thereby also reaffirms and strengthens the ego from which it derives its energy. Until a desire has been fulfilled in action, or else dissipated by wisdom, it may remain dormant, like a seed, in the subconsciousness for incarnations. The stronger the mental tendency, the greater the ego's commitment to it. The amount of energy diverted toward these myriad commitments is incalculably great. Paramhansa Yogananda used to tell us, "There is enough latent energy in one gram of your flesh to supply the city of Chicago with electricity for a week. Yet you imagine yourselves powerless in the face of a few difficulties!" The reason we can tap so little of the energy potentially available to us is that most of what we attract to ourselves from the surrounding universe has already been "spoken for"; it is absorbed by countless eddies of prior egoic commitments.

I had an interesting experience a few years ago relative to this energy-drain. Having, as I thought, seriously overextended myself in my work, I had reached a point of exhaustion. One evening I had a class to give, and half an hour before leaving for it lay down to rest. But I didn't sleep; instead, I reviewed in my mind as dispassionately as I could all the reasons I had for feeling so tired: the endless activities (daily lectures, classes, a radio program), the unceasing stream of correspondence, the constant telephone calls, the numerous requests for interviews, the incessant demands for decisions from people who could have made just as good decisions on their own. As I recalled each reason to mind, I reacted with an instinctive feeling of rejection: "Oh, no—it's just too much!"

But then came the dispassionate challenge: "*Is* it? It is a fact of your life now, whether you like it or not. Why not simply accept it?" In each case, as I applied this advice, I felt as though I had closed some psychic door through which energy had been pouring from me in my anxiety to push the unwanted experience out of my life. As each door closed, I found more energy being retained in myself.

The results were extraordinary. By the end of that half hour my exhaustion had completely vanished; I was fairly bursting with energy! A friend who had seen me earlier that day and pleaded with me to cancel my class saw me now and exclaimed, "What a wonderful sleep you must have had. You look so refreshed!" Interestingly enough the subject of my class that evening was "Energization." It was perhaps the best I have ever given on this subject. Afterwards I still felt so full of energy that I stayed up until two o'clock the next morning, talking, reading, then meditating.

And the energy that I rechanneled that day was only a minute fraction of the energy pre-empted by millions of other vortices in my subconscious mind!

If we could only channel all our energy in any one direction—if, for example, we could learn with our whole being to say *Yes* to life, instead of mixing so many "yeses" with "nos"—our powers of accomplishment would be greater than most people deem possible. But it is important, at the same time, to channel this energy wisely. For if we use it to achieve goals that are external to our true nature, our very success will bring us disappointment.

To understand how to utilize rightly the enormous amounts of energy that are available to us, we must understand how energy functions in the body. Its main channel is the spine. The spine, like a bar magnet, has its north pole at the spiritual eye, and its south pole at the base, in the coccyx. In a bar magnet, all the molecules, each having its own north-south polarity, are turned in the same direction. In an unmagnetized bar the molecules, though similarly polarized, are turned every which way, and cancel one another out. A common man, similarly, may lack the dynamic power that one associates with human greatness, but it isn't because he has less energy than the mightiest genius; it is only that the "molecules" of his subconscious desires and impulses pull him in conflicting directions, and cancel one another out.

A steel bar becomes magnetized, not by the introduction of any new element, but simply by the realignment of its molecules. Human magnetism, similarly, results when the "molecules" of conflicting desires are realigned unidirectionally. Limited power can be achieved, for a time, by directing them one-pointedly toward *any* goal. Many modern psychiatrists, in fact, cognizant of this fact, have recommended to people that they seek fulfillment through the outward release of subconscious repressions. But deeper realities of human nature, and the fact that the very way our bodies are made reflects those realities, make it impossible for us to bring *all* our "molecules" into alignment until we adjust them to the north-south polarity of the spine. That is to say, all our desires and aspirations must flow upwards, toward the spiritual eye: the "doorway" to Infinity.

Likes and dislikes, and their resultant desires and aversions, are the root cause of mortal bondage. The progressive stages of involvement with *maya* may be traced through the basic functions of human consciousness: *mon, buddhi, ahankara,* and *chitta:* mind, intellect, ego, and feeling. Paramhansa Yogananda explained these basic functions by the illustration of a horse seen reflected in a mirror. The mirror is the mind (*mon*), reflecting the image just as it appears through the senses, without in any way qualifying or defining that image. *Buddhi* (intellect) then defines what it sees, informing us, "That is a horse." *Ahankara* (ego) steps in next to say, "That's *my* horse." Up to this point we are not yet really bound by the thought of ownership; the identification, though personal, remains more or less abstract. But then comes *chitta* (feeling), which says, "How *happy* I am to see my horse!" *Chitta* is our emotional, reactive process, our likes and dislikes, and is, as I said, the true source of all our delusions. Thus, the ancient sage Patanjali, classical exponent of the yoga science, defined yoga itself as "the neutralization of the vortices (*vrittis*) of *chitta*."*

Master once told me, "When I applied to the Maharaja of Kasimbazar for permission to transfer my school to his Ranchi property, he called in several pundits to test my knowledge of spiritual matters, since the request involved a religious institution. I could see they were all set for a theological bullfight, so I turned the tables on them. I said, 'Let us talk only of truths we have actually realized. An ability to quote the Scriptures is no proof of wisdom.' I then asked them a question for which I knew there was no answer in any text. 'We read,' I said, 'of the four aspects of human consciousness: *mon, buddhi, ahankara,* and *chitta*. We also read that these have their respective centers in the physical body. Can you tell me where in the body each center is located?' Well, they were completely stumped! All they knew was what they had read. I then told them, '*Mon* (mind) is centered at the top of the head;

---

* *Yoga Sutras* 1:2. *Chitta* is usually translated "mind-stuff." Paramhansa Yogananda himself, in his autobiography, accepts this translation. But in a series of classes on Patanjali, and in private discussions with me, he defined the word more exactly as I have given it here.

buddhi (intellect), at the point between the eyebrows; *ahankara* (ego), in the medulla oblongata; and *chitta* (feeling), in the heart.' "*

"Blessed are the pure in heart," said Jesus, "for they shall see God." The teachings of the Galilean Master and those of India's great yogis were cut from the same cloth of Self-realization. Only when the likes and dislikes of the heart, and their resultant vortices of desire and aversion, have been dissolved—in short, when the heart has been purified—can Self-realization be attained. The vortex of ego itself is then dissipated with relative ease, for without objective attachments it soon loses its momentum, and is dispersed at last by the currents of divine inspiration.

Most efforts to transform oneself involve a laborious struggle to correct an endless array of individual faults—a tendency to gossip, over-attachment to sweets, physical laziness, and the like. The devotee must, of course, fight such battles as they present themselves to his mind. But to attempt to win the whole war in this piecemeal fashion would be like trying to realign each molecule in a bar of steel separately. Purely psychological efforts at self-transformation are a never-ending task. Even after one has succeeded, finally, in turning a few mental "molecules" in the right direction, there is no guarantee they'll remain turned that way once one leaves them to work on the next lot.

The way to magnetize a bar of steel is to introduce a south-north current into it, by placing it in close proximity to a magnetized bar. The way to become spiritually magnetized, similarly, is to place oneself in spiritual "proximity" to one's guru; that is to say, to attune oneself to him mentally. Because the energy of an awakened master flows naturally upwards, toward the spiritual eye, attunement with him generates a similar flow in the disciple.

But of course, more is involved here than passive acceptance of the guru's blessings. Any disciple, indeed, who relies on those blessings alone will make only negligible progress. For man is not inert metal; he can and must cooperate in the process of self-transformation. As Yogananda put it, "The path is twenty-five percent the disciple's own effort, twenty-five percent the guru's effort on his behalf, and fifty percent the grace of God." The guru needs the disciple's cooperation. And the disciple can cooperate best when he

---

* I have referred earlier to the fact that love is experienced in the heart center. It may be of interest to note also that intense intellectual effort is often accompanied by a slight frown: evidence that energy is being directed to the point between the eyebrows. Again, note how pride tends to draw the head backward: a sign that energy is being focused in the medullary region. That is why we speak of a proud person as "looking down his nose" at others.

understands how this magnetic influence actually works in his body, raising subtle currents of energy through the spine to the brain. Cooperation with the guru's efforts, and with divine grace, means doing what one can himself to direct energy upwards through the spine.

The correlation between spiritual awakening and this upward movement of energy can be observed somewhat in ordinary human experience as well. When, for example, a person feels an increase of happiness or inspiration, or when he makes a firm resolution to do something wholesome and positive, he will, if he introspects, observe an accompanying upward flow of energy to his brain. He may even find himself standing or sitting more erect, holding his head higher, looking upward, turning the corners of his mouth up in a smile. On the other hand, if he feels depressed or discouraged, he will note a corresponding flow of energy, downward, away from the brain. He may even slump a little, look down at the floor, turn the corners of his mouth downward, and actually *feel* physically a little heavier.

Spiritual awakening takes place when *all* one's energy is directed upward to the spiritual eye. Hence the saying of Jesus, "Thou shalt love the Lord thy God with all thy *strength*": that is, "with all thy *energy*."

This upward flow is obstructed in most people by countless eddies of *chitta,* which, once formed in the heart, get distributed along the spine according to their anticipated level of fulfillment—the lower the level, the more materialistic the desire; the higher the level, the more spiritual. These eddies, or *vrittis,* can be dissipated by a flow of energy through the spine strong enough to neutralize their centripetal force. Numerous techniques of yoga have as their main objective the awakening of this energy-flow.

Of all such yoga techniques, the most effective, according to Paramhansa Yogananda and his line of gurus, because the most central and direct in its application, is Kriya Yoga. This was the technique, they said, that was taught in ancient times by Lord Krishna to Arjuna. And Krishna, in the *Bhagavad Gita,* states that he gave this technique to humanity in an incarnation long prior to the one in which he taught Arjuna. Of all the techniques of yoga, Kriya is quite probably the most ancient.

Kriya Yoga directs energy lengthwise around the spine, gradually neutralizing the eddies of *chitta.* At the same time it strengthens the nerves in the spine and brain to receive cosmic currents of energy and consciousness. Yogananda stated that Kriya is the supreme yoga science. Beside it, other yoga techniques that work on calming the breath, concentrating the mind, etc., though important in themselves (Yogananda also taught a number of them), must be classed as subsidiary.

He often said that Kriya Yoga strengthens one in whatever path—whether devotion, discrimination, or service; Hindu, Christian, Moslem, or Judaic—one is inclined by temperament, or by upbringing, to follow.

A visitor who once came to his Ranchi school had been practicing *Bhakti Yoga,* the path of single-minded devotion, for twenty years. Though deeply devoted, he had never yet experienced the Lord's blissful presence.

"Kriya Yoga would help you," the Master suggested to him earnestly.

But the man was fearful of being disloyal to his own path.

"No, Kriya won't conflict with your present practices," Master insisted. "It will only deepen you in them."

Still the man was hesitant.

"Look here," Master finally said, "you are like a man who for twenty years has been trying to get out of a room through the walls, the floor, the ceiling. Kriya Yoga will simply show you where the door is. There is no conflict, in that kind of aid, with your own devotional path. To pass through the doorway you must still do so with devotion."

The man relented at last, and was initiated. Hardly a week passed before he received his first deep experience of God.

"I wasn't sent to the West," Yogananda often told his audiences, "by Christ and the great masters of India to dogmatize you with a new theology. Jesus himself asked Babaji to send someone here to teach you the science of Kriya Yoga, that people might learn how to commune with God directly. I want to help you to attain actual experience of Him, through your daily practice of Kriya Yoga."

He added, "The time for knowing God has come!"

CHAPTER 35

The Monks

As often as the heart
Breaks—wild and wavering—from control, so oft
Let him re-curb it, let him rein it back
To the soul's governance.

T HESE WORDS OF Lord Krishna in the *Bhagavad Gita* offer valuable counsel for all stages of the spiritual journey. For it often happens on the path that selfish desires spring up with surprising vigor out of the subconsciousness, to attack one's devotion. The devotee may be progressing steadily, confident that God is all he wants in life, when all of a sudden worldly opportunity knocks, and he thinks "Here's my chance—perhaps the only one I'll ever have—to become a great concert pianist"; or, "to acquire riches and worldly respect"; or, "to make a great scientific contribution to mankind"; or, "to marry my soul mate!" I've never seen such desires, when followed *as an alternative* to serving God selflessly, lead to anything but disappointment in the end. The concert pianist tires of playing for a fickle public. The would-be millionaire soon finds that life without God is truly hell, especially if he has known soul-peace before. The hopeful scientist finds the world either indifferent to his discoveries, or anxious to divert them to ignoble ends. And the devotee who forsakes spiritual practices to marry his "soul mate" as likely as not gets divorced after a year or two. (What, indeed, can human love offer to compare with the sweetness of God's love, which he has already tasted in his soul?)

Among my saddest memories are those of erstwhile devotees who, having left their divine calling, have returned to their former brothers and sisters on the path to show off their newly acquired worldly goods. With what pride they display their new cars, new suits, new wives! You see in their eyes a will to explain away the good they have lost. You hear in their voices some of the self-conscious laughter of people who boast of getting drunk—as though they hoped by making noise to silence the stern voice of their conscience. Yet sooner or later these erstwhile devotees lose confidence in the choices they have made, and, too sadly often, in themselves for having made them.

Worst of all, inconstancy to God creates in them a pattern of further inconstancy. They end up rarely succeeding at anything, for they have spurned a quality that is necessary for success in *any* endeavor: steadfastness. Fortunate are those who, having realized their mistake, abandon it and return resolutely to the divine search. I have often admired one such devotee who, when others asked her how she dared to show herself at Mt. Washington again having once left it, replied joyously, "Do you expect me to worship my mistakes?"

Few, alas, are blessed with such resolution. Of one fallen disciple Master told me, "He hasn't known a day of happiness since he left here. I tried hard to save him, but his mind was set.

"We were together in New York, when one day he told me he wanted to go to Philadelphia.

" 'To buy a wedding ring?' I challenged him.

"Well, he couldn't deny it, but tried instead to convince me what an angel the girl was.

" 'She isn't at all what you imagine,' I warned.

" 'You know nothing about her,' he argued. 'You've never even met her!'

" 'I know *everything* about her!' I assured him.

"Well, he wouldn't listen. But—he has found out." Master's eyes expressed grief for his erring disciple.

"All things forsake thee who forsakest Me," Francis Thompson wrote in his beautiful poem, *The Hound of Heaven*.

Devotion is the greatest protection against delusion. But that devotee can hardly be found whose devotion *never* wanes, who never experiences times of spiritual emptiness or dryness, or never feels the tug of worldly desire. What is one to do when what Master called the "karmic bombs" of restlessness and desire strike, particularly in the midst of a dry period? In preparation against such a time, it is important to fortify oneself with regular habits of meditation, and with loyalty to one's chosen path. Once the habit of daily meditation becomes firmly established, one will cruise steadily through many a storm, succumbing neither to despondency when the way seems hard, nor to over-elation when it seems easy.

Loyalty to one's chosen path nips in the bud the temptation to seek easier, pleasanter pathways to God—perhaps a more "sympathetic" teacher, or practices that make fewer demands of the ego.

"Loyalty is the first law of God," Yogananda often said. He was not referring to the superficial, sectarian loyalty of those who feel impelled constantly to prove how dedicated they are, and to discredit anyone whose views happen to differ from their own. (Such flag-waving is usually done to conceal subconscious doubts.) Master's reference, rather, was to that calm acceptance of one's own path which admits of no change of heart, which cannot be swayed by any obstacles that one might encounter on the way. This quality, alas, is not often stressed nowadays in America, except perhaps as the need for steadfastness to Ambition. Ours is a tradition of pioneers of men and women who repeatedly affirmed their freedom by pulling up roots and settling in new territory. Even today, when there are no new lands on this continent to conquer, our youths are urged to court novelty, to follow the will-o'-the-wisp of "fulfillment" wherever it might lead them, and to pay scant heed to such inconvenient considerations as commitment and duty.

"They change jobs, wives, and gurus at a moment's notice," Master lamented. "How can they expect to get anywhere, when they keep on changing direction whimsically?"

"Quite a few heads will fall," he had told me when speaking of the period of testing that began a few months before my trial at Twenty-Nine Palms. I grieved deeply when some of those I loved most left the ashram. I had known for some time that Boone was pulling away, but when Norman left, and then Jean, I was badly shaken.

Poor Norman! He loved God deeply, but moods of despondency came, and he allowed them to undermine his meditative routine to the point where it no longer sufficed to protect him from worldly delusions. But I knew he would always love God, and would continue to seek Him.

"This is the first time in many lives that delusion has caught Norman," Master remarked sadly. He added, "Divine Mother wants him to learn responsibility. But wherever he is, he is with me."

Norman visited Mt. Washington a few months later. "Do you remember how hard it was for me to get along with Jerry?" he asked me. "He was one of the main reasons I left here. Well, where I work now there are *six* men just like him!"

Over the years I have observed that when devotees try to avoid facing their karmic lessons, they only attract these very lessons again in other forms—and often in larger doses!

Jean had great will power, but he didn't concentrate so much on developing devotion. Master always taught us that we should meditate with no other motive than love for God, and the desire to please Him. "Mercenary devotion" he called meditation for personal spiritual gain. " 'Lord, I have given You so many Kriyas. Now You have to keep Your side of the bargain and give me so much realization.' God never responds to that kind of devotion! He will accept nothing less from us than our unconditional love." When, after two or three years of determined meditative efforts, high spiritual experiences still eluded Jean, he grew discouraged. "I didn't come here to rake leaves!" he was reported as saying the day he left. Alas, dear friend, had you forgotten the teaching of the *Bhagavad Gita,* that, to the devotee who offers God even a leaf or a flower with deep *love,* the Lord Himself responds in person?

Of one of the women disciples, who left during this period of intense testing to get married, Master commented sadly, "The desire for human romance had attracted her for years." She had been with him a long time. Her karmic test must have come to a head shortly before she left, for he added, "Had she remained here just twenty-four hours longer, she would have been finished with that karma forever!"

Particularly awe-inspiring was his warning to one disciple, who later left: "Yours is a very complex karma. If you leave here now, it may take you two hundred incarnations to return to the point you have already reached on the path."

But though Master said that it was not unusual for the fallen devotee to wander in delusion for one or more incarnations, he also said that the good karma accrued from yoga practice would bring him back in the end. He never saw life in the hell-or-heaven terms of orthodox dogmatists.

"Sir," Boone asked him one day, "will I ever leave the spiritual path?"

"How could you?" Master replied. "Everyone in the world is on the spiritual path."

"Is it possible, Master," I once asked him, "for the soul to be lost forever?"

"Never!" he replied firmly. "The soul is a part of God. How could any part of God be destroyed?"

Most of those who left the work have remained devoted to Master, even while pursuing for a time the chimera of a few worldly dreams. They are, after all, his spiritual children, his destined disciples. Of only one who left did I ever know him to say, "He won't be back; he was never in." This was in response to a question of

Jerry's: "How long will it be before he returns to you?" But of another disciple, who for years after leaving Mt. Washington rejected him, Master said, "He will never find God except through this instrument, designated to him by God."

"People are so skillful in their ignorance!" Master exclaimed once exasperatedly after trying to help someone. And then, in a discussion with a small group of us, he said, "I see the spiritual path as a race course. Some of the devotees are sprinting; others are jogging along slowly. Some are even running backwards!"

"The spiritual life," he told the monks on another occasion, "is like a battle. Devotees are fighting their inner enemies of greed and ignorance. And many are wounded—with bullets of desires."

Loyalty, devotion, regular meditation, attunement with the guru—armed with these, every devotee can win the battle—not easily, perhaps, but in the end gloriously. "The more you do what your mind tells you," Master admonished us, "the more you become a slave. The more you do Guru's will, the more you become free." The difference between those who stayed in the ashram and those who left it seemed to boil down to two alternatives: the desire to live only for God, and the desire to cling still to the little, human self. Jesus said, "Whosoever will save his life shall lose it." Leaving the ashram did not, of course, in itself constitute a fall, spiritually. Nor was such a fall, when it occurred, necessarily permanent for this lifetime. It all depended on whether one still put God first in one's life, and on whether one refused to accept even the severest setback as a final defeat. Whatever the circumstances, however, it was an unwise disciple who thought he could leave the ashram with impunity, certain that he would never forget God. "Delusion has its own power," Master warned us.

I was, as I said, deeply saddened when any brother left—particularly anyone who had inspired me in my own spiritual efforts. Being in charge of the monks now, I determined to do everything in my power to improve the steadfastness of those who were weak by organizing our routine so that regular spiritual practice would no longer be wanting in any of their lives. Master encouraged me in these efforts. So also did a number of my fellow monks—though not all of them, unfortunately. Human nature does not easily relinquish outer for inner freedom. I could see in the eyes of a few men the thought, "All right, so Master has put you in charge. That doesn't give you the right to *do* anything about it!" When I persisted in trying to organize them, they dubbed me, sarcastically, "The monk." It was no joy for me, either, to have to impose my will on them, despite the fact that my purpose was to carry out

Master's wishes, and to strengthen them on the path. But my sadness over those we'd lost goaded me on to develop a routine that
would prove a buttress for others in times of trial.

"I don't ask your obedience," I told them, "but I know you
want to obey Master, and I'd be disobedient to him myself if I
didn't ask your *cooperation*. At the same time," I added, "I pledge to
each of you *my* cooperation in return. Anything that any of you
wants from me, so long as it doesn't conflict with our rules, I will
do for you gladly." Thus, by seeking to place myself in a position
of service to them, I gradually won their support. In my own
meditations I often sang the chant "O God Beautiful!" and repeated over and over the line, "To the serviceful Thou art service." Daily I filled my mind with the joyous thought that the only
work worthy of a devotee is humble service to his Cosmic
Beloved.

Ultimately my organizing efforts were successful. Thereafter,
partly as a result of them, more and more of those who came to
Mt. Washington remained on the path.

For me personally, however, there was a certain poignancy in
these organizational struggles. For I sensed deeply that, the better I
succeeded in them, the less Mt. Washington would remain for me
the wonderful spiritual home I had found it when I first came
there. In boarding schools as a child, particularly in this country, I
had developed a deep aversion to group-consciousness. To be instrumental in developing such a consciousness at Mt. Washington,
though I knew it was needed, made me feel a little as though I had
volunteered for a suicide mission.

It relieved me that Master, too, didn't seem much in tune with
the thought of organizing. Sister Gyanamata used to say, "You will
never be able to organize the work so long as Master is alive."
Sometimes he would speak with longing of the informality of the
life of a spiritual teacher in India, "roaming by the Ganges," as he
put it, "drunk with God." He preferred the flow of divine intuition
to constricting rules and regulations. By nature, indeed, I think he
might have responded as Ramana Maharshi, the great Indian master, did when disciples complained to him about a certain eminently sensible, but generally inconvenient, rule that his own
brother had imposed on the ashram community. The rule read,
"Do not use the office as a thoroughfare. Walk around it on your
way to the dining room." Ramana Maharshi's reply to the protest-
ers was, "Let us leave this place. It no longer feels like ours!"
(Needless to say, the offending rule was abandoned.)

The cultural attitudes of India have never conduced very much to organization. "Don't make too many rules," Master told me. "It destroys the spirit." From him I imbibed a principle that has served me well, especially in recent years, when I have been responsible for directing the spiritual lives and activities of many people. That principle is, *Never put the needs of an organization ahead of those of even one of its members.* For service is the true and sole purpose of any spiritual work.

In addition to organizing our routine at Mt. Washington, and to making a few rules, as necessary, I also developed a series of classes in discipleship, the notes for which are, I believe, still used by the monks and nuns. Master worked with me in all these efforts, and talked often about the future directions in the work as they related to the monks.

During the last two years of his life he also spent many hours with the monks, teaching, encouraging, and inspiring them.

"Each of you must individually make love to God," he told us one evening. "Keep your mind at the Christ center, and when you work, all the time think you are working for God and Guru. Always: God and Guru—God, Christ, and Guru. Many come here, then talk and joke all the time—and play the organ." Master glanced meaningly at one of the monks. "They won't get God that way! There are many mice living in the canyon on this property, but they are not developing spiritually! They haven't God. Don't think you can make spiritual progress merely by living here. You yourself must make the effort. Each of you stands alone before God."

One evening he praised the spirit of those disciples (Daya Mata, Virginia Wright, and Miss Darling) who had long served him personally. During their early years at Mt. Washington, especially, they had often followed a full day's work with all-night office labors as well.

"Sir," I inquired, "didn't they get much time to meditate?"

"Well, working near this body as they did, they didn't need as much meditation; they evolved spiritually just the same. But you all must meditate more, because you haven't that outward contact as much as they had."

Often he urged us to be steadfast in our practice of Kriya Yoga. "Practice Kriya night and day. It is the greatest key to salvation. Other people go by books and outer disciplines, but it will take them incarnations to reach God that way. Kriya is the greatest way of destroying temptation. Once you can feel the inner joy it gives you, no evil will be able to touch you. It will seem like stale cheese, then, compared with nectar. When others are idly talking or passing time, *you* go out into the garden and do a few Kriyas. What more do you need? Kriya will give you everything you are looking for. Practice it faithfully night and day."

He added, "After practicing Kriya, sit still a long time; listen to the inner sounds, or practice *Bhakti Yoga* (devotion), or watch the breath in the spine. If you eat your dinner and then run, you won't be able to enjoy the meal; your enjoyment will be greater if you rest afterwards. Similarly, after doing Kriya don't jump up right away. Sit still and pray deeply; enjoy the peace that you feel. That is how soul-intuition is developed."

"Give both the good and the bad that you do to God," he told us one evening. "Of course, that does not mean you should deliberately do things that are bad, but when you cannot help yourself because of too-strong habits, feel that God is acting through you. Make *Him* responsible. He likes that! For He wants you to realize that it is He who is dreaming your existence."

"Sir," Clifford Frederick, one of the disciples, addressed him one afternoon, "how can one become more humble?"

"Humility," Master replied, "comes from seeing God as the Doer, not yourself. Seeing that, how can you feel proud for anything you have accomplished? Humility lies in the heart. It is not a show put on to impress others. Whatever you may be doing, tell yourself constantly, 'God is doing all this through me.' "

One of the disciples was being tormented by self-doubt. "As long as you are making the effort," Master consoled him, "God will *never* let you down!"

To Henry one day he said, as he was preparing to go out for a drive, "Whenever you see wrong in the world, remember, it's wrong with you. When you are right, everything is right, because you see God there. Perfection is inside."

Vance Milligan, a young black boy, first came to Mt. Washington at the age of seventeen. Being not yet of legal age, he was forced by his mother to leave. As soon as he turned eighteen, however, he returned.

"How does your mother feel now about your being here?" Master asked him.

"This time she says it's all right," Vance replied.

"That's good that you have her consent. Without it you should still have come, but with it is even better.

"Swami Shankara," Master continued, "was only eight when he decided to leave home in search of God. His mother tried to prevent him. Shankara, reluctant to leave without her permission, jumped into a nearby river and allowed himself to be caught by a crocodile. He was highly advanced from past lives, and had the power to save himself. 'Look, Mother,' he cried, 'I'm going to let myself be pulled under if you don't give me your consent. Either way you will lose me!' Hastily she promised to let him leave home. He then released himself from the crocodile, came out of the water, and left home to begin his mission.

"One day, many years later, he cried, 'I taste my mother's milk. She is dying!' Hastening to her side, he helped her in her final moments, then cremated her body with a divine fire shooting out from his upraised hand."

Master continued: "Another born sage who left home at an early age was Sukdeva. He was only six at that time, but wanted to go in search of his guru. Byasa, his father, was the author of the *Bhagavad Gita*. He was fully qualified to be the guru himself. But Sukdeva could see that he had a little attachment to him, as his son. As the boy was leaving, Byasa followed him, pleading with him to seek God at home.

" 'Keep away from me,' the boy said. 'You have *maya*.'

"Byasa then sent him to the royal sage, King Janaka, for training."

I asked Master one day, "Sir, in what way ought one to love people?"

"You should love God first," he replied, "then with His love, love others. In loving people for themselves, rather than as manifestations of God, you might get attached."

Speaking of love another time, he told us, "Human love is possessive and personal. Divine love is always impersonal. To develop devotion in the right way, and to protect it from the taint of possessive, personal love, it is better not to seek God above all for His love until one is highly developed. Seek Him first of all for His bliss."

"Don't joke too much," Master often told us. "Joking is a false stimulant. It doesn't spring from true happiness, and doesn't give true happiness. When you joke a lot, the mind becomes restless and light so that it can't meditate."

To one of the younger renunciates° he said one day, "You have devotion, but you are always joking and keeping the others rollicking. You must learn to be more serious."

° *Renunciate:* This noun form is in common usage in India but is not to be found in either *Webster's International* or the *Oxford* dictionaries, both of which favor the relatively uneuphonic *renunciant*. In Self-Realization Fellowship we used the word *renunciate,* following Master's lead. But sometime in the mid-1950s one of the sisters happened to notice that this form wasn't given in *Webster's. Renunciant* was then adopted. Yet Indian English is quite old enough to be accepted as a

"I know it, Sir," the young man replied sadly, "but my habit is so strong. How can I change without your blessing?"

"Well, *my* blessing is there already. *God's* blessing is there. Only *your* blessing is lacking!"

"It's awfully hard to change my ways, Sir," Jerry lamented one day, "but I'll go on to the end of life."

"That's the spirit," Master said approvingly. "Anyway the wave cannot leave the ocean. It can protrude farther from the surface, but it is still a part of the ocean, and has to return to it at last."

"Never count your faults," he once told us. "Be concerned only that you love God enough. And," he added, "don't tell your faults to others, lest someday in a fit of anger they hold them against you. But tell your faults to God. From Him you should try to conceal nothing."

Some of the monks grew discouraged at seeing the departure of others. Master once told them, " 'Devotees may come, and devotees may go, but *I* go on forever.' *That* must be your attitude." To those who, seeing others fall, doubted their own spiritual chances, Master said, "You have to live anyway! Why not live in the right way?"

The American "go-getter" spirit drew praise from him. " 'Eventually? Eventually? Why not now!' *That* is the American way that I like. Seek God with that kind of determination and you will surely find Him!"

Concerning some of the monks who had left, he told me one evening, while walking about the grounds at SRF Lake Shrine, "Many will have their own centers someday—David, Jan, et cetera, et cetera."

My own feeling was that the best possible place to serve the work was at Mt. Washington. But one day we were discussing our need for disciples with certain talents, and I mentioned Adano Ley, our center leader in Montreal, Canada. "Why don't we invite him to come here, Master? He is doing very good work there."

"If he is doing good work there," Master replied somewhat indignantly, "why bring him here?"

Work qualifications were never in any case the real reason he accepted anyone. We had long been in need of a printer, when

---

legitimate branch of the English language—particularly where, as in this case, the word involves a concept that is *their* specialty, not ours. I opt for the much more pleasant-sounding *renunciate*. Like *initiate* (the noun), *renunciate* is grammatically legitimate. And this, after all, is how new words get accepted into the language. *Renunciate* has only to gain wide circulation for future editions of *Webster's* to give it full recognition.

one evening I came to Master with what I thought was good news: "We have a new man for the print shop, Sir!"

"Why do you tell me that?" he demanded indignantly. "First see if a newcomer has our spirit; accept him only on that basis. Next, help him to develop our spirit more deeply. Only *then* think where he might fit into the work. Two others have already come and told me we have a new printer. I never ask people first what they can do. I see the spiritual side."

"Believe me, Sir," I replied, abashed, "that's my interest, too. I should have expressed it. This man said to me, 'I'm so glad you all pray with such devotion here.' And I had him in my cave for a long time, chanting, and playing Hindu devotional records. He loved it."

Master nodded approvingly. "That is what I like to hear."

But in fact, though he hadn't yet met the new man, his response was based on sure intuition. For the man left not many months afterward. Master then remarked to me, "I knew he wouldn't stay."

By the time of that new printer's acceptance, Master had turned over to me the task of accepting new men disciples, while he himself spent much of his time in seclusion to complete his writings. It was difficult for me to face the fact that many who sought admission were simply not ready for our way of life. To me, Mt. Washington was so wonderful that I wanted to share it with as many people as possible.

One student wrote from an Eastern state that he wanted to come, despite certain difficulties that he was having with his health. Master replied that, since his health was poor, he should not come. But the man wrote back pleadingly, "My doctor assures me I'll be fine as long as I take regular medication." Master was in seclusion when this letter came, so I answered it. The only objection I knew of to the man's coming was his physical condition; otherwise he seemed to me deeply sincere. Since this objection had been met, I wrote to tell him he could come and give our way of life a try.

When Master returned to Mt. Washington and learned what I had done, he scolded me, "That wasn't my only reason for telling him not to come. It was simply the *kindest* reason. I knew he was not spiritually ready for our way of life." He added, "You will see."

Shortly thereafter the young man arrived. A short week later he was gone.

I took in one man who even *I* could see was not ready for acceptance. Despite a sincere desire to live spiritually, he was steeped in worldly habits. It was his strong desire to change that had moved me to take him; I simply hadn't the heart to say no. For several months the newcomer applied himself earnestly, though often he shook his head in wonderment at the change his life had undergone. He didn't stay long, but while at Mt. Washington he did improve greatly. Master was pleased.

"I left it up to your own will to change," he told him one day. Then, referring to the man's rather checkered past, he added, "But it is much easier to be good than bad, really. If one is bad, he is always in terror. But the good man is afraid of nothing and no one. The gods themselves have to look out for him, for the God of all gods is on his side!"

Because I'd accepted this man, Master did his best to help him. But when he first learned of his acceptance, Master exclaimed to me, "I'm going to have to give you intuition!"

His words may have been meant seriously as a blessing. At any rate, soon thereafter I found I could often tell at a glance whether a man belonged at Mt. Washington or not. Sometimes, even before he'd mentioned anything about coming, I would tell him, "You belong with us." As nearly as I remember, when such feelings came to me they always proved justified.

Master, in his talks with us, always sought to turn our minds toward God. He urged us to see the Lord manifested in everything and everyone. "Respect one another," he once told us, "as you respect me."

Many hours he spent talking with us, giving us help and encouragement. Above all he urged us to seek our inspiration inwardly, in meditation.

Hearing one of the monks chanting in the main chapel one evening, to the accompaniment of an Indian harmonium, he paused during the course of a conversation downstairs. Blissfully, then, he remarked, "That is what I like to hear in this hermitage of God!"

CHAPTER 36

The Wave and the Ocean

"DIVINE MOTHER once said to me, 'Those to whom I give too much, I do not give Myself.'"

Master was explaining to us the difference between joyous acceptance of divine favors, vouchsafed by God as a sign of His love, and a desire for the favors themselves.

"Seek God for Himself," he told us, "not for any gift that He might give you." Unlike many proponents of spiritual "new thought," who seem to equate spiritual progress with the ability to "manifest" increasing material abundance, Paramhansa Yogananda taught us that the true test of spirituality is indifference to everything but God's love. To the sincere devotee, he said, God's lesser gifts are meaningful in one sense only: as demonstrations of His love.

A touching episode, illustrative of this teaching, occurred two or three years after I entered the work. Master, in his travels between Los Angeles and Encinitas, sometimes stopped in the town of Laguna Beach, in a little Scottish tea shop where shortbread was a specialty. One day, going there for this delicacy, he sent Virginia Wright (now Ananda Mata) in. She returned to report that the last batch had been sold.

Surprised, Master prayed, "Divine Mother, how come?" It wasn't that he was disappointed. Accustomed, rather, to receiving divine guidance in even the minor details of his life, he wondered whether some lesson might be intended in this unexpected denial. Suddenly he saw a shaft of light shine down onto the little shop. Moments later the door opened; the owner came out.

"Wait! Wait!" she called. Hastening over to the car with a little package, she said, "I was saving this order for a local customer. But I want you to have it. I can make more for him."

Master had had no real desire for the shortbread. What touched him deeply about this episode was the divine love it exemplified. For the more inconsequential the need to which God responds, the greater, in a sense, the proof of His love. Divine intervention in time of serious need might be attributed to other motives—perhaps the wish to see some important work finished. But what motive could there possibly be for such intervention in trivial matters, save love alone?

To Master, *all* gifts, short of divine love itself, came under the general heading "lesser gifts." To make religion a matter of "manifesting" an endless succession of worldly goods would be, he implied, to make a religion of materialism. And while he said that we had a right, as children of the Infinite, to God's infinite abundance, he reminded us that this birthright could be claimed *fully* only in cosmic consciousness.

The sincere devotee prefers rather to "manifest" a simple life, and usually seeks only as many of this world's goods as he needs to sustain him in his spiritual search. If God gives him more than that, he employs it for the welfare of others. And all that he owns he considers God's property altogether, to be returned joyously to its Owner at a moment's notice.

Even for worldly people, simple living is an important key to happiness. Across the road from Master's retreat at Twenty-Nine Palms there lived a man in a small one-room cabin, alone. He had no garden, and, indoors, few modern conveniences. Yet his happiness was transparent. He was burdened with no debts. There were no unnecessary chores to pilfer away his precious hours of freedom. Again and again he proudly played a recording of a popular song, expressive of his perfect contentment with life: "I've Got My Home in Twenty-Nine Palms."

Master, gazing over toward this man's place one day, remarked, "He is like a king in his palace! Such is the joy of simple living."

Master used to say, "Whenever I see somebody who needs something of mine more than I do, I give it away."

"A few years ago," he told us, "I had a fine musical instrument, an esraj from India. I loved to play devotional music on it. But a visitor one day admired it. Unhesitatingly I gave it to him. Years later someone asked me, 'Weren't you just a *little* sorry?' 'Never for a moment!' I replied. Sharing one's happiness with others only expands one's own happiness."

Master kept only enough money personally to finance his trips to the different ashrams. Even this amount he often gave away. So strong, indeed, was his urge to share that he sometimes gave away more than he had. I remember him asking me once to lend him five dollars, that he might give them to someone else. When traveling, too, he liked to go simply. He would take with him for his meals only a few nuts, dates, and raisins in a clear plastic box. Generally he ate in the car, to avoid what he termed the "heterogeneous vibrations" of restaurants.

He enjoyed cooking for others, and was an excellent cook. "It is a form of service," he told me, simply. After preparing an especially tasty dish for us one day, he explained, "I always know just how much spicing to add: I can taste it in the spiritual eye. I never have to sample the food with my tongue." The inimitable ingredient in his cooking was, of course, his blessing. One always felt spiritually uplifted afterwards. But although he sometimes fed us sumptuously, I noticed that he himself generally ate little.

He displayed the same indifference to all outward enjoyments. It wasn't apathy; enthusiasm for all aspects of life was a hallmark of his personality. But it was clear that he enjoyed things not for their own sake, but because they manifested in various ways his one, infinite Beloved. Often, as he was expressing joy outwardly, I would note in the still depths of his gaze a fathomless detachment.

I once experienced this detachment in a matter that seemed, to me, pressingly important. It was in the summer of 1950. For months I had been looking forward eagerly to our trip to India. Master had said we would be leaving only if and when God gave him the definite guidance to go, but all I heard in his statement was the "when" of it not the "if." In July, finally, he announced that it was God's will that we not make the voyage that year.

"Will we be going another time, Master?" I asked.

"That is in God's hands," he replied, indifferently. "I am not inquisitive about these things. What He wants, I do."

Not inquisitive—about a trip to *India?* Mentally I tightened my belt of expectations, telling myself that it was all the same to me, too. I wasn't completely successful, I'm afraid.

On August 20th of that year Master dedicated the SRF Lake Shrine. The impressive public ceremony was attended by some 1500 people. Guests of honor were California's Lieutenant Governor, Goodwin J. Knight, and his wife. Present also were many civic dignitaries and other people of worldly prominence. I was impressed to see with what ease, respect, and complete inner freedom Master could mix with all sorts of people, great and humble, famous and obscure, giving to each his full and loving attention, yet never defining himself in terms of what others expected of him, nor in terms of what he gave. He was simply and entirely what he always was: a divine mirror to everyone he encountered, completely devoid of any "complexes" of his own.

After the opening, Master occasionally sponsored evening

concerts in the open-air temple by the lake. Large crowds attended these events, attracted by a series of well-known concert artists, and by the beautiful, star-lit setting. To Master the concerts were a service to others, based on the fact that divine inspiration often reaches man through the medium of music. But above all he saw these events as a means of drawing people to the spiritual path. For until inspiration becomes rooted in actual God-contact, it is, he reminded us, ever fleeting and uncertain.

One evening he sat chatting with a few of us after a concert. Reflecting on the numbers of visitors who attended these events for merely temporary upliftment, he remarked, "Outsiders come, and see only the surface. Not understanding what this place has to offer them, they go away again. But those who are our own see beneath the surface. *They* never leave."

He was referring, I knew, not only to the casual public, but also to the disciples, not all of whom were discerning enough to recognize the priceless gifts he had to bestow on them.

Not long after the opening of the Lake Shrine, Chuck Jacot, a monk there, was trying to repair a pump that sent water up a little hill, at the top of which stood a statue of Jesus Christ, his hands outstretched in blessing on the grounds. From a point below the statue, the water descended in a graceful cascade. Chuck, a trained plumber, couldn't get the pump to work.

Finally he hit on a spiritual solution. At least, he hoped it was a solution. Recalling, in *Autobiography of a Yogi,* a passage that says, "Whenever anyone utters with reverence the name of Babaji, that devotee attracts an instant spiritual blessing," Chuck sat down and called mentally to that great master. Suddenly, to his awed amazement, Babaji appeared in vision before him, blessed him, and offered priceless spiritual counsel. Later, when Chuck returned to outward consciousness, he found the pump functioning smoothly, and the water again flowing.

"Logically, that pump just *couldn't* work," he told us. "It hadn't even been primed!"

"I asked Babaji to give Chuck that experience," Master told us later.

Many others have acted upon those words of promise in *Autobiography of a Yogi,* and received extraordinary blessings.

Pedro Gonzales Milan, who later became our center leader in Merida, Mexico, told me of the first time he had read the *Autobiography.* When he came to the above passage, he put the book down, moved to his depths. "If these words be true," he thought, "I must prove them so! Babaji, heed the cry of my heart: Come to me!

"Instantly," he told me, "the room became filled with a glorious light. And my heart was filled with bliss."

I, too, have experienced Babaji's blessings on the occasions when I have prayed to him. In 1960, on my second visit to India, I wanted to find a place for a few days of seclusion before returning to Calcutta to resume activity in our society there. But I had no idea where to go. Part of my difficulty was that Indians often found a Western swami rather a curiosity. Villagers, especially, would sometimes gather in scores outside my room, waiting for hours, if need be, for me to come out. I was staying in a hotel in Madras at this time, having entered India from Ceylon. One morning I prayed to Babaji, "Please help me to find a *quiet,* secluded place."

Soon afterward I was eating breakfast in the hotel dining room, when a man at the table next to mine introduced himself. "I have a house," he informed me without further preliminaries, "in a secluded section of Kodaikanal. I would be honored if you would use it for meditation. I shall be away from there for the next few weeks; no one will bother you. It occurred to me that since Kodaikanal is in the mountains, its cool climate might be congenial to you. Westerners often go there to escape the heat of the plains."

I took advantage of his offer. The place proved ideal in every respect.

Sometime after the Lake Shrine opening, I attended a concert with Master in another outdoor setting: the famous Hollywood Bowl. Vladimir Rosing, an old friend and student of his was conducting Johann Strauss's comic operetta, *Die Fledermaus.*

A minister from one of our other ashrams wanted to demonstrate to Master his talent for leadership. His way of doing so this evening was to boss me about.

"Master needs a blanket, Don. Would you please fetch him one?" Or, "Don, be so good as to get Master a glass of water."

I obeyed him eagerly, aware that the real prize in the spiritual life is the opportunity for service, especially to one's guru. It delighted me further when Master, to see if I could be drawn into a competitive attitude, pretended to accept my offerings with a slight sneer of condescension—as though receiving ministration from one of obviously inferior leadership abilities. It was quite enough for me that I felt Master's smile in my heart.

After the concert I glimpsed a touching side of his personality. Miss Lancaster (now Sister Sailasuta), one of the women disciples, had been invited to come along. She joined us on the way out, and remarked amusedly on the operetta's worldly theme. Certainly Master would not have attended *Die Fledermaus* on its merits alone;

if anything, I imagine he'd have told us all to give it a miss. But the conductor in this case was a friend of his. Therefore, with solemn loyalty, he answered Miss Lancaster, "It was a *good* show."

After the Lake Shrine opening we concentrated on completing India Center, a large new building on our church grounds in Hollywood. Well, hardly a *new* building, exactly. Master, re-enacting the strategy he had pursued in building the church, had bought a large, very old, very dilapidated structure in some dying neighborhood, and had had it moved, shaking and creaking, onto the church grounds. I imagine his purpose was to circumvent some of the cumbersome building code restrictions that applied only to new construction. And so, once again, the neighbors had to put up with an unsightly relic of (one hoped!) better days. And, once again, their dismay turned to pride as we transformed this relic into a beautiful, new-looking hall.

"We," I say? Well, perhaps this pronoun is a euphemism. My own contribution had little to do with the building's ultimate beauty. I dug the ditches, shoveled sand into the cement mixer, and did miscellaneous little jobs that it was generally understood, would later be hidden, conveniently, by coats of plaster.

"I've sure learned a lot on this job!" I exclaimed one day to Andy Anderson, our foreman, as the project was nearing completion. Andy gazed at me for a moment in stunned silence. Obviously wanting to be charitable, he simply couldn't think of anything to say.

During the months while Andy supervised our work at India Center, he developed a deep love for Master. Master, in return, was touched by his devotion, and by his simple, kindly nature. As Christmas 1950 approached, Andy took pains to buy his guru an appropriate present. During our luncheon break one day he made a special journey to Mt. Washington and, with trepidation, went up to the third floor. Placing the present by Master's door, he fled.

"Oh," he cried, on returning to India Center, "what a fool I am! I forgot to put my name on that package. Now Master will never know who gave it to him!"

Just then the telephone rang. It was Master, asking to speak with Andy. Andy returned to us minutes later, beaming from ear to ear.

"Master just wanted to thank me for my present!"

Andy, like many in the construction trade, rather liked his beer. Sometimes, in fact, he came to work a little "under the influence." One day Master asked him to construct a concrete driveway at Mt. Washington.

"Heavy trucks drive up here," Master explained, "with paper for the print shop. How thick do you suggest we make the driveway to bear all that weight?"

After a few moments' thought, Andy replied, "Four inches would be quite enough, Master."

"Make it six," Master said with a sweet smile.

Andy was about to object, when he saw Master's smile. "All right, Sir," he gulped, swallowing his professional knowledge.

I wondered at the time why two extra inches of concrete should have inspired Master to request them so sweetly. Later I understood. For when the day came for pouring the concrete, one could tell from the look in Andy's eyes that he was feeling no pain. Not fully conscious of what he was doing, he sprayed too much water on the new driveway, diluting the mixture. If it hadn't been for those extra inches, the cement would have cracked. Master, out of loving respect for Andy, wouldn't allow anyone to replace him. Indeed, it was to compensate for this problem, which he'd foreseen, that he'd requested those extra two inches of concrete. The sweetness of his smile had been due to his compassion for Andy.

India Center was formally opened to the public on April 8th, 1951. "The first cultural center of its kind in America," the press called it. A large hall downstairs was dedicated as a "meeting place for men of goodwill of all nations." Upstairs, a public restaurant served delicious vegetarian meals, the recipes for which were Master's own creations. Over the years both meeting hall and restaurant were to become famous.

India Center (as our Hollywood property was now named) and the SRF Lake Shrine were, in a sense, Master's outward gifts to the world. There was another gift, one infinitely more precious to us, his disciples, which he bestowed on us during the last two years of his life.

Great masters have the power to assume others' karma, much as a strong man might take onto his own body blows intended for a weaker person. They can sustain a considerable number of such karmic "blows" without themselves suffering any noticeable ill effect. Occasionally, however—especially toward the end of their lives, to help their disciples through years of spiritual effort without the Guru's physical presence—they assume large amounts of karma. At such times their own bodies may suffer temporarily.

It was such a gift that Master now bestowed on us. His legs became affected. The result was that, for a time, he couldn't walk. It was an "astral disease" primarily, he explained to us. He described a frightful array of demonic entities that were wreaking havoc on his body, especially the subtle body, though the physical body took some of the punishment also.

"I held my mind down to the body during the worst period," he told us, "because I wanted to experience pain as others do."

Daya Mata, in profound sympathy, cried out one day, "Why does Divine Mother treat you like this?"

"Don't you *dare* criticize Divine Mother!" Master scolded. Personal likes and dislikes formed no part of his nature. His only will was to do what God wanted.

Even at the height of his illness, he could still walk whenever he needed to. Sometimes it was with divine assistance. In August 1951, he was scheduled to speak before a large convocation of members on the tennis courts at Mt. Washington. Unwilling to publicize his condition, which he viewed as a sacred offering to his disciples for their spiritual growth, he determined to walk when the time came. The car took him as far as the edge of the courts. The door was opened. Master lifted his legs with his own hands, and placed his feet on the ground. "Instantly, a brilliant light surrounded my body," he told us later. "I was able to walk with ease." We saw him go up onto the lecture platform, stand through his long lecture, and walk back unaided to the car. "Once back in the car," he told us, "my legs became helpless again."

"Carry my body," he laughed one day, as we bore him up a flight of stairs, "and I'll carry your souls!"

Another time he remarked smiling, "This body is not everything. Some people have feet, but can't walk all over!"

Gradually his condition improved. One afternoon I was helping him into his car. "You are getting better, Sir," I exclaimed thankfully.

"Who is getting better?" Master's tone was impersonal.

"I meant your body, Sir."

"What's the difference? The wave protruding from the ocean bosom is still a part of the ocean. This is God's body. If He wants to make it well, all right. If He wants to keep it unwell, all right. It is best to remain impartial. If you have health and are attached to it, you will always be afraid of losing it. And if you are attached to good health and become ill, you will be always grieving for the good that you have lost.

"Man's greatest trouble is egoism, the consciousness of individuality. He takes everything that happens to him as affecting *him,* personally. Why be affected? You are not this body. You are *He!* Everything is Spirit."

As Master's condition improved, he began spending more time again with the monks. One day he was conversing with a group of us on the front porch at Mt. Washington, when a woman student, Miss Lois Carpenter, passed by on her way into the building. In one hand she carried a paper bag, evidently containing something she'd just purchased. Seeing Master, but not wanting to intrude on his discussion with us, she greeted him silently as she proceeded toward the door. Master stopped her.

"What are you carrying in that bag?"

"A few dates, Master, for you. I was going to place them by your door."

"Thank you very much. I shall be glad to accept them here."

Master, taking the fruits, passed them out among us. "I had been wanting to give you all something," he explained. "As soon as I saw her with that bag, I knew my wish had been fulfilled."

Early one rather mild autumn evening he was seated in his car, chatting with a few of us before going out for a drive. He was explaining some philosophical point, when, midway through the explanation, he paused and inquired, "Isn't it rather hot today?"

We hesitated, knowing that he had it in mind to give us money for ice cream. He looked at us expectantly. At last I said, smiling, "Well, it *was* hot, Sir, but by now it has cooled off."

"Too bad!" Master laughed playfully. "You cheated yourselves out of some refreshments!" He returned to his discourse. Several more minutes passed, then he paused again.

"You're *sure* it isn't a bit warm this evening?"

"Well," we replied laughingly, "it is if you say so, Sir!"

Decisively he concluded, "I can't keep money and I won't! Here, take these dollars for ice cream. I like having money only so that I can give it away."

I still have three dollars that he gave us one evening for ice cream. I spent three dollars of my own, and kept the gift he had touched.

One evening he spoke briefly of his recent illness. To our expressions of deep sympathy he said unconcernedly, "It was nothing! When the wisdom dinner from the plate of life has been eaten, it no longer matters whether you keep the plate, or break it and throw it away."

On another occasion he remarked, "I forget myself so much these days, I have to ask others if I have eaten!"

"Man was put here on earth to seek God," he reminded us one evening. "That is the only reason for his existence. Friends, job, material interests: All these by themselves mean nothing."

"Sir," one of the monks inquired, "is it wrong to ask God for material things?"

"It is all right, if you need them," Master replied. "But you should always say, 'Give me this or that, *provided* it is all right with You.' Many of the things people want would prove harmful to them if they got them. Leave it to God to decide what you ought to have."

On the subject of prayer, he told us, "God answers all prayers, but restless prayers He answers only a little bit. If you tried giving away something that didn't belong to you, your 'generosity' wouldn't be very impressive, would it? So it is when you try to give your mind to God: You should first own it yourself. Gain control over your thoughts; give Him your full attention when you pray. You will see, when you pray in that way that He answers marvelously!"

Whatever Master's topic of conversation—whether some aspect of the spiritual path, or some perfectly ordinary task that he wanted done—if one "listened" sensitively enough one always felt a subtle power emanating from him. If one took this awareness within, one felt blessed with a heightened sense of joy and freedom. Sometimes in Master's company, and again years later in India, in the ashrams of saints, I observed disciples that were so fascinated by their guru's gestures, words, and facial expressions that they neglected to commune with his magnetizing influence in their own selves, in their spines. Master saw his own personality quite impersonally, as a necessary aspect of functioning in this physical world.

"Before taking a physical body," he once told me, "I see the personality I am to assume, and feel slightly uncomfortable with it. It is like having to put on a heavy overcoat on a hot day. I soon get used to it, but inwardly I never forget that this personality is not my true Self."

At the same time, Master never sanctioned an irresponsible denial of mundane realities. "You should combine idealism with practicality," he once told me. In down-to-earth matters he himself was completely practical. He taught us the importance of meeting every reality on its own level. One minute he might be instructing us in some fine point of meditation, and the next telling us how to keep our rooms tidy. ("Put everything away as soon as you finish with it.")

When he invited guests to lunch, he often had me serve them. After the meal I would demonstrate the yoga postures, then sit in the room while he conversed. Whenever possible, I would write down his remarks. If sometimes I found it difficult to keep up with him, he would take notice, and speak more slowly. Occasionally, after the guests had departed, he would keep me with him to discuss my work, usually as it related to the public, or to correct something I might have said in private conversation at church, or in a lecture. Once I expressed astonishment at his complete awareness of things I'd said and done when he was physically distant.

"I know every thought that passes through your mind," he assured me calmly.

Two visitors to Mt. Washington who got to meet Master were Mother and my cousin Bet. Mother he received graciously in his upstairs sitting room. Before their meeting I had asked him to give her a special blessing. He'd agreed to do so, but in a manner so parenthetical to our discussion at the moment that I wasn't sure my request had really registered with him. To my joy, then, at the end of his interview with her he held her hand by the door, and prayed to God and our line of gurus for the blessing I'd solicited. I've no idea what Mother thought of this unexpected departure, but, with tears of gratitude, I touched Master's feet, convinced that his blessing could not fail. (Nor, indeed, has it done so.)

Bet I introduced to Master as he was leaving one afternoon for a drive. From his remarks later on it was clear that she had made an excellent impression on him.

"Would she make a good yogi, Master?"

"Oh *yes.*"

In addition to lecturing in the churches, and to organizing the monks, I wrote letters for Master.

"Sir," I said one day, "what letters we are getting from Germany. Such sincerity and devotion! Letter after letter pleads with us for Kriya Yoga initiation."

"They have been hurt," Master replied with quiet sympathy, "that's why. All those wars and troubles! Kriya is what they *need,* not atom bombs."

"How wonderful it would be to send Henry there, with his knowledge of German."

"Well, maybe I will send *you* there someday."

Recalling his intention to send me to India, I replied, "I thought you had other plans for me, Sir. But of course I'll go wherever you send me. I'm familiar with Europe, certainly."

"There is a great work to be done there."

"Is this work a new religion?" I asked him one day.

"It is a new *expression,*" he corrected me.

Truth is one: *Sanatan Dharma* as it is known in India—"the Eternal Religion." The great world religions are all branches on that single tree.

Sectarianism is divisive. "The one Ocean has become all its waves," Master told me once, when I questioned him about his own role in the religious evolution of this planet. "You should look to the Ocean, not to the little waves protruding on its bosom."

Self-Realization Fellowship Lake Shrine dedication ceremony. August, 1950. On the far left in the white robe is Rev. Bernard. Next to him is Rev. Stanley, then Dr. Lewis, Master, and me. At the extreme right of the picture is Roy Eugene Davis. Roy is now the founder and director of the Center for Spiritual Awareness in Lakemont, Georgia, and is well known as an author, lecturer, and teacher.

Monks sitting in meditation around the old pepper tree in the Temple of Leaves at Mt. Washington. In the early days, Master taught classes here.

The monks working on building India Center in 1951.
(back row) Second from left, Norman Paulsen; far right, Roy Eugene Davis *(middle row)* Second from left, Daniel Boone; next to the right, Leo Cocks; fifth from the left, Rev. Bernard; then to the right, Jean Haupt, Jerry Torgerson, Joe Carbone (Brother Bimalananda), Henry Schaufelberger (Brother Anandamoy), Chuck Jacot. *(front row)* Second from left, Debi Mukerjee; next to the right, me.

I am standing with Yogacharya Oliver Black during my visit to his SRF center in Detroit, Michigan, in 1955.

James Coller, fellow disciple, much-loved by Master.

Shortly before my first trip to India in 1958.

Sri Daya Mata, third president of Self-Realization Fellowship.

Moments before this picture was taken, Master was asked if he would let himself be photographed. "Just a moment," he replied, "let me first go into *samadhi*." Two or three seconds later he said, "All right." So perfect was his control over his mental processes!

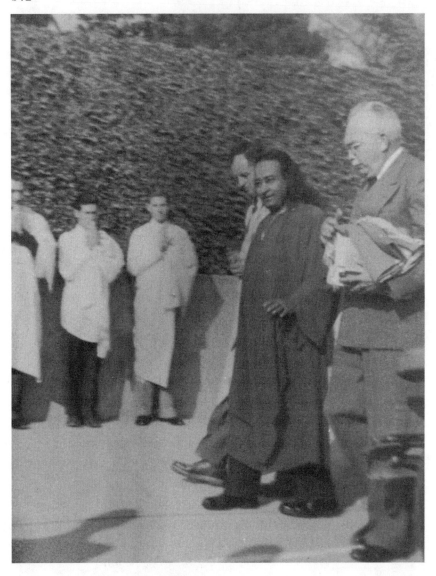

August 1951. At the time this photograph was taken, Master was suffering from an illness that had affected his legs, and he was unable to
walk. He was scheduled to speak to a large convocation of members.
Unwilling to publicize his condition, he determined to walk when the
time came. A car took him near the outdoor lecture platform. Master
lifted his legs with his own hands, and placed both feet on the ground.
"Instantly a brilliant light surrounded my body," he later told us. "I was
able to walk with ease." We saw him go up onto the lecture platform,
stand through his long lecture, and walk back, unaided, to the car.
"Once back in the car," he told us, "my legs became helpless again."

CHAPTER 3 7

Reminiscences

"I N THE EARLY DAYS of Mt. Washington, a visitor once inquired superciliously, 'What are the assets of this organization?'

" 'None!' I replied, 'Only God.' "

Master was sitting with us in the basement, reminiscing about his early years in America. Toward the end of his life, in addition to counseling us, he spent many hours trying to make us feel a part of that long period of his life before most of us had come to him.

"My reply on that occasion was literally true, too," Master chuckled. "We hadn't *any* money! But it would be just as true to-day, when our work is financially strong. For our strength has always been God alone. We might lose everything, materially speaking, and in His love we would still possess all that really mattered.

"Years ago a rich man came here who thought to buy me with his wealth. Knowing we badly needed money just then, he tried in certain ways to get me to compromise my ideals. I refused. Finally he said, 'You'll starve because you didn't listen.' Leaving here, he talked against me to a rich acquaintance of his, a student of this work. And *that* was the man God chose to give us the help we needed!

"Another time, years later, we were facing another financial crisis: Mt. Washington was threatened with foreclosure. I went out into the desert and meditated all night long. 'Divine Mother,' I prayed, 'why did You give me this responsibility? I came here to the West to speak of You, not to worry about organizational problems! If You took everything away, it would mean nothing to me except only my freedom! Say the word, Mother, and I will walk out into the desert and never once look back!'

"At three o'clock in the morning came Her answer: '*I* am your stocks and bonds. What more dost thou need than that thou hast

Me? Dance of death and dance of life—know that these come from Me. My child, rejoice!'

"The next day a check came in the mail for the exact sum of money that we needed."

Master often said, "He is happiest who gives everything to God." He told an amusing story to illustrate his own preference for simple living, free of all ostentation.

"A wealthy student of mine wanted to buy me a new overcoat. Taking me into a well-known clothing store, he invited me to select any coat that I wanted. Seeing one that looked nice, I reached out for it. But then, seeing the price tag, I quickly withdrew my hand. It was a very expensive coat.

" 'But I'd be *happy* to buy it for you,' my friend insisted. He added an expensive hat to match. I appreciated his kindness in giving me these gifts. But whenever I wore them, I felt uncomfortable. Expensive possessions are a responsibility.

" 'Divine Mother,' I finally prayed, 'this coat is too good for me. Please take it away.'

"Soon afterwards I was scheduled to lecture in Trinity Auditorium. I sensed that the coat would be taken away from me that evening, so I emptied the pockets. After the lecture the coat was gone. What a relief!

"But then I spotted an omission. 'Divine Mother,' I prayed, 'You forgot to take the hat!' "

Master went on to tell us about someone he'd met long ago in New York. "This man told me, 'I can never forgive myself for taking thirty-five years to make my first million dollars.' 'You still are not satisfied?' I asked. 'No. I will not be satisfied until I have made *forty* million!' Well, before he could make those forty million and settle down to spending the rest of his life in unalloyed happiness, he suffered a complete nervous breakdown. Not long afterward, he died."

As I write these lines, less than a week has passed since the death of Howard Hughes, one of the richest men in the world. The radio carried his reply to a recent question, "Are you happy?" "No," answered the billionaire, "I can't say that I'm happy."

"You don't have to *own* a thing to enjoy it," Master told us. "To possess things is all right, provided your possessions don't possess you, but ownership often means only added worries. It is much better to own everything in God, and not to cling to anything with the ego."

Smiling, he continued, "Years ago I visited Radio City Music Hall in New York. Having paid the price of admission, I told myself, 'For the hour or so that I am here, this building is mine!' I walked about, enjoying this beautiful acquisition. After I had enjoyed as much of it as I cared to, I gave the building back to the management, with thanks, and walked out a free man!"

Master told us of a time when his non-attachment had been tested. "I was standing alone one evening on a dark street corner in New York, when three hold-up men came up from behind me, one of them pointing a gun.

" 'Give us your money,' they demanded.

" 'Here it is,' I said, not at all disturbed. 'But I want you to know that I am not giving it to you out of fear. I have such wealth in my heart that, by comparison, money means nothing to me.' They were so astonished! I then gazed at them with God's power. They burst into tears. Returning my money, they cried, 'We can't live this way anymore!' Then, overwhelmed by the experience, they ran away.

"On other occasions, too, I have changed the hearts of criminals—not I, but God's power through me. One evening during the depression years I lectured to thousands at Carnegie Hall. I spoke out against the way certain rich people were taking advantage of the poor. I actually mentioned a few names. Afterwards, several people urged me, 'Please don't go home alone tonight.'

" 'God is with me,' I replied. 'Whom have I to fear?'

"Alone I entered a dimly lighted part of the station, when a man came up brandishing a gun. 'Why did you talk against those people?' he demanded.

" 'Why shouldn't I?' I replied. 'God is for the common man as much as for the rich. Both are His children. And He is not pleased when His rich children take advantage of His poor ones.' "

Listening to Master, we chuckled at this point in his story. How incongruous seemed this ingenuous explanation beside the man's threat of assassination!

Master continued: "Gazing steadily into the man's eyes, I said, 'Why do you live the way you do? You aren't happy. I *demand* that Satan come out of you, and that you change!'

"The man began to tremble. All of a sudden, dropping his gun, he fell to his knees before me. 'What have you done to me?' he cried. 'I was sent to kill you.'

" 'You can never win,' I said. 'Pick up your gun and throw it away.' His life was completely transformed by that meeting."

Master told of a similar conversion after another Carnegie Hall lecture. "We had chanted 'O God Beautiful!' for over an hour. Three thousand people had joined me joyously in singing this chant. Many were in ecstasy. Afterwards, a man burst into my interview room. Flinging a revolver emotionally onto the desk, he cried, 'I ought to kill you for what you've done to me this evening! I can't go back to that way of life any more.'

"Such is the power of God's love!

"But there have been times," Master continued, "when His power flowed through me in other ways. I follow only His will. One evening in Chicago I visited a park. It was during the depression years, and Chicago, as you know, was notorious for its gangsters at the time. A policeman stopped me as I was about to enter the park, and warned me that it was unsafe there after dark. 'Even we are afraid to go in,' he said.

"Well, I went in anyway, and comfortably took a seat on a park bench. After some time a tough-looking man, much larger than I, stopped in front of me.

" 'Gimme a dime!' he snarled.

"I reached into a pocket and gave him a dime.

" 'Gimme a quarter!' I gave him a quarter.

" 'Gimme fifty cents.' I gave him fifty cents.

" 'Gimme a dollar.'

"By this time I could see that matters weren't going to improve. So, with the consciousness of God's power, I leapt to my feet and shouted:

" 'GET OUT!!!'

"The man started to tremble like a leaf. 'I don't want your money!' he mumbled. Backing fearfully away, he kept on repeating, 'I don't want your money! I don't want your money!' Suddenly he turned and fled as though his life depended on it.

"I sat down peacefully once more, and watched the moonrise. Later, as I was leaving the park, the same policeman saw me and asked, 'What did you say to that man? I saw him with you, and didn't dare to interfere. He's a dangerous character!'

" 'Oh,' I replied, 'we came to a little understanding.' "

Whether Master protected himself by love, or by sterner measures, depended on the guidance he received inwardly. Perhaps love was what he gave to persons of innate sensitivity who had succumbed to the influences of an evil environment, and sternness to those whose cruelty was self-generated, or who, though not insensitive to finer feelings, suppressed them deliberately. In this last connection he told us of a guest at Mt. Washington during the 1920s. The man's sister was a resident disciple there.

"I was sitting on my bed one morning, meditating," he said, "when God showed me this man coming upstairs to beat me up. He wanted to boast publicly of what he'd done, you see, so as to discredit this work.

" 'Give it to him!' the voice said.

"Moments later the man appeared in the doorway. 'I know why you have come,' I said. 'You may not realize it, but I am very strong; I could easily best you in a fight if I wanted to. But I won't meet you on that level. Still, I warn you: Don't cross that threshold.'

" 'Go on, prophet!' he replied contemptuously. 'What could you do?'

" 'I've warned you. You'll be very sorry.'

"Ignoring my words, he stepped into the room. The instant he did so, he fell to the floor screaming, 'I'm on fire! I'm on fire!' Leaping up, then, he ran downstairs and out of the building. I followed quickly behind, and found him rolling about on the front lawn, still crying, 'I'm on fire! I'm on fire!' When I placed a hand on him he was all right, though still terrified of me. 'Don't touch me!' he cried. 'Don't come near me!' He sent his sister into the building for his belongings, and departed at once."

Many were surprised to learn how physically powerful Master was. He was quite short—five feet five or six inches—and, though well built, didn't impress one as being particularly strong. But his strength came primarily from his complete command over the energy in his body.

"In Symphony Hall in Boston," he told us, "I was lecturing once on the merits of the energization exercises, and mentioned the great physical strength one derives from them. I then threw out the challenge: 'Would anyone here like to *try* my strength?'

"Six tall, burly policemen jumped up onto the stage! The audience gasped. They were certain I'd fail the test.

"Well, I placed my back against the wall, facing them. Then I asked the men all together to push on my stomach as hard as they could. They did so. 'Is that the best you can do?' I demanded.

" 'Yeah!' they grunted between clenched teeth.

"Suddenly I arched my back. All six of them went tumbling backwards into the orchestra pit!"

People who know only of Paramhansa Yogananda's extraordinary love and compassion, his sweetness, his childlike simplicity, are sometimes taken aback when they encounter his power. Few realize that power and divine love are opposite sides of the same coin. For divine love is no gentle sentiment, but the greatest force in the universe. It couldn't exist without power. Great saints would never use that power to suppress or coerce others, but power nevertheless is inextricably a part of what it means to be a saint. It took extraordinary power, for example, for Jesus Christ, alone in a crowd, to drive the money-changers from their tradition-sanctioned seats in the temple. Worldly people fear this power in the saints, and, fearing, persecute them. They don't realize that it is rooted in love, or that it threatens nothing but their delusions and ignorance-induced suffering.

Yogananda's power was not only a product of his divine awareness; his human personality, too, reflected past incarnations as a warrior and conquering hero. In Calcutta, in his youth, he was several times approached by people who wanted him to lead a revolution against the British. There was that in his very bearing which bespoke the intrepid leader.

Master could also be very outspoken when occasion demanded it. It simply wasn't in him to be insincere. One time, not able to beg off giving a speech after a high-society banquet to which he'd been dragged in New York City, he spoke what was in his heart. Sternly he upbraided his listeners for the shallowness of their lives. It wasn't condemnation. The indignation he showed rather, was on *their* behalf. Graphically he described their delusions to them, and exhorted them to stop wasting an entire incarnation in spiritual sloth. His hearers were stunned. Many wept.

Yet the experience, painful though it was for them, was also their good karma. For how many people get to hear what they need from a man of divine wisdom? Master himself once told Dr. Lewis, "No one's path has crossed mine in this life except for a reason."

Another story that shows how outspoken Master could be concerns a visit he once paid to a certain vegetarian organization. "I was invited to inspect their facilities," he told me. "They believed in raw foods, or, as they called the unfired foods.' They took me around their kitchen, and then into the dining room, where they served me the worst meal I have ever eaten in my life. After this epicurean disaster, they asked me to address them!

" 'Please,' I said, 'I'd rather not.'

" 'Oh, but you must,' they insisted. 'Everyone is eager to hear you.'

" 'You won't like what I have to say,' I warned. But they wouldn't take no for an answer. At last I stood up.

" 'In the first place,' I said, 'I have never in my life tasted worse food. What makes you think there is virtue in preparing meals so unpalatably? Enjoyment of what one eats aids the digestion. But you all imagine that what you are eating is healthful. In no way is it. It is seriously lacking in nutritive balance.'

"Well, by this time they were all greatly agitated! 'You don't know what you are saying,' they shouted.

" 'I urge you to take me seriously,' I replied, 'for unless you improve your diet, fifteen days from now one of you will die of malnutrition.'

" 'You are cursing us!'

" 'I'm doing nothing of the kind,' I said. 'You are cursing yourselves by your fanaticism!'

"Well, they wouldn't listen. Fifteen days later one of them died, and soon after that the organization disbanded."

Master usually accepted evil as a regrettable, but necessary, part of the cosmic drama. He fought it only in those who sought his spiritual aid. "The villain's role on the stage," he used to say, "is to get people to love the hero. Evil's role, similarly, in the drama of life is to spur people on to seek goodness." There were times, however, when he became an avenging angel, particularly when the lives of his own disciples, or of those dear to them, were affected.

The mother of one close disciple was afflicted with cancer of the breast. Finding a sanatorium that advertised a newly discovered, supposedly miraculous cancer cure, she entered it hopefully.

"All they gave their patients," Master told us, "was water! They took their money, fed them nothing, and simply waited for them to die. When I found out their scheme, I cried, 'Divine Mother, destroy that place!' Within a month the police came in and closed it. The leaders all went to prison."

Master went on to speak of that woman's subsequent death. "I contacted her in the astral world. When I came upon her, she was being led away by an angel, and was marveling at the beauty of the flowers in the field she was in. I called to her, but she didn't hear me. Again I called; this time she turned, but didn't recognize me. In the transition of death, you see, she had forgotten. But I touched her, and recognition came. 'I will never again forget you,' she promised. Then, opening her flowing robe, she showed me where the cancer had been. 'See?' she said, smiling. 'It is gone now!'

"Soon thereafter I saw her again, in the sunset."

Master explained to us that after the death of the physical body, the soul remains encased in a subtler body of energy, known as the "astral body." This body is the prototype for the physical body. The astral universe, similarly, forms the prototype for the grosser material universe. When a person dies, he lives on in an astral body, and may, if he is spiritually even slightly developed, inhabit an astral planet with vibrations harmonious to his own. His length of stay there is determined by his karma.

In one of the most inspiring chapters of *Autobiography of a Yogi,*
Paramhansa Yogananda gives a lengthy description of the astral
universe. It is composed, he tells us, of endlessly varied vibrations
of energy. Compared to this physical world, the astral heavens are
inexpressibly beautiful. Not everyone, however, goes to those heavens after death. As Jesus put it, "In my Father's house are many
mansions."* Many souls are vibrationally attracted to less exalted,
though still harmonious, spheres. Others, having created nothing
but disharmony in their own lives on earth, are vibrationally
drawn to astral hells. Materialistic people often are only dimly conscious of the astral world between earthly sojourns. People who
developed good qualities while on earth, however, especially those
who meditated and acquired a measure of soul-awareness, are attracted to higher astral worlds after death.

To Master, death was no "undiscovered country from whose
bourne no traveller returns." He told us he spent much time in the
astral world. Thus, to him, it was no tragedy when people died.
But at the same time he was too warmly human not to feel the
reality of people's bereavement, or to offer loving sympathy to
them in their grief. Indeed, he sometimes offered far more than
sympathy: He actually brought loved ones back "from the grave."

One case involved a lady in Encinitas. Master told me the story:

"A real estate agent in Encinitas, hearing that I had healing
power, came to me to request a healing for his wife, who had been
ill for ninety days. I prayed, but God told me not to go to her
bedside. Shortly thereafter, she died. Only then was I given the
guidance to go to her.

"About thirty people were present in the room when I arrived.
Her husband was weeping and shaking her, almost out of his mind
with grief. He wouldn't accept the fact that she was already dead.
I motioned him away.

"Putting one hand on the dead woman's forehead, and the other
one under her head, I began invoking the divine power. Five minutes passed. Ten minutes. Suddenly her whole body began to
tremble like a motor. After some time, a deep calmness stole over
her. Her heartbeat and breathing returned. Slowly her eyes
opened; they held a far-away expression, as though she had just
returned from a long journey. She was completely healed."

Another episode concerned a man in Dakshineswar, a Calcutta
suburb. I first heard the story from Master, and then again years
later from Sri Tulsi Bose, a childhood friend of his, and a cousin

* John 14:2.

of the man who had died. As Sri Bose told the story, it was because the man was his cousin that Master performed this miracle.

"I was passing the house," Master told us, "when I heard a loud outcry within. God told me to go inside. I found a man there stretched out on a bed. Five or ten minutes earlier the doctors had pronounced him dead. The family were all weeping and crying.

"I requested them to leave the room, then remained alone with the dead man for some time, praying. Breath returned to his body at last. His eyes opened. He was completely cured."

Master was equally at home on all levels of reality. To those who identified with this physical plane of existence and its sorrows, he was compassionate. In the astral world, where physical sufferings are unknown, he was like a sea captain, returning to port as often as he wished. But his own true affinity was with spheres far subtler than either of these: the timeless bliss of divine union. It was amazing to see how effortlessly he would enter *samadhi*. For most of us struggling devotees it took time even to touch the hem of superconsciousness. For him, the vastness of cosmic consciousness was only a breath away.

I remember someone asking his permission one evening to photograph him. "Just a moment," Master replied, "let me first go into *samadhi*." Two or three seconds later he said, "All right."

"I used sometimes to go to movies," Master told us, "to get away from the unceasing demands of the work. Sitting in the movie theater, I would enter *samadhi*. Later, if people asked me how I liked the movie, I replied, 'Very much!' I had been watching the cosmic 'movie,' with stars and planets whirling through space!"

No environment was wholly mundane to him. Everywhere he saw God. "Do you know where I wrote my poem '*Samadhi*'?" he asked us one day. "It was on the New York subway! As I was writing, I rode back and forth from one end of the line to the other. No one asked for my ticket. In fact," he added with a twinkle, "no one saw me!"

Visitors sometimes boasted of their own high experiences in meditation. Boastfulness would make any discerning person skeptical; true experiences of God, after all, should make one humble. But Master could tell at a glance what level a person had reached in his spiritual development.

"People have a very distorted notion of what the path is all about," he said. "Visions and phenomena aren't important. What matters is complete self-offering to God. One must become absorbed in His love.

"I remember a man who came forward after a lecture in New York and claimed he could enter cosmic consciousness at will. Actually, what he meant was that he could travel astrally, but I saw right away that his experiences were imaginary. Still, I couldn't simply tell him that. He wouldn't have believed me. So I invited him up to my room, and there asked him to favor me by going into cosmic consciousness.

"Well, he sat there fidgeting, his eyelids flickering, his breath pumping away—signs, all, of body-consciousness, not of cosmic consciousness! At last he could contain himself no longer.

" 'Why don't you ask me where I am?'

" 'Well,' I said, to humor him, 'where are you?'

"In rounded tones, as if hallooing from afar, he answered: 'On top of the dome of the Taj Mahal!'

" 'There must be something the matter with your own dome!' I remarked. 'I see you sitting fully here, right in front of me.' He was utterly taken aback.

"I then made a suggestion. 'If you think you can travel all the way to the Taj Mahal, why not see if you can go to somewhere nearby, as a test of the validity of your experience?' I suggested that he project himself to the hotel dining room downstairs, and describe what he saw there. He agreed to the test. Going into 'cosmic consciousness' again, he described the dining room as he saw it. He actually believed in his visions, you see. What I wanted to do was demonstrate to him that they were the result of a vivid power of visualization. He described a number of things in the restaurant, including a big piano in the right-hand corner.

"I then described the scene as I saw it. 'In the right-hand corner,' I said, 'there are two women seated at a table.' We went at once downstairs, and found the room as I had described it, not as he had. At last he was convinced."

Master often told us stories of his boyhood in India. Years later I wrote and published several of these accounts in a small book titled *Stories of Mukunda*. Here is one that was omitted from that book; it didn't quite fit the mood of it.

"The first time I fed the poor in India," Master said, "I decided to feed two hundred people. I was just a boy. Everybody wondered how I planned to do it. Another boy, a friend of mine, objected, 'You haven't any money. Neither have I. There's just no way we can feed that many people.'

" 'All I need,' I replied, 'is twenty rupees. And that money will come through you.'

" 'Impossible!' he cried, shocked.

" 'It will happen,' I assured him, 'but on one condition: that you take care not in any way to antagonize your mother today.'

"Later that day his mother told him to go to his rich aunt's house and deliver something. He was about to refuse, when he remembered my warning. Docility was hardly his usual attitude, but he went this time without a murmur, and delivered the package.

"When he arrived at his aunt's house, she began scolding him, 'Who is this boy you've been running around with?' Her reference was to me. Like many wealthy people, she tended to harbor suspicions of strangers. My friend grew angry. He was about to leave when she cried, 'Stop! I hear he is planning on doing some good. Take this money and use it.' She gave him twenty rupees.

"The word had already been making the rounds that we were planning to feed the poor. Those twenty rupees bought a sizable amount of rice and lentils. When the neighbors saw such tangible support for our plans, they became enthusiastic. Money began pouring in from all sides. People volunteered their services to help with cooking and serving. Instead of two hundred poor people, we fed two thousand!"

Talk turned one evening to the attributes of success. "Will power," Master told us, "is more important to success than knowledge, training, or even native ability. Some people, when you shake them, reply with a groan, 'Don't bother me; I'm sleeping.' Others wake up a little bit, but if you leave them alone for a few minutes they start dozing again. But some people are wide awake the moment you speak to them, and keep going without having to be stirred again. Those are the kind of people I like!

"When I first started on my own in the spiritual life, I settled in a little mud hut with two other boys. One of them was about my size: short and slight. The other was a big, stalwart fellow. One day I said to them, 'Let's lay a cement floor in the main room.'

" 'Impossible!' protested the big fellow. 'We don't have the cement; we don't have the equipment; we don't have the know-how. For a technical job like this you need experience.'

" 'If we make up our minds,' I replied, 'we can do it'

" 'Wishful thinking!' he scoffed, walking away to show what he thought of the scheme.

"That day the other boy and I went around to the neighbors. Bit by bit we gathered donations of materials, and loans of equipment. Two men added careful instructions on how to mix and lay the cement. That whole night we stayed up, mixing and pouring. By the following morning the job was finished. Later on the big fellow returned to our hermitage.

" 'Well,' I sighed, teasing him, 'I guess you were right.' "

" 'Aha,' he cried. 'You see? I told you so!' "

"I then asked him please to fetch me something from the next room. He opened the door. And there was our new cement floor! We'd even colored it red. He was dumbfounded."

Master went on to emphasize that miracles become possible when man unites his will with God's will.

"Not many miles from our school in Ranchi, there was a high waterfall, above which was a rock ledge, dangerous to walk on. Sometimes I would take the boys across there.

" 'Do you believe in God?' I would shout to them over the noise of the water.

" 'Yes!' they all shouted back. And so, chanting God's name, we always crossed over in safety.

"One day, some years after I had come to America, another teacher in the school tried to lead a group of boys across there, repeating the words I had used. One boy slipped off the ledge and was drowned. It was because that teacher didn't have the power. Faith must be rooted in spiritual realization, otherwise it lacks vitality.

"And then, too," Master added, "one's motives must be pure. A few years ago two young boys in India decided that, because they believed in God, He would surely protect them no matter what they did. To prove their point they took a sword, and went out into a nearby forest. One of them kneeled; the other aimed a sweeping blow at his neck with the sword. Well, God didn't consider their presumption deserving of a miracle. The kneeling boy was killed instantly. Had their faith been pure, those children would have had the understanding not to behave so rashly. A person with pure motives doesn't try to coerce God. When you act in tune with Him, things always turn out well."

On another occasion Master was talking to us about the power of true faith. "One evening I had just returned to Mt. Washington when a sudden, violent wind struck the main building. It was an effect of the evil karma of the war. People little realize how greatly the very elements are affected by mass consciousness. I told one of the ladies living here to remove a shoe and strike the front porch with it three times, repeating certain words. She did as I said. On the third blow, the wind stopped instantly. In the newspaper the next day there was an item about the violent wind that had started in Los Angeles, then, minutes later, abated.

"The mind's potential," Master added, "is considerable, even without the addition of divine power. One day I was traveling in this country by train. It was a very hot summer day, and the train had no air conditioning. Everyone was suffering in the heat. I said to those who were with me, 'See what a little concentration can do. I will dwell on the idea of icebergs.'

"Minutes later I held out an arm for them to feel. It was cold."

Master often regaled us with amusing anecdotes of his beginnings in America. "Because of my robe and long hair, people sometimes thought I was a woman. Once, at a Boston flower exhibition, I wanted to find the men's room. A guard directed me to a certain door. Trustingly I went in. My goodness! Ladies to the left of me, ladies to the right of me, ladies everywhere! I rushed out, and once more approached the guard.

" 'I want the *men's* room,' I insisted. Eyeing me suspiciously, he finally pointed to another door. This time as I entered a man cried out, 'Not in here, lady! Not in here!'

"In a basso profundo voice I answered, 'I know what I am doing!'

"Another time on a train the conductor kept walking up and down the aisle, eyeing me. Finally he could restrain his curiosity no longer. 'Is yo a man,' he asked, 'or is yo a woman?'

" 'What do you theenk?'* I demanded in a deep, booming tone.

"I used to wear a beard. On the ship coming over from India, a fellow passenger, a Muslim by the name of Rashid, persuaded me to shave it off. Americans, he insisted, might accept me if I had *either* long hair *or* a beard, but definitely not if I kept both. Since my master had expressed a wish that I keep my hair long, I decided to sacrifice the beard. Rashid volunteered his services as a barber. I placed myself trustingly in his hands. He lathered my face, then proceeded carefully to shave half of it. At that point he abandoned me! And I had no idea how to shave! I was left there until, sometime later, he returned laughing to complete the job.

"Rashid was a great prankster. But he was also very helpful to me when I began my first lecture tour. He got the halls, prepared the publicity, and acted as my secretary. Still, he did play pranks!

"But one evening I got the better of him. He was always avoiding his work, and running after girls. He didn't realize that I knew what he was doing. On this particular evening he'd promised to come in and work with me. When he didn't show up, I knew just where to find him. I went to a nearby park, and there he was, sitting on a bench with a new girl friend. (He certainly had a way

---

* Master spoke English with a pronounced Bengali accent. I've emphasized his pronunciation here because it was part of the charm of the story.

with them!) I crept up stealthily from behind, and stood nearby, hidden by a bush. He put his arms around the girl, and was just about to kiss her. At that instant I called out in a loud, deep voice, 'Rasheeeed!' You should have seen him jump! He came into the office after that, and worked quite docilely!"

We laughed uproariously at Master's story, which was delivered with suitably droll gestures and facial expressions.

"But," he concluded, "Rashid more than made up for all his pranks, years later. He was living in India when I returned there in 1935. He prepared a huge public reception for me in Calcutta. I was deeply touched."

I myself got to meet Rashid in Calcutta in 1959. By that time he was much older, but even then it was easy to imagine him as the debonair prankster of his youth.

"When I first came to America," Master continued, "my father used to send me money. But I wanted to rely wholly on God, so I returned it. In the beginning God let me taste a little hardship, to test my faith in Him, but my faith was firm, and He never failed me."

Master continued his reminiscences of those years. "A student of this work in Boston told me he wanted to be a renunciate. I said to him, 'Your path is marriage.'

" 'Oh, no!' he vowed, 'I'll *never* marry!' Well, a week later he met a beautiful girl and swore he was deeply in love with her!

" 'She isn't the one for you,' I warned.

" 'Oh, but she *is!* he cried. 'She is my soul mate.'

"Well, it wasn't long after that that he returned shamefacedly. 'I want to be a renunciate,' he announced fervently once again. The girl had left him, after enjoying his money.

" 'You have yet to meet the right one,' I said.

"Some time later, laughingly, he told me of a fat, quite unattractive-looking girl who had been taking an unwelcome interest in him.

" 'Aha, I said, 'she sounds like the one!'

" 'No Swami, no!' he cried, horrified. 'You were right before. *Please* don't be right this time!'

" 'She sounds like the one for you.'

"It took him some time, but gradually he discovered what a good nature she had beneath her unglamorous exterior, and fell deeply in love with her. Eventually they were married.

"People are so often blinded by outward appearances," Master continued. "Marriage in this country is often a union between a pretty shade of lipstick and a smart-looking tie! They hear a little music, fall into a romantic mood, and end up pledging their lives away.

"I remember a couple who came to me in Phoenix and asked me to marry them 'immediately.' I told them, 'I must know the people I marry. I want to meditate on your request. Please come back tomorrow.' At this proposed delay, the man was furious. When they returned the next day, he pressed me, 'Is it all right?'

" 'No,' I said.

"He was enraged once more. 'Let's get out of here, *dear!* We can get married by somebody else.'

"They were almost to the door when I called to them. 'Remember my words: You will never be happy together. You will find that out when it is too late. But please, I urge you, at least don't kill each other!'

"They were married elsewhere. Soon afterward they came to Mt. Washington just to show me how happy they were. I said nothing, but inside I thought, 'You don't know what is hidden under that lid!'

"Six months later they returned. This time they knelt humbly before me and confessed, 'We didn't realize how different our natures were. If you hadn't warned us, we would surely have ended up killing each other.' Under the influence of emotional intoxication, you see, they hadn't observed the explosive violence that was inherent in their relationship.

"People must learn to look behind the veil of superficial attraction. Without soul harmony there can be no true love."

Master saw every human experience, including that of marriage, primarily as an opportunity for inner development. Romantic notions of "wedded bliss" were, to him, purely and simply delusions. It wasn't that he denied the satisfactions of a harmonious marriage, but rather that he wanted devotees to see human experiences as stepping stones to the soul's only true state of being, in God. Thus, he recommended to people seeking marriage that they look first for spiritual compatibility in their mates, and only secondarily for mental, emotional, and physical compatibility. He saw marriage not only as a fulfillment, but, much more importantly, as an opportunity for learning essential spiritual lessons in selflessness, loyalty, kindness, respect, and trust. To devotees who, in the name of dispassion, considered it unnecessary to express these qualities outwardly towards their fellow creatures, he said, "Don't imagine that God will come to you if you behave unkindly to others. Until you know how to win human love, you will never be able to win God's love."

To Master, human experience was, in a sense, part of a process of divine healing. Man's supreme disease, he said, is spiritual ignorance. His own life was devoted to healing people on all levels, in keeping with his philosophy that religion should serve humanity's total needs: physical, emotional, and mental, as well as spiritual. Though the supreme "cure" he offered was divine bliss, he healed many that I knew, including myself, of various physical ailments.

One case of physical healing that stands out in my memory occurred years before I entered the work. Master told us the story:

"It was during the Chicago World's Fair, in 1933. Dr. Lewis telephoned me in Los Angeles to report that a friend of his had a blood clot on the heart, and was dying. Could I help him? I sat in meditation and prayed. Suddenly a great power went out from me, like an explosion. In that same instant the man, who had been in a coma, was healed. A nurse was in the room with him—not a spiritual woman at all. She testified later that she'd heard an explosion in the room, and seen a brilliant flash of light. The man at once sat up, completely recovered."

Master then spoke of the most important kind of healing: the dispelling of soul ignorance. "That is why we have these ashrams," he said, "for those who want to give their lives to God, to be healed of *all* suffering forevermore." He talked on about those earlier years at Mt. Washington.

Looking at us sweetly, he concluded, "How I wish you all had been with me then! So many years had to pass before you came."

CHAPTER 38

His Last Days

Oh, I will come again and again!
Crossing a million crags of suffering,
With bleeding feet, I will come—
If need be, a trillion times—
So long as I know
One stray brother is left behind.
            —from "God's Boatman"
            by Paramhansa Yogananda

RAINDROPS FALL to earth, play their countless separate dramas, then rise, to fall again in endlessly repeated cycles. Similar is the tale of each soul. Through unnumbered cycles of return we refine our understanding, till we become convinced to our very depths that the fulfillment we are seeking is ours already—in the bliss of our own being!

Why should it take so long to make such a simple discovery? Why is it so difficult to realize that earthly pleasures are but reflections of our inner joy? Alas, in a house of mirrors one is less inclined to introspect. The reflections are too fascinating! If one gives thought to oneself, it may be only for the sake of changing those reflections. With human life, similarly, the reflections of our inner joy that we perceive in outward fulfillments are simply too tantalizing! Many lifetimes pass, usually, ere we realize that our fascination has been with mere images, and that we have been living in an unreal world.

Normally, when a soul achieves final emancipation, ending its long cycle of incarnations, its joy in victory is so overwhelming that it feels no desire to return to this earthly dungeon. Even the spiritual hunger of other seekers can't suffice to lure it back. For such a soul feels—justifiably, surely—that after untold millions of years in bondage it has a right to claim its hard-won reward of eternal bliss. Only a few extraordinary souls, having once earned their freedom, postpone the perfect enjoyment of it to return to this dark plane and lead other struggling mortals out of delusion into light. Of such rare souls Paramhansa Yogananda is a shining example. Indeed, even among those few it must be the exception who promises to come back "if need be, a trillion times." Yogananda's compassion simply staggers the imagination.

Devotees sometimes ask, "Do souls that have been born on this earth keep reincarnating here?" Master's reply, when once I posed this question to him, was, "No, there are innumerable planets to go to." He added, "If they returned always to the same one, they might find out too quickly!" Divine perception, in other words, must be earned. It is not the "plot" of this cosmic drama for wisdom to be thrust upon man uninvited; he must employ the sword of discrimination himself. The house of mirrors must lose its fascination for him because he has seen through its tricks, and not merely because, by constant repetition, the reflections have ceased to interest him.

In one respect, however, the soul does tend toward a long repetition of outward associations: in its relationships with other souls.

An example may help here. In the nebulous gasses of infinite space, the atoms drift about at great distances—the average is several miles—from one another: much too far for their gravitational fields to attract one another. But if two atoms happen to drift together, their combined field makes it easier for them to attract a third. For three it is still easier to attract a fourth. Thus, an occasional ball of matter may keep on growing, until its gravitational field at last encompasses a radius of many millions of miles. At some point in this process a mighty implosion will occur, as nebulous gasses from vast distances get sucked inward. The gravitational force of this huge mass becomes so great that changes occur within the structure of the atoms themselves: A shining star is born.

The soul, similarly, in its gradual progress toward divine wisdom, develops the "gravitational" power by which it attracts and holds the understanding it needs for enlightenment, until at last, in the firmament of living beings, it becomes a veritable "star."

In the same way, too, the soul develops the gravitational power to form meaningful and lasting relationships with other souls. Gradually, in its outer life, it and others who are spiritually compatible with it form great families of souls that return to earth, or to other planets, to work out their salvation, not only inwardly on themselves, but through interaction with one another. For divine emancipation it is necessary to spiritualize one's relations with the objective world, and with other human beings, as well as with God.

The stronger the family, spiritually speaking, the greater its attractive pull on new souls that may still be wandering about, searching for an identity of their own. A family evolves as its individual members evolve. It too, becomes a "star" in the firmament of humanity, once it begins to produce great souls of Self-realization.

As spiritual "stars," such great families become powerful for the general upliftment of mankind. Like stars, too, they then draw "planets" of less-evolved families into their beneficial auras, vitalizing them with rays of divine truth. Such families are like mighty nations. To them is given the real task of guiding the human race—not in the way governments do, by ordinances, but by subtler, spiritual influence.

Yogananda's is one such spiritual family. His forms part of a greater spiritual "nation" in which Jesus Christ and Sri Krishna (in this age, Babaji) are also leaders. Yogananda, like William the Conqueror at Hastings, came to America to establish a beachhead—not, in this case, of worldly conquest, but of divine communion. Many have been born and are being born in the West to assist him in his mission. Many others are being attracted to it for the first time by the radiant magnetic influence, the spiritual "gravitational field," it has created.

During the last year and a half of Master's life, long-time disciples gathered around him, as though somehow aware that his end was approaching. Some who, for a variety of reasons, had not seen him for years, visited him now. Others who hadn't met him yet, but whose destiny it was to meet him in this life, came, as if hurrying to get in before it was too late.

Recalling Master's panoramic vision in 1920 of all his destined disciples in America, I asked him in June 1950, "Have you already met most of those you saw in your vision at Ranchi?"

"Practically all," he replied. "I am waiting for only a few more to come."

Among close disciples who visited him during his last year were Señor Cuaron from Mexico, Mr. Black from Detroit, Michigan, and Kamala Silva from Oakland, California.

After Mr. Black's departure, Master remarked to me with loving reminiscence, "Did you see God in his eyes?"

Of Kamala he said to us one day, "Look at that girl. For twenty-seven years she has been in this work. She is very near freedom. After she had been with me a long time, living here at Mt. Washington, I told her she should marry.

" 'Oh, no, Master,' she said, 'I don't want to.' But I urged her to, and promised her she would be safe. It was a little past karma she had to work out. I picked out her husband myself.° What a wonderful soul he is—a true *sannyasi,* just like one of you all!"

Señor Cuaron came in 1950, then again in 1951. I first met him moments after someone had delivered a huge suitcase of shapeless dimensions onto the carpet by the door of the front lobby. I was smiling at the sight of this amorphous bag, when a voice somewhere above me announced, "That's mine." I looked up, and there, in human form, was the bag's exact counterpart! There was nothing to smile at, however, except lovingly, in Señor Cuaron's spiritual nature. I soon discovered that he had a heart as large as his body.

Master had great love for him. "I lost touch with you for a few incarnations," he told him, "but I shall never lose touch again." Thereafter, from time to time, Señor Cuaron lovingly reminded him of his promise. "Never again," Master reassured him.

Mme. Galli-Curci, the famed opera singer, settled near Encinitas. "Has she advanced far spiritually?" I once asked Master, who sometimes discussed with me the spiritual states of the disciples. "She is soaring in God!" he replied blissfully.

Arthur Cometer, who had accompanied Master on his lecture tour across the country in 1924, and inspected Mt. Washington the first time with Master in 1925, visited also during this period. Master spoke of him with warm appreciation.

At about this time also, Jesse Anderson, an elderly disciple in San Jose, California, gave Master a picture of Sri Yukteswar that he had stitched in colored yarn. Retired from work now, and living on a small income, Mr. Anderson had financed the purchase of the yarn by gathering walnuts from the ground on the roadside, and selling them.

Master was deeply touched by the gift. He had it hung in the hallway at the top of the staircase outside his quarters. Frequently, when passing this picture, he would pause silently, placing his palms together in solemn salute to his great guru. Master's reverence for Sri Yukteswar was all the more touching because he himself had long ago outgrown the status of a disciple.

° Her husband, Edward Silva, was a school teacher in Oakland, California.

There is a saying, "No man is great in the eyes of his own valet." In the case of saints this saying is falsified, for it is those who know them best, their own close disciples, who regard them the most highly. Sri Yukteswar's nature was stern; he had not been an easy guru to follow. Many a would-be disciple, seeing only his surface personality, had fled at the first crack of his whip of discipline. But Master had seen the divine consciousness behind the mask.

"One day," he told us, "a group of disciples got fed up with the strictness of his training, and decided to leave him. 'Come,' they said to me, 'we'll follow you. He is too severe for us.'

" '*You* go if you like,' I said sternly. '*I* stay here with my guru!' "

In Master's case, too, I observed that those disciples who knew him best were invariably those who held him in the highest esteem.

One such disciple was Sister Gyanamata. Much older than he, the dignified widow of a university professor, and a person who seldom praised anybody, she yet displayed a respect for Master so undeviating, so humble, so profound that the worldly person, visiting the ashram for the first time, might have supposed her the merest neophyte.

In Master's presence, so I was told, she always remained standing.

"I was once in the main room of the Encinitas hermitage with Sister and a few others," said Eugene Benvau, a brother disciple, "when Master entered. Sister, though an old woman, stood up immediately with the rest of us. Master never glanced at her, nor did he say a word. Walking over to the window, he gazed out at the ocean. Sister wasn't looking at him, either. But after awhile I noticed both of them smiling quietly—a sort of inward smile. Several minutes later Master left the room, having addressed not a word to anyone. But I had a strong feeling that he and Sister had been in silent communication with each other.

"I have only to hold a thought about Sister," Master told us, "and the next day a letter comes from her." A number of her letters to Master, and to fellow disciples about her relationship with Master, appeared in the book *God Alone.**

"Dear Children," she once wrote to some of the younger nuns, "Yesterday you put the question, 'What is the last word in discipleship? What would be the distinguishing mark of the perfect disciple?'

"You know that I am always quiet when in the presence of the

° Self-Realization Fellowship, 1984.

Master. This is not a pose, intended to win his approval, nor is it altogether because I know this to be the proper way to behave. It is because I have an inner feeling of stillness. I seem to be listening intently. So his words sink into my mind and heart to be pondered upon, sometimes for years. Because of this, I often get the answer to a mental question in his very words."

She went on to describe how the answer to her sister-disciples' question had come to her this time, too, in Master's words. A lady student, to whom he had given a red rose to be worn during a special ceremony, had protested, "But I don't *want* a red rose. I want a pink one." Master had answered, "What *I* give, *you* take."

"Here is *my* answer," Sister concluded. "The quick, or at least open, mind. The willing hands and feet—these, brought to perfection, would be the last word, the distinguishing mark, the very perfection of discipleship."

Someone once told her of having had a vision of her as she was in some past incarnation. Sister later wrote Master, ending her letter with the words, "Whatever, whoever I have been in the past, in this—the most important incarnation of all—I am Gyanamata, the work of your hands. Please pray for me that I may stand firm and unshaken to the end. With reverence, gratitude, devotion, and love—but not enough. Oh, not enough!"

Ah, what unutterable sweetness! Tears well into my eyes as I type these words. Small wonder, I think, when I recall how Master, paying tribute to her at her funeral, cried out in divine love, "Darling Sister!"

Sister Gyanamata died November 17, 1951, at the age of eighty-two. "I have searched her life," Master said, "and found not a single sin, *not even of thought.*"

For the past twenty years Sister had suffered physically. She had borne her burden of ill health heroically, as a priceless gift from God and Guru. Master, speaking about her to a group of us shortly before the funeral, said, "One day as I visited Sister's room I could hear her heart from as far away as the door, wheezing and making terrible sounds. It was barely pumping. Seeing me, she said, 'I don't ask you to heal me. All I ask is your blessing.' What faith she had! It saved her instantaneously from death. I made a covenant then with God for her life; I knew she would not go until I prayed for her release.

"Another time," Master continued, "she and Mrs. Maley were sitting on the porch at Encinitas, when a voice they both heard plainly said, 'Tell Paramhansaji I am taking you.' She told me about it afterwards. I replied, 'The next time he talks to you, tell him it isn't true. I have made a covenant with God for your life. He won't break His word.'

"A few days later she and Mrs. Maley were sitting on the porch again, when they heard the same voice, 'I am going to take you soon.' Sister answered, 'Paramhansaji says it isn't true.' The voice fell silent.

"A little while later her doctor, whom I'd never met, came by on his regular visit. As he was leaving I went to intercept him. 'Tell me, Doctor,' I said, 'how do you find Sister?'

" 'Oh, all right,' he replied.

" 'But tell me,' I said, 'isn't there something you don't understand about her case?'

" 'Well, it *is* a little confusing,' he admitted.

" 'Don't you think,' I suggested, 'that her trouble might be malnutrition? How would it be to have her placed under observation?'

" 'By Jove, perhaps you're right!' he exclaimed. They took her to the hospital, and there discovered that she hadn't enough nourishment left in her body to keep her alive another twenty-four hours. She'd been having sores on her lip, and had been taking nothing but tea—no other nourishment of any kind. They fed her again, and she recovered. But that was what the voice on the porch had meant."

Sister's life was spared repeatedly At last, after twenty years, Master gave her her release. "Such joy!" she cried with her last breath. "Too much joy! Too much joy!"

"I saw her sink into the watchful state of Spirit, beyond creation," Master said later. Sister's reward for years of perfect surrender to Guru's will was final liberation.

"She attained God through wisdom," Master said. "My path has been through joy."

On his return to Mt. Washington, Master spent some time discussing Sister with a group of us. He mentioned again her attainment of complete liberation. The recollection passed through my mind of what he had told me at Twenty-Nine Palms, that the soul must free others before it can itself receive final freedom. Catching my thought, Master said, "She *had* disciples."

"In all the years I have known her," Daya Mata told me during Sister's final hours, "I have never once heard her say anything unkind about anyone." What a beautiful tribute! I reflected that it said much about Daya Mata, too, that she had singled out this one quality for special praise. Kindness was the hallmark of her own personality.

We all felt, with Sister's passing, that the time was fast approaching when Master, too, would leave this world. Master himself hinted as much. To Dr. Lewis he remarked one day, "We have lived a good life together. It seems only yesterday that we met. In a little while we shall be separated, but soon we'll be together again."

His next life on earth, Master told us, would be spent in the Himalayas. Having devoted so much of his present life to public service, he planned to remain for many years of that incarnation in deep seclusion. "In my later years," he told us, "I will gather about me those who are close to me now." To most of his close women disciples he said, "You will come as men in that life." Only to Mrs. Brown, as far as I know, did he say that she would come again as a woman. Two hundred years would elapse, he told us, before his next incarnation.

During his last months, especially, he found his greatest earthly joy in those disciples who had lived up to his divine expectations of them. Often he praised Saint Lynn, Sister Gyanamata, Daya Mata, Mrs. Brown, and others. Of Merna Brown (Mrinalini Mata) he said, "She has wonderful karma! You will see what she will do for the work." She had been a saint, he told us, in more than one of her past lives. Of Corinne Forshee (Mukti Mata) he exclaimed to me once, "She is a *wonderful* soul!" Of Virginia Wright (Ananda Mata) he never spoke in my hearing, but it was clear from the way he treated her that she had pleased him very deeply. Another disciple who had, I know, pleased him greatly was Jane Brush (Sahaja Mata). In my years of work with her in the editorial department I never saw her anything but cheerful, even-tempered, and kind.

Master showed himself much pleased also with Henry's spirit. Henry (Brother Anandamoy) had one trouble after another. First he broke a rib; next he had a rash of some sort which made his life miserable; then he broke another rib. Minor misfortunes seemed to haunt him. One day, when he found himself afflicted anew with something, Master said to him, "Always more troubles, isn't it so? But that's good! You have lots of work to do, that's why you get them. God wants to make you strong. We produce more than D.D.s here. Our ministers win their spirituality in the fires of testing."

To Oliver Rogers (Brother Devananda) he remarked one day, "You have clear sailing!"

Mr. Rogers told us of an amusing occurrence in his recent work for Master. Master, as I've said earlier, gave great emphasis to the importance of positive thinking. It was his own positiveness that was partly responsible for his extraordinary productivity. By visualizing clearly the things he wanted to accomplish, he succeeded where few could have done so. Sometimes, however, his mental projections were so clear to him that their subsequent manifestation on this material plane may have struck him as a mere signature to a finished painting.

"Master asked me to paint a room," Mr. Rogers said. "One or two days later, before I'd even had time to buy the paint, I found Master in the room, conversing with Saint Lynn, both of them in a state of ecstasy. Seeing me, Master began praising me to Saint Lynn, ending with the remark, in a tone of childlike wonder, 'And he painted this whole room all by himself!' Saint Lynn looked at the unpainted walls, the ceiling, then at me. We smiled at each other, but said nothing."

Before coming to Mt. Washington, Mr. Rogers had been a professional house painter. "In heaven," Master told him, "you will be creating beautiful astral flowers by simply wishing for them."

"Sir," I said to Master one day, "after you are gone, will you be as near to us as you are now?"

"To those who *think* me near," he replied, "I will be near."

His last months passed quickly. Far *too* quickly, for in our hearts we knew that the end was approaching.

"It will be very soon, I feel," Daya Mata remarked to me one day in her office.

"But surely," I protested, "Master will return once more to India first." He was planning to go again that year, and had mentioned to me how sad the Indian disciples were that he had missed going there the last two years.

"Do you think so?" Gazing at me deeply, she said nothing more. Her presentiment, however, proved accurate.

One day Master visited an antique shop to purchase a few canes. In whatever he did, he assumed the consciousness appropriate to that activity. Now, therefore, since he was conducting business, he bargained carefully. But once the transaction was over he ceased playing the role of the conscientious buyer saving money for his monastery. Gazing about him, he noticed marks of poverty in the shop. Sympathetically, then, he gave the owner much more money than he'd saved by bargaining with him.

"You are a gentleman, Sir!" exclaimed the man, deeply touched. To show his appreciation, he gave Master a particularly fine antique umbrella.

When Master returned home, he sighed, "What a poor-looking floor that man had in his shop! I think I'll buy him a new carpet."

How perfectly he manifested in his life the truth that, to the man of Christ Consciousness, all men are brothers.

The last issue of *Self-Realization Magazine* to come out during Master's lifetime contained an article titled "The Final Experience." It was the last in a series of Master's commentaries on the New Testament Gospels that had been running continuously for twenty years. In this issue Master expanded on the words: "And when Jesus had cried with a loud voice, he said, Father, into thy hands I commend my spirit: and having said thus, he gave up the ghost."* Surely the perfect timeliness of this article was more than a coincidence. It appeared in the March 1952 issue. Master passed away on March 7, 1952.

As a further interesting note, the writing of the account in these pages about Master's passing has coincided closely with the season of Christ's passing. Yesterday was Good Friday, 1976.

Several days before the end, another disciple posed Master a question similar to the one I'd asked him two years earlier: "Have all your disciples of this life come to you yet, Sir?"

"I am waiting for two or three more to come," Master replied.

In that week two more disciples arrived: Leland Standing (now Brother Mokshananda) and Mme. Erba-Tissot, a well-known and highly successful lawyer from Switzerland who, not long afterwards, gave up her profession to organize centers for Master's work in Europe. There was, I believe, one other who came at this time, but if so I don't recall who it was.

We had been impressed by Leland's spirit from months of correspondence with him. Master had written him at last, suggesting that he come live at Mt. Washington. Leland met Master shortly after arriving there. "You have good spirit," Master told him. "Remember, loyalty is the greatest thing."

Master had been staying at his Twenty-Nine Palms retreat. He returned to Mt. Washington on March 2nd to meet His excellency, Binay R. Sen, India's recently appointed Ambassador to the United States. On the evening of his return, he embraced each of us lovingly, and blessed us. To some he gave words of personal help, to others, encouragement to be stable in their efforts, to still others the advice to meditate more. Afterwards I got to see him briefly upstairs, alone.

Many times over the past three and a half years Master had scolded me, mostly for my slowness in understanding him perfectly, sometimes for not weighing in advance the possible consequences of my words. I knew that he often said, "I scold only those who listen, not those who don't," but in my heart there

*Luke 23:46.

lingered a certain hurt. Try as I would, I couldn't rationalize it away. For some months I had been hungering for a few words of approval from him.

Now, alone with me, he gazed into my eyes with deep love and understanding, and said, "You have pleased me very much. I want you to know that." What a burden lifted from my heart at these few, simple words!

On Tuesday, March 4th, the Ambassador and his party visited Mt. Washington. I served Master and his guests in his upstairs interview room. During their visit Mr. Ahuja, India's Consul-General in San Francisco, remarked to Master, "Ambassadors may come, and ambassadors may go. You, Paramhansaji, are India's real Ambassador to America."

Thursday evening, March 6th, Master returned from a ride in the car. He asked Clifford Frederick, who was driving, to take him behind Mt. Washington, to Rome Drive. There, gazing at the main building, he remarked quietly, "It looks like a castle, doesn't it?"

The monks had just finished their group practice of the energization exercises when Master's car entered the driveway. As we gathered around him, he touched each of us in blessing. He then spoke at length about some of the delusions devotees encounter on the path.

"Don't waste your time," he said. "No one can give you the desire for God. That is something you must cultivate yourself.

"Don't sleep a great deal. Sleep is the unconscious way of contacting God. Meditation is a state beyond sleep—superconsciousness, as opposed to subconsciousness.

"Don't spend too much time joking. I myself like to laugh, but I have my sense of humor under control. When I am serious, nobody can tempt me to laugh. Be happy and cheerful within—grave, but ever cheerful. Why waste your spiritual perceptions in useless words? When you have filled the bucket of your consciousness with the milk of peace, keep it that way; don't drive holes in it with joking and idle speech.

"Don't waste time on distractions—reading all the time and so on. If reading is instructive, of course it is good. But I tell people, 'If you read one hour, then write two hours, think three hours, and meditate all the time.' No matter how much this organization keeps me busy, I never forego my daily tryst with God."

In the basement, minutes later, Master saw a box of green coconuts that had just arrived from Abie George's brother in Florida. "Back at the car Divine Mother was trying to tell me these coconuts had come, but I didn't listen—I was talking too much!"

Master, laughing delightedly, opened a coconut and drank from it. But his enjoyment seemed to me for some reason tinged with unreality. I looked into his eyes, and saw them deep, still, utterly untouched by what he was doing. In retrospect it seems like the heartiness of one who knew he was bidding us goodbye, but didn't want us to know he was doing so.

Catching my glance, he became all at once almost grave.

"I have a big day tomorrow," he said. Walking toward the elevator, he paused at the door, then repeated, "I have a big day tomorrow. Wish me luck."

The following day, March 7th, he came downstairs to go out. He was scheduled to attend a banquet that evening at the Biltmore Hotel in honor of the Indian Ambassador. "Imagine!" he said, "I've taken a room at the Biltmore. That's where I first started in this city!"

Then again he repeated, "Wish me luck."

Master had asked me to attend the banquet with Dick Haymes, the popular singer and movie actor. Dick had recently become a disciple, and had taken Kriya initiation from me.

Years ago Master had said, "When I leave this earth, I want to go speaking of my America and my India." And in a song about India that he had written, to the tune of the popular song "My California," he paraphrased the ending of that popular version with the words, "I know when I die, in joy I will sigh for my sunny, grand old India!" Once, too, in a lecture he had stated, "A heart attack is the easiest way to die. That is how *I* choose to die." This evening, all these predictions were to prove true.

Master was scheduled to speak after the banquet. His brief talk was so sweet, so almost tender, that I think everyone present felt embraced in the gossamer net of his love. Warmly he spoke of India and America, and of their respective contributions to world peace and true human progress. He talked of their future cooperation. Finally he read his beautiful poem, "My India."

Throughout his speech I was busy recording his words, keeping my eyes on my notebook. He came to the last lines of the poem:

> Where Ganges, woods, Himalayan caves and men dream God.
> I am hallowed; my body touched that sod!

"Sod" became a long-drawn sigh. Suddenly from all sides of the room there was a shriek. I looked up.

"What is it?" I demanded of Dick Haymes, seated beside me. "What happened?"

"Master fainted," he replied.

Oh, no, Master! You wouldn't faint. You've left us. You've left us! The forgotten playwright in me cried silently, *This is too perfect a way for you to go for it to mean anything else!* I hastened to where Master lay. A look of bliss was on his face. Virginia Wright was stooped over him, trying desperately to revive him. Mr. Ahuja, the Consul-General, came over to me and put an arm around my shoulders to comfort me. (*Never, dear friend, will I forget that sweet act of kindness!*)

They brought Master's body to Mt. Washington and placed it lovingly on his bed. One by one we went in, weeping, and knelt by his bedside.

"Mother!" cried Joseph. "Oh, Mother!" Indeed, Master had been a mother to us all—ah, and how much more than a mother! Miss Lancaster glanced at me in anguish.

"How many thousands of years it took," marveled an older disciple, gazing upon him in quiet awe, "to produce such a perfect face!"

Later on, after we'd left the room, Daya Mata remained alone with Master's body. As she gazed at him, a tear formed on his left eyelid, and slowly trickled down his cheek. Lovingly she caught it with her handkerchief.

In death, as in life, he was telling his beloved disciple, and through her the rest of us, "I love you always, through endless cycles of time, unconditionally, without any desire except for *your* happiness, forever, in God!"

The banquet at the Biltmore Hotel, in honor of Binay R. Sen, India's Ambassador. In this room, a short time after this photo was taken, Master entered *mahasamadhi* (a yogi's final conscious exit from the body).

At the head table *(circled, l. to r.)* are Mr. M. R. Ahuja, Consul General of India; Ambassador Binay R. Sen; Mrs. Sen; and Master. I am seated in the center of the room.

Jesse Anderson and the picture of Sri Yukteswar he made out of colored yarn as a present for Master. Retired, and living on a small income, Mr. Anderson had financed the purchase of the yarn by gathering walnuts from the ground on the roadside, and selling them. Master was deeply touched by the gift. He had the picture hung in the hallway outside his quarters.

Sister Gyanamata, Yogananda's most advanced woman disciple.

I am presenting a box of *singharas* (an Indian savory) to Master on the occasion of the visit of India's Ambassador, B. R. Sen, and his wife to Mt. Washington, three days before Master's *mahasamadhi*.

Master in the last years of his life.

Master chanting "Om" with his hands raised, registered his thoughts in the ether. After a lecture in Beverly Hills, California, in 1949 he said: "We must go on—not only those who are here, but thousands of youths must go North, South, East and West to cover the earth with little colonies, demonstrating that simplicity of living plus high thinking lead to the greatest happiness!"

PART III

CHAPTER 39

Spiritual Organizing

"To those who *think* me near, I will be near."

How often since Paramhansa Yogananda's lips were sealed in death have we, his disciples, experienced the fulfillment of that deathless promise. Truly, his was not death at all, but *mahasamadhi,* "the great *samadhi*"—a perfected yogi's final, conscious merging in the Infinite.

One of the first proofs we received of our guru's victory over death came from Forest Lawn Memorial-Park, in Glendale, California, where the casket that contained his body was kept unsealed for twenty days pending the arrival of two disciples from India. On May 15th of that year Mr. Harry T. Rowe, Forest Lawn's Mortuary Director, sent Self-Realization Fellowship a notarized letter:

"The absence of any visual signs of decay in the dead body of Paramhansa Yogananda offers the most extraordinary case in our experience. . . . No physical disintegration was visible. . . . This state of perfect preservation of a body is, so far as we know from mortuary annals, an unparalleled one. . . . The appearance of Yogananda on March 27th, just before the bronze cover of the casket was put into position, was the same as it had been on March 7th. He looked on March 27th as fresh and as unravaged by decay as he had looked on the night of his death."

The casket was closed after twenty days, when word came that the two Indian disciples would be unable to make the journey. Later one of them reported that Master, after his *mahasamadhi,* had appeared to him in his physical form and embraced him lovingly.

Norman had a similar experience. "I was lying in bed one night," he told me, "when the door suddenly flew open. Master walked in, just as plain and as solid as I see you now. He gave me a few strong words of advice, then left. The door, which he never touched, closed behind him."

Daya Mata tells of how Master appeared to her in his physical form—years, I believe, after his *mahasamadhi*—when once she faced a serious decision in the work. "I touched his feet," she says. "They were as solid as my own. Though he said nothing, I understood his meaning as clearly as though he'd spoken."

I have told earlier the story of Master's appearance also, and warning, to Professor Novicky in Prague, Czechoslovakia, when a communist informer tried to get him to betray his interest in yoga.

Most of us were, for a time, grief-stricken at Master's passing. But Mrs. Royston told me of going one day with a few of the nuns to his crypt at Forest Lawn. "The others were standing in front of the crypt," she said, "weeping. But I didn't at all feel we'd lost him. I called to him silently. Suddenly I knew he was standing beside me. I felt rather than saw him, but I heard him quite distinctly. 'I'm not in *there!*' he exclaimed. It seemed to surprise him that disciples, schooled in his teachings, should be devoting so much attention to his mere body!"

One disciple, disconsolate for weeks after Master's passing, received a telephone call one day from Rajarsi Janakananda in Encinitas.

"I didn't realize you were suffering," he told her, gently. "Master appeared to me last night and asked me to comfort you. He said to tell you that you *must* be happy; he is always with you."

Disciples naturally felt hesitant to report such experiences, uniquely precious as they were. Master warned that to talk of deep blessings might dissipate them. That a few devotees have shared these experiences with others must be attributed to their special generosity, but it would not surprise me if Master had visited many others.

I myself have not, to date, been blessed with Master's physical manifestation since his *mahasamadhi,* but increasingly through the years he has made his presence known to me. Often, after praying to him, I have received clear answers to difficult problems. Many times, too, guidance has come from him in my work; inspiration in teaching and counseling others; strength in meeting difficult tests; consolation and understanding during periods of sorrow; sudden healing in times of illness; and, above all, increasing inner joy while meditating on him.

Master's blessings and protection have become a reality for many also who never knew him, physically. A recent example springs to mind: a lady in northern California who had studied with me, and who subsequently accepted Master as her guru. Unfortunately, her husband, as sometimes happens, became intensely jealous of her new interests. One evening, when they were out for a drive, he began berating her angrily.

"It was a miserable ride," she later confided to me. "After Jim had been shouting at me for some time, he began insulting Master. This, I felt, was just too much. 'Master,' I prayed, 'make him be still!'

"Suddenly: complete silence! For the rest of that ride—in fact, for the rest of the evening—Jim behaved toward me with unusual respect, but he uttered not another word!"

During the weeks following Master's passing, the thought uppermost in our minds was, "How, from now on, can we please him best?" None of us, I'm sure, doubted that he was fully conscious of us, and as capable of helping us spiritually as ever. Paramount in our thoughts were his general commandments to us, to meditate deeply and regularly, to love and respect one another, and to cooperate harmoniously in spreading his teachings. For those of us to whom he had added other, more personal instructions, it became more important than ever to meditate on them, and apply them.

For years thereafter I continued to write down everything I could recall his saying, both to me and to others. Reliving each scene again and again in my mind, I drew from it what lessons I could for my own, and others', spiritual development. The time came when people rarely asked me a question about his teachings, or about life and truth in general, that I wasn't able to answer instantly from something he himself had said or done. The more I pondered his life and teachings, the more I marveled to see how perfectly they responded to the needs of this age. Only the Cosmic Dramatist Himself, it seemed to me, could have designed such a role. In his teachings Yogananda had touched on every important aspect of modern life—from marriage, friendship, and human relations in general to secrets of fulfillment and success, schooling, business practices, artistic expression, politics, economics, formal religion, science, health and hygiene, diet: the entire gamut—and had shown how to spiritualize each aspect and make it a stepping stone to cosmic awareness. His was by no means a one-sided teaching, directed only toward inspiring people to meditate and pray. He himself often said that religious teaching should help man on all levels: physical, mental, and spiritual. While never sacrificing his own vision of the highest Truth, he also addressed himself to where people actually were in their personal development, with a view to helping them move forward from their present state toward life's divine and ultimate goal.

I had come to Master with a keen longing not only to find God myself, but to help others to resolve their spiritual doubts, and thereby to feel inspired to seek Him. For people feel impelled to serve others according to the ways in which they themselves erred in the past, and suffered, and learned from their suffering important lessons. Those, in other words, whose desire is to help others to find good health suffered in their own health in the past, and learned the importance of living in accordance with physical laws. Those whose desire is to help others on a mental level suffered mentally in the past. Those who feel a desire to work for the prevention of crime quite possibly erred against society's laws in the past. And in my case, Master told me, my greatest past error was doubt. This explains why, in the present life, I have always longed to help others to resolve doubt, and acquire faith.

It was towards the fulfillment of this deep-seated desire that Master directed all my own training. "No more moods, now," he said, "otherwise, how will you be able to help people?" Even when I balked at teaching publicly, he insisted that this was my calling. "You'd better learn to like it," he replied. "That is what you will have to do."

By contrast, he spoke little to me about organizing the work, except where the monks were concerned, and actually seemed willing at one point to consider my replacement in that job, when, because I was experiencing temporary ill health, I suggested to him that he give it to someone else. But he never showed such willingness with respect to my occasional pleas not to be left in the ministry. The only consolation he threw me, when one day I expressed fear of the delusions attendant upon a public life, was to promise me solemnly, "You will *never* fall because of ego."

The energy at Mt. Washington after his *mahasamadhi,* however, was centered mainly in organizing his work. "After I am gone," he had told the disciples, "you all must work very hard to organize the work. Otherwise you won't be able to handle the thousands who will be coming to you." For some years I joined this trend, partly just because it *was* the trend, and partly because, whatever my actual karmic duties in this life, I discovered in myself a certain flair for organizing. My deepest interest remained what it had always been: to help people. But I considered myself insufficiently trained, as yet, to offer writing and lecturing as a serious service to others, and told myself that if for now I could help coordinate various functions of our work, those who joined the work later would be better served. Thus it befell that, from a background of almost fervent opposition to institutionalism, I found myself, in the present institutional context, almost as fervently devoted to developing Self-Realization Fellowship as an instrument of divine service.

Shortly after Master's *mahasamadhi,* I spent two weeks in seclusion at Twenty-Nine Palms. There I prayed deeply to Master to direct me in my service to him. Should I, I asked him, concentrate right away on writing and lecturing? "Not yet," was the reply as I understood it. But what, then, was I to do? I felt too much enthusiasm for serving him to sit quietly on the sidelines, preparing myself for writing and lecturing as my eventual work.

And then it was that, indirectly, the answer came. Accompanying me on this retreat was Andrew Selz, a brother monk. Toward the end of our stay there, we began discussing the need in the Mt. Washington office for simplifying the procedures, particularly with a view to serving our members better. An office job we shared was letter writing. Our special concern, therefore, was to shorten the time it took for letters to reach the letter-writers' desks. Ideas for streamlining procedures soon began flooding our minds. In the very inspiration we felt I recognized Master's answer to my prayer those two weeks for guidance. Soon Andy and I were formulating plans for reorganizing the entire office.

On our return to Mt. Washington, we proposed the changes we had worked out. There were a few old-timers who objected, perhaps not surprisingly, but Rajarsi Janakananda, our new president, gave us his stamp of approval. Soon Andy and I were deep in reorganization. The task, which I had expected would take about two weeks, took a year and a half! By the end of this long time I was thoroughly inured to the idea of organizing. I completed my organization of the monks, then went on to organize the SRF centers, the center department, the churches, and the lay-disciple order.

My center activities came about as an extension of my work of organizing the monks. Something Master had often told me was that he wanted the monks and nuns to live in separate communities after his death. My concern, when contemplating the mechanics of such a separation, was to ensure an equable division of responsibility for the work in the years to come. Meditating on this problem, and trying to tune in to the "blueprint" for the work, which, Master told us, was "in the ether," I received what I believed was the right solution: to place membership activities under the nuns, who ran the main office at Mt. Washington; and center and church activities under the monks, whom Master had designated particularly for the ministry. I proposed also that the centers be made less the "fiefdoms" of individual leaders by designating *two*

speakers instead of one at Sunday services, and by naming them
"service leaders," rather than, as they had been known until then,
"center leaders." For the services themselves, I suggested the inclusion of a story from *Autobiography of a Yogi,* and a sermon outline
which the first service leader might use as a basis for his talk, with
proposed, but not obligatory, readings from Master's books. The
purpose of all these suggestions was to make sure our centers were
truly representative of Master's work. Realizing, however, that
there were also many members who preferred to meet informally,
I recommended a new designation as well: informal Meditation
Groups. These groups would be at liberty to adopt as little, or as
much, of our center program as they chose. Our interest would be
to serve and inspire them, not to direct.

These proposals also were agreed to by Rajarsi Janakananda and
the Board. The job of implementing the proposals was given to
me.

From this point, a natural next step for me was the development
of a lay-disciple order in the churches. By this time, I had become
generally regarded as Self-Realization Fellowship's "compleat organizer." Considering my own deep-seated aversion to institutionalism, it was ironic. But the logic of our position demanded these
steps. I consoled myself that this aversion of mine, which I think
most of the disciples shared, constituted at least a natural safeguard
against organizing excesses. My own motives remained unchanged:
I saw these activities not as ends in themselves, but as means to
uplifting people, starved as they were for inner joy. The logic of
our position, as I say, dictated the need for uniformity in certain of
the aspects of our work, but I saw no particular virtue in uniformity itself. The whole point, where center activities were concerned, was simply to ensure that our centers didn't *mis*represent
us. It was a fine line to walk. Too many rules would engage
people's attention too much outwardly, and cause them to lose
sight of what Master's teachings were all about: personal, *inner,*
spiritual development. "Don't make too many rules," Master had
told me, "or you'll destroy the spirit." It was important to balance
even the need for rules that were sensible in themselves against the
equally great need, in the centers, for a certain spontaneity and joy.
The alternative would be a preoccupation with externals, and the
attendant evils of such preoccupation: gossip, suspicion, and the
desire for personal power.

I say these things partly because almost everyone at one time or
another finds himself caught between an institution's need for uniformity, and his own need for inward development. People on

either side of this issue would do well to recognize the inherent validity of the other side, for only by such recognition can a necessary balance be achieved, avoiding the twin pitfalls of ossification
and chaos.

As a matter of fact, I myself was forced, finally, to concede that,
while it is important for the workers in any organization to defer
to the organization's directives, it is not a sound policy to try to
ensure such deference by discouraging leadership ability in the
organization's representatives. I tried for some years to establish
safeguards against what I viewed as individual "fiefdoms," only to
recognize at last that in every successful center there was always
someone whose spirit it reflected, someone on the scene, someone,
usually, acting in a capacity of leadership. To discourage such personal influence in the name of down-grading "personality," as the
communists do in their monolithic system, was, I discovered, simply to fly in the face of reality. I observed, for instance, our center
in Oakland, California, which, when Kamala was its minister, was
perhaps the most spiritually inspiring of all our centers, filled with
a spirit of devotion, humility, and love. But in 1956 poor health
forced Kamala to resign from all center activities. She invited me to
develop the center along our new organizational lines. I did so
with full enthusiasm, viewing this as a test case. Despite my best
efforts, however, I was forced at last to admit that the real spirit of
the center was no longer there. Leadership, I gradually came to
realize, is vital to the success of any group. Like every other human quality, of course, it has its pitfalls. A leader might, for example, feel tempted to assert his independence by disobeying the
parent body he serves. But this is simply a risk that must be
taken—both by him, and by the parent body. A tree must drop
many seeds to produce a few saplings. As Jesus put it, "Many are
called, but few are chosen." Yogananda never shielded his disciples
from the tests they needed for their own spiritual growth. Though
many center leaders failed him, he continued to recognize and foster leadership as that rare human quality, *the willingness to bear responsibility,* without which no venture can truly succeed. Where a
person shows promise of doing well, more actual, positive control
may be exercised over him by encouraging him to do his best than
by discouraging him from doing his worst.

But Master, shortly before his *mahasamadhi,* gave us the ultimate
secret of spiritual organizing. Daya Mata had asked him, sadly,
"Master, when you are gone, what can ever replace you?"

"When I am gone," he replied, smiling tenderly, "only love can
take my place."

In August 1952, during our annual convocation, we had an India Fair at Mt. Washington. I dressed up for the occasion as a Hindu storyteller, and sat in the Temple of Leaves telling stories from the Indian Scriptures.

Here, I am conducting a service in Hollywood Church.

The Jaganath Temple in Puri, Orissa, one of the most sacred temples of the Hindus. We were among the first Westerners ever allowed to enter the temple.

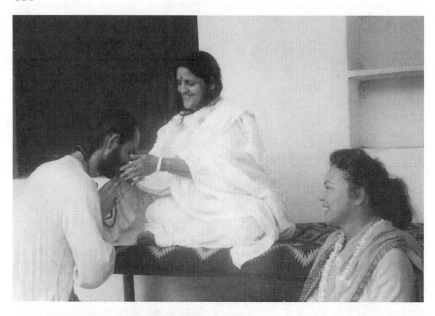

Daya Mata and I on a visit to the great Indian saint, Sri Ananda Moyi Ma, at her ashram in Benares. Ananda Moyi Ma has just given me a *rudraksha mala,* or garland of prayer beads, which I still use in my meditations.

An outdoor class at Master's school in Ranchi, Bihar, India. He believed that education should take place as much as possible in a natural setting.

I stand with Sri Rama Yogi, a great disciple of Sri Ramana Maharshi. Of Sri Rama Yogi Master said, "If I had spent another half hour in his company, I could never have brought myself to leave India again." I stayed four days with Sri Rama Yogi at his ashram outside the city of Nellore, in South India.

420

I spent the month of February 1962 in seclusion in this Himalayan cave on the River Ganges.

A painting of Lahiri Mahasaya before his meeting with Babaji in 1860, done from the photograph shown at the lower right. I discovered them at the Benares home of Sri Satya Charan Lahiri, the great master's grandson. Included here *(insert upper right)* are Lahiri Mahasaya's sandals and his copy of the *Bhagavad Gita.* The long bundle is a printing on bark of *Sri Chandi,* an ancient scripture devoted to God in the aspect of Divine Mother.

The monks welcome me back to Mt. Washington on my return there from India in April, 1960. *(front row, l. to r.)* Leland Standing, Henry Schaufelberger, and Rev. Michael (now Brothers Mokshananda, Anandamoy, and Bhaktananda respectively).

Taken in the courtyard of the home of Dewan Balkishen Khosla, in Patiala, Punjab, where I was a guest. I gave a series of lectures and classes in Patiala in November 1959.

Lord Krishna

An artist's conception of the great Hindu *avatar*. Lord Krishna is often depicted in legend as a youth playing his flute by the banks of the River Jumna, calling his playmates away from worldly pursuits to the divine search within.

Another photograph of me taken in Patiala, 1959.

CHAPTER 40

"Feed My Sheep"

NINETEEN FIFTY-FIVE WAS AN important year for Self-Realization
Fellowship. In February, Rajarsi Janakananda died. The Board
of Directors elected Daya Mata to replace him, making her the
third SRF president. Her activities prior to that time had been
more or less behind the scenes. We who knew her, however, and
who knew the high esteem in which Master held her, hailed the
choice as the best possible one.

Nineteen fifty-five was an important year also for me, personally.
In May and June I went on a lecture tour to SRF centers in
America, Canada, and Europe. Shortly after my return to Mt.
Washington, I was appointed the main minister of our Hollywood
church. And on August 20th, three other monks and I took our
final vows of renunciation in solemn ceremony, receiving *sannyas,*
or ordination into full monkhood, from Daya Mata. On that occasion we symbolically cremated our bodies in sacrificial flames, to
signify that we looked upon ourselves thenceforth as dead to the
world, and alive only in God.

*Sannyasi*s (those who embrace *sannyas*) usually belong to the
Swami order of monkhood, which Swami Shankara—or, as he is
also known, Swami Shankaracharya—established many centuries
ago in India. There are ten subdivisions of Shankaracharya swamis
in India. Ours is the *Giri,* or "mountain," branch. Acceptance into
the monastic order of Self-Realization Fellowship entails acceptance
also into the Giri order of swamis. Thus my *full* name and title
became, properly speaking, Swami Kriyananda Giri.

The *sannyasi* schools himself to view the world and everything in it
as a dream. Seeing God as the Sole Reality, he seeks to live his life
by the divine will alone, without any personal attachment or desire.

Traditionally excluded from initiation into the Swami order were
non-brahmins (that is, those born outside the priestly caste of
Hindus), foreigners, and women. Great masters in this age, however,

have broadened the tradition as it applied to non-brahmins and foreigners, and discarded it altogether as it applied to women.

As regards the former, they have pointed out that caste was not originally intended as a hereditary system. Rather, it constituted a simple recognition of universal realities of human nature. The whole human race, Yogananda explained, consists of four natural castes, known in India as *sudras, vaisyas, kshatriyas,* and *brahmins. Sudras* are those who live uncreatively, on a purely physical plane. *Vaisyas* live more *creatively,* but for personal gain. *Kshatriyas* devote their energies primarily to society. And *brahmins* are those whose interests are essentially spiritual. Obviously, those only whose nature places them in this fourth category are fit for *sannyas,* the definition of which is a life lived for God alone, and for the spiritual upliftment of others. Nationality is not a consideration here. India's millenniums-old adoption of the caste system constituted a recognition, merely, of universal stages in human evolution.

The barring of women from taking *sannyas,* on the other hand, has no basis in the eternal truths propounded by India's Scriptures. In no age have women been denied the highest spiritual attainments. Their non-acceptance into the Swami order was based on purely transitory, sociological considerations. Greater social freedom in the present age has encouraged increasing numbers of women to enter ashrams, and to embrace *sannyas.* Their admission into the Swami order has been fully endorsed by several of the greatest masters of our age.

During the course of a *sannyas* initiation ceremony in Puri, Orissa, on May 27th, 1959, Swami Bharati Krishna Tirth, the then-presiding Shankaracharya of Gowardhan Math, and the recognized leader of all the Shankaracharya swamis in India, formally redefined those ancient traditions by recognizing Daya Mata's initiation into the Swami order by Paramhansa Yogananda.

Kriyananda, the name I took on the occasion of my own ordination, derives from two Sanskrit words and means "divine bliss through Kriya Yoga," or, alternately, "divine bliss in action." Rev. Michael, Joe Carbone, and Carl Swenson also took their vows with me on this occasion, receiving respectively the names Bhaktananda, Bimalananda, and Sarolananda.

In my heart that day I pledged my life more earnestly than ever to Master's service.

As the minister-in-charge now at our principal church, I realized that the time had come for me at last to take lecturing seriously, according to Master's instructions. The truth is, I hadn't seriously believed, heretofore, that I could do much good through the medium of mere words. But now I decided at least to try, and prayed deeply to my guru to inspire me to help others. Interestingly, it wasn't long before his blessings began to take effect.

It is curious. We naturally tend to think, if we believe in divine guidance at all, that God alone can decide how He will operate in our lives. But the truth is, His grace flows through whatever channels *we ourselves* open up to Him. We may want with all our hearts to do His will, but the principle of free will is part of His law. He guides us, therefore, according to the *kind* of inspiration we ask of Him. One might say that it is the magnetic quality of our interest that *draws* His response. If, for example, we write music, the inspiration we receive will be in terms of music. If we are immersed in religious organizing, the guidance we attract will be related to organizing. And if we seek divine assistance as lecturers, the inspirations God gives us will be for how to lecture well.

Thus it was that, during my years of organizing, most of the guidance I received related to organizing. Consequently, I kept feeling I wasn't yet ready to get into lecturing seriously. But when outward necessity forced me to concentrate more on public speaking, I began receiving guidance primarily as a speaker. People now began telling me that something I had said in a lecture had changed their lives, or answered some long-standing doubt, or awakened love for God in their hearts for the first time.

More was involved here, however, than guidance. For organizing hadn't actually been God's long-range will for me. Now that I was doing more specifically what Master had asked of me, I felt a growing sense of inner fulfillment and joy.

At first I approached public speaking with an attitude developed over years of organizing activities. That is to say, though a minister, I spoke more as one representing my church than as one deeply concerned for the people I was serving. But I soon discovered that, just as organizational activity has its own logic, so also do teaching and counseling. For a minister, it is important to give the highest priority to people's needs. Only by attuning oneself to them may one hope to reach them.

I was aware that, in my evolving understanding of the ministry, I was not treading any well-paved highway. Most of the ministers I'd met seemed to view themselves rather as spokesmen for their churches than as ministers to hungry souls. They reverted hastily to monologue, whenever dialogue looked threatening. I myself, as an SRF minister, had a tendency to begin with to let Master's teachings speak for themselves, rather than apply those truths creatively to my specific listeners.

Sincerity in the ministry came to mean to me, above all, sincerity to the people I was serving. If, I thought, a minister's duty were to answer every question with a dogma, he might as well record whatever he has to say and ask his secretary to play the appropriate tape. But one who sincerely wants to help people cannot but discover in time, because he *listens* to them, that the guises truth wears are many. His aim then becomes, not to bind people to his church and make "dyed-in-the-wool" believers of them, *but to awaken in them a sense of the divine truth within themselves.* As Paramhansa Yogananda put it, "Our only goal is to 'dye people in the wool' of their own Kriya Yoga practice." —

Often Master told us, "Self-Realization Fellowship is not a sect." As long as my own focus was on organizing, his statement seemed less relevant to me. But it assumed vital significance once I began serving the public. For as I attuned myself to the true task of the ministry, I understood that such service, to be effective, must be centered in truth itself; it must be free of any hidden, sectarian motive.

Sometimes I would actually recommend to someone that he join some other spiritual work. In India once during a question-and-answer period after a public lecture, I urged a listener to spend his weekends at a nearby Sri Aurobindo Ashram. Afterwards this man approached me and asked, "How did you know that I'm a member of that ashram?" I *hadn't* known, actually, but something about him had brought that society to mind as being on his spiritual "wavelength." Probably this particular degree of nonsectarianism will not be found in any textbook for the ministry! Because I placed people's own, actual needs ahead of normal institutional considerations, however, thousands, satisfied that I wanted only to share with them truths I myself deeply believed in, joined our work as a result of my lectures and classes.

I first went to India in 1958. There, virtually for the first time, I found myself lecturing to audiences consisting mostly of people who were unfamiliar with our work. It was a priceless opportunity to learn how to apply Master's teachings creatively.

In the autumn of 1959 I was invited to address the student body of a men's college in Simla, a hill station in the Himalayas, at the end of their school day. I set out on foot. Misjudging the distance, however, I arrived twenty minutes late. The student-body president, on whose recommendation I'd been invited to speak, met me apprehensively on the street below the hilltop campus.

"I don't know how they're going to receive you, Swamiji. The problem isn't only that you've arrived late. It's that we have just concluded a protest rally against China's latest incursions onto

Indian soil. We ended by signing a petition to the Government *in blood!*" He paused, cocking an ear up the hill. "Just listen to them!"

From the hilltop, sounds of angry tumult were distinctly audible: hundreds of voices raised in a hum of protest, hundreds of feet stamping impatiently on the hall floor.

"Swamiji," my host pleaded, "please allow me to cancel the talk."

"But I can't do that," I remonstrated. "It would mean breaking my word to them."

"I'm only afraid they may mistreat you!"

Climbing the hill, I hoped for the best. During the principal's subsequent, and somewhat nervous, introduction of me, I noticed students glancing meaningly at the door. Obviously, the circumstances were anything but ideal for a lecture on the benefits of meditation!

Instead, therefore, I launched into a vigorous dissertation on the subject uppermost in their minds: China's incursions. I restated their own case to them, perhaps better than they had heard it stated that day. As I spoke, I sensed a flicker of interest, and then mounting approval. Gradually, once I felt their support, I introduced the suggestion that warfare, hatred, and other kinds of disharmony in society are due primarily to disharmony in man himself. Even we, I suggested, who perhaps hated no one, might yet feel that we hadn't as much inner peace as we'd like. The first thing, then, if we would bring peace to others, was to change, not *them,* but *ourselves.*

By this time the students were eager to hear more. I went on to speak about yoga and meditation. At the end of my talk they plied me with questions. Many wanted to know how they could study yoga. At last the principal pleaded with them repeatedly to stop questioning me, as the last buses would shortly be leaving Simla for their villages.

In India, by psychically "listening" to my audiences as I lectured to them, and reflecting the truth back to them as their own higher natures understood it, I learned how to reach people on many levels of spiritual unfoldment and get them to take up meditation. After a lecture at Mahindra College, Patiala, in 1959, the professors told me that never in the history of their college had so much interest been awakened by a speaker. Response to my talks and classes in the auditorium of the public library of Patiala was, people said, "unprecedented" for that city. A few weeks later, in New Delhi, thousands enrolled in my yoga classes. I became known in northern India as the "American yogi."

I had entered the ministry reluctantly. Now, however, the more willingly I served God through people in this capacity, the more clearly I experienced His blessings in everything I attempted.

Before the first of my class series in New Delhi, I invited our local members to my hotel room to discuss plans. There weren't many of them. They came cautiously, sat cautiously, and cautiously suggested we engage a small school room where I might address them and their families, and perhaps a few friends. But I felt that Master wanted me to make his message known to thousands.

"Let us rent a large tent," I said.

"A large . . . tent?" They gulped apprehensively. "For how many?"

"About eighteen hundred," I replied. The look in their eyes implied that I'd taken complete leave of my senses. But at last they gave in. The tent was set up on a large, empty lot in Main Vinay Nagar, an outlying district of New Delhi.

The day of my introductory lecture, I was meditating in a nearby home. At four o'clock, the announced time of the lecture, a member came over to fetch me.

"It's a good crowd, Swamiji," he announced dolefully. "About a hundred people."

A hundred people—in a tent large enough to hold eighteen hundred! Later I was told that one member, of somewhat timid disposition, had already begun pacing up and down outside the tent, moaning, "Our reputation will be ruined!"

"Master," I prayed, laughing inwardly, "I had the feeling we'd get at least eighteen hundred people. That wasn't my *desire*. If no one had come, it would have been the same to me." But then, recalling people's tendency to be late, I said, "Let us wait a bit."

Seven minutes later the man returned. "There are two hundred there now, Swamiji. Hadn't we better start?"

"Not yet," I replied. He left, wringing his hands.

At four-fifteen, smiling with relief, he returned. "About six hundred people are there now. Shall we begin?"

I rose to my feet. During the brief time it took us to reach the tent, crowds more arrived. By the time I'd reached the dais, the tent was full to overflowing. Two thousand people heard me that day. Most of them later enrolled for the classes.

At the end of my lecture, I announced, "For this week of classes, it would be easier, for those who might want private interviews with me, if I were housed nearby. Would anyone here like to invite me to stay in his home?" Afterwards fifty or more people approached me to invite me. Dismayed, I realized I'd have to refuse all of them but one. "Master," I prayed, "whose offer should I accept?" Then all at once, seeing one man, I was attracted by the look in his eyes. "I'll stay with you," I said.

Later Sri Romesh Dutt, my host for that week, confided to me, "I read Paramhansaji's *Autobiography of a Yogi* years ago, and wanted very much to receive Kriya Yoga initiation. But I didn't know where to get it. At last I read in the newspaper about your recent lectures in Patiala, a hundred miles away. I decided to request time off from my office and go there to seek initiation from you. But my wife said to me, 'Why go all that distance? If you have faith, Swamiji will come to New Delhi and give initiation here. Not only that, *he will stay in our own home!*' Truly, Swamiji, your visit in this humble dwelling of ours is an extraordinary proof of God's grace to us!"

Lecturing and speaking to people around India, I gradually came to understand how I might also carry out Master's other instructions: to write. For years I had puzzled over what I could say in writing that would approach even remotely his depth of philosophical and spiritual insight. My usefulness, whether as teacher or writer, was to acquaint people with *his* message. *He* was the master. I was only his instrument.

Yet he had told me, "*Much* yet remains to be written." To what, I wondered, had he been referring? After two or three years in India, it occurred to me that I might be able to "reach out," through writing, in the same way that I had been reaching out to people in my lectures, by "listening" psychically, as it were, to their needs. I could show them how even the worldly fulfillments they were seeking could be achieved, in the fullest sense, only by including spiritual values in their lives. Master himself, I reflected, had touched on numerous fields of human interest. Perhaps I could expand on what, from him, had often amounted to no more than a hint. Taking his teachings, metaphorically, as the hub of a wheel, I would try to show that many spokes led inward to that same hub.

One of the principal goads to my own spiritual search had been the spreading evil, in our times, of nihilism. Many people, after exposure to the teachings of modern science, found it difficult to accept any moral and spiritual values. Idealism they discarded as "sentimental." Of the college-trained intellectuals that I encountered, even in spiritual India, many insisted that truth is only relative, that no higher law exists, that the best justification for any act is the ability to get away with it. A number of these people, unable to abandon their moral sense altogether, embraced communism, with its materialistic moralism, simply because it at least makes a show of believing in *something*. And all too often, especially in the West, the educated people I met who accepted spiritual values found themselves unable to counter the challenges of modern science, and therefore swept those challenges under the carpet rather than acknowledge their existence. Their beliefs, while constructive, seemed to me to lack a certain intellectual integrity.

Trained as I was in Master's teachings, and familiar with the clear insights they offered to the confused thinking of our age, I longed to help people to find an *honest* basis for spiritual faith.

By no means all of my time, during the nearly four years I spent in India, was devoted to lecturing. Much of it was given to organizational work for our society. Among other things, I reorganized our lessons, which went out twice monthly from our Indian headquarters. By placing techniques and fundamental yoga teachings earlier in the series, and offering them first in large doses, I tried to make the lessons more responsive to the expectations of new students. I also wrote a set of rules and guidelines for our Indian monastic order, and performed numerous assignments for Daya Mata.

Among my happiest memories of those years are the frequent opportunities I got for visiting living saints, some of whom were well known, and others whose names, though little known in the world, must surely be written in shining letters in the Book of Life. I've already mentioned my four-day visit to Sri Rama Yogi, the highly advanced disciple of Ramana Maharshi. Another great saint with whom I got to spend considerably more time was Ananda Moyi Ma, the "Joy-Permeated Mother" whom Paramhansa Yogananda described lovingly in his autobiography. Memories of weeks passed in her sacred company are among the most precious of my life; to me she seems veritably an incarnation of the Divine Mother. I also met Sitaramdas Omkarnath and Mohanananda Brahmachari, two devotional saints of Bengal; Sanyal Mahasaya, the last-surviving disciple of Lahiri Mahasaya; Deoahara Baba, 140 years old at that time, but possessing the body of a man of forty; Neemkaroli Baba, the well-known guru of the American devotee, Ram Dass; Swami Sivananda, whose saintly disciples—Swamis Chidananda, Satchidananda, Venkatesananda, Sahajananda, Vishnudevananda, and others—have done much in recent years to make India's teachings known in the West; Swami Purushottamananda, a blissful hermit near whose Himalayan cave, "Vashishta Guha," on the River Ganges I spent four weeks in seclusion; His Holiness the Dalai Lama of Tibet; His Holiness, Bharati Krishna Tirth, the Shankaracharya of Gowardhan Math, whom I had met previously in America; His Holiness the Shankaracharya of Kanchipuram; and others.

Something that touched me deeply was the extraordinary regard many of those saints showed for my beloved guru. The Shankaracharya of Kanchipuram told me, "I met your guru in Calcutta in 1935. I have been following his activities in America ever since. As a bright light shining in the midst of darkness, so was Yogananda's presence in this world. Such a great soul comes on earth only rarely, when there is a real need among men."

One thing that impressed me deeply about India was the intensely individual nature of religious worship there. Several of the saints I met were unabashedly, one might almost say gloriously, eccentric—as though wanting to challenge people to live for God alone, and not merely to please mankind. How much fresher and more vital, their deeply individual approach to devotion, than the rigid formats of congregational worship! When a religion tries to ensure the preservation of its sanctity by generalizing its standards of outward comportment, it loses responsiveness to the needs of individuals, endlessly varied as they are. Thereby losing elasticity, it becomes moribund.

In May 1960, during a six-month visit to America, the SRF Board of Directors unanimously elected me as a member of the Board, and as the vice-president of Self-Realization Fellowship. After my return to India later that year, I was elected to the same positions in our sister organization, Yogoda Satsanga Society of India.

My new position in the organization, albeit a high honor, heightened also a conflict that had been stirring within me for some years: How to reconcile my organizing activities with my role, which Master had assigned me, as teacher, lecturer, and writer? Most of my co-workers, who seldom if ever attended my public lectures, saw me primarily as an organizer and tried to involve me further in organizational activities. Sri B.N. Dubey (later he was given the name Swami Shyamananda), the secretary of our work in India, wanted me to accept the position of office manager at our Dakshineswar headquarters. (The headquarters was subsequently relocated to Ranchi.)

"Why, it would take me twenty years," I exclaimed, "just to see the light of day again!"

"Quite right," he replied matter-of-factly.

I knew that Master didn't want me in office work any longer.

"Your work," he had told me, "is writing, editing, and lecturing." How to persuade others, however, that these were his wishes? The impetus I'd established over years of organizational activities made it difficult even for me to redirect my energies, what to speak of redirecting other people's expectations of me.

There are tides in the more-or-less predictable flow of all lives that draw us, drive us, or sometimes heave us into situations for which we consider ourselves ill prepared, and which may leave us convinced that we are the victims of an evil fortune. Then, with the passage of time—months, perhaps, even years—we come to realize that what happened was not only inevitable, but divinely right for us—perhaps even a source of extraordinary blessings.

In retrospect, I see that it was such a karmic tide that entered my life at this time and swept me along with it. I found myself at a crossroads. My dilemma was brought into focus by the realization that what the world needed from these teachings was not a smoothly run organization, but a dynamic, joyful, compassionate outreach. We needed to reach people where *they* were, and not only to serve efficiently the few who came to us.

It wasn't that I didn't see also the need for an organization that functioned with a semblance, at least, of efficiency. Master, however, had often told us (quoting his guru, Sri Yukteswar), "Organization is the hive; God is the honey." I was inwardly certain that what my Guru wanted of me now was that I concentrate on bringing the "honey" of his teachings to truth-hungry souls, and to work less on perfecting the hive.

Master's example in this respect was an encouragement. He, too, had sought by various means to improve the spiritual "atmosphere" in the West: for example, through schools and colleges, through "world brotherhood colonies," and by showing people in all walks of life the sheer common sense of living spiritually. Much spade work was needed, he realized, before India's teachings could win wide acceptance in the West.

The guidance I felt from him with growing insistency was to devote myself to furthering this aspect of his work: through the medium of ideas—especially of books and lectures—to help cultivate the spiritual "soil" of our times, so as to make it more receptive to the liberating message of inner, divine communion and Kriya Yoga.

Given this direction, how was I ever to get my books published, after I'd written them? And how, for that matter, was I to justify to co-workers my need for the time to write them? Our editorial department would, I was perfectly certain, take a jaundiced view of any such activity; it was inconceivable that they would publish the kind of books I had in mind. The main editor had quite enough on her hands as it was, getting out Master's books.

Yet when I had asked Master, "Hasn't everything been said already in *your* books?" (in response to his statement that my life work would include writing), he replied almost as if taken aback by the narrowness of my vision, "Don't say that! *Much* more is needed."

The crossroads at which I found myself amounted to a conflict of premises: the one, that the organization was the priority, to which people must adjust if they would receive what it had to give them; the other, that people and their spiritual needs were the priority, to which the organization must work constantly to be responsive. It was assumed for me that my direction lay primarily in organizational activities. My own assumptions in that regard, however, were changing. It wasn't so much that I disagreed with anyone as that a deep urgency within me—inspired, as I still believe, by my Guru—insisted on making people's individual spiritual needs my priority.

How the conflict developed is a story I prefer not to go into. Conflicts are always best left to third parties to describe.

To shorten the proverbial long story, destiny intervened. Nothing I did or could possibly have done would have changed the outcome. I myself had been feeling deep within me that some sort of change had to happen, though I could never, in my conscious mind, have anticipated or accepted what actually did happen.

The accusation was made that, in my desire to reach out and help people, *en masse* and individually, I was seeking personal power. I did my best, thereafter, to "toe the line," and would, I believe, have continued to do my best all my life, whatever the frustrations involved, to adjust what I deeply felt to be the needs of the work to what others expected of me. For my first priority had nothing to do with any work that I might do during this brief lifespan on earth. That priority was, as it had always been, to find God. And to find Him, my basic assumption was that my spiritual development depended on serving Master *within* the framework of his organization. My "ulterior motive," if one may call it that, was always to please God through service to my Guru. I held strong views on loyalty, both to him and to the organization he had founded. The solution as I saw it, then, was to learn how to live with others' rejection of my convictions about the needs of the work, and at the same time to do what I could, when I could, to continue recommending those needs to my fellow disciples.

As things turned out, I was powerless to change the course of events no matter what I did. Every attempt on my part to influence the powerful currents in which I found myself struggling only worsened my predicament.

Finally, over my anguished protests, I was dismissed—cast adrift, so it seemed to me, in a rowboat on a vast ocean. This happened in July, 1962, at a meeting in New York to which I'd been summoned by cablegram from India.

Because the separation caused pain to others as well as to me, I prefer not to dwell on the attending circumstances, which in any case were but the mechanics of the matter. I understand, now, that my dismissal was a good thing.

Was it a good thing for SRF? My fellow disciples there may continue to think so.

Was it good for me? Very definitely! For, as circumstances have since proved, there were things Master had to do through me that could never have been done, had I not been out on my own.

CHAPTER 41

"He Will Be Your Strength"

T HE STORM THAT beats upon the countryside in unbridled fury, hurling rain from lowering clouds in malediction, seems the sworn enemy of earthly happiness. Yet its ultimate effect is beneficial. It rejuvenates the land. From the rainfall come healing herbs; the grasses rise to new heights; flowers emerge, smiling; forests and meadows are left fragrant and refreshed. Even the gusty winds are a blessing, for they help the wild plants to grow hardy, stronger in themselves. Their large, pampered cousins in city greenhouses cannot achieve their strength; life for them is too easy.

So is it also with the storms of misfortune that descend from time to time on human life. Aristotle defined the beneficial impact of tragedy in literature as a *catharsis*. The vicarious experience of utter loss, he said, leaves one feeling purified, lifted for a time above earthly attachments, inwardly tranquil. Similar is the case with personal tragedy. Though its effect is seldom so immediate, in the long run it leaves one feeling uplifted and at peace. But if there is attachment in the heart, the purification may be delayed—years, perhaps, even incarnations, until bitterness is resolved at last in understanding acceptance.

True happiness depends on *attitude,* not on outward circumstances. With right attitude it is possible to recover quickly even from great sorrow. The quicker the recovery, moreover, the greater the spiritual gain, for it requires an extraordinary surge of inner strength to combat suffering while the storm is still raging. Indeed, in the inner fortitude thus acquired, suffering may prove a doorway to sainthood. Thus it became in the German concentration camps, during World War II, for those heroic few who refused to surrender to the spiritual darkness surrounding them.

My own life weathered its greatest storm so far in my separation from Self-Realization Fellowship. That I even survived seemed to me, at the time, but my added misfortune. Partly I suffered because of my attachment to the work, and partly also because, although I clung as hard as possible to positive attitudes throughout, incomprehension rushed upon me repeatedly in such violent gusts that often I found myself swept away like a leaf in a hurricane. Why? I demanded—*why* this loss of everything I believed in and cared about in life? Ceaselessly I sought answers in prayer. But alas, all my answers seemed locked away in vaults of uncaring silence. Hope seemed utterly lost to me.

Ah, Master! For a time I even doubted your love for me—this perhaps worthless disciple whom you had, as I thought, completely abandoned. To listen to recordings of your voice, even to read your words, caused me almost unbearable pain. I clung mentally to your feet, and reminded you that I was yours eternally, even if you rejected me. But, I confess, in my intense loneliness I felt rejected. It was only with the passing years that I came to understand, and accept, that what had happened was for my good, and for whatever good you might be able to accomplish for others through me.

At first my predicament bewildered me utterly. I knew, of course, that God can be reached by many paths, but Master's was *my* path; I was completely committed to it. How was I to reconcile this fact with that of my severance from his work? A major part of my commitment was to serving him, yet I wondered if continued service now were even possible. As long as I had been working within his organization, the issue had been fairly clear-cut: Serving Master meant, quite simply, serving SRF. But now that I was on my own, I feared lest any attempt to serve him might in some way prove a *dis*service. My anxiety was brought sharply into focus by the fact that, next to Daya Mata, I was probably the best known of Yogananda's living disciples, particularly since it was I alone, so far, who had gone out lecturing around the world. SRF members would be upset, certainly, when they discovered that I was no longer in the work. Wouldn't it be best for the work if I were never heard from again?

Yet the fact remained that I still had *my* life to live, a life that had been pledged irrevocably to Master's service. It was unthinkable, surely, that the only way for me to serve him now was by *not* serving him!

Truth, fortunately, is never an impossibility. It is the one secure island in the vast sea of human ignorance. My error lay in limiting Master to his organization—Master, that great Guru whose consciousness was in the very air I breathed! True, he had founded an organization, and it was the appropriate and official custodian for his teachings, but this didn't mean that the rest of the world had therefore to cease functioning! How often he himself had said that he hadn't founded a sect. Those disciples who were able to function within his organization did well to do so, but what of those who could not? They were not relieved thereby of the duty to serve him according to their best lights, and to their best opportunities. As a world teacher, Paramhansa Yogananda belonged to the world. And I, as his disciple, had blessings to share of which the world stood in urgent need.

My error lay also in the fear that, by continued service to the divine cause—a cause which ever embraces harmony—I might create disharmony. How could harmony ever be a *cause* of disharmony? Even when harmonious activity is not received harmoniously, it cannot rightly be blamed, any more than good symphony music deserves blame if a few listeners happen to prefer jazz.

My own attitude towards Self-Realization Fellowship had not altered at all with my altered circumstances. I believed in it as deeply as ever. My feelings toward it, moreover, despite the pain of separation, were as supportive as ever. For I *knew* what the work was, and what the disciples were like who served in it so devotedly. How, then, if I continued to serve harmoniously in my way, could I be blamed if a few people reacted disharmoniously because I represented an anomalous position in the work. It is no part of spiritual teaching to shield people from reality.

These conclusions I arrived at by no means easily, or presumptuously, but painstakingly, over a period of years, testing every step of the way to see whether the ground on which I was treading had the strength to support me. At first, I asked myself how it would be possible for me to dishonor my vows by accepting any other calling than service to Master. It would, I felt, be far better if I died. Indeed, for months I prayed fervently to be allowed to die. But at last it became clear that this prayer, like my earlier one, was not going to be answered. Finally I resolved to spend the rest of my days in seclusion and meditation. But even this desire was denied me.

I sought repeatedly for a suitable place. But I had no income, and knew of no one to sponsor me. Without money for food, at least, where was I to live a hermit's life in America? I might possibly have pitched a tent in the forest, and waited for God to feed me—like St. Paul of the Desert, who, legend tells us, was visited daily by a raven carrying him a loaf of bread. But I couldn't live on private land without permission, and, as far as I knew, the maximum stay permitted on government land was two weeks. On the other hand, if it be true that God would have sustained me had I gone out into some forest anyway, with faith, I must answer that it was precisely in my faith that I was the most severely shaken.

I would have returned gladly to India. There, I knew, one can survive as a hermit. I wrote to Ananda Moyi Ma, the great woman saint with whom I had spent many weeks, to see if she would invite me to stay in one of her ashrams. But meanwhile the Divine Will made certain that I didn't take this way out: My application for a re-entry visa into India was denied. Someone in that country, it seems, out of jealousy, had accused me to the Indian Government of being a CIA agent, and (supreme horror!) a Christian missionary in disguise. Repeated efforts to refute these absurd charges proved futile. It was only when, ten years later, I felt God's inward direction to return there that all obstacles to my return evaporated like mist.

And so it was that my search for a solitary haven continued in the West. I tried every place I could think of: investigated Episcopalian monasteries in Michigan, Massachusetts, and southern California; lived for a time in a Roman Catholic hermitage near Big Sur, California; and even considered a little-known religious site in Lebanon. I applied for permission to live in out-of-the-way obscurity, pursuing my own path, on a variety of religious properties; for I preferred if possible to live on consecrated ground. I traveled extensively about California, Oregon, and Arizona, and visited central Mexico, seeking everywhere I went a place to stay. I even studied sales brochures from little countries in the Caribbean, thinking I might someday be able to afford land there. Nothing came of any of these efforts.

In retrospect I see now that divine assistance was always given me in direct proportion to my willingness to serve others. So long as I sought a place only for myself, not a single door opened to me. It was only when I accepted that Master still wanted me to serve that the doors opened wide. Indeed, the assistance I received from then on was often miraculous.

Marvelous to relate, throughout this period, which was certainly the bleakest of my life, abandoned as I felt by God and man, I experienced, on some deep level within me, a subtle joy that never left me. How to account for it? These contradictory states of consciousness might be compared to looking through a spyglass. Though my present focus was on the problem of what to do with my life, and on the pain that attended that problem, at the same time, and within the same range of vision—closer, however, and therefore blurred—was this joy. Dimly I could perceive its outlines, while its presence somehow eluded me.

During the late summer and autumn of 1962 I lived at my parents' home in Atherton, a small community thirty miles south of San Francisco, California. One evening in September they invited me to accompany them to a dinner party at the home of Mr. and Mrs. Watson Defty, neighbors of theirs on Walsh Road. I was on the point of declining when the thought came to me, "What is my alternative? To lie in my room and gaze at the ceiling?" I decided to go.

Present at the Deftys' that evening were an Indian couple, Dr. and Mrs. Haridas Chaudhuri. Learning that the Chaudhuris came originally from Calcutta, I began conversing with them in Bengali. We hit it off from the start. Their simple dignity, mingled with sweetness, keen intelligence, and unaffected simplicity, was deeply appealing to me.

"But where did you learn to speak Bengali so fluently?" they demanded. When I explained that I'd spent some years in Bengal, they inquired what I'd been doing there. My parents, strangers as they were to Indian traditions, had introduced me that evening as "our son Don." Now I introduced myself by my monastic name.

"Kriyananda!" they cried. "Why, we've heard your recordings of Yogananda's chants. What a beautiful voice you have! Oh, please, you *must* come and sing at our ashram on October 7th. We are having a Mahatma Gandhi Memorial Service there that day." Dr. Chaudhuri, as it turned out, was the founder and spiritual director of a well-regarded religious institution in San Francisco, the Cultural Integration Fellowship.

I was alarmed. "Oh, I'm very sorry, but I'm not doing any public speaking these days."

"But this isn't a lecture. We're only asking you to sing. *Please* come!" They smiled appealingly.

Still I refused as graciously as I could. But Dr. Chaudhuri wouldn't take no for an answer. "I felt guided to insist," he told me later. "From that first meeting I felt toward you as toward a younger brother. Inwardly I felt certain that it was God's will for you to get back into the activity for which your guru had trained you. You have much to give; it would be a great pity not to share it with others." In the following days he wrote me once, and telephoned several times, pleading with me to accept.

Finally I asked myself, "Could this be the guidance I've been praying for?" Certainly I had received no other. To test that possibility, and see how it felt, I finally agreed to come.

On October 7th I sang *"Gokula Chandra"* ("Moon of Gokula"). This popular *bhajan,* or devotional song, depicts the devotee's pangs of separation from God in the form of Krishna, the eternal Companion: "If my Beloved won't return to Gokula, life will lose all meaning for me. Ah, my friends, I will leave everything and go to find Him. If I succeed, though I know His consciousness is as infinite as the ocean, yet will I bind Him with my love, and keep Him forever a prisoner in my heart!" In my anxiety lest, by this public appearance, I displease Master, I was intensely nervous at first. But soon I lost myself in the inspiration of the words, so particularly meaningful to me as they were at this time. For the first time in over two months, I felt Master's blessings once again in my heart.

After the service, two people—one from the Indian Students' League of the University of California at Davis, and the other from the Unitarian Church in San Francisco—invited me to lecture to their respective groups. It surprised me that a mere song should have prompted two such notable invitations. Putting it down to coincidence, however, I declined, remaining firm even when they begged me to reconsider.

What was my astonishment, then, over the next several weeks to find them, like Dr. Chaudhuri, persistent. First they wrote, then phoned me repeatedly, long distance. Finally I prayed, "Master, could this be *your* will?" Certainly, on the only occasion so far that I'd appeared publicly, my feeling of attunement with him had deepened, not lessened. These invitations, moreover, constituted at least *some* kind of guidance. My inner voice, by contrast, seemed committed to total silence. I accepted at last.

To my astonishment it happened again: During those two lectures I felt Master's blessings as I hadn't felt them during weeks of desperate prayer at my parents' home. Yet while lecturing, anxious as I was not to displease him, I might well have felt *worse*. Might it be, I wondered, that in my resistance to public activity I had actually been *thwarting* his will? His two specific commandments to me, after all, had been to write and lecture. "But," I cried silently, "miserable as I am, what could I share with anyone but my pain?" Yet, almost incredibly, what people told me they'd derived above all from those lectures was a sense of joy!

Dr. Chaudhuri invited me to give a lecture in his ashram, backing his invitation with the earnest counsel, "I really feel this is the kind of work God wants you to do." This time I was better disposed to heed his advice, and let him schedule the talk. He also persuaded me to give a series of classes in Raja Yoga at the American Academy of Asian Studies in San Francisco, with which he was affiliated. Both lecture and classes meant for me, among other things, some badly needed income.

Still, however, I continued actively to pursue every possible lead for a place of seclusion.

One place I visited was New Camaldoli, south of Big Sur, California, the Roman Catholic hermitage mentioned earlier. Dom Pedro Rebello, the Retreat Master, a venerable-looking man with kindly eyes and a long white beard, was a native of south India. We took to one another instantly. Dom Pedro agreed to let me stay in their retreat house, despite the fact that I wasn't a Roman Catholic. He frankly expressed the hope that I'd become a convert and join their order. I remained there six months, deeply grateful for the respite it gave me. But was this, I asked myself, where Master wanted me to be? I couldn't feel that it was. Nor would it have been possible for me to convert sincerely to Roman Catholicism. Quite apart from my own deep feelings about serving Master, the church held tenets that I simply couldn't accept, including what I must call a certain *lack* of catholicity, a narrowness, though I think a few of the hermits mellowed in this respect during my stay there. As it happened, far from converting me, several began requesting me to teach them yoga meditation techniques. Dom Pedro himself ended up requesting Kriya initiation, and accepting Master as his guru "in Christ."

Then, after some months, a few of the novices began trying to convert me. It wasn't at all my desire to shake their faith by giving them answers for which their dogmas hadn't prepared them, but I found myself unable to shake off their persistent challenges. As an unfortunate result of their proselytizing efforts, they began to question some of their own beliefs. By now I could see that the only proper solution was for me to remove myself from their community altogether. I'd hardly reached this decision when the prior himself suggested that it would be better for the novices' peace of mind if I were no longer around.

My stay at New Camaldoli helped me in many respects, despite the fact that, with all the theological discussions I got involved in, I didn't find it exactly the quiet place of seclusion I'd been seeking. Among other things, the hermits introduced me to several exceedingly interesting books, some of them by Christian saints. It was, indeed, from those works that I culled many of the quotes in the chapter in this book on "Original Christianity." I was inspired to begin research for the book I had envisioned writing prior to my separation from SRF. Back in the San Francisco Bay Area, after leaving New Camaldoli, I continued my research at Stanford University. Dr. Chaudhuri helped me also with leads and suggestions. Thus, gradually, I found myself drawn into the other side of Master's commandment to me: writing.

Dr. Haridas Chaudhuri and his wife, Bina.

Father Rebello, Retreat Master of the Catholic monastery, New Camaldoli, south of Big Sur, California. Father Rebello accepted Master as his "guru in Christ."

Even now, to Dr. Chaudhuri's loving exasperation, I still insisted that all I wanted was seclusion. My feeling was that unless Master in some way actually *announced* his will to me, I didn't want, even in the face of the blessings I felt from him when I did lecture, to presume that public service was actually his will for me.

In the autumn of 1963 I decided to drive to Mexico and seek a place where I might live inexpensively, stretching the little money I had over enough months to get my bearings again.

Dr. Chaudhuri, ever solicitous for my welfare, maneuvered to head me off from what he viewed as a mistake. At his suggestion, I stopped in Sedona, Arizona, at the home of friends of his, Mr. and Mrs. Nicholas Duncan. He also wrote them, I suspect, to suggest they invite me to stay on their ranch. At any rate, they did so. The next three months I lived, rent-free, in a cabin on their property. Surviving sparely on only ten dollars a month, I meditated long hours, and, when, not meditating, worked on my book.

Did Master *want* me to write this book? This was my latest doubt. Urgently I prayed for direction. One night reassurance came to me in the form of a vision. First came an ordinary dream, in which I was discussing my proposed opus with a few friends. "To write a book of this sort," I exclaimed, "one would have to be willing for every bone in his body to be broken!" Then, with deep fervor, I cried, "And I *am* willing!" The moment I said this, a great surge of energy shot up my spine. I was thrown first into wakefulness, and thence into superconsciousness. An open book, which I recognized as the book I intended to write, appeared before me. My dream-willingness that every bone in my body be broken referred, I later understood, to my need for complete mental openness—even if, in the process, it meant breaking my every single preconception. Only by such intellectual sincerity could one be worthy of writing such a book. I would have, in other words, to approach with a completely open and fair mind views against which all my own nature, training, and convictions militated.

As it turned out, this was the supreme test that I faced in writing that book, the first volume of which I published several years later under the title *Crises in Modern Thought*.

During my stay in Sedona, Dr. Chaudhuri wrote to ask if I wouldn't give a series of classes that winter in his San Francisco ashram. His persistence puzzled me. "He *knows* I want to be in seclusion," I thought. I wrote back, declining his invitation. Yet, strange to say, I knew that I would not only be teaching those classes that winter, but *living* in his ashram! How would these things come to pass, I wondered?

Three months after my arrival in Sedona, the Duncans decided to go to India. Their departure left me without a place to stay. At the same time, my parents urged me to visit them in Atherton for Christmas. After some deliberation, I decided to return there for the holidays, then resume my search for a place of seclusion in Arizona or Mexico after the New Year.

Back in the San Francisco Bay Area, I attended a Saturday evening dinner party in the city with the Chaudhuris. We parted company afterwards on the street outside. My plan was to leave for Arizona the following Wednesday. The Chaudhuris lovingly wished me a safe journey. Yet, strange to say, even now as we said goodbye I *knew* I wouldn't be leaving.

The following morning, Dr. Chaudhuri, midway through his Sunday sermon, collapsed with a heart attack. He was rushed to a hospital, where the doctors informed him that it would be months before he could lecture again. There was no one to take his place at the ashram. When I learned what had happened, I realized that my only possible choice was to offer my services as his replacement. The friendship he had given me during these times of spiritual need merited everything I could do for him in return. I telephoned his wife, Bina.

"Oh, thank God!" she exclaimed. "I was debating whether I dared ask you to postpone your journey, knowing how badly you wanted to leave. But if you can stay and help us for awhile, it will be truly a God-send!"

Thus it happened that I took Dr. Chaudhuri's place as the minister of the ashram, where I lived for a year, and for several years gave Sunday services and taught mid-week classes there.

For the past year and a half, Master had repeatedly closed every door to me but that of continued public activity, finally *pushing* me through this one. This then, it seemed clear now, was the direction he wanted my life to take: a direction of continued service to him through "writing and lecturing."

Living and teaching in San Francisco, first in the ashram, and later in an apartment of my own at 220 Sixteenth Avenue, I devoted myself to the study of some of the leading philosophies of our times, and to considering how I might bridge the gap between materialism, with its attendant spiritual barrenness and consequent suffering, and the truths that, I knew now from personal experience, could serve man as a bulwark against even intense sorrow. "People are so skillful in their ignorance!" Master had once exclaimed. I set myself the task of sparring with that ignorance, and of turning it, wherever possible, to spiritual advantage. I studied the writings of atheists—Jean-Paul Sartre, and others; of "New Age" thinkers who offered merely worldly solutions to age-old spiritual needs; of scientists who claimed to find in physics, chemistry, and biology the disproof of ancient scriptural teachings; of neo-"ethical" thinkers who believed they saw in relativity the disproof of universal moral law; of theologians who, by defending spiritual truths without first gauging the opposition's strength, offered pale arguments that all but surrendered their own position. Many of the fruits of this study found their way into my slowly developing book, *Crises in Modern Thought,* as well as into my lectures and classes, which were being increasingly well received everywhere.

I began also writing songs, hoping through them to touch people's hearts along with their minds. Many of these songs expressed a philosophy of joy. "Say 'YES' to Life!", the first album I recorded, was released in 1965. People wrote from afar to say that, by listening to these songs, their hope in life had been renewed.

"My brother," wrote one lady from the East Coast, "has a long history of chronic depression. Since receiving your record from me as a gift he's been playing it constantly. He simply won't listen to anything else! And he seems so much happier now."

Sometimes people remarked to me, "Well, *you* can write happy songs. *You've* never suffered!" My reply was, "It is *because* I've suffered, and learned the lesson of pain, that I've earned the right to sing happy songs! For true happiness isn't something one feels only when things are going well. The test of it is its power to transcend suffering."

In addition to *Crises in Modern Thought,* I wrote and published several other books, each of which was designed to reach people of different interests, and to show them that those interests could be fulfilled truly only by the adoption of spiritual values.

In time I founded a meditation retreat and spiritual community along the lines Master had envisioned in his "world brotherhood colonies."

Gradually, I learned to trust my intuitive feelings once again. The more I did so, the stronger the awareness of inner guidance became. No longer was I afraid to follow my inner voice, for I found that obedience to it resulted in success, harmony, and an expanding vision of life, whereas disobedience resulted in disharmony and loss.

During the years following my great test, divine help has been demonstrated to me repeatedly.

In 1968 I faced a serious financial crisis. Building costs at

Ananda Meditation Retreat, which I was constructing at that time, rose many thousands of dollars higher than the original estimate, and than the money I'd saved. My various creditors agreed to let me pay them in monthly installments until my debts were liquidated. Monthly, with God's grace, I was able to honor those commitments.

A local lumber company, however, whom I'd been paying regularly, saw what looked like a "heaven-sent" opportunity to seize our land, and placed a lien on it. Next, a letter arrived from their lawyer to inform me that if I didn't pay off my entire debt in two weeks, they would foreclose on us.

"Divine Mother," I prayed, "what am I to do?" I could see no way of raising so much money in time.

Two evenings later I gave a showing of color slides, which I had taken in India, to a group of people in a private home in Palo Alto, California. Only the hostess knew me, and not even she had any idea of the crisis I was facing. I said nothing of it that evening. Afterwards, however, one of the guests approached me.

"I'd like to help your work," he said. "Would you accept a donation?"

"Very gratefully," I replied, expecting him to give me a five- or ten-dollar bill.

The check he handed me was for three thousand dollars! After paying my bills that month, including the full debt to the lumber company, I had $1.37 left in my bank account!

"Divine Mother," I prayed, "how wonderful is Your kindness— and how exact!"

In 1972 I felt inwardly guided to go to India. Money for the trip came from friends, and from classes that I had given months earlier. But an emergency came up suddenly; the only way I could meet it was by spending most of the money I'd saved for the journey.

"Divine Mother," I prayed, "if You really want me to go to India, You will have to return this money to me right away. Otherwise I won't be able to afford the ticket."

So saying, I paid out $1,100. That was on a Friday evening. The following Monday morning I received in the mail, from a complete stranger, a personal check for $1,000! An accompanying letter requested me to use the money "in whatever way Divine Mother wishes." Gifts in such large amounts rarely come to me, personally, and when they do so I usually use them for our work. But in this case I felt justified in applying that money to the journey.

At Ananda World Brotherhood Village, where I now live, I once received in meditation a design for a publications building. The plan called for an unusually shaped, curved roof. When our carpenters reached that point in the construction, they were unequal to the task. Advice sought elsewhere produced no results. Eventually, for lack of this knowledge, the work came to a halt. The carpenters sat down, meditated, and prayed for assistance. Finally, receiving, as they thought, no guidance, they rose and prepared to leave the job.

Just then a car drove up, and a man stepped out. Explaining that he was a building contractor from Santa Barbara, hundreds of miles away, he said, "I was wondering if you needed help."

The men explained their predicament.

"It's lucky for you I happened to come here," said the contractor. "I am probably the only man in California who knows the special technique this job needs!"

"Prove me now herewith, saith the Lord of hosts, if I will not open you the windows of heaven, and pour you out a blessing, that there shall not be room enough to receive it."*

Our publications building stands today as a beautiful tribute to God's constant solicitude for His devotees.

Thus, by offering my life up to God's guidance, and no longer holding back for fear of displeasing Him and Master, I found that everything in my life began working for the best. With joy now I was able to say that God had watched over me lovingly, even in my darkest hour.

To worldly people, the thought that God really cares for His human children seems preposterous. Indeed, demonstrations of divine solicitude are withheld from skeptics, who weigh all things—the most sensitive feelings no less than the specific gravity of metals—on the crude scales of logic. To such people, "All that is real is rational," as the philosopher Hegel put it, "and all that is rational is real." Seen in this light, cosmic law seems indeed impersonal, even cruel. Against the claim that God is Love, the rationalist sets the sufferings of untold millions, the blatant injustices, the outrages against innocent childhood and helpless old age. How, he asks, could any God who permits such colossal wrongs feel love for His creatures? Small wonder that even among religious believers there are many who, faced with this rational dilemma, see God as a Lord of wrath, not of love.

But the treasure hunt for the "pearl of great price" would lose much of its appeal if every truth promoted itself like a vote-hungry

---

* Malachi 3:10.

senator running for re-election. Jesus said, "Thou hast hid these things from the wise and prudent, and hast revealed them unto babes."[*] The fact is, the childlike devotee who opens his heart to God, especially in meditation, finds himself filled with a love so exquisite that doubt of the divine Goodness can simply no longer exist. Beholding the universe with transformed vision, he recognizes a higher destiny for all creatures than the fleeting fulfillments of earthly life. In suffering he sees valuable lessons for the soul. He understands what great blessings follow apparent misfortunes, once one has learned to accept all things even-mindedly as gifts from God. With increasing wonder, he receives repeated proofs that God really does care.

Foolish sentimentalism? So judges the crowd, having, by its egotism, self-preoccupation, and unbelief rejected the help that God tenders lovingly to all His creatures. A musician who refuses to play his instrument in harmony with the orchestra has no grounds for complaint if the notes he plays sound dissonant. A person who creates disharmony in his own life perceives disharmony everywhere. Is God then to blame?

"God really talks," Yogananda said, "if you don't think about saving for yourself first." Again and again, in my own life and in the lives of others, I have seen that God responds lovingly, in even the smallest matters, to devotees who give their lives to Him without reservation, and who seek to please Him above all else.

"If only you knew Whose son you are," Master said to us, "and how much territory you own, you would give up everything else!"

As I learned to depend on God wholly once more, the greatest storm in my life passed. It left my heart feeling cleansed, strengthened, and lovingly grateful. During the time of my deepest unhappiness, Ananda Moyi Ma sent me the message: "Take this experience as your guru's grace." *Grace?* If any one word was unacceptable to me at that time as an explanation for the grief I was experiencing, surely it was this one! But now I realized that grace was indeed what my loss—the greatest imaginable for me at the time—had brought me.

---

[*] Luke 10:21.

Ananda means "joy."

(above) Performing selections from *The Mystic Harp* with Derek Bell of The Chieftains.

(above right) A class held out of doors begins with enthusiastic excercises.

(above) Sunday Service at The Expanding Light.

(left) Here I am with some of our Ananda Singers.

Ananda Village (1996)

(*above*) Ananda Publications Building, overlooking downtown Ananda.

(*above*) One of our housing clusters, with dwellings built in a circle around a common courtyard and garden. (*above right*) Ananda is home to some 200 adults and 75 children. (*right*) The Rajarsi Ridge Business Park, built in 1995 around the Publications Building.

ht) A workday dedicated
the memory of St. Lynn
ajarsi Janakananda),
ananda's foremost disciple.

ow) Participants in a
rkday chanting and
ditating before lunch.

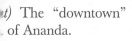

t) The "downtown"
of Ananda.

w) Ananda member
ph "Bharat" Cornell,
or of *Sharing Nature*
Children, leads some
ur children in a game
his popular book.

The Expanding Light (1996)

The amphitheatre, the open-air classroom at our guest retreat, The Expanding Light.

The Expanding Light offers programs to the public year round. We host thousands of guests each year from around the world.

Education for Life

anda's ucation for e" system udes training moral and itual values addition to ademics. ldren learn peration with rs, and sen- ity to their r and outer The system ased on the cational methods of Paramhansa Yogananda as presented in my book *Education Life*. *(below left)* An Ananda student receives from his teacher the personalized ntion that is essential to Ananda's "Education for Life" system of instruction.

Crystal Hermitage (1996)

Crystal Hermitage, where I live, is in many ways the spiritual heart of the community. *(above)* The upper garden, with the museum on the left, and the chapel on the right.

(above) An interior shot of the museum, which displays artifacts from the lives of our line of gurus, including a water pot that belonged to Lahiri Mahasaya.

(right) The Crystal Hermitage chapel, used for many ceremonies, and also daily meditation.

(right and bottom) Crystal Hermitage garden, the scene of many informal gatherings, as well as summer evening concerts.

(below) A view of the colonnade and fountain.

(below right) A view of the garden outside my house.

Ananda World Brotherhood Colonies (1996)

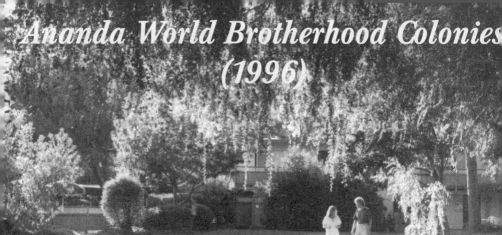

(above) The Ananda Palo Alto Community *(left and below)* Ananda Church of Self-Realization in Portland, and in Palo Alto. We have over 6 meditation groups worldwide, as well as communities in Portland, Dallas, Italy, and, soon, in Australia.

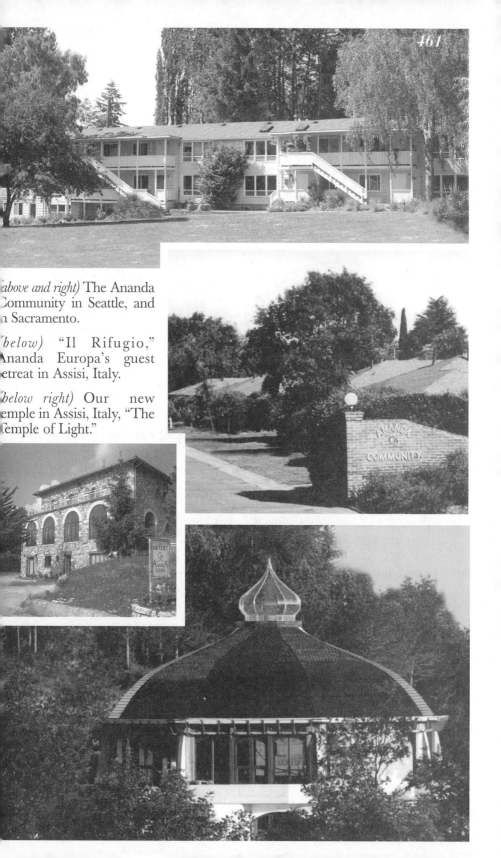

(above and right) The Ananda Community in Seattle, and in Sacramento.

(below) "Il Rifugio," Ananda Europa's guest retreat in Assisi, Italy.

(below right) Our new Temple in Assisi, Italy, "The Temple of Light."

CHAPTER 42

Less Is More

L ORD KRISHNA is depicted in legend as a boy playing his flute by the banks of the River Jumna, calling his playmates away from worldly pursuits to the divine search within. All men, consciously or unconsciously, hear in their souls this call to divine awareness. Every time a bird's song charms them with the reflection of how sweet life might be, were it tuned to simpler melodies, it is this call they hear. They hear it when a sunset reminds them of Beauty overlooked in the frenzied struggle for success; when a starlit night reminds them of Vastness and Silence, driven afar by noisy self-preoccupation. How well they heed the call depends on how ensnared they are by desires. The less they think of serving themselves, the more they can expand their consciousness into the Infinite.

Modern society, alas, is committed to an almost diametrically opposite principle. It firmly believes that the more one owns, and that the more one experiences of outward diversity, entertainment, and excitement, the happier one will be. Consumerism is propounded as if it were a moral value: "Spend more, so that there will be more jobs, and more things produced, so that you can spend still more." It is not wrong, of course, per se, to possess the conveniences that modern civilization has made available to us through its highly developed methods of mass production and distribution. What is wrong is the amount of energy that is directed toward these outward goals, at the expense of inner peace and awareness. What is wrong is that the quest for possessions tends to fool people into thinking that getting is more important than giving, and self-aggrandizement more important than service; that one's commitments need be honored only as long as they continue to serve one's own ends; that the most valid opinions and ideas are those which have gained the widest circulation; and that wisdom, fulfillment, and happiness can be mass-produced, like the parts for a radio. What is wrong, finally, is that people are losing touch with themselves, and are thereby *losing* their happiness, not gaining more of it. Probably there has never been an age in which so many people felt alienated from their fellow men, and from life itself, so unsure of themselves and of their neighbors, so nervous, fearful, and *un*happy.

Consumerism, elevated as it has been in modern times to the status of a moral law, sets aside as old-fashioned some of the fundamental teachings of the ages—as if the ability to build airplanes and TV sets qualified us to say that we know better how life should be lived than Jesus, Krishna, Buddha, or Lao-tzu. Were a prophet of modern consumerism to give us his Sermon on the Mount, he might start with, "Blessed are they who dig in and get theirs." But at least we have had an opportunity to observe the results of this sort of philosophy, and they are not pleasing. Human nature has not changed. Those who ignore its guiding principles pay all the usual penalties, whether as restless and unhappy camel drivers or as restless and unhappy jet airplane pilots, or corporate executives.

It is not that what we have nowadays is wrong. The solution lies not in reverting to primitivism, or to any other culture that imagination may cast for us in a romantic glow. Those cultures had their problems, too. We are living today. What is needed is a change in our *priorities*. We need, as every age has needed, to subordinate material to human and spiritual ends. The principles taught by Paramhansa Yogananda will, if adopted, correct the spiritual imbalances of our times.

One of the pressing needs nowadays is for what Yogananda called "world brotherhood colonies," as places to facilitate the development of an integrated, well-balanced life, and as examples to all mankind of the advantages of such a life. Such cooperative communities ought not to be isolationist, like medieval villages, nor in any sense a step backwards in time, but an integral part of the age in which we live.

Cooperative spiritual communities are needed especially as a means of fostering deeper spiritual awareness. Paramhansa Yogananda used the simile of a young sapling, which requires protective hedging against herbivorous animals until it grows large and strong enough to stand exposed to them. The devotee, too, he said, requires the protection of a spiritual environment until he can develop the strength in himself to be able to move through the world unaffected by its swirling currents of worldly desire. People today who recognize the need in society, and in themselves, for a more

spiritual way of life need hardly have pointed out to them the difficulties involved in such a development. For every affirmation of
spiritual values, the world cries out a thousand times from all sides
that opulence is the answer to all human needs. The result is spiritual confusion. In a recent survey, children in America were asked
who their heroes were. The largest number named actors in their
favorite television programs. The next largest chose prominent ath-
letes. Then came well-known politicians. Only two percent chose
famous writers or scientists. None chose people for their spiritual
qualities. When Dr. Radhakrishnan was vice-president of India, he
once told me, "A nation is known by the men and women its own
people look up to as great." By this standard alone it must be clear
that America's spirituality, though potentially, indeed, enormous,
requires careful cultivation. Cooperative spiritual communities, or
"world brotherhood colonies," provide a vital solution to one of
the most pressing needs of our times—an opportunity for those
who want to develop spiritually to do so in a supportive environment, and a dynamic example to the rest of the world that spiritual
principles really work.

One of the fundamental needs of our age is for putting down
roots again. We have extended ourselves too far outward, away
from the Self within, and away from the natural rhythms of the
planet on which we live. Even in our outward, human associations
we have lost touch with reality. The average person in America
today moves fourteen times in his life—not to new homes in the
same community, but to different communities altogether. Loneliness has become chronic. Friendships tend to be of the cocktail
party and patio barbecue variety, and not the deep bonds that
people form as a result of trials and victories shared. We know
people to smile at, but not to weep with, not to confide in, not to
go to for help in times of physical, emotional, or spiritual distress.
Small, spiritual villages offer a viable alternative to the
depersonalizing influences of our times. People living and working
together, sharing with one another on many levels of their lives,
suffering, growing, learning, rejoicing, winning victories together,
develop a depth in their outward relationships as well that helps
them, inwardly, to acquire spiritual understanding.

Small, cooperative communities offer more than a simple opportunity to demonstrate the value of already-fixed teachings and techniques to the world. Throughout history, the greatest advances
have always come from the cross-pollination that occurs when
relatively small groups of people with similar ideals have interre-
lated with one another. We see it in the golden era of Greek

philosophy; among the small bands of early Christians; among the artists and writers of the Italian renaissance; in the golden age of music in Germany; and in the days of England's great colonial power. Again and again, cultural advances have been defined by small groups of people with the opportunity to relate meaningfully to one another, people whose relationship was one of friendship, of give and take, people with an opportunity to know *whom* they were talking to, and not only what they were talking about. On a mass level such interrelationship is impossible: Nobody can know well more than a handful of people. But elitist cliques like that of England's aristocracy during her colonial days are no longer feasible. Ours is an egalitarian society. The solution now is for small groups of people to set themselves, not in a position of superiority to the rest of society, but somewhat apart from it in meaningful relationships to one another.

It is already happening. During the late 1960s and early 1970s many people went out into the country, bought land, and formed small cooperative communities. To be sure, thousands failed, but a few proved remarkably successful. And the lessons these few learned in the process are making it increasingly easy for other, similar communities to get started.

Among the successful communities, moreover, there is developing a consciousness of community *with one another,* of sharing in an experiment of national, even international, dimensions. New definitions are slowly emerging, and are being shared among them—definitions of marriage, education, friendship, cooperation, business, life's true goals, and other departments of life, definitions that are meaningful for people living in cities as well as in the country. It is a movement of potentially tremendous importance to modern civilization as a whole.

More than most people realize, the communitarian ideal was given its modern impetus by Paramhansa Yogananda, through his lectures and writings, and by the sheer power of his thought, which, he said, he was sending out into "the ether."

To further his ideals, I myself have founded what has become one of the handful of successful new communities in America. Its name is Ananda World Brotherhood Village. *Ananda,* a Sanskrit word, means "Divine Joy." Ananda Village is a place for devotees of all walks of life, whether married, single, or monastic, who feel a need to integrate their work with a life of devotional service to God, and of meditation. The members of Ananda are all disciples of Paramhansa Yogananda. Taking his teachings as our basis, we study how to relate them to every aspect of life.

Situated on 650 acres of land in the Sierra Nevada foothills of northern California, Ananda presently comprises over a hundred full-time residents, a meditation retreat (to which the public is invited), three "how-to-live" schools (from preschool through high school), a farm, various supporting businesses, private homes for families, two monasteries—in short, the essentials of a complete spiritual village.

Ananda's most obvious inspiration was Yogananda's "world brotherhood colonies" ideal. But it is possible also that I, as his destined disciple, acquired early in life a special attunement to this aspect of his mission, for even at fifteen, long before I met him, the strong thought came to me someday to found such a community. In a sense, indeed, I believe there never was a time in my life when this idea was not somehow forming in my mind.

In college I pursued the dream further, through months of thinking and study, and actually tried, albeit unsuccessfully, to get my friends to join me in founding a community. Later, when I abandoned my previous, outward goals in life, and accepted Paramhansa Yogananda as my guru, I was thrilled to find that he himself shared this particular goal. The day of his forceful lecture in Beverly Hills, when he exhorted "not only those who are here, but thousands of youths . . . to cover the earth with little colonies, demonstrating that simplicity of living plus high thinking lead to the greatest happiness!" I vowed to do my utmost to see that his dream became a reality. Thereafter, I took every opportunity I could get to study his ideas on the subject. Through the 1950s I researched other communities, past and present, consulted people who I thought might help me with suggestions on various practical aspects of communitarian life, read and meditated on the reasons many such communities had failed, and took whatever occasion I could find to visit active communities in Europe, Israel, and India. My very work as head of the monks, in the center department, and in the ministry afforded me ceaseless opportunities for studying the intricacies of group dynamics.

I had always expected that, if I started such a community, it would be under the auspices of SRF. After my separation from that organization, and once I'd sorted out the problem of personal seclusion versus service to others, I realized that if I was to continue working for Master, this was one aspect of his mission that could be fulfilled without intruding on anything his own organization was doing. Indeed, of all the disciples, I was, as far as I knew, the only one dedicated to the fulfillment of this aspect of his work.

In 1967, by a series of extraordinary events, I discovered and purchased sixty-seven acres of beautiful, wooded land in the foot-hills of the Sierra Nevada mountains. There, with the aid of a few friends, I began constructing what finally became Ananda World Brotherhood Village.

Then, in the spring of 1968, finding a growing interest among my friends in forming a spiritual community, I wrote and pub-lished a small book, *Cooperative Communities—How to Start Them, and Why,* to explain the sort of community that I envisioned.

The difficulties I faced in the beginning were twofold: financial, of course, primarily, and secondarily the fact that, because my ideas were still "in the air," many people with substantially differ-ent ideas tried to sidetrack my energies toward helping them to fulfill *their* ideas. One person offered me $70,000—enough money to get the community off to a good start—on the condition that I build the kind of community *he* wanted. But I saw that our ways were not compatible. Even if I failed, I decided, I must go on as I felt Master wanted me to. Indeed, success or failure alike mattered little to me. I only wanted to serve my guru.

The financial crises, especially, that we faced were considerable. They included two attempts to foreclose on us and seize our prop-erty. God, however, always gave us the money and help we needed to pull through. One reason He did so, I think, was that I refused to subordinate the welfare of individuals to the needs, how-ever desperate, of our work. One man came to me with $200,000, a sum we certainly could have used, and asked whether I thought he ought to join Ananda and give this money to the community.

"Your place," I told him, "is India."

By placing primary emphasis on spiritual values, and on God-contact in meditation, Ananda developed, gradually, as a place of selfless dedication to God, and to God in man. In his letter to the Galatians (5:22), St. Paul wrote, "The harvest of the Spirit is love, joy, peace, patience, kindness, goodness, fidelity, gentleness, and self-control." These attitudes are difficult, if not impossible, for man to develop to any significant degree on his own, but they evolve naturally in the hearts of those who attune themselves to God.

Often I have felt Master's smile in my heart to see his "world brotherhood colony" dream a material reality. His blessings on the land, an almost tangible aura of peace, are felt by all who come here.

The spiritual energy that is developing here extends far beyond Ananda's boundaries. Thousands in America and abroad find in Ananda's example the inspiration, and also the practical direction, for spiritualizing their own lives. This, indeed, is the broader purpose of cooperative spiritual communities, for while relatively few people may ever live in such places, everyone can be helped by examples—augmented by the large numbers involved in a flourishing community—that spiritual principles are both inwardly regenerative and outwardly practical. Every devotee, moreover, can be helped by the realization that he is not alone in his spiritual search. Thus, Ananda already provides people in many lands with a sense of spiritual family, a sense which serves them as a bulwark in times of trial, and of encouragement and shared inspiration in times of joy.

Often, as I stand and gaze out over Ananda's green fields, woods, and rolling hills, I am reminded of a poem I wrote in Charleston, South Carolina, not long before I came to Master. Since then I have set it in the legendary golden era of Lord Rama, whose kingdom of Ayodhya, in ancient India, was a place of universal harmony, peace, and brotherhood. Thus may all men learn to live, wherever their paths take them outwardly. For now, as then, true, divine peace is possible only when people place God and spiritual values first in their lives.

June in Ayodhya

>Listen! Fair June is humming in the air,
>And Ram's Ayodhya sings of lasting peace.
>The growing grass nods heavy to the wind,
>Patient till cutting time. The hay is stored;
>The fields spring up with adolescent plants,
>Laughing flowers, berries, and graceful corn.
>In the orchards, every hand is quickly busy
>To catch the ripest fruits before they fall.
>Men's hearts are strong with that perfected strength
>That smiles at fences, lays aside old hates,
>Nurtures true love, and finds such earnest pleasure
>In seeking truth that every private mind
>Seems drawn to virtue, like a public saint.
>The women's words are soft with kindliness;
>The children answer with humility;
>Even the men are like so many fawns,
>Modest and still, sweet with complete respect.
>June in Ayodhya is so roused with joy
>The earth can scarcely keep its boundaries,
>Swelling with energy and waking strength
>Till not a mountain, not a valley sleeps,
>Straining to burst, and flood the world with laughter.

> Such harmony flows everywhere when men,
> With grateful hearts, offer their works to God.
> Then brotherhood needs no enforcing laws,
> No parliaments, no treaties sealed in fear:
>
> True peace is theirs to whom the Lord is near.

Musing on these words, I recall with gratitude the people here whose lives exemplify its meaning so beautifully. Embodiments they seem to me, truly, of Babaji's words to Sri Yukteswar in *Autobiography of a Yogi:* "I perceive potential saints in America and Europe, waiting to be awakened."

By odd coincidence, as I write these lines it is my birthday: May 19, 1976. Exactly fifty years have passed since the life here chronicled began. Community festivities celebrating the event have, in one form or another, taken up most of the day. This afternoon, gazing on the smiling faces that were gathered around me in blessing, I thought of our Divine Beloved whose love they reflected. "Blessed are they," I quoted, "who come in the name of the Lord!"

It is evening now. I sit peacefully in my home. My gaze takes in an expansive view through the large living-room window: hills, sky, and slowly wakening stars. Such, I reflect, is The Path: Wherever man stands upon it, his soul-evolution stretches out before him to infinity. The stages on the spiritual journey are only temporary. Temporary, too, are its tests, as also its fulfillments. God alone is real.

"Lord," I pray silently, "may I never become attached to Thy dream of creation, nor yet to the path that leads out of the dream, but only to Thee: to Thy love, to Thy eternal joy!"

Afterword

January 5, 1996

Nearly twenty years have passed since I wrote those last lines. Twenty years is a significant portion of anyone's life. I myself, nearing as I am the Biblical age of threescore and ten,[*] can look back on countless blessings over these two decades. Much has transpired—too much for me to enumerate in an afterword. My primary purpose has been to describe what it was like to live with a great man of God.

Yet Paramhansa Yogananda's full life story encompasses far more than his visible accomplishments. His was a world mission, in many ways not definable in terms of any sort of outward structure. A new phase of that mission began the day he relinquished his physical body.

Over the years since then I have understood with increasing clarity that his work had always embraced more than his words and deeds, more than the organization he founded, more than any one group of followers. For these are but *manifestations* of his mission.

His mission was the spiritual upliftment of all aspects of society; it was not only the salvation of a few. His message was directed toward truth seekers of every persuasion, and not only toward those who studied his actual teachings. It was not and never could be circumscribed. The message he brought was catholic in the fullest and truest sense of the word: universal. Nor was it even so much a message, really, as a special ray of God's consciousness— a "new dispensation," to use a Biblical expression that he himself applied to the mission God had entrusted to him.

I now have a better understanding of that statement he made to me at Twenty-Nine Palms in 1950: "*Much* yet remains to be written." His teachings were both qualitative (for the salvation of his students and disciples) and quantitative (for the upliftment of

---

[*] Psalms 90:10

mankind generally). From his statement to me, "*Much* remains to be written," and from other statements he made to me for my personal guidance, I see now that his plan was for me to serve his work *outside* of his own organization. Thus, as subsequent events have made clear, I would be able to reach people in many walks of life and, from a central point of attunement with him, show the relevance of his message to their special needs.

In keeping with that plan I have so far written over sixty books, developing seed thoughts that were already expressed in his teachings, and demonstrating their applicability to a wide variety of human needs. I have composed over 300 pieces of music with the hope of awakening in people the soul-aspiration to which his teachings called all humanity.

Increasingly, his reality has become for me primarily the consciousness of his liberating presence within. I think of him only secondarily in terms of his outer words and actions. Thus, while writing a book or composing a piece of music, I seek guidance first from my inner awareness of attunement with him. Once I feel that inner guidance, examples arise spontaneously in my mind of things he said or did that endorse that guidance. I then search my memory for words or episodes that might contradict that presumptive insight.

Thus, I can say truthfully that none of my writings or compositions are really mine at all: They are my Guru's—filtered, admittedly, through the imperfect instrument of my human brain and understanding.

Part III of this book ended with a brief description of Ananda Village, the first "world brotherhood colony" to be founded on the ideals of Paramhansa Yogananda. Ananda, at the time I finished this book, was metaphorically speaking still a child. It was not even eight years old. Since then the child has grown and matured. Following the Biblical commandment to "be fruitful and multiply," Ananda has also produced spiritual offspring. Branch Ananda communities flourish in several places. In California there is an Ananda community and church in Sacramento, and another in Palo Alto. In Oregon Ananda has a church in Beaverton and a community on the outskirts of Portland. In the state of Washington there is an Ananda church in Seattle and a community in Lynnwood. There is an Ananda church, but not yet a community, in Dallas, Texas. And in Italy, finally, we have a community and retreat center near Assisi, the birthplace of Saint Francis.

Ananda's total resident membership today stands at about 800 adults and children, natives of countries around the world. Our far-flung spiritual family includes congregation members and friends numbering many thousands. And our two retreat facilities, The Expanding Light at Ananda Village, and *Centro della Gioia* near Assisi, attract thousands of visitors every year from points as far away as Japan and China, Australasia, India, China, Russia, Africa, and Europe, as well as from all parts of North and South America.

Ananda Village, where I live, has grown from Spartan beginnings to become a place of man-made as well as natural beauty. Simple but charming homes, school buildings, offices, and places of business express in architecture the twin principles Yogananda recommended: "plain living and God-thinking."

My own home, which I gave the name Crystal Hermitage, is the spiritual center of Ananda Village. Its graceful gardens open up from a succession of flowered terraces onto an expansive view of the Sierra Nevada foothills. Above the house stands a small stone chapel that was inspired by the Porziuncola of Saint Francis in Santa Maria degli Angeli. Further terraces above that stands a little museum, housing relics of our gurus and of other great saints of Self-realization.

Sant Keshavdas, a well-known spiritual teacher from India, once remarked to me, "What a lot of *tapasya* [spiritual austerities] you had to perform to make this place possible!" Indeed, is anything worthwhile ever accomplished without arduous effort? There are countless opposing currents to be struggled against for every single-minded effort in this world. Every major development in Ananda's history has been preceded by periods of testing.

If, after reading this account, you should desire further information, please write to us at Ananda Village, 14618 Tyler-Foote Rd., Nevada City, CA 95959. Better still, we'd love to have you visit us. The Expanding Light, our retreat facility, is open to you the year around.

Resources

A Selection of Other Crystal Clarity Books

Superconsciousness—A Guide to Meditation

J. Donald Walters

trade paperback

Many books have been written about meditation. But this new book is something more. There is a power to this work that will give you an entirely new understanding of your potential—to expand your consciousness beyond anything you can now imagine, to the state of superconsciousness. This is not a book based on theory alone. The author writes with a simple, compelling authority, born of actual experience of the truths he presents. Glimpse into the heart and soul of someone who has spent nearly fifty years exploring the innermost reaches of human consciousness, and who has dedicated his life to helping others on the sacred journey to self-transcendence. (Published by Warner Books)

Meditation for Starters

J. Donald Walters

trade paperback, available with or without companion CD

Learn the secrets of deep, *joyful* meditation! J. Donald Walters, an internationally respected spiritual teacher, has practiced meditation daily for nearly fifty years. *Meditation for Starters* offers simple but powerful guidelines for attaining inner peace. This is a book for long-time meditators as well as for beginners. It is also "for starters" in the secondary sense that all of life's activities are enhanced if they are started with meditation.

Autobiography of a Yogi

Paramhansa Yogananda

trade paperback

One of the great spiritual classics of this century. This is a verbatim reprinting of the original, 1946, edition of *Autobiography of a Yogi*. Although subsequent reprintings, reflecting revisions made after the author's death in 1952, have sold over a million copies and have been translated into more than 19 languages, the few thousand of the original have long since disappeared into the hands of collectors. Now the 1946 edition is again available, with all its inherent power, just as the great master of yoga first presented it.

The Rubaiyat of Omar Khayyam Explained
Paramhansa Yogananda
edited by J. Donald Walters
hardcover

Omar Khayyam's famous poem is loved by Westerners as a hymn of praise to sensual delights. Throughout the East, his quatrains enjoy a very different reputation: They are known as a deep allegory of the soul's romance with God. But their inner meaning has remained veiled, until this century. Yogananda writes in the introduction, "I suddenly beheld the walls of its outer meanings crumble away. The vast inner fortress of golden spiritual treasures stood open to my gaze." First penned nearly 60 years ago, *The Rubaiyat of Omar Khayyam Explained* is available at last, aflame with the fire of spiritual ecstasy.

"Yogananda's interpretation of The Rubaiyat *is a must-read for all spiritual seekers."*   —Louise L. Hay, author, *You Can Heal Your Life*

The Essence of Self-Realization—The Wisdom of Paramhansa Yogananda
Kriyananda (J. Donald Walters)
trade paperback, hardcover, and book-on-tape

Here are jewels from a master of yoga. Yogananda's words of wisdom have been lovingly preserved and recorded by his disciple, Kriyananda. The scope of this book is vast. It offers as complete an explanation of life's true purpose, and the way to achieve that purpose, as may be found anywhere.

"A wonderful book! To find a previously unknown message from Yogananda now is an extraordinary spiritual gift."   —Body, Mind, Spirit Magazine

How to Meditate
John (Jyotish) Novak
trade paperback

This handbook on meditation is an aid to calmness, clarity of mind, and, ultimately, inner communion with God. *How to Meditate* offers clear instruction on the basic preparation for meditation, how to quiet the mind and senses, and breathing techniques. Much loved by readers for its clarity, *How to Meditate* is written by a disciple of Yogananda who has been teaching and practicing meditation for 28 years. An indispensable aid to the sincere meditator, and a glimpse into the ancient science of yoga.

Ananda Yoga for Higher Awareness
Kriyananda (J. Donald Walters)
trade paperback

This unique book teaches hatha yoga as it was originally intended: as a way to uplift your consciousness and aid your spiritual development. Kriyananda's inspiring affirmations and clearly written instructions show you how to attune yourself to the consciousness of the poses, so that each posture becomes a doorway to life-affirming attitudes, clarity of understanding, and an increasingly centered and uplifted awareness. Excellent for beginning and advanced students.

Expansive Marriage—A Way to Self-Realization
J. Donald Walters
trade paperback

Marriage, understood and lived expansively, is a path to transcendent love—to the realization of our higher spiritual potential. This book is a practical and inspiring guide to help you deepen your relationship. Discover the fundamental attitudes that lead to greater love and fulfillment; they will enrich not only your marriage, but your whole life.

Do It NOW!
A Perennial Calendar and Guide to Better Living
J. Donald Walters
trade paperback

There is greatness within each one of us that lies waiting to be tapped, if only we knew how. J. Donald Walters' new book offers 365 fascinating and practical suggestions for deepening your awareness—of yourself, and of the world around you. Open the doorway to fresh creativity and a blossoming of your own highest potential. *Do It NOW!* is the distillation of a lifetime of creative endeavors.

Money Magnetism
J. Donald Walters
trade paperback

This book has the power to change your life. It contains techniques and keys for attracting to yourself the success that everyone seeks. It offers fresh, new insights on ways to increase your own money magnetism. This is a book about money, but also about a great deal more. Its larger purpose is to help you attract whatever you need in life, when you need it. Chapters include: What Is True Wealth? / You Are Part of an Intelligent Reality / How Much Wealth Is Available? / To Live Wisely, Give.

The Art of Supportive Leadership
A Guide for People in Positions of Responsibility
J. Donald Walters
trade paperback and cassette

This practical guide is recommended for managers, parents, and anyone else who wishes to work more sensitively with others. Become an effective leader who gets the project done by involving and supporting the people working with you.

Affirmations for Self-Healing
J. Donald Walters
trade paperback

This inspirational book contains 52 affirmations and prayers, each pair devoted to improving a quality in ourselves. Strengthen your will power; cultivate forgiveness, patience, health, and enthusiasm. A powerful tool for self-transformation.

Intentional Communities
How to Start Them, and Why
J. Donald Walters
trade paperback

This classic handbook is the fruit of more than 50 years of study, thought, and practical experience: hard-won lessons gleaned from human nature, not abstract theory. Drawn from Mr. Walters' experience founding Ananda Village, one of the most successful intentional communities in the world today. Chapters include: Communal Economics / Intentional Communities Past and Present / Self-Realization vs. the Megalopolis / What Is Ananda?

AUDIO Selections from
Clarity Sound & Light

Meditation for Starters—J. Donald Walters
cassette/CD, narration and music, 60 minutes

Learn how to meditate, step by step, and discover a new world inside yourself. This recording begins with instruction in meditation. The simple, powerful, and clear explanation is an excellent refresher even for those who have been meditating for years. A guided meditation follows, taking you on a meditative journey to "The Land of Mystery," with beautiful music and soaring melodies. This is the companion audio for the book of the same name.

Metaphysical Meditations—J. Donald Walters
cassette, 73 minutes

Kriyananda's soothing voice leads you in thirteen guided meditations based on the soul-inspiring, mystical poetry of Paramhansa Yogananda. A great aid to the serious meditator, as well as those just beginning their practice. Each meditation is accompanied by beautiful classical music to help you quiet your thoughts and prepare you for deep states of meditation.

Guided Meditations on the Light—J. Donald Walters
cassette, 40 minutes

One of our most popular tapes. You'll be sensitively guided on an inner journey of ever-expanding awareness. Beginning and advanced meditators alike can learn how to draw to themselves the deep states of consciousness evoked in these powerful guided meditations. Gentle sitar music in the background. Side one: Meditation on the Moonrise. Side two: Expansion of Light.

Meditation: What It Is and How to Do It—J. Donald Walters
cassette, 60 minutes

Learn how to meditate, and how to achieve deep states of inner peace. Meditation is the key to direct, personal experience of the Divine. It offers a scientific approach to expanding your awareness beyond the limits of the senses. Included are many short guided meditations to inspire your meditation practice. Extremely clear and helpful.

Mantra—Kriyananda (J. Donald Walters)
cassette/CD, vocal chant, 70 minutes

For millennia, the Gayatri Mantra and the Mahamrityunjaya Mantra have echoed down the banks of the holy river Ganges. Allow the beauty of these sacred sounds to penetrate every atom of your being, gently lifting you to a state of pure awareness. Chanted in Sanskrit by Kriyananda to a rich tamboura accompaniment.

"Ancient, unhurried majesty." —NAPRA Review

Himalayan Nights—Ferraro/Howard
cassette/CD, instrumental, 60 minutes

Seamless sitar, tabla, and tamboura on one continuous track—a soothing tapestry of sound. Use *Himalayan Nights* as a relaxing musical background for any daily activity.

" . . . will gently refresh and purify the spirit." —Music Design in Review

The Mystic Harp—Derek Bell
cassette/CD, instrumental, 70 minutes

Derek Bell, of Ireland's four-time Grammy Award winning **Chieftains**, captures the haunting, mystical quality of traditional Celtic music on this solo album of original melodies by J. Donald Walters. Derek plays Celtic harp on each of the nineteen richly orchestrated melodies, and is joined on the duet "New Dawn" by noted violinist Alasdair Fraser.

I, Omar—J. Donald Walters
cassette/CD, instrumental, 61 minutes

If the soul could sing, here would be its voice. *I, Omar* is inspired by *The Rubaiyat of Omar Khayyam.* Its beautiful melody is taken up in turn by English horn, oboe, flute, harp, guitar, cello, violin, and strings. The reflective quality of this instrumental album makes it a perfect companion for quiet reading or other inward activities.

Life Is the Quest for Joy— J. Donald Walters
cassette/CD, instrumental, 69 minutes

This beautiful instrumental reaches deep into the heart, producing a feeling of profound relaxation, and an inward, meditative awareness. One melody embraces the human condition: the love, hope, disappointment, and pain that human beings experience in their quest for joy. A thrilling experience in music, and in consciousness.

"An intimate, meditative stream of lush music." —NAPRA Review

Secrets of Life—J. Donald Walters
cassette/CD, instrumental with occasional sayings, 61 minutes

Here are exquisite, haunting melodies, reminiscent of the world's most treasured classical music, as well as something entirely fresh. You'll hear the kind, beautiful voice of J. Donald Walters offering occasional inspirational thoughts woven into the music. This is an experience designed to uplift your consciousness in wonderful ways.

"Lovely, soul-stirring music." —Atlantis Rising Magazine

For a **free** Crystal Clarity catalog
or for additional information
please call **1-800-424-1055.**

Other Resources of Ananda

Ananda World Brotherhood Village

Ananda World Brotherhood Village, founded in 1968, is one of the most successful intentional communities in the world. Several hundred people live together on 750 acres of land near Nevada City, California, and work in harmonious cooperation developing spiritual models for marriage, child raising, interpersonal relationships, work, and the arts. Ananda members are guided by the inspiration of Swami Kriyananda in following the teachings of Paramhansa Yogananda.

Ananda incorporates many aspects of public and private enterprise, including a school system, two health food stores, a medical clinic, an auto shop, a thrift shop, and several publishing and recordings businesses. The community also operates two retreat centers which offer a variety of programs throughout the year.

Ananda also has World Brotherhood Colonies in Seattle, Portland, Dallas, Sacramento, and Palo Alto (CA), and a retreat center and European community in Assisi, Italy. Ananda also has more than 75 meditation groups worldwide. For more information on Ananda World Brotherhood Colonies or meditation groups near you, please call **916-292-3462**.

The Expanding Light

Ananda's guest facility, *The Expanding Light,* offers a varied, year-round schedule of classes and workshops. You may also come for a relaxed personal retreat, participating in ongoing activities as much or as little as you wish. The beautiful serene mountain setting, supportive staff, and delicious vegetarian food provide an ideal environment for a truly meaningful, spiritual vacation. Programs offered at *The Expanding Light* include:

Ananda Yoga for Higher Awareness—You can take weekend or week-long intensives in the original Hatha Yoga, as taught in the book *Ananda Yoga for Higher Awareness* by Kriyananda (J. Donald Walters). Experienced instructors will give you individual attention at your own skill level, from beginning to advanced. Also offered is the **Yoga Teacher Training Course**—a month long course that gives certification in hatha yoga instruction.

How to Meditate—Meditation is the key to Self-realization. In these weekend and week-long intensives, you'll receive personal instruction in the basic meditation techniques taught by Paramhansa Yogananda and learn how to bring the benefits of meditation into every aspect of your life.

ya **Preparation**—Kriya Yoga is the highest technique of meditation taught by Paramhansa Yogananda. This course will help you prepare for initiation in this ancient and sacred science of Self-realization.

Other programs offered at *The Expanding Light* include courses on yoga philosophy, spiritualizing your daily life, relationships, healing, "Experience Ananda" weekends, and much more. For a catalog of programs or information call **1-800-346-5350**.

Ananda Course in Self-Realization
Ananda Church of Self-Realization offers you a complete and practical training program in yoga, meditation, diet, the fundamentals of the spiritual path, health and vitality, affirmations, and much more—all a part of one mutually reinforcing whole designed to bring every aspect of your life into uplifted balance. The course includes 22 lesson booklets, 1 book, 13 audio tapes, and a variety of optional videos that will deepen your understanding and practice of Paramhansa Yogananda's teachings. It also prepares you for initiation into Kriya Yoga, Yogananda's most advanced technique. This course can be completed in as little as a year, or may be studied over a longer period, depending on your individual needs, and offers extensive training and deep insights for the new or experienced seeker. To order call *Ananda Church of Self-Realization* at **916-478-7561**.

Hand-Crafted Meditation and Yoga Aids
Meditation pillows (zafus), half-moon pillows, padded and unpadded meditation benches, meditation and yoga mats, incense, malas, and more. For information call *The Ananda Collection* at **1-800-537-8766**.

Index